ALSO BY RICK BAYLESS

. . . . .

Authentic Mexican

REGIONAL COOKING FROM
THE HEART OF MEXICO

(WITH DEANN GROEN BAYLESS)

RICK BAYLESS'S MEXICAN KITCHEN

Capturing the Vibrant Flavors
of a World-Class Cuisine

WITH DEANN GROEN BAYLESS
AND JEANMARIE BROWNSON

PHOTOGRAPHS BY MARIA ROBLEDO
ILLUSTRATIONS BY JOHN SANDFORD

SCRIBNER

SCRIBNER
1230 Avenue of the Americas
New York, NY 10020

Designed by Barbara M. Bachman

SET IN ADOBE FAIRFIELD AND OPTI NAVY BLACK

Manufactured in the United States of America

1 3 5 7 9 10 8 6 4 2

Library of Congress Cataloging-in-Publication Data is available.

ISBN 0-684-80006-3

To

Lane Ann Groen Bayless,

WITH LOVING HOPE THAT THE WORLD YOU GROW UP INTO

IS BLESSED WITH GENEROUS GARDENS,

COMFORTABLE KITCHENS AND

WELCOMING TABLES.

ACKNOWLEDGMENTS

All creations are to some extent collaborations, and you'll find *Rick Bayless's Mexican Kitchen* more than a little collaborative. I am a lover of Mexico and its cooking—a translator of and believer in Mexican cuisine as one of the world's greatest—but I am not Mexican. Nearly everything I've included here I have learned from the generous and ingenious cooks of Mexico; still, any mistakes, oversights, confusions or omissions are mine.

My first thanks, without hesitation, go to Mexico's cooks. Without the benefit of status or many physical means (but with fertile land, welcoming climate and a vibrant cultural spirit), those cooks have created, re-created, refined and innovated along a steady, though regularly bumpy, path for millennia.

Marilyn Tausend of Culinary Adventures in Gig Harbor, Washington, and her Mexican partner, Carmen Barnard in Morelia, Michoacan, know a remarkable number of impressive cooks throughout Mexico. I'm thankful not only for their generosity to me through the years (they plan our yearly trips for the staff of Frontera Grill and Topolobampo) but for their dedication to Mexico. They have led me to many, many well-laid tables. Beverly Karno of Karno Books has enriched these pages immeasurably by sending a steady supply of Mexico's hard-to-find and out-of-print cookbooks.

Mary Jane Mendoza, Nancy Mayagoitia and Toni Sobel have opened the wonders of Oaxaca for me. Ofelia Toledo and Abigail Mendoza have given those wonders an aroma and flavor. Carmen Ramírez Degollado, Ricardo Múñoz, Lula Bertrán, Alicia D'Angeli and María Dolores Torres Izábel, all of Mexico City, have spent many hours teaching, talking and offering tastes. Each has contributed something unique. And Silvio Campos of Tixkokob, Yucatan, taught me more about flavor and a sense of place, with just one bite of his *cochinita pibil,* than you could write in volumes. (What I learned, however, didn't deter me from bringing him to Chicago to make his pit-cooked masterpiece—but that's for another book.)

As you read these pages, you will realize that I have also learned a good amount about Mexican cooking in our restaurant kitchens. Little of it would have been possible without the dedication, inexhaustible curiosity, talent and imagination of the restaurants' sous chefs (especially Kevin Karales, Generoso Bahena, Gonzalo de Santiago, Tracey Vowell, Richard James, Peter Goad and Paul Kahan) and so many of our co-workers in the kitchen that have traveled this road with us for over five years (Raúl Arreola, Bertha Gómez, Rodolfo Neri,

Patricio Sanisaca and Mark Segura). Any who have found themselves totally consumed in a project know the need for someone to keep "real life" flowing; thank you Pat Schloeman, my unbelievably efficient assistant, for doing anything and everything that is needed.

Rather than Chicago being the Mexican-ingredient wasteland most imagine it to be, my fair city offers perhaps the best availability of traditional ingredients in the United States. And with suppliers like Tom Cornille (Cornille and Son) and Allan Heymann (Bruss Company), no ingredient is too far afield. Paula Lambert (Mozzarella Co.) worked tirelessly with me to create *queso fresco* (what she sells as *queso blanco*) that's just like Mexican fresh cheese.

I owe a special debt to many chefs and cooking teachers specializing in Mexican and Southwestern cuisine for helping me familiarize people with Mexican ingredients. Because of their hard work, ingredients are more widely available everywhere. And to the Culinary Institute of America, especially to Greg Drescher, director of education at Greystone, for a commitment to showcasing Mexican cuisine with the integrity it deserves. And to Dun Gifford and Sara Baer-Sinnott at Oldways Preservation and Exchange Trust, for believing in and tirelessly promoting sustainability and the genius of traditional diets.

Maria Guarnaschelli, our insightful and scrupulous editor at Scribner, deserves the loudest thank you here. Without her gentle persistence over several years, I never would have figured out when to put these words on paper, and thanks, too, Maria, for living with us in the "process," until this beautiful book was born. To Doe Coover, our nurturing and ever-positive agent, you're the best.

I would never underestimate the role this book's design plays in achieving our goal of clarity and usability. Barbara Bachman's design is exquisite. Amy Hill, Erich Hobbing and Jay Schweitzer at Scribner worked diligently and set all the details beautifully in place.

My heroes, friends and family are my lifeblood. The example, words and perfectly simple food of Alice Waters always right my course when I've strayed, and Julia Child never fails to inspire with insightfulness, boundless energy and humor. Floyd and Bonnie Groen are the best family anyone could dream of. Levita Anderson, my mother, and LuAnn Bayless Tucker, my sister, are, through thick and thin, my ever-supportive flesh and blood. Olivia Wu, Bob and Jewel Hoogstoel, Georgia and Dan Gooch, Peg Tappe and Dan Spike have nourished me well for many years. And John Sandford, together with Frances and Eleanor, have blessed our lives with a flood of beauty (including the drawings in this book) that we treasure as much as the Sandford friendship.

For a concentrated decade, Michael Horowitz and I have explored the uncertain terrain of human development together. Without his commitment and stamina along lightless and rugged paths, I would have faltered. The freedom, happiness and understanding I enjoy would doubtless never have come my way.

You will all want to voice appreciation to JeanMarie Brownson, as I do, for her masterful insight, discerning editing and careful recipe testing (which she did in her home with ingredients from the local groceries). She has made these Mexican dishes within everyone's easy reach. Jean's tireless, positive persistence, vast knowledge and love of good food (from Mexico and beyond) have made this project a dream from which I hope never to awaken.

All who know Deann understand what an incredibly lucky man I am. Not only are we soulmates, sharing a passionate respect for Mexico, but she brings to our collaborations a steady, far-sighted and quick understanding of everything from financial management to the flavor of a well-made *mole*. Deann, without your insight and perseverance, neither this book nor our restaurants would have blossomed so beautifully.

Is it appropriate to thank a five-year-old girl named Lanie, whose boundless and innocent curiosity, whose joie de vivre, inspires me everyday? I certainly hope so.

Rick Bayless

Though Rick has sung the lead, I will add harmony in the chorus of thank yous to friends in Mexico and in the United States who are passionate about Mexican culture, food and art: The things I have learned from them extend far beyond the pages of this book. And the love of our good friends all these years is sustenance I have counted on.

The support of my family, Pep and Ilene Peterson and Paul and Macky Groen, has never faltered; to Floyd and Bonnie Groen my thanks are continuous and concrete, for their hours spent working in our office and, especially, for loving and caring for Lanie. Thanks also to Susan Sances for her intelligent insights and guidance through the ups and downs that accompany our many projects.

Not only do we learn about preparing Mexican food in our restaurants, but we learn from serving it, helping others to understand it. I am grateful to our front-house managers, Elizabeth Bolger, Jim Fessler and Larry Butcher for their conscientious running of our dining rooms. Thanks also to our wait staff and hosts, especially those who for more than five years have been helping our diners find their way through all the foreignness to the food that is most satisfying for them: David Beckman, Melissa Bucher, Wilson Cuzco, Silvia De Santiago, Eric Hubbard, Antone Jacobs, Tom Keating, Albaro Márquez, Armando Márquez, Nancy O' Connor, José Pacheco, Alfredo Rodriguez, Kathe Royball, Irene Santiago and Julio Villa.

I feel honored to add a personal thank you to Maria Guarnaschelli (for patiently pushing us through to completion), to Doe Coover (for never-failing reassurance and understanding that is only a phone call away) and to JeanMarie Brownson (for vivacious dedication through both the excitement of progress made and the tedium of checking measurements and commas).

Muchísimas gracias, Lanie, for shedding your sunshine on my life. Your smile is the most amazing treatment for exhaustion, anxiety and frustration. And finally, thank you to you, Rick. From those first honeymoon months on Mexican back roads to last night's service of dinner, your ceaseless exploration and desire to learn, your striving for perfection, and your love of life inspire and challenge me every day. Thank you for helping make life so rich.

Deann Groen Bayless

Many friends and family members deserve thanks for helping me be part of this extraordinary book. First, foremost and forever to my husband Scott—the most adventurous recipe taster and patient partner anyone could wish for. Thank you also to Claire and Glen for always offering small hands to husk tomatillos and push the buttons on the blender.

I would like to thank my parents, Marty and Dolores Kaiser and Bill and Mickey Brownson for their boundless love and support. My sisters, brothers and in-laws, too, deserve a special thanks for their many hours spent amusing my children during our recipe testing sessions and for their years of enthusiasm for all of my culinary journeys.

Thank you also to my friends and colleagues for their willingness to offer advice and encouragement including Suzanne Checchia, Karen and Jim Fleming, Mary Abbott Hess, Dodie Hofstetter, Marcia Lythcott, Jeanny McInerney-Lubeck and Lisa Schumacher. A special thank you also goes to my co-workers at the *Chicago Tribune,* especially Carol Mighton Haddix and the food department.

Finally my unending gratitude to Rick and Deann Bayless for offering me the dream of a lifetime: to work with gifted, passionate and thoughtful people on a book filled with magic.

JeanMarie Brownson

CONTENTS

INTRODUCTION

THIS BOOK IS FOR PEOPLE WHO SIMPLY LIKE TO COOK AND EAT. Which, admittedly, is an obvious audience for a cookbook, although I buy cookbooks for many reasons. Occasionally I want to learn more about what I'm eating (and how cooks get it that delicious); I want to be carried away to an exotic culinary byway; I've invited some folks for dinner and feel I have to make something different (not to mention impressive); or I want to give our home that certain feeling only a beautiful cookbook on the counter or coffee table can create.

Then again, many of us simply love the process of cooking and the pleasure of eating, and we want a cookbook to help us enjoy both experiences. Maybe we don't put a made-from-scratch dinner on the table every night, but we've found great satisfaction in spending time getting to know a culture through its flavors, in creating meals of those flavors and sharing them with friends. If you're at all like me, you get as much pleasure from roasting ripe tomatoes and inhaling the earthy perfume of tomato-jalapeño sauce, as you do sitting at the table savoring a plate of *huevos rancheros*. We're invigorated by meals that taste of love and heritage, dishes that show a spark of creativity. We relish gustatory exploration and culinary challenge. You might say that the pursuit of good food (both cooking and eating) has become a hobby, and one that richly nourishes us while allowing us to nourish others.

MANY OF US can make pesto, even roll out our own pasta. Grilled rare tuna with sundried-tomato relish no longer poses much of a challenge. But handed a recipe for guajillo chile sauce or peanut *mole*—in fact, practically any traditional Mexican recipe—and we feel all thumbs. Buying, cleaning, toasting, soaking, pureeing and straining the dried chiles for either of those sauces seem as exotic as the Amazonian custom of pounding cassava into meal for bread. When faced with any of those dried-chile tasks (or even the simple matter of roasting fresh chiles), many North American cooks will simply retreat to a modern recipe for grilled chicken breasts with corn-and-black-bean salsa or the like. Delicious and comfortable as those "Southwesternesque" dishes may be, I simply cannot let them pass for real Mexican food. The *real* thing is rich with complex flavors, remarkably delicious, invigorating and satisfying. And it is not difficult to put on the table with ease and confidence: We just need a little experience.

After some twenty years of day-in, day-out experience with Mexican cooking, I've distilled what I believe are its essential flavors. Though the Mexican repertoire is enormously varied and regionally distinct, there are common building blocks that weave their way through the national cuisine.

I've picked 14 of those building blocks and set them apart in the first chapter of Essential Recipes. Each of these straightforward culinary blueprints produces a salsa, sauce or seasoning (I've also tossed in the indispensable recipe for corn tortillas as Essential Recipe #15). Most of them may be served as condiments, but all (and I think this is the exciting part) can become the flavorful cornerstone around which to create numerous dishes. So rather than learning dozens of distinct recipes, you can start your exploration of real Mexican cooking by working through the Essential Recipes, then springboarding comfortably to a wide variety of preparations. In fact, about half the recipes in this book spring from one of the Essential Recipes.

These Essential Recipes help bring real Mexican cooking (the spirited ingredients and simple, distinctive techniques) into the everyday repertoire of our contemporary American kitchens. They are the simmered-down essence of Mexican flavor, and they are within easy reach of North American cooks these days. You need virtually no specialized equipment, the ingredients have become easily obtainable and the dishes are precisely what we want to eat—in terms of flavor *and* nutrition.

Now the questions: Are the recipes in this book authentic? Can a gringo guy with popular Stateside restaurants flesh out the nuances of Mexico's real cooking?

If you agree with me that authentic cooking respectfully utilizes traditional ingredients and time-honored techniques to prepare dishes that express the spirit of a particular people, then, yes, this is authentic cooking at its best. But, if your vision of authentic is only recipe-as-artifact spelled out in ethnographic detail, then know that what I do goes a step further.

I start with the artifact recipes I've collected from 25 years of traveling and living in Mexico (as well as from my hundreds of Spanish-language cookbooks from Mexico), then, with utmost passion and deference to Mexican culinary heritage, I spell out dishes that embrace both sides of the border: dishes that give life to the brilliance of traditional Mexican cooking in the context of the contemporary American kitchen.

In essence, I see my role as that of translator. Frequently, the translation is easy: Ingredients, techniques and ways of serving are equivalent here and in Mexico. Other times, I have to translate the delicious integrity of authentic Mexican cooking into a vernacular my compatriots can understand.

Purely ethnographic collections of recipes often leave me frustrated in the kitchen, wondering how to to use ingredients from my markets and equipment in my kitchen to achieve the wonderful flavors I'm reading about. To my way of thinking, if authentic cooking is truly going to mean something to us, we actually have to get the great flavors on the table. Anything short of that is as incomplete an experience as reading gardening manuals without ever setting a pot in the window.

The recipes in this volume provide a rich understanding of the ingredients, techniques, whys and wherefores of the Mexican kitchen, all set forth within the cultural context you need to create authentic meals. As you return to your favorite preparations time and again, you'll find your expression of Mexican spirit becoming more and more "authentic," more fluent and more satisfying.

So let's start filling the kitchen with the aroma of toasting chiles and roasting garlic. Let's get on the phone to invite friends and family. *¡Buen Provecho!*

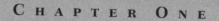

CHAPTER ONE

ESSENTIAL FLAVORS OF THE MEXICAN KITCHEN

EVERY CUISINE HAS CLASSIC COMBINATIONS OF FLAVOR THAT EMANATE FROM ITS PLATTERS and plates. As distinctly recognizable as these combinations are (everyone knows when a dish tastes Italian or Moroccan or Thai), rarely are they as easy to isolate into building-block recipes as they are in Mexico. No one, though, has attempted this project—the dislodging of these cornerstones from full-built Mexican dishes—yet it's an exercise I think can be very useful when getting to know the Mexican kitchen. So I'm formalizing a first pass at it here, and what follows is the way my 15 Essential Recipes naturally group.

All recipes, except the one for tortillas, make a salsa, sauce or seasoning. One group focuses on tomatoes (with fresh or dried chiles as flavorings), another on tomatillos (again with fresh or dried chiles), and a third on purees of rehydrated dried chiles. In addition, there's an essential recipe that focuses on fresh poblano chiles and one on the classic Yucatecan spice, achiote. These recipes together illustrate the principal flavor choruses that sing their way through dishes in Mexico. Some are utilized more than others, though I think most Mexican cooks would agree that each plays an essential role in the cuisine.

Within the recipes that feature tomatoes, one (the Essential Simmered Tomato-Jalapeño Sauce) slowly simmers them into a sauce spiked with jalapeños and seared white onion, a second (Essential Simmered Tomato-Habanero Sauce) sizzles them in a pan with fruity, renegade habaneros, and a third (Essential Quick-Cooked Tomato-Chipotle Sauce) does the same with smoky chipotles and sweet garlic. Each has a different tomato texture, each a distinct profile resulting from its featured chile.

Roasted tomatoes that don't receive any additional cooking (no further sizzling or simmering) get worked together with jalapeños, garlic and cilantro into a salsa (Essential Roasted Tomato-Jalapeño Salsa) that has both richness and robust freshness—a combination of characteristics you don't find in any of the cooked sauces. And if freshness is your passion, then one of the two chopped salsas will satisfy—either the classic mix of raw tomato, white onion, serrano and cilantro (Essential Chopped Tomato-Serrano Salsa) or the fiery close cousin (Essential Chopped Tomato-Habanero Salsa) made with habaneros, plus radishes for crunch.

Tomatillos offer a tangier backdrop than tomatoes. When they're simmered with serranos, onions and garlic in the Essential Simmered Tomatillo-Serrano Sauce, there is a mellow transformation in flavor and texture. Simply working together the same basic ingredients— no further cooking—creates a salsa (Essential Roasted Tomatillo-Serrano Salsa) with a rough texture that springs into a very zesty mouthful. Simply blend together roasted tomatillos with the smokiness of chipotles and the sweetness of roasted garlic, and you wind up with a salsa (Essential Roasted Tomatillo-Chipotle Salsa) that emphasizes tangy sweetness and fire.

The seasonings and sauces made from purees of rehydrated dried chiles transform each chile's concentrated flavor into an even more concentrated (but less raucous) experience, filled in and balanced with herbs, spices and garlic. When you make the Essential Sweet-

and-Spicy Ancho Seasoning Paste you'll notice that the rich, dried cherrylike ancho comes to the fore, while natural bitterness fades: The near-molasses edge on the wc dried-fruit punch of black pasillas is the focus of Essential Bold Pasilla Seasoning Paste, tangy vegetal qualities of the chile are much less apparent.

The Essential Simmered Guajillo Sauce pulls together the whirl of brilliant raw flavo into a well-proportioned sauce that casts sweetness against natural sharpness. And Essen tial Sweet-and-Smoky Chipotle Seasoning Salsa is an exercise in boldness: smokiness made even smokier by frying the dried chiles, roughness smoothed and piquancy concentrated by slowly cooking the puree, and everything balanced by plenty of sweetness from dark sugar and roasted garlic.

We're a long way into these essential recipes to be just arriving at Essential Roasted Poblano *Rajas*. This simple mixture of rich-tasting roasted peppers, seared white onions, garlic and herbs, is without doubt quintessentially Mexican and thoroughly useful—it works with everything from condiments and salsas to salads, soups and casseroles.

While you'll find several flavors of seasoning pastes in Yucatecan markets, the rusty-colored achiote one is known and used throughout Mexico. All the garlic, herbs and spices give it a baroque quality, though the earthy flavor of achiote is what this seasoning (Essential Garlicky Achiote Seasoning Paste) is all about.

Corn tortillas are a backdrop to all Mexican flavor—more so than beans and rice, cer-tainly more than flour tortillas. The Essential Corn Tortilla recipe gives detailed directions for how to make them. I include this recipe not because ready-made tortillas are difficult to find, but because I want to encourage you to (occasionally) make your own: The feel of the dough, the smell of a griddleful of golden rounds and the taste of a just-baked tortilla will teach you more about the Mexican table than anything else I can imagine.

As you page through the rest of the book, you'll find that when one of these Essentials is the cornerstone of a recipe, we've highlighted it. I hope this will bring them to your atten-tion, as well as bring to mind ways to utilize these basic flavors in dishes of your own cre-ation. You may even find yourself making double or triple batches of your favorite Essentials to have on hand as a head start. In each dish that uses an Essential, I list the amount you'll need; if you already have the Essential made, simply measure out the appropriate quantity and move straight on to finishing the dish.

SIMMERED TOMATO-JALAPEÑO SAUCE

Salsa de Jitomate Cocida

...e sear and sizzle in every spoonful of this well-known classic. Here the
...of charred tomatoes and blistered chiles are all blended to a rough puree
...hot pan. But why does tradition dictate that we go to the fuss of roasting and
...a comforting sauce of canned tomatoes (perhaps with the familiar touch of
...ste) could be slow-simmered with a little diced jalapeño? Because we want the
...gustiness of Mexico here, not the slow-simmered sweetness of a typical pizza sauce.
...e talking inimitable *huevos rancheros* of energetic tomato-doused sunnyside-up eggs on
...asty corn tortillas.

Choose plum tomatoes for a thicker texture, round tomatoes for a lighter, brothier consistency. This sauce is so versatile you can substitute it for any tomato sauce called for in this book.

MAKES 4 CUPS

Generous 1 pound (about 2 large round, 8 to 10 plum) tomatoes

1 to 2 (about ¾ ounce total) fresh jalapeño chiles, stemmed

1 tablespoon vegetable oil or rich-tasting lard

½ small (about 2 ounces) white onion, thinly sliced

1½ cups chicken broth

Salt, about 1½ teaspoons, depending on the saltiness of the broth

1. *Roasting the tomatoes and chiles.* Roast the tomatoes and chiles on a baking sheet 4 inches below a very hot broiler until blistered and blackened on 1 side, about 6 minutes, then use tongs or a spoon to turn them over and roast the other side. Cool, then peel the tomatoes, collecting all the juices. Roughly chop the chiles. Coarsely puree the tomatoes (with juices) and the chiles in a food processor or blender. Pulse the mixture only a few times leaving it quite chunky for *huevos rancheros,* for instance, or run the machine until the sauce is quite smooth if you're preparing, say, enchiladas.

2. *Cooking the sauce.* In a medium (8- to 9-inch) deep, heavy skillet or medium-size (2- to 3-quart) saucepan heat the oil or lard over medium. Add the onion and fry until browned, about 10 minutes. Increase the heat to medium-high, and, when very hot, add the tomato-chile mixture. Stir for 5 minutes or so as the mixture sizzles, darkens and thickens, then reduce the heat to medium-low, stir in the broth and let the sauce cook at a gentle simmer for about 15 minutes, until beginning to thicken (though it shouldn't be as thick as spaghetti sauce). Taste and season with salt and it's ready to use.

ADVANCE PREPARATION—This useful sauce can be made several days in advance; it can be frozen successfully but may need to be boiled briefly to look as it did before freezing.

SHORTCUTS—Three-quarters of a 28-ounce can of tomatoes can replace the fresh ones.

OTHER CHILES YOU CAN USE—The same quantity of serranos can replace the jalapeños, as can ½ to 1 habanero chile.

TRADITIONAL DISHES THAT USE THIS ESSENTIAL AS A STARTING POINT
Spicy Tomato-Sauced Enchiladas (page 176)

SIMPLE IDEAS FROM MY AMERICAN HOME

Huevos Rancheros—Steam-heat (page 145) 8 corn tortillas. Fry 8 eggs sunny-side up. On each of 4 plates, slide 2 eggs onto 2 slightly overlapping warm tortillas, liberally spoon the sauce over everything, then sprinkle with sliced raw onion, chopped cilantro and a little crumbled Mexican *queso fresco, queso añejo* or Parmesan.

Layered Tortilla-Ricotta Casserole—Steam-heat 12 tortillas (page 145), smear a little of the sauce over a baking dish, then make 4 "stacks" in the dish: Spread out 4 tortillas, spoon 3 tablespoons of ricotta (seasoned with salt) onto each, sprinkle with some sautéed mushrooms or grilled vegetables and some chopped cilantro or fresh thyme, splash with a little sauce, then repeat the layers of tortilla, ricotta, mushrooms (or vegetables) and sauce. Finish each stack with a tortilla. Spoon sauce on to cover the tortilla well, sprinkle with grated Chihuahua or other melting cheese and bake until they're bubbly and brown.

Seared Jalapeño Beef Tips—Make the sauce with beef stock if you have it. In a large, heavy skillet filmed with oil, sear about 1¼ pounds of beef sirloin or other steak (cut into 1-inch cubes) over medium-high heat until browned on all sides. Add 2 cups of the sauce, then briskly boil until slightly reduced and the meat is as done as you like it.

FRESH JALAPEÑO CHILES

. . . . .

As my wife Deann says, "Jalapeños are being bred to boredom." The raw flesh of some of the cultivars has as little flavor and heat as a green bell pepper, with the same kind of juicy, grassy qualities. Others will be richer in flavor and medium hot (or more). The bigger ones seem to be blander, and I think their only good use is for stuffing, because it is easy. Jalapeños sold in the Mexican markets are often smaller and more flavorful. If the jalapeños in your recipe are chopped or pickled whole, they could easily be replaced with serranos (and in some instances probably should be, if you like a spicy green-chile zing).

Jalapeños are found in practically every market in Mexico and most supermarkets in the United States. It's in Veracruz, though, that they have their homeland and grow in the greatest variety. You'll find Christmasy red ones, and ones they call *gordos* (fat chiles), or *huachinangos*, or *cuaresmeños*—locals swear they all taste different, though I think you need to be raised there to get some of the differences. The smallest ones are dried into *chile chipotle colorado* (also known as *chile mora* or *morita*); large ones that dry with a corky covering become *chile chipotle meco*.

Stats: An average jalapeño is bell-pepper green (lighter than a poblano), about ½ ounce, about 2½ inches long by ¾ inch wide, the smooth-skinned, torpedo-shaped body (with rounded shoulder) quickly tapering to a point near the end.

fresh jalapeño chiles

ESSENTIAL ROASTED TOMATO-JALAPEÑO SALSA
FROM THE STONE MORTAR
Salsa de Molcajete

*T*HE FIRST TIME you hear that gravelly, rock-against-rock rotation of the mortar, the first time you smell the irascible aroma of crushed roasted garlic and chiles, the first time you taste the jazz band of seasoning playing through the juicy ripe tomatoes—you've come face to face with the real Mexico. It's a simple first step, partly because it looks like what we think of as "salsa," partly because we can find the ingredients so easily. But do go to the extra effort to buy good tomatoes. Then *roast* them and the garlic and chiles with a confident hand—that's the technique that sets these flavors apart. With a lava-rock mortar from Mexico, you'll feel centuries of tradition as your hands work the ingredients together.

MAKES ABOUT 2 CUPS

1 pound (2 medium-large round or 6 to 8 plum) red, ripe tomatoes

2 large (about 1 ounce total) fresh jalapeño chiles

3 garlic cloves, unpeeled

Salt, about a scant ½ teaspoon

½ small (about 2 ounces) white onion, finely chopped

A generous ⅓ cup loosely packed chopped cilantro

About 1½ teaspoons cider vinegar (optional)

1. *Roasting the basic ingredients.* **The broiler method:** Lay the tomatoes on a baking sheet and place about 4 inches below a very hot broiler. Roast until blistered and blackened on one side, about 6 minutes; with a spoon or pair of tongs, flip the tomatoes and roast on the other side. **The griddle method:** Line a griddle or heavy skillet with aluminum foil and heat over medium. Lay the tomatoes on the foil and roast, turning several times, until blistered, blackened and softened, about 10 minutes. Don't worry if skin sticks to the foil.

Cool, then peel the skins, collecting all the juices with the tomatoes.

While the tomatoes are roasting, roast the chiles and unpeeled garlic directly on an ungreased griddle or heavy skillet (you already have one set up if you've griddle-roasted the tomatoes) over medium. Turn occasionally until both chiles and garlic are blackened in spots and soft, 5 to 10 minutes for the chiles, about 15 minutes for the garlic. Cool, pull the stems off the chiles and peel the papery skins from the garlic.

2. *Grinding the salsa.* **The mortar method:** In a large mortar, use the pestle to crush and grind the chiles, garlic and ¼ *teaspoon* of the salt to a coarse-textured paste (this will release

a wonderfully pungent aroma), paying special attention to breaking up the chile skins. A few at a time, grind in the roasted tomatoes, transferring the ground mixture to a bowl if the mortar gets unmanageably full. **The food processor or blender method:** In a food processor or blender, grind the chiles, garlic and ¼ *teaspoon* of the salt to a coarse paste, stopping to scrape down the sides of the bowl a couple of times. Add the tomatoes and pulse a few times until you have a coarse-textured puree.

Transfer the salsa to a serving bowl, and stir in any reserved tomato juices.

3. *Final seasoning.* In a strainer, rinse the onion under running water, shake off the excess and stir into the salsa, along with the cilantro and optional vinegar. Add water, if necessary, to give the salsa a thickish, but easily spoonable, consistency (2 to 4 tablespoons is the norm). Taste and season with salt, usually a scant ¼ teaspoon, and the salsa's ready to serve.

ADVANCE PREPARATION—This salsa comes into its own a few hours after it's finished, especially if left at room temperature. It can be made through step 2 a day or two ahead, covered and refrigerated. Add the cilantro and onion shortly before serving.

OTHER CHILES YOU CAN USE—Besides jalapeño, serranos (3 to 5 for this quantity) are also classic. It's also made with habanero (½ to 1) or manzanos (½ to 1). With habaneros, this typical Yucatecan salsa, called *chiltomate,* is frequently made without chopped onion or cilantro and is flavored with sour orange juice in place of the cider vinegar.

TRADITIONAL DISHES THAT USE THIS ESSENTIAL AS A STARTING POINT
Classic Red Tomato Rice (page 250); Rustic Red-Sauced Eggs (page 266); Seafood Rice *Cazuela* (page 339)

SIMPLE IDEAS FROM MY AMERICAN HOME

A Different (but Traditional) Guacamole—Make the salsa as directed, but don't add any water. Coarsely mash 3 avocados, stir in a cup or so of the salsa, add a little more chopped cilantro if you wish, taste for salt and the guacamole is ready.

Spicy Chicken "Hash"—In a large nonstick skillet over medium heat, fry an onion (sliced) in several tablespoons of oil until golden. Add about 1½ cups of the salsa and cook until thick and reduced, then stir in 3 cups of boiled-until-tender, roughly mashed red-skin potatoes. Keep frying and turning and working everything together until the potatoes brown and the mixture holds together. Stir in a cup of shredded smoked (or roasted) chicken and some chopped cilantro or green onion, warm through and the hash is ready.

Jalapeño-Baked Fish—Lay four 5- or 6-ounce fillets—such as snapper, mahimahi, grouper or bass—in an oiled baking dish in a single layer and sprinkle with salt. Spoon 2 cups of salsa over them. Bake in a 400-degree oven until the fish just flakes when firmly pressed (it'll take about 8 minutes if your fillets are ¾ inch thick). If you like richer flavors, sear the fillets on both sides in an oiled skillet over medium-high before laying them in the pan. If the sauce seems too juicy, pour it into a saucepan and boil gently until reduced. Sprinkle the whole dish with some chopped cilantro before serving.

What's Best? Mortar versus Blender versus Food Processor

Those chiseled-out bowls of basalt (lava rock) called *molcajetes* in Mexico—the ones that sit on counters in *taquerías*, home kitchens, even fancy eateries—are so tangled up in Mexican culinary history that it's nearly impossible to think there could be a replacement. But, in all honesty, for some jobs there is.

If you're talking about a chunky salsa made from roasted jalapeños, garlic and tomatoes, what you'll get from the mortar—juicy, elegantly textured, clear in flavor—is much better than the pulp you'll get from a blender or food processor that you've turned on and just let run. However, carefully pulsing a machine with sharp blades can yield a decent salsa.

Very few cooks these days (in Mexico or beyond) use a mortar (or its larger cousin, the *metate*) to make dried chile sauce; the chile skins are hard to grind. A food processor works remarkably well for such a sauce, as does a blender, though the latter usually requires the addition of a little extra liquid and repeated stopping to scrape down the blender jar. For sauces thickened with nuts and seeds (like *moles* and *pipianes*), the blender works far better than the food processor because its blades go faster and can pulverize even the smallest seeds.

I would be remiss if I didn't say that those who've been raised on *mole de la abuelita* (grandma's *mole*) say that when she grinds everything by hand the flavors and textures are better. This makes perfect sense: in the mortar or on the *metate*, you're crushing ingredients, hence extracting more flavor, rather than finely chopping them as you do in a blender.

Bottom line: I have a mortar and I use it for grinding spices and for certain salsas (I've noted this in the recipes). The extra muscle power I expend is easily made up for by my enjoyment of the aromas and texture. In my recipes, I call for a mortar, blender and food processor; whichever I list first is my preference.

Choosing, Seasoning and Using a Mexican Mortar

It's not likely you'll find a good, heavy *molcajete* made of the densest basalt (lava rock) for sale in the United States, simply because the best ones weigh and cost a lot, and there's not a huge call for them here. Lightweight "tourist" models look nice on the shelf but are so rough and porous that you'll forever be grinding grit into your food. In Mexico, I suggest you search through the markets for a stall that primarily sells mortars and *metates* (the sloped flat grinding stones). Choose a heavy, compact, smooth-textured mortar—the surface should look a little like unpolished granite—that will hold three to four cups. I am partial to the ones with a decorative pig or ram's head carved on the side.

To season your *molcajete,* grind a handful of wet, raw rice in it once a day for several days, until you've smoothed out the roughest edges in the bowl and the rice no longer looks dirty. When grinding, hold the *metlapil* (the pestle) so that your fingers are parallel to its length (not wrapped around it), with the smallest end toward your palm. Keep your wrist rather loose to allow you to rotate the pestle easily around the bowl while exerting an even pressure from your palm.

When making salsa in the mortar, the idea is to work the ingredients together a little at a time. Start with the hardest (or most difficult to grind) items, then, work in the softer, juicier stuff.

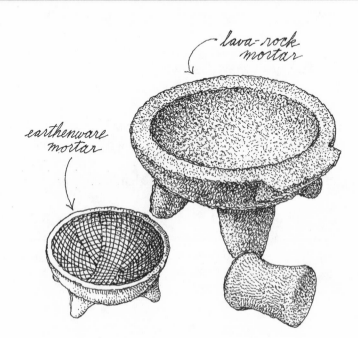

lava-rock mortar

earthenware mortar

ESSENTIAL CHOPPED TOMATO-SERRANO SALSA

Salsa Mexicana Clásica

THE TENDERNESS of ripe tomato against the crunch of raw onion, the tap dance of serranos backed up by aromatic cilantro, garlic and lime—this is Mexican cooking at its most beguiling.

Of course, *Salsa Mexicana* is best when each ingredient is perfect—from warm, just-picked tomatoes to green-tops-on white onions—but don't miss the pleasure of this salsa even when the tomatoes are less than perfect. Chop everything with a sharp knife so nothing gets bruised and finely enough that the flavors really meld. Make your salsa within an hour or so of serving for great texture and vibrant flavors.

MAKES ABOUT 2 CUPS

12 ounces (2 medium-small round or 4 or 5 plum) ripe tomatoes

Fresh serrano chiles to taste (roughly 3 to 5, ½ to 1 ounce total, or even more if you like it really picante*), stemmed*

A dozen or so large sprigs of cilantro

1 large garlic clove, peeled and very finely chopped (optional)

1 small (4-ounce) white onion

1½ teaspoons fresh lime juice

Salt, about ¾ teaspoon

Core the tomatoes, then cut in half widthwise and squeeze out the seeds if you wish (it will give the sauce a less rustic appearance). Finely dice the flesh by slicing it into roughly ¼-inch thick pieces, then cutting each slice into small dice. Scoop into a bowl.

Cut the chiles in half lengthwise (wear gloves if your hands are sensitive to their piquancy) and scrape out the seeds if you wish (not only will this make the salsa seem less rustic, but it will make it a little less *picante*). Chop the chiles as finely as you can, then add them to the tomatoes. Carefully bunch up the cilantro sprigs, and, with a sharp knife, slice them ¹⁄₁₆ inch thick, stems and all, working from the leafy end toward the stems. Scoop into the tomato mixture along with the optional garlic. Next, finely dice the onion with a knife, scoop it into a small strainer, then rinse it under cold water. Shake to remove excess water and add to the tomato mixture. Taste and season with lime juice and salt, and let stand a few minutes for the flavors to meld.

ADVANCE PREPARATION—This salsa tastes best within a few hours of the time it's made, though if using as the base of a cooked dish you can make it early in the day.

OTHER CHILES YOU CAN USE—Three to five jalapeños can be substituted for serranos, as can habaneros, though in the last case you'll want to use just $\frac{1}{2}$ to 1 chile.

TRADITIONAL DISHES THAT USE THIS ESSENTIAL AS A STARTING POINT
Guacamole (page 78); Roasted Cactus Salad (page 94); Classic Seviche Tostadas (page 84); Mexican Rice Supper (page 262); Deluxe Scrambled Eggs (page 272); Shrimp *a la Mexicana* (page 332)

SIMPLE IDEAS FROM MY AMERICAN HOME

Great Summer Supper—When you're making the salsa, chop an extra 2 garlic cloves and 2 serranos and mix them with 2 or 3 tablespoons of Worcestershire sauce and a little grated lime zest. Use this mixture to marinate about 1¼ pounds of trimmed skirt steak (to serve 4) for an hour, then charcoal-grill and serve with a liberal sprinkling of the salsa.

Simple Confetti Pasta—Make the salsa without the lime juice. Boil 12 ounces of fresh pasta for 4 people until *al dente,* drain, return to the pan and drizzle on a little olive oil. Mix in the salsa, tossing until everything is warm, then divide onto plates and sprinkle with finely crumbled Mexican *queso añejo* or Parmesan and chopped cilantro.

A Different Potato Salad—Cube a pound of boiling potatoes and boil in salted water until just tender. Drain, and, while hot, gently toss with olive oil and a little mellow vinegar. When cool, gently stir in about a cup of the salsa and more cilantro if you like.

FRESH SERRANO CHILES

In the workaday world of my kitchen (restaurant or home), fresh serranos are indispensable. They're hot and intense with a pure-and-simple flavor that only can be described as "green chile," unless of course they've matured to a sweeter—but still hot—red. Many Americans know instinctively to chop up serranos to add zing to a dish, yet few of us think of pickling them. We should, since just about anywhere jalapeño is appropriate, so is a serrano, especially if you like spiciness and bold flavors. And keep in mind that a serrano is more predictably hot than a jalapeño. It is certainly more beloved in Mexico, where most people call it simply chile verde, "green chile."

The compact texture of a serrano's raw flesh is compact in flavor, too: green apples and raw green beans mixed with a sharp heat and what I think of as the perfect, bright-green, almost limey, green-chile flavor that lingers with hints of olive oil and cilantro.

fresh serrano chiles

Stats: An average serrano is the color of a green bell pepper with some ripening to yellow or red. There are about 6 to an ounce, each 1½ to 2 inches long by about ½ inch wide, having a bullet-shaped body, with rounded shoulders that tapers to a point near the end.

Tomatoes

Great tomatoes are a critical ingredient in Mexican cuisine, second only to chiles. So what do you do when it's winter, you want to make great Mexican food and you live in St. Louis? Well, the situation has improved. Sinaloa, in northwestern Mexico, ships crates of plum tomatoes our way during the winter months. Though they're picked pretty green and gassed to ripen, they are certainly okay in cooked sauces. In fact, if you let the tomatoes ripen on the counter, and never refrigerate them unless they're so ripe they'll spoil, the sauce will be quite good.

Plum tomatoes (called *tomates guajes* or *jitomates guajes* in much of Mexico) work well in cooked sauces because they have a pulpier, less juicy texture that cooks up rich and thick. For chopping raw or for roasting and crushing into a salsa, I prefer the juicy texture of round tomatoes (called *tomate* or *jitomate* with or without the adjective *redondo*). Cherry tomatoes taste riper than round tomatoes in off-peak months, but their skins are tough in salsas; the small round hothouse varieties (especially those imported on the vine) are a better, though expensive, option.

Bottom line: Ripeness is more important than shape, and by "ripe" understand that I mean "very ripe, soft ripe, riper than you'd usually think of as ripe." For cooked sauces, canned tomatoes (preferably plums) may be substituted for fresh (a 28-ounce can is equivalent to 1½ pounds fresh), though you're sacrificing some texture and all the flavor you'd get from roasting the tomatoes.

At farmer's markets, look for a high-acid tomato if you want your dishes to really sing. I love an heirloom variety they sell in Chicago called *costoluto*. It's very similar to a deeply fluted tomato folks seem to like so much in Oaxaca—medium pulpy and good both for cooking and eating raw. I highly recommend roasting and peeling lots of late-summer ripe tomatoes to freeze for the winter.

Stats: An average plum tomato weighs 2 to 3 ounces, a medium-small round weighs 6 ounces, a medium-large weighs 8 ounces, and a large weighs 10 ounces.

ESSENTIAL CHOPPED TOMATO-HABANERO SALSA

Xnipec

*Y*UCATECANS LIVE in a tasty world of bright flavors. The natural sweetness of ripe tomatoes invigorated with the ignitable potential of habanero, the aroma of cilantro, the zing of sour orange or lime, and the resonant crunch of raw radish and onion. That's *xnipec* (say "shnee-pek," Mayan for "nose of the dog" the books say, refraining from further comment). If you leave out the tomatoes, most Yucatecans call the resulting mix *salpicón*, an enlivened sprinkle for their otherwise quite simply flavored fare. I doubt you'd think of the tomatoless version as a salsa (especially one for chips), but its possibilities as a relish are numerous. Either version is essential in my kitchen to accompany anything flavored with achiote.

MAKES ABOUT 2 CUPS

1 small (4-ounce) red onion

2 tablespoons fresh sour orange or lime juice

10 ounces (2 small round or 3 or 4 plum) ripe tomatoes

6 radishes

½ to 1 whole fresh habanero chile, depending on your personal attraction to the "burn"

A dozen or so large sprigs of cilantro

Salt, about ½ teaspoon

Very finely chop the onion with a knife (a food processor will make it into a quickly souring mess), scoop it into a strainer and rinse under cold water. Shake off as much water as possible, then transfer to a small bowl and stir in the juice to "deflame" the onion's pungency. Set aside while you prepare the remaining ingredients.

Core the tomatoes, then cut them crosswise in half and squeeze out the seeds if you want (it'll make the sauce seem less rustic). Finely dice the tomatoes by slicing them into roughly ¼-inch pieces, then cutting each slice into small dice. Scoop into a bowl. Slice the radishes ¹⁄₁₆ inch thick, then chop into matchsticks or small dice. Add to the tomatoes. Carefully cut out and discard the habanero's seed pod (wear rubber gloves if your hands are sensitive to the piquancy of the chiles), mince the flesh into tiny bits, and add to the tomatoes. Bunch up the cilantro sprigs, and, with a very sharp knife, slice them ¹⁄₁₆ inch thick, stems and all, working from the leafy end toward the stems.

Combine radishes, chile and chopped cilantro with the tomato mixture, stir in the onion and juice mixture, taste and season with salt and it's ready to serve in a salsa dish for spooning onto tacos, grilled fish and the like.

Advance Preparation—The salsa is best within a few hours of its completion, and be forewarned that the longer it sits, the more *picante* it will seem.

Other Chiles You Can Use—Jalapeños and serranos (3 to 5) can replace the habanero. Manzano chiles (½ to 1) also would taste good in this salsa.

Traditional Dishes that Use this Essential as a Starting Point
Spicy Yucatecan Beef "Salad" Tacos (page 148)

Simple Ideas from My American Home

Spicy Chicken Salad—Mix cubed cooked chicken (try smoked chicken for even more flavor) with mayonnaise until you get the chicken salad as moist as you like it. Stir in salsa a spoonful at a time (draining off as much liquid as possible) until the salad is spicy and nicely flavored. Diced jícama adds a nice crunch; a little more cilantro adds liveliness.

Seafood or Asparagus Salad—As a substantial appetizer for four, very briefly boil 1 pound of shrimp or steam 1 pound of asparagus until tender; cool. Mix 2 to 4 tablespoons of olive oil with 2 tablespoons sour orange or lime juice, stir in a cup or so of the salsa and taste for salt (it should be a little salty). For seafood: Combine salsa and cooked seafood, and let stand an hour or so, stirring regularly, before serving on a bed of sliced lettuce. For asparagus: Divide the asparagus among 4 lettuce-lined plates and spoon the salsa mixture over them. You may want a little extra chopped cilantro.

Seared Fish with Tangy Habanero—In a large, heavy skillet filmed with oil, sear 4 fish fillets over medium-high heat until brown on both sides. Remove from the pan, add the salsa and stir until wilted and the liquid reduces. Stir in ¼ to ⅓ cup of heavy cream or *crème fraîche,* then nestle the fish back in the pan. Cover and simmer over medium-low heat until the fish barely flakes. Transfer to dinner plates. If the sauce is thinner than you'd like, boil it briskly to reduce, then spoon over the fillets.

Fresh Habanero Chiles

· · · · ·

Wow! The aromatic of a fresh raw habanero—I'm talking about an orange, ripe one—smells like passion fruit or guavas, apricots and orange blossoms, all mixed up with green herbs and a piquancy your nose can detect. All the flowers and fruit come through in the taste as well, along with sweetness and a tangerine tang—and a glorious heat that overtakes the front two-thirds of your mouth and heightens your senses.

These are *not* Scotch bonnet peppers, the latter being more aggressively flavored (though noticeably similar) and equally hot. The related Scotch bonnet looks different, too, usually smaller and sunken at the shoulder with a stem that rises from a nipple-shaped bump.

A final note about habaneros: we use so little of them in each dish that I recommend buying a handful when you find them and storing them whole in the freezer up to 3 months. Frozen ones slice in half easily and taste as good to me as fresh ones in cooked sauces and even in fresh salsas, where there's so little chile that the textural difference is hard to notice.

Stats: An average habanero ranges from light green to bright orange, is about ⅓ ounce, about 1½ inches long by 1 inch wide at the squared-off but not sunken shoulder, the lantern-shaped body quickly tapering to a point just before the end; almost all will be deeply dimpled and the points of some will look like a nipple.

habanero chiles

"Deflaming" Onion

I'm not a scientist, but am thankful they can give us useful information about why onions make us cry. Listen to Harold McGee in *On Food and Cooking*: "The volatile substance in onions that makes the eyes water . . . arise[s] from another cysteine derivative that is rearranged by enzymes when the cell contents are mixed." By *mixed*, I think he means when we cut into the onions. And the juice that flows out (the mixed contents of the cells) is that same aggressive juice that's responsible for what I call the "American-Mexican Restaurant Syndrome," that rather annoying repetition of flavors you experience hours after you've left one of the less-careful Mexican restaurants.

From good cooks in Mexico, who love to put raw onion in and on just about everything, I've learned to take the "flame" out of the cut-up vegetable by scooping it into a strainer and rinsing it under cold water. If you need to chop an onion several hours ahead, soak it for a few minutes in a bowl of cold water to which you've added a splash of vinegar, then drain it well. In some recipes that call for citrus juice or vinegar, I've directed you to deflame the onions right in the acidy liquid.

ESSENTIAL SIMMERED
TOMATO-HABANERO SAUCE

Tomate Frito

*H*OW THE METTLE of roasted tomatoes changes when simmered with habanero! Sure, the hot chile gives them some piquancy (though the chile in this recipe is just cut in half in traditional Yucatecan style, so it won't impart much), but they also take on that flavor so many of us have grown to love—fruity, herby, complex. In short, deliciously, unusually habanero.

This is a cooked mixture (hence the name *sauce*), but it's thought of more as a salsa in Yucatan, set out at room temperature to spoon on another preparation. That's mostly how we've used it throughout the book, but feel free to add 1 cup of chicken broth to it once it's reduced and simmer for an additional 15 minutes. You'll have an all-purpose habanero sauce to use on enchiladas or eggs.

Yucatecans roast lots of their vegetables, usually on a griddle since ovens with broilers are not common. I've described the traditional method for the tomatoes, then given you the simpler, more controlled broiler method. Replacing fresh tomatoes with good-quality canned is an option (you'll need a 28-ounce can); you'll miss the roasty flavor, but the sauce will certainly be worth making.

MAKES ABOUT 2 CUPS

1½ pounds (3 medium-large or 9 to 12 plum) ripe tomatoes

1½ tablespoons rich-tasting lard or olive or vegetable oil

1 small (4-ounce) white onion, thinly sliced

1 fresh habanero chile, halved

Salt, about ½ teaspoon

1. *Roasting the tomatoes.* **The griddle method:** Line a griddle or heavy skillet with aluminum foil and heat over medium. Lay the tomatoes on the foil and roast, turning several times, until blistered, blackened and softened, about 10 minutes. Don't worry if some of the skin sticks to the foil. **The broiler method:** Lay the tomatoes on a baking sheet and place about 4 inches below a very hot broiler. Roast until blistered and blackened on one side, about 6 minutes; flip the tomatoes and roast the other side.

Cool, then peel, collecting any juices with the tomatoes. Coarsely puree tomatoes and juices in a food processor or blender.

2. *The sauce.* In a medium-size (2- to 3-quart) saucepan, heat the lard or oil over medium. Add the onion and fry until deep golden, about 8 minutes. Add the tomatoes and chile

halves and simmer 15 minutes or so, stirring often, until nicely reduced but not dry (it should be an easily spoonable consistency). Taste (it will be wonderfully *picante* and nicely perfumed), season with salt, remove the chile if you want and it's ready to use.

ADVANCE PREPARATION—Covered and refrigerated, the sauce will keep for several days; it also freezes well.

OTHER CHILES YOU CAN USE—Jalapeños and serranos (3 to 5) and manzanos (1 to 2) can replace the habaneros.

TRADITIONAL DISHES THAT USE THIS ESSENTIAL AS A STARTING POINT
Motul-Style Eggs (page 270); Yucatecan Tamales (page 301); Campeche Baked Fish Fillets (page 348)

SIMPLE IDEAS FROM MY AMERICAN HOME

Spicy Stuffed Zucchini—Slice 2 large zucchinis in half lengthwise and scoop out the center with a small spoon to make 4 "boats." Warm ½ cup cream cheese in a microwave, then mix in 1½ cups fresh corn kernels and ⅓ cup soft bread crumbs; salt. Stuff into the zucchini boats and bake at 350 degrees on an oiled baking sheet until the zucchini is crisp-tender, about 20 minutes. Spoon warm salsa over the boats and sprinkle with cilantro.

Simple Black Bean Dinner—If you have a pot of seasoned, cooked black beans on hand, simmer it for 20 or 30 minutes with ½ cup chorizo sausage or with cubed smoked sausage. Serve topped with big dollops of this sauce and chopped cilantro.

Where to Buy Chiles

These days, I'm glad to say, you can find a variety of chiles in most grocery stores, especially in areas with large Mexican populations or in stores that offer specialty items. You'll find fresh chiles in the produce section, of course, dried chiles with ethnic ingredients or spices. In grocery stores and specialty food shops, dried chiles are often sold in small packages; you'll need to go there with an idea of what you're looking for (they're sometimes mislabeled) and be prepared to pay the specialty-store price. Mexican groceries are the best places to buy your chiles, since a greater demand usually translates into freshness. There, too, you'll need to know what you're looking for, since the chiles may not be labeled at all.

To find a Mexican grocery, ask around for a Mexican community, then visit its business district, preferably on a Sunday afternoon when the grocery stores tend to be hopping and have special offerings (like *carnitas, barbacoa,* cactus salad, *chicharrón, masa* for tortillas or tamales—all the special stuff for a great Sunday dinner). If there's no Mexican grocery nearby and no specialty food shop that is Mexican-friendly, refer to Sources (page 425), where I've listed a few mail-order companies that offer good variety of high-quality dried chiles and other ingredients.

. . . .

Onions in Mexican Cooking

Onions (and garlic) form the warp in a Mexican sauce, into which more assertive flavors are woven. They add texture and brightness when stirred in raw (see notes on Deflaming Onions, page 30, for the Mexican way to tame their bite); they enrich with a delicate sweetness when cooked.

North of the Río Grande, we think of onions as yellow; south they are white. Yet despite the similarity of the two, they really are not interchangeable. Yellows have a more complex, herbal, sweeter flavor; whites are tangy and sharp with a clean, crisp flavor and texture. In Mexican food, that yellow-onion complexity translates as a muddy taste, I feel, especially when used raw.

Thankfully, white onions are readily available in most grocery stores throughout the United States. The green-tops-on variety that Mexicans love to slice raw over finished dishes can be found in Mexican groceries and farmer's markets.

Red onions are used extensively in Yucatan and regularly throughout the rest of the country (though, to my understanding, they're thought of as a specialty onion—one used for pickling). Supersweet types like Vidalia are not part of the general offerings in Mexico, and I doubt they ever will be. Their pure sugariness seems inappropriate for the role of onions in the cuisine.

Stats: All the recipes in this book were cooked using an exact *weight* of onion that corresponds to whole white onions as follows: a small onion weighs 4 ounces, a medium 6 ounces and a large 8 ounces. A medium red onion weighs 8 ounces.

. . . .

ESSENTIAL QUICK-COOKED
TOMATO-CHIPOTLE SAUCE
Salsa de Chile Chipotle y Jitomate

THIS EARTHY-HUED Essential Sauce, gently balanced between smokiness and natural sweetness, is used as the starting point for more dishes in this book than is any other dried red chile Essential.

The concentrated, roasty flavor of blackened tomatoes gets focused in this classic when they're blended with the smokiness of chipotles and sweetness of garlic, then seared in a hot oiled pan (I do hope you won't be afraid to use a little high-heat-rendered pork lard; the sauce tastes all the better). Leaving the sauce fairly thick makes it more versatile (you can use it as the base for shrimp cocktail, for instance), though if you're looking for that tomato-sauce sauciness for *huevos rancheros,* stir in 1 cup of chicken broth and simmer over medium-low heat for 15 minutes or so. You can make the sauce with good canned tomatoes—a 28-ounce can here—if there were no ripe tomatoes to be found, skipping the tomato roasting step, of course.

MAKES ABOUT 2 CUPS

3 to 4 (*about ¼ ounce total*) *dried black-red* chiles chipotles colorados (*chiles moritas*)

OR 2 to 3 (*about ¼ ounce total*) *dried tan* chiles chipotles mecos

OR 3 to 4 *canned* chiles chipotles en adobo

4 garlic cloves, unpeeled

1½ pounds (*3 medium-large round or 9 to 12 plum*) ripe tomatoes

1 tablespoon rich-tasting lard or olive or vegetable oil

Salt, about ½ teaspoon

1. *Toasting and roasting the key ingredients.* Set a heavy ungreased skillet or griddle over medium heat. If using dried chiles, break off their stems. Toast the chiles a few at a time: Lay on the hot surface, press flat for a few seconds with a metal spatula (they'll crackle faintly and release their smoky aroma), then flip and press down to toast the other side. Transfer the toasted chiles to a bowl, cover with hot water and let rehydrate for 30 minutes, stirring regularly to ensure even soaking. Pour off all the water and discard.

If using canned chiles, simply remove them from the *adobo* they're packed in.

On a heavy, ungreased skillet or griddle over medium heat (you'll already have it on if you're using dried chiles), roast the unpeeled garlic, turning occasionally, until blackened in spots and soft, about 15 minutes. Cool, slip off the papery skins, and roughly chop.

Lay the tomatoes on a baking sheet and place about 4 inches below a very hot broiler. When they blister, blacken and soften on one side, about 6 minutes, turn them over and roast on the other side. Cool, then peel, collecting all the juices with the tomatoes.

2. *The sauce.* Scrape the tomatoes and their juices into a food processor or blender and add the rehydrated or canned chiles and garlic. Pulse the machine until the mixture is nearly a puree—it should have a little more texture than canned tomato sauce.

Heat the lard or oil in a heavy, medium-size (2- to 3-quart) saucepan over medium-high. When hot enough to make a drop of the puree sizzle sharply, add it all at once and stir for about 5 minutes as it sears and concentrates to an earthy, red, thickish sauce—about the consistency of a medium-thick spaghetti sauce. Taste and season with salt.

ADVANCE PREPARATION—The sauce will keep for several days, covered and refrigerated; it freezes as well, though upon defrosting, boil it briefly to return its great texture.

OTHER CHILES YOU CAN USE—You can replace the chipotles with dried cascabel, árbol or dried serrano (*serrano seco*) chiles.

TRADITIONAL DISHES THAT USE THIS ESSENTIAL AS A STARTING POINT
Smoky Shredded Pork Tacos (page 150); Layered Tortilla-Tomato Casserole (page 201); Seared Zucchini with Roasted Tomato, Chipotle and Chorizo (page 216); Browned Vermicelli with Roasted Tomato, Zucchini and Aged Cheese (page 228); Smoky Shredded Chicken and Potatoes with Roasted Tomatoes (page 322); Smoky Braised Squab (page 328)

SIMPLE IDEAS FROM MY AMERICAN HOME

Sweet-and-Smoky Pork Chops—Lay 4 thick pork chops in a baking dish and pour the sauce over them. Bake in a 325-degree oven until tender but still a little pink inside (allow about 35 to 40 minutes for 1-inch chops and warm sauce). Remove the chops to a baking sheet and increase the oven to 500 degrees. Pour the sauce into a saucepan and simmer briskly until as thick as you like. Mix 3 tablespoons with 3 tablespoons honey and brush over chops. Bake until nicely browned. Serve with the remaining sauce spooned around.

Simple Chilaquiles—To feed 4, combine in a large skillet a full recipe of the sauce with 2 cups of broth, 8 cups (8 ounces) of tortilla chips (preferably thick ones), a handful of *epazote* leaves (or 1 cup or 2 of sliced chard or spinach if that's easier). Cover and simmer over medium-high heat for 3 minutes, until the chips are softening. Uncover, stir well (the chips should be soft but not mushy; the mixture should be a little saucy), then spoon out onto plates and sprinkle generously with crumbled Mexican *queso añejo* or Parmesan.

DRIED CHIPOTLE CHILES

. . . . .

These darlings hardly need an introduction these days. We've become enamored with their smoky heat, but few of us understand that there are really two main types of chipotles, a black-red one and a light-brown one. They have different smoky flavors, though both are smoke-dried cultivars of fresh jalapeño. Most of us, I believe, are familiar with and attracted to the dried-fruit fruitiness of the black-red ones, the ones we know from the can that are packed in a vinegary, tomatoey, slightly sweet sauce (*adobo*).

Black-Red Chipotle—This category is called most often, I've found, *chile chipotle* or *chile chipotle colorado* in the Gulf region, or *chile mora* or *chile morita,* depending on size, in the Central region. A puree of toasted, rehydrated black-red chipotles is a very spicy but near-complete flavor—it'll remind you of great, sweet smoked ham, if ham were naturally *picante*. Or smoky dried sweet cherries, or dried orange rind. And its full (and forward) heat is backed up by a flavor that's rich and lingering. The black-red chipotle puree comes out a dark, rosewood red.

I usually don't distinguish between black-red and light-brown chipotles in the recipes throughout this book; use what you can get, they'll both be good. For any chipotle-based salsa or cooked sauce, I generally prefer the black-red ones; for stuffing with a warm, shredded-pork or smoked fish *picadillo,* I like the larger light-tan chipotles.

Stats: An average black-red chipotle is purple-red to black with an intense, sweet smoky aroma; it'll be 1 to 1½ inches long by a good ½ inch wide, 8 to 12 to an ounce, wrinkle-skinned (a good one will be slightly flexible), a little twisted and pointed.

Light-Brown Chipotle (*chipotle meco*)—Through the years, I've known these beauties (they look like well-worn suede) to have a variety of flavors, from very hot, grassy smokiness to sugar-and-smoke medium spiciness. In front of me right now is a puree of toasted, rehydrated light-brown chipotle that isn't very hot at all. I'm thinking of brown sugar, ripe pineapple, tobacco and mesquite chips as I taste it—all in a good way, though the sum isn't as rich, complete and lingering as the flavor I find in black-red chipotles. The puree is mincemeat brown.

Stats: Typical light-brown chipotles are a jute (or craft-paper) brown, 6 to 8 to an ounce, about 4 inches long by 1 inch wide, their striated, slightly wrinkled body (with rather square shoulders) tapering gently to a point.

dried black-red chipotle chiles

dried light-brown chipotle chiles

The Whys of Soaking Chiles

When you taste a bit of dried ancho chile, chewing it and turning it over in your mouth until it softens up, an intense flavor seeps out that's untamed, even brash. But when toasted, then plumped in hot water, that ancho can be worked into a beautifully balanced salsa or sauce.

Over the years, I've tested different ways of rehydrating chiles and decided I don't think boiling them is a good idea; it takes out too much of their flavor. Instead, I use hot tap water for softening the chiles.

The chiles should be in enough water to float freely. Stir them now and again to ensure they're plumping evenly (you may find it easier to lay a small plate on top of them to keep them submerged). Soaking longer than half an hour leaches out too much flavor for me, and for salsas where I want a pungent punch, I suggest in the recipes soaking the chiles only long enough to make them pliable, usually 15 to 20 minutes.

I usually discard the soaking liquid (it often adds a bitter edge) and use water or broth to blend the chiles and finish the dish. If pouring out the soaking liquid goes against your grain, taste the liquid, and, if it's not bitter, use it.

ESSENTIAL SIMMERED
TOMATILLO-SERRANO SAUCE
Salsa Verde Cocida

*T*OMATILLOS ARE WONDERFULLY ADAPTABLE. Sure, any dish that employs them for sauciness will showcase their lovely, earthy-green tartness. But depending on which steps of preparation are chosen, what balance of flavors in the dish and what variety is at hand, tomatillos can contribute a wide range of flavors.

This simmered sauce is the perfect example of the tomatillo's congeniality. For a light (both in color and flavor), bright sauce that's great for fish or enchiladas, I've given directions for barely boiling the tomatillos during the first stage of preparation. For a rich, more complex sauce that I love with beef or lamb, there are directions for roasting the tomatillos first. A thorough frying of the tomatillo puree mellows the tartness by concentrating the sweetness. The richer-flavored the broth (meat broth being the richest in flavor), the more genial the sauce. And, if it seems appropriate for your finished dish, incorporating practically any dairy product (from yogurt or cream *in* the sauce, to fresh, aged or melted cheese *over* the dish), offers even more balance.

MAKES ABOUT 2 1/2 CUPS

1 pound (10 to 12 medium) tomatillos, husked and rinsed

Fresh serrano chiles to taste (roughly 3, 1/2 ounce total), stemmed

1 1/2 tablespoons olive or vegetable oil or rich-tasting lard

1 medium (6-ounce) white onion, roughly chopped

2 large garlic cloves, peeled and roughly chopped

2 cups chicken, beef or fish broth (depending on how the sauce is to be used)

1/3 cup roughly chopped cilantro

Salt, 1/2 to 3/4 teaspoon, depending on the saltiness of the broth

1. *The tomatillos and chiles.* **The roasting method:** Lay the tomatillos and chiles on a baking sheet and place about 4 inches below a very hot broiler. When the tomatillos and chiles blister, blacken and soften on one side, about 5 minutes, turn them over and roast the other side. **The boiling method:** Half fill a medium (2- to 3-quart) saucepan with water, salt generously and bring to a boil. Add the tomatillos and chiles and simmer vigorously over medium heat until the tomatillos have softened a little and lost their brightness everywhere except on the indented stem end, 2 to 4 minutes. Drain and cool.

Transfer tomatillos, chiles and any accumulated juices to a food processor or blender.

2. *The puree.* Heat *1 tablespoon* of the oil in a deep, medium-large (9- or 10-inch) heavy skillet over medium. Add the onion and cook, stirring often, until deep golden, about 8 minutes. Stir in the garlic and cook a minute longer, then scrape the browned mixture into the processor or blender. If using a blender, cover it *loosely.* Now, pulse whatever machine you're using to reduce the ingredients to a rough-looking puree—smooth enough to hold together, but rough enough to keep it from that uninteresting baby-food blahness.

3. *Finishing the sauce.* Wipe the skillet clean; then heat the remaining ½ *tablespoon* of the oil over medium-high. When hot enough to make a drop of the puree sizzle sharply, pour it in all at once and stir constantly for 4 or 5 minutes, as your sauce base sears and sizzles into a darker and thicker mass. (You'll notice that characteristic roasty, tangy aroma fill the kitchen.) Stir in the broth, let return to a boil, reduce the heat to medium and simmer briskly until thick enough to coat a spoon, about 10 minutes. (You can check the consistency by spooning a little on a plate: If it looks watery, solids separating quickly from the broth, simmer it longer; if it mounds thickly, stir in a little broth or water.) Stir in cilantro, then taste and season with salt.

ADVANCE PREPARATION—The sauce can be prepared 4 or 5 days ahead. If frozen, whiz it in the blender or processor to get it back to a beautiful texture.

OTHER CHILES YOU CAN USE—Fresh jalapeños can stand in for the serranos.

TRADITIONAL DISHES THAT USE THIS ESSENTIAL AS A STARTING POINT
Tacos of Tomatillo Chicken (page 146); Tangy Tomatillo-Sauced Fish Enchiladas (page 174); Roasted Mexican Vegetables in Green-Sesame *Pipián* (page 221); Pan-Roasted Salmon in Aromatic Green *Pipián* (page 351); Tomatillo-Braised Pork Country Ribs (page 382)

SIMPLE IDEAS FROM MY AMERICAN HOME

Simple **Enchiladas Suizas**—Steam-heat 10 or 12 corn tortillas (page 145); shred about 1¼ cups of cooked chicken into a skillet and warm with a moistening of the sauce. Roll a portion of the filling into each tortilla, lay them in a baking dish, douse with more of the hot sauce and sprinkle with about 1½ cups of grated Chihuahua or other melting cheese. Broil until browned and bubbly, then serve topped with rings of white onion.

Mexican Scalloped Potatoes—Slice 3 pounds of boiling potatoes into a large bowl, toss with salt, then spread half of them into a 13 x 9-inch baking dish. Drizzle in ¾ cup each of the tomatillo sauce and whipping (heavy) cream; sprinkle on ¾ cup shredded Chihuahua or other melting cheese. Repeat with the remaining potatoes and equal amounts of sauce, cream and cheese. Bake at 400 degrees for about half an hour, until browned.

Grilled Pork Tenderloin Encebollado—For 4 servings, cut 2 large pork tenderloins in half. Sprinkle with salt. In a large skillet filmed with lard, bacon drippings or vegetable oil, fry 2 sliced white onions over medium-high, stirring, until nicely browned but still crunchy. Add the sauce and bring to a simmer; taste for salt. Grill the pork tenderloins over a medium-hot charcoal fire until just losing the pink at the center, about 15 minutes. Lay on warm plates and spoon the sauce over the pork. Sprinkle with chopped cilantro and serve.

Tomatillos

Those walnut-size, pale-green globes covered with a pretty, papery, lantern-shape husk are one of the primary colors on the Mexican palette of flavors. They're called *tomate verde* (green tomato) in most of Mexico, confusing North Americans, since they are *not* green tomatoes. We call them tomatillo in the States (after the northern Mexican moniker), and they have a tangier, more citrusy flavor and richer texture than green tomatoes.

It's wonderful to know that fresh tomatillos don't have the ripeness problems that tomatoes do, and that they are available from coast to coast in the States. In fact, in the decade since I wrote *Authentic Mexican,* good-quality fresh tomatillos have replaced canned tomatillos at almost every grocery. If canned is all that's available to you, remember that an 11-ounce can is equivalent to 1 pound fresh. Fresh tomatillos keep very well, several weeks at least, loose in the vegetable bin of your refrigerator.

Enormous (golf-ball size and bigger) tomatillos seem to have the least flavor, and what flavor they have is sharp and slightly bitter. Smaller, yellower tomatillos would be my first choice; they're sweeter and fuller in flavor. Occasionally at the restaurant, we get the purple-blushed tomatillos (they're common in much of Mexico), and they have a wonderfully rich, herbal flavor; if you get them, be forewarned that they make a sauce or salsa that veers toward golden, rather than green. The tiny, wild *miltomates* that are so prized in Oaxaca for their intensely sweet-tart, deeply complex flavor look like the closely related wild ground cherries around Chicago; *miltomates* are less golden, less sweet than ground cherries.

Choose tomatillos that have grown to fill their husks. They're not fully mature if they haven't. When you're ready to use them, peel off the papery husk, then rinse off the sticky coating that makes the husk occasionally difficult to remove.

Tomatillos are commonly cooked, since that's when their best flavors emerge. If you boil them, as many Mexican cooks suggest, do so only briefly, to soften them a little. I haven't given you details for roasting tomatillos in the traditional way on the griddle, because I find the process difficult. The thin skin of the tomatillos tends to burn (and stick to the griddle) before the fruit is soft. I prefer to roast the tomatillos until dark on a baking sheet under a very hot broiler to concentrate their natural sweetness. If your finished sauce seems tart, season it with a hint of sugar to bring it into balance.

Stats: A medium tomatillo weighs about 1½ ounces.

stem

husk breaking away from tomatillos

tomatillos

ESSENTIAL ROASTED TOMATILLO-SERRANO SALSA

Salsa Verde Cruda

SOPHIE COE, MY guru when it comes to early Meso-American cooking, in her master-piece, *America's First Cuisines,* tells us that the tomatillo (also known in Mexico as *milto-mate, tomate verde,* or simply *tomate*) was likely the most-consumed *tomatl* (Nahuatl for a general class of plump fruit) in pre-Columbian times. Yes, more than the *jitomate* or red, ripe tomato to us English speakers. That explains, I think, why a mouthful of tomatillo salsa transports you straight to Mexico. It is the gustatory essence of the country—a gleaming contour of fresh green spiciness, herbal perfume and zest.

Though most initiates to Mexican cooking probably will start with a recipe for tomato salsa, I'd encourage this tomatillo one as a first foray. Besides being clearly authentic, it's easier: Ripe tomatillos are easier to find than ripe tomatoes; tomatillos don't get peeled; they give the salsa a consistently lovely thickness; and they come out a better texture than toma-toes when chopped in the blender or food processor.

For a salsa that's the quintessence of freshness and spiciness, make the recipe that fol-lows with just a half pound of raw tomatillos, roughly chop them, then coarsely puree them in a blender or food processor with all the rest of the ingredients (left raw), and add a tablespoon or two of water (it should be the consistency of a relish or fresh chutney). Clearly, this all-raw version is very quick to make, but you need to enjoy it within an hour or so.

MAKES ABOUT 2 1/2 CUPS

1 pound (10 to 12 medium) tomatillos, husked and rinsed

Fresh serrano chiles to taste (roughly 5, about 1 ounce total)

2 large garlic cloves, unpeeled

1 small (4-ounce) white onion, finely chopped

1/4 cup loosely packed, roughly chopped cilantro

Salt, about 1 generous teaspoon

Sugar, about 1 scant teaspoon (if needed)

1. *Roasting the key ingredients.* Lay the tomatillos on a baking sheet and place 4 inches below a very hot broiler. When the tomatillos blister, blacken and soften on one side, about 5 minutes, turn them over and roast the other side. Cool completely on the baking sheet.

Roast the chiles and garlic on an ungreased griddle or heavy skillet over medium heat, turning occasionally, until blackened in spots and soft, 5 to 10 minutes for the chiles, about 15 minutes for the garlic. Cool, then pull the stems from the chiles and peel the garlic.

2. *The puree.* Scrape the roasted tomatillos (and any juices that have accumulated around them) into a food processor or blender, along with the roasted chiles and garlic. Pulse the machine until everything is reduced to a rather coarse-textured puree—the unctuously soft tomatillos will provide the body for all the chunky bits of chiles and garlic.

Scrape the salsa into a serving bowl, then stir in between ¼ and ½ cup water, to give the sauce an easily spoonable consistency. Scoop the onion into a strainer, rinse under cold water, shake off the excess and stir into the salsa, along with the cilantro. Taste and season with salt and a little sugar.

ADVANCE PREPARATION—This salsa should be eaten within several hours after you've added the onion and cilantro, though you can make the puree a day or more ahead.

OTHER CHILES YOU CAN USE—Fresh jalapeños can replace the serranos.

TRADITIONAL DISHES THAT USE THIS ESSENTIAL AS A STARTING POINT
Tomatillo-Green Guacamole (page 81)

SIMPLE IDEAS FROM MY AMERICAN HOME

Scrambled Eggs with Mushrooms and Spicy Tomatillo—For 4 servings, beat 8 eggs with 3 tablespoons cream or yogurt and a generous teaspoon of salt. Heat 2 tablespoons of olive oil in a large (12-inch) skillet over medium-high, then add 2 cups sliced mushrooms (I'd choose shiitakes, portobello or any wild mushrooms I could find). Stir-fry until thoroughly wilted, then stir in ⅔ cup of the salsa. Continue to stir until the salsa is reduced and thick. Stir in the eggs, then stir every 10 or 15 seconds until the eggs are done to your liking. Divide onto warm plates, spoon on a little more salsa and sprinkle with chopped cilantro.

Tangy Seared Chicken and Spinach for Pasta—For 4 servings, cut 1 pound (a little more if you like larger servings) of boneless, skinless chicken breasts into one-inch cubes and season with salt. Heat a tablespoon of oil in a large skillet or wok over medium-high. Stir-fry the chicken until nicely browned and barely done, then remove with a slotted spoon. Add 12 ounces of stemmed spinach to the pan along with 1 cup of the salsa; stir until the spinach is wilted. Taste for salt. Serve over pasta, sprinkled with fresh Mexican cheese, feta, goat cheese or Parmesan.

Avocado Soup with Orange and Tomatillo—For 6 servings, roast 6 cloves of garlic on a griddle or skillet over medium heat, turning regularly, until soft. Peel and puree in a blender or food processor with ⅔ cup of the salsa, 2 ripe avocados, about a tablespoon of orange zest and ⅔ cup roughly chopped cilantro. Stir in 2⅓ cups beef broth (the richer, the better) and season with salt. Serve cool with a dollop of salsa and sprinkle of chopped cilantro on top.

The Rich Sweetness of Roasted
Tomatoes and Tomatillos

Many modern recipes call for roasted vegetables these days, no matter what the cuisine, so the whole procedure seems less foreign than it did a decade ago. And, I think most of us are aware that the payoff of roasting is enormous—sweet, concentrated, caramely flavors that quite simply make just about everything taste better.

Although the tidy cleanliness of the television-ad kitchens certainly has appeal, it's precisely that modern tidiness that's meddling with Mexican flavor, even in Mexico. It has led cooks to replace the Mexican grandma's charcoal- or dry-heat roasting with *boiling* in many cases, and the flavor's just not the same. Boiling is simple, bland.

I love old-fashioned roasted flavors and up-to-date convenience, so I adapt the modern kitchen to achieve traditional results. Roasting tomatoes and tomatillos on a baking sheet (one with sides to catch juices) under a very hot broiler is as effective as roasting them directly on the griddle or in the fire: It's simpler and you don't have to watch them constantly. When properly roasted, they should be *blackened* on the outside (splotchy) and completely *soft* within; they should not be hard and carbonized. With tomatoes, I usually peel off the blackened skin (though I don't try to get every bit) and I find that the tomatoes still have a rich, roasty flavor. Some cooks like to leave the charred skin on to add texture, flavor and black flecks throughout the sauce. Tomatillos are not peeled; you'll find that dark-roasted ones taste sweeter than lightly roasted ones.

Tomatoes and tomatillos can be roasted (and peeled, if appropriate) up to several days ahead; cover them and refrigerate. At the height of tomato season, I recommend freezing roasted, peeled tomatoes for later use.

· ·

ESSENTIAL ROASTED TOMATILLO-CHIPOTLE SALSA

Salsa de Chile Chipotle y Tomate Verde

THESE ARE THE MOST attractive salsa flavors I know: tangy (almost citrusy) from the tomatillos, smoky and hot from the chipotles and sweetly aromatic from the roasted garlic. Add anything else but salt (and a pinch of sugar if the tartness of your tomatillos seems to be prominent) and you're gilding a naturally perfect lily. I just love this salsa.

Unlike salsas that have lots of raw ingredients, this one can be kept for days in the refrigerator. As you approach the final step of this simple salsa, you can choose whether you like the rusty-colored, fully integrated flavors of the smoother version, or the olive-colored, flecked with red, rougher-looking version that'll offer surprise bursts of chipotle in every mouthful. When you have the time, try a third alternative in the mortar, crushing together the garlic and chiles, then working in the tomatillos; the garlic and chiles will be noticeably richer and fuller, the texture of the tomatillos beautifully coarse.

MAKES ABOUT 1 1/4 CUPS

3 to 6 (1/4 to 1/2 ounce total) *dried* chiles chipotles colorados (chiles moritas)

OR 2 to 4 (1/4 to 1/2 ounce total) *dried* chiles chipotles mecos

OR 3 to 6 *canned* chiles chipotles en adobo

3 large garlic cloves, unpeeled

8 ounces (5 to 6 medium) tomatillos, husked and rinsed

Salt, about 1/2 teaspoon

Sugar, about 1/4 teaspoon

1. *Toasting and roasting the key ingredients.* Set an ungreased griddle or heavy skillet over medium heat. If using dried chiles, break off their stems. Toast the chiles a few at a time: Lay them on the hot surface, press flat for a few seconds with a metal spatula (they'll crackle faintly and release their smoky aroma), then flip and press down to toast the other side. Transfer the toasted chiles to a bowl, cover with hot water and let rehydrate for 30 minutes, stirring regularly to ensure even soaking. Pour off all the water and discard.

If using canned chiles, simply remove them from the *adobo* they're packed in.

On a heavy, ungreased skillet or griddle over medium heat (you'll already have it on if you're using dried chiles), roast the unpeeled garlic, turning occasionally, until blackened in spots and soft, about 15 minutes. Cool, slip off the papery skins, then roughly chop.

Lay the tomatillos on a baking sheet and place about 4 inches below a very hot broiler. When the tomatillos blister, blacken and soften on one side, about 5 minutes, turn them over and roast the other side. Cool completely on the baking sheet.

2. *The salsa*. **Method 1 (the smoother alternative):** Scrape the tomatillos (and any juices that have accumulated around them) into a food processor or blender and add the rehydrated or canned chiles and garlic. Pulse the machine until everything is thick and relatively smooth. **Method 2 (the chunkier alternative):** Scrape the tomatillos and juices into a food processor or blender and add the garlic. Pulse until everything is coarsely pureed. Chop the rehydrated or canned chiles into tiny bits, then stir them in.

   Transfer to a serving bowl and stir in enough water, usually 3 to 4 tablespoons, to give the salsa an easily spoonable consistency. Taste and season with salt, plus a little sugar to soften the tangy edge.

ADVANCE PREPARATION—The finished salsa will keep about 1 week in the refrigerator, though the tomatillos have the brightest flavor for the first 24 hours.

OTHER CHILES YOU CAN USE—Dried árbol (use 3 to 6) or cascabel (use 2 to 3) can replace the chipotles. Dried *chile pasilla oaxaqueño* taste delicious here (use 1 to 3) if you can lay your hands on them.

TRADITIONAL DISHES THAT USE THIS ESSENTIAL AS A STARTING POINT
Smoky Braised Mexican Pumpkin (page 219); Grilled Catfish Steaks (page 358); Chipotle-Seasoned Pot Roast (page 368); Seared Skirt Steak with Chipotle and Garlic (page 366)

SIMPLE IDEAS FROM MY AMERICAN HOME

Crusty Chipotle-Beef Sandwich—Marinate very thinly cut (minute) steaks (*bistec* in Mexico) with lime juice and salt, then sear them in a large, very hot, lightly oiled pan or on a grill. Slice into thin strips and, in a pan over medium heat, toss with enough salsa to coat nicely. Split crusty submarine rolls or Mexican *teleras*, hollow them out slightly, then pile in the meat and sprinkle with crumbled Mexican *queso añejo* or Parmesan. I love these sandwiches with a smear of leftover fried black beans on the bun.

Great Chicken Livers—For 4 people, rinse a generous pound of chicken livers, pat dry, then toss with a little salted flour. In a large, hot, heavy skillet filmed with oil or bacon fat, fry the livers in an uncrowded layer until crusty and still pink in the center. Pour in a full recipe of the salsa, let come to the boil, then serve with rice or pasta.

Salsa versus Sauce

Salsa, surveys tell us, now outsells ketchup in the United States. Salsa—the stuff you eat with chips, spoon on crunchy tacos, even slather over hamburgers. You know, the cool and zesty condiment, usually made from chunky tomatoes with at least a hint of green chile.

In Mexico, the word *salsa* embraces a wider range than it does in the States. Yes, it includes the condiments, but they're more varied, spicier and less chunky, meant to be drizzled on a soft taco rather than scooped up with a crispy tortilla chip. But the word *salsa* reaches out to embrace "sauce" too, as in "spaghetti sauce" or "cream sauce."

In these pages, I've used the word "salsa" in the English titles for anything that's a condiment (they're all served cool): Roasted Tomato-Jalapeño Salsa, for example. I've used "sauce" for something that's cooked (they're nearly always served warm), as in the Simmered Tomato-Jalapeño Sauce. The only possible confusion you may encounter will be the Spanish titles: both condiments and simmered sauces are called, appropriately, *salsa* (always in italics); the first of our examples is *Salsa de Molcajete,* the second, *Salsa de Jitomate Cocida.*

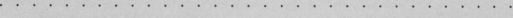

ESSENTIAL SWEET-AND-SPICY ANCHO SEASONING PASTE
Adobo de Chile Ancho

$\mathcal{I}$F YOU TAKE a few minutes to make this medium-spicy seasoning paste from toasted, rehydrated ancho chiles, sweet roasted garlic and spices, you'll have a gold mine in the refrigerator. More versatile than salsas (which are spooned on as condiments), this deep-burgundy, almost fluffy puree can be turned into the most complex dishes in the Mexican collection, from slow-simmered, rich, red *mole* and quick-seared red-chile enchiladas to garnet-colored rice. I even use it to flavor American-style baked beans.

Start with this seasoning to learn how to clean, toast, soak, puree and strain dried chiles—it'll seem awkward if you haven't done it before, but when you taste what the seasoning does to different dishes, you'll keep making it until the process seems second nature.

MAKES ABOUT 1 CUP

8 large garlic cloves, unpeeled

8 medium (about 4 ounces total) dried
   ancho chiles

1½ teaspoons dried oregano, preferably
   Mexican

½ teaspoon black pepper, whole or
   freshly ground

⅛ teaspoon cumin seeds, whole or
   freshly ground

A scant ¼ teaspoon cloves, whole or
   freshly ground

⅔ cup beef, chicken or fish broth
   (even vegetable broth or water),
   whichever is appropriate for the
   dish you're going to use the adobo
   in, plus a little more if needed

Salt, about 1 teaspoon

1. **The garlic and chiles.** Set a heavy ungreased skillet or griddle over medium heat. Lay the unpeeled garlic on the hot surface and let it roast to a sweet mellowness, turning occasionally, until soft when pressed between your fingers (you'll notice it has blackened in a few small spots), about 15 minutes. Cool, then slip off the papery skins and roughly chop.

While the garlic is roasting, break the stems off the chiles, tear the chiles open and remove the seeds. Next, toast the chiles a few at a time on your medium-hot skillet or griddle: Open them flat, lay them on the hot surface skin-side up, press flat for a few seconds with a metal spatula (if the temperature is right you'll hear a faint crackle), then flip them. (If pressed long enough, they'll have changed to a mottled tan underneath. If you see a slight wisp of smoke, that's okay, but any more will mean burnt chiles.) Now, press down again to toast the other side. Transfer to a bowl, cover with hot water and let rehydrate for 30 minutes, stirring regularly to ensure even soaking. Pour off all the water and discard.

2. *The seasoning.* If using whole spices, pulverize the oregano, pepper, cumin and cloves in a spice grinder or mortar, then transfer to a food processor or blender, along with the drained chiles and garlic. Measure in the broth and process to a smooth puree, scraping and stirring every few seconds. (If you're using a blender and the mixture won't move through the blades, add more broth, a little at a time, until everything is moving, but still as thick as possible.) With a rubber spatula, work the puree through a medium-mesh strainer into a bowl; discard the skins and seeds that remain behind in the strainer. Taste (it'll have a rough, raw edge to it), then season with salt.

ADVANCE PREPARATION—Covered and refrigerated, the marinade will keep for about 2 weeks; it also freezes well.

OTHER CHILES YOU CAN USE—Though I want you to learn the unique flavor of ancho by making this seasoning solo, it's very commonly made with half ancho (for rich sweetness) and half guajillo (for tangy brightness); a few chipotles in the mix adds heat and complexity. Always substitute an equivalent weight of chiles.

TRADITIONAL DISHES THAT USE THIS ESSENTIAL AS A STARTING POINT
Spicy Chile-Baked Oysters (page 90); Street-Style Red Chile Enchiladas (page 182); Simple Red *Mole* Enchiladas (page 178); Chile-Glazed Sweet Potatoes (page 226); Red Chile Rice (page 252); Red Chile–Braised Chicken (page 314); Ancho-Marinated Whole Roast Fish (page 356)

SIMPLE IDEAS FROM MY AMERICAN HOME

Very, Very Good Chili—In a large, heavy skillet or Dutch oven filmed with oil or bacon drippings, fry 2 pounds of coarse-ground beef (or half beef, half pork) and one large chopped onion over medium-high heat, stirring to break up clumps, until nicely browned; drain off most of the fat. Add a full recipe of the seasoning, stir for several minutes to temper the raw flavor, then stir in enough water or beef broth so that everything's floating freely. Partially cover and simmer gently for an hour, until it looks like chili; season with salt and a touch of sugar. If you like a less intense flavor, add 1 cup or so of blended canned tomato along with the water, and, if you prefer your chili with thickened juices, mix together a little *masa harina* and water, and whisk it into the chili during the last few minutes of simmering. I like my chili with whole boiled beans stirred in at the end.

Ancho-Broiled Salmon—Mix 4 or 5 tablespoons of the seasoning with 1½ tablespoons of balsamic vinegar and 1 tablespoon of brown sugar. Use this to marinate 4 salmon fillets (you can also choose sea bass, mahimahi or snapper) for a few minutes, then lay on a baking sheet and set about 6 inches below a hot broiler. After about 4 minutes, flip them over, drizzle on any marinade left in the bowl and broil a few more minutes, until the fish flakes under firm pressure.

DRIED ANCHO CHILES

· · · · ·

If I could have but one dried chile to work with, it would be ancho. The solidity of its earthy sweetness mixed with a small dose of heat, gives ancho that Robert De Niro character that is as perfect in a tux as it is in boxing trunks.

Anchos are mostly grown and sun- or force-dried in West-Central Mexico, but you can buy them in practically every town in Mexico and most towns in the United States. They suffer from the Michoacan Nomenclature Predicament (that is, they're called *pasillas* there), which means you often hear "pasilla" in California, too. One of my suppliers in California distinguishes between Mexican ancho and what he calls California pasilla, saying the California pasilla is a variety of ancho/mulato grown in Baja California; it is smaller, redder, milder and more wrinkled than Mexican ancho. To his knowledge there are no anchos grown in the United States. Now, if that's not enough to confuse anyone . . .

Tasting a bit of pureed, toasted, rehydrated ancho, I sense a mix of earth and fruit: sweet dark cherries, prunes, fresh tobacco (with all its licorice and dried-leafy bitterness) and dried calimyrna figs. It is rich and unctuous, and ranges from mild to medium-hot. The puree is the color of henna on black hair.

Though anchos are used almost exclusively in cooked dishes (cooking definitely rounds their flavor), crumbled toasted bits are a common garnish on soup in Michoacan (there's a great appetizer of almost-crisp-fried anchos and onions, too) and whole ones (pickled or not) are occasionally stuffed (see page 108).

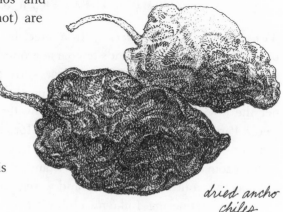

Stats: An average ancho is very dark cranberry (if you tear it open and hold a single layer up to the light, you'll see that beautiful cranberry color), about ½ ounce, 4 inches long by 3 inches wide, the wrinkled-skin, heart-shaped body tapering slowly to a point; notice that the stem is recessed a bit.

dried ancho chiles

Why Toast Dried Chiles?

To my tongue, toasted dried chiles have more flavor. Toasting adds complexity, a hint of char and a bit of smokiness, all elements that balance a chile's natural astringency.

Toasting chiles isn't a very exact science; in fact, you could skip it altogether and your dish would come out all right, though a bit less rich. Overtoasting is a greater problem than not toasting at all, since overtoasted chiles have an acrid flavor.

Many Mexican cooks prefer to toast whole dried pods on their medium-hot *comales* (griddles), turning them until they're fragrant and slightly browned at the spots the chiles directly touched the hot surface; those cooks break off the stems and shake out the seeds after toasting. I use that method for small chiles like chipotle and árbol. For toasting large chiles (like ancho, pasilla, mulato, guajillo and New Mexico), I feel more comfortable following the lead of a Pueblan cook who first stems and seeds the chiles, tears them into flat pieces, then presses them against the hot surface with a spatula. The toasting seems to be more even, though a bit slower, since you can only work with one or two chiles at a time.

The actual time each chile is on the griddle may surprise you. If you have an even, medium heat under your griddle (or heavy skillet), you'll hear a faint crackle when the chile is pressed flat, skin-side up. In a few *seconds*, you'll smell a roasty, chile-spiked perfume, and, when you flip the chile, you'll notice it's changed to a mottled tan. Press it down to toast the other side and that's it.

Another widely used toasting method is frying in oil (we've used it here for Braised Turkey in Teloloapan Red *Mole,* page 277). The flavor difference is remarkable—so much so that even a novice can tell the difference in the finished dish. You sense a richer toastiness and texture.

Our restaurant-style chile-toasting method involves a broiler, though only when you've mastered griddle-toasting should you try this. We open the stemmed and seeded chiles flat on a baking sheet and place them about 6 inches below a commercial salamander heated to its lowest setting (about medium on a home broiler); the chiles begin to move about (it's quite a sight), and within seconds we catch their aroma and see a faint wisp of smoke. That's when we quickly pull them out, flip them over and toast the other side.

When pulverizing chiles into powder, you can toast them thoroughly on the griddle or bake them in the oven until thoroughly crisp. Oven-crisping is okay for powder (where thorough, dry toasting and crispness is important), though it doesn't add the complexity you get from the direct-surface or oil toasting.

. . . .

ESSENTIAL SWEET-AND-SMOKY CHIPOTLE SEASONING SALSA

Salsa Negra

*H*AVING AROUND a jar of this swarthy, very concentrated, yes, very smoky-spicy stuff opens even more seasoning possibilities than a bottle of Asian chile paste or hoisin or Worcestershire. Skillet-seared shrimp tossed with a little salsa will attract any spice-loving friend; smeared on a warm tortilla with a little crumbled cheese, it becomes an addictive snack.

The first time around, you have to convince yourself that it's okay to cook something calling for 50 chipotles that are fried in an oil bath, then soaked in dark sugar water, blended and fried again. For years, even *I* avoided following the strange-sounding directions of this recipe, until Carmen Ramírez Degollado, one of Mexico's most dynamic cooks, walked me through the traditional Veracruz preparation when she came to teach at our restaurant. Now we're all converted.

The first time you stir a spoonful into that bowl of black beans you're having for dinner, the first time you add a little to that bland barbecue sauce you bought, you'll know why I think of it as "essential," even when it isn't widely known or used in Mexico.

MAKES ABOUT 1 1/4 POTENT CUPS

2½ ounces (roughly 2½ small cones) piloncillo (Mexican unrefined sugar)
OR ⅓ cup dark brown sugar plus 2 teaspoons molasses
Vegetable oil to a depth of ¼ inch, for frying

4 ounces (about 50) dried chipotle chiles (preferably the cranberry-red colorados [moritas], not the sandy brown mecos), stemmed
3 garlic cloves, peeled
Salt, about ½ teaspoon

1. *Salsa basics.* Into a medium-size (2- to 3-quart) saucepan, measure 1¼ cups of water, add the *piloncillo* (or brown sugar and molasses), bring to a boil, remove from the heat and stir until the sugar is dissolved.

Set a medium-size (8- to 9-inch) skillet of oil over medium heat. When the oil is hot but not smoking, add half of the chiles. Stir as they toast to a spicy smelling, mahogany brown, about 2 minutes. Use a slotted spoon to scoop them out, leaving as much oil as possible behind, then drop them into the sweet water. Treat the remaining chiles the same way.

Pour off all but a thin coating of oil in the skillet and return to medium heat. Add the garlic cloves and cook, stirring regularly, until golden, 4 minutes. Add to the chiles. Pour the chile mixture, water and all, into a blender or food processor, and whir into a smooth puree.

2. *Frying the salsa.* Return the well-oiled skillet to medium-high heat. When hot, add the chile puree all at once. Stir for a minute, scraping up anything that sticks to the bottom of the skillet, then reduce the heat to medium-low and cook for about 20 minutes, stirring frequently, until the salsa is as thick as tomato paste. (It will be very spicy smelling and will have darkened to nearly black. If you've left a nice coating of oil in the skillet, it'll be shiny on top when perfectly reduced.) Taste gingerly and season with salt.

If you're planning to use the salsa as a condiment on the table for each of your guests to spoon on or stir in, you'll probably want to stir in a little water to give it a more saucy consistency. For use as a seasoning, you can simply scrape it into a glass jar, store in the refrigerator and dole it out a tablespoon or so at a time.

ADVANCE PREPARATION—This salsa keeps for weeks, covered and refrigerated.

OTHER CHILES YOU CAN USE—This unique preparation is really best made with *chipotle colorado/chile morita. Chipotle meco* is an option, though you'd get a different taste and color; canned chipotles shouldn't be used.

TRADITIONAL DISHES THAT USE THIS ESSENTIAL AS A STARTING POINT
Puffed Black Bean–*Masa* Cakes (page 188); Broiled Chipotle Chicken (page 319); Chipotle Shrimp (page 334)

SIMPLE IDEAS FROM MY AMERICAN HOME

Spicy Clams or Mussels—For 4 people, fit 32 to 40 well-scrubbed medium-size clams or mussels into a good-size pot. Mix together 1 tablespoon or 2 of the seasoning salsa and a cup of fish broth, water or white wine. Pour over the mollusks, cover and boil over high heat until the shells have opened, usually 3 to 5 minutes. Pile into bowls. Taste the pan juices and season with salt, then served with chopped cilantro.

Cheese Spread for Sandwiches or Nibbles—Mix together ½ pound *each* cream cheese and goat cheese with 3 chopped green onions, 2 or 3 tablespoons of the seasoning salsa, enough chopped fresh thyme or cilantro to taste and salt and fresh pepper. Spread on crusty bread, lay on slices of tomato and you'll have quite a meal.

ESSENTIAL BOLD PASILLA SEASONING PASTE

Adobo de Chile Pasilla

$\mathcal{P}$ASILLA IS ONE of the most sophisticated chile flavors: pungent and tangy, deeply rich and woodsy. When you're used to using the gentler Ancho Seasoning Paste, graduate to pasilla. The techniques for making it are the same as those you encounter with the ancho seasoning. Here, we accentuate and balance their muscley, less-sweet flavor by using their soaking water, adding more garlic and elaborating their woodsiness with more herbs, fewer spices.

The near-black pasilla tastes perfect with black beans, mushrooms and richer meats like lamb and duck. Its spicy pungency becomes more focused when dark sugar or honey are part of the finished dish. If you enjoy rich, bold flavors, you'll love dishes made from pasilla.

MAKES ABOUT 1 1/2 CUPS

1 small head of garlic, broken apart into cloves but not peeled

12 large (about 4 ounces total) dried pasilla chiles

2 teaspoons dried oregano, preferably Mexican

1/2 teaspoon black pepper, whole or freshly ground

1/4 teaspoon cumin, whole or freshly ground

Salt, about 3/4 teaspoon

1. **The garlic and chiles.** Set a heavy ungreased skillet or griddle over medium heat. Lay the unpeeled garlic on the hot surface and let it roast to a sweet mellowness, turning occasionally, until soft when pressed between your fingers (you'll notice it has blackened in a few small spots), about 15 minutes. Cool, then slip off the papery skins and roughly chop.

While the garlic is roasting, break the stems off the chiles, tear the chiles open and shake and/or pick out all the seeds; for the mildest sauce, be careful to remove all the stringy, light-colored veins. Next, toast the chiles (to give them a richer flavor) a few at a time on your medium-hot skillet or griddle: Open them flat, lay them on the hot surface skin-side up, press flat for a few seconds with a metal spatula (if the temperature is right you'll hear a faint crackle), then flip them. (If you pressed them just long enough, they'll have changed to a mottled tan underneath. If you see a slight wisp of smoke, it's okay, but any more than that will mean burnt chiles and bitter taste.) Now, press down again to toast the other side (you won't notice as much change in color on the skin side). Transfer the toasted chiles to a bowl, cover with hot water and let rehydrate for 30 minutes, stirring regularly to ensure even soaking. Pour off the water, reserving about 2/3 cup.

2. **The puree.** If you're using whole spices, pulverize the oregano with the pepper and cumin in a mortar or spice grinder, then transfer the ground spices to a food processor or

blender, along with the drained chiles, the garlic and the reserved soaking liquid. Process to a medium-smooth, thick puree, scraping and stirring every few seconds. (If you're using a blender and the mixture won't move through the blades, add water a little at a time until everything is moving, but still as thick as possible. Not only is a soupy mixture a watery, uninteresting marinade, but the pureeing capabilities of the blender are much reduced when too much liquid is added.) Taste and season with salt.

ADVANCE PREPARATION—Covered and refrigerated, the seasoning will keep for a week or more; it can be successfully frozen.

OTHER CHILES YOU CAN USE—While this recipe looks similar to that for ancho, the fact that it uses the soaking liquid and more garlic gives it a balance just right for pasilla. Mulato could work here, though it doesn't have the roundness of pasilla. As with Ancho Chile Seasoning Paste, you can embroider pasilla with chipotle for a smoky edge.

TRADITIONAL DISHES THAT USE THIS ESSENTIAL AS A STARTING POINT
Spicy Pasilla-Mushroom Tacos (page 156); Layered Pasilla-Tortilla Casserole (page 208); Seared Lamb in Swarthy Pasilla-Honey Sauce (page 370)

SIMPLE IDEAS FROM MY AMERICAN HOME

Robust Lentil Soup—As a hearty supper for 4, simmer 2 cups (about 12 ounces) lentils in 8 cups water with 3 chopped bacon slices until the lentils are very tender and beginning to fall apart and the broth is thickening a bit (allow 30 to 45 minutes). Stir in as much of the seasoning as you like (since it's pretty *picante*, I'd start with ¼ to ⅓ cup), 2 large chopped tomatoes and 6 chopped green onions. Simmer 15 minutes, season with salt and ⅓ cup chopped cilantro (or a couple of tablespoons of chopped thyme or slightly less rosemary). Serve in big bowls topped with a little more chopped tomato and herbs.

Hardy Hamburgers—For 4 good-size hamburgers, mix together 10 ounces of coarse-ground chuck and 8 ounces of ground lamb or pork with 3 or 4 tablespoons of the seasoning and 3 chopped green onions. Form into patties and sear in a hot skillet or over glowing coals.

DRIED PASILLA CHILES
· · · · ·

It took me years to get comfortable with pasillas, but now I understand their swarthiness. Jean Andrews, the most careful and easy-to-understand chile writer I have read, points out that these chiles never lose their chlorophyll when they ripen and redden (these are *chilacas* when fresh), and that's what accounts for their deep chocolaty brown color. It's the dark, rich *flavor,* though, that I've grown to love, as much when it's seared and simmered to a concentrated near-black (think of balsamic vinegar's depth) or toasted and crumbled onto tortilla soup.

Woodsy and tangy come to my mind when I taste a puree of toasted, rehydrated pasillas. The prunelike, dried-fruit flavor of ancho and mulato seems more in the background, so you notice the tang; a spicy, dark flavor reminiscent of dried tomatoes and baked-potato skin is what you're working with here. The puree is mahogany brown, with a voluptuous texture.

The Michoacan Nomenclature Predicament affects pasillas: In Michoacan (and often in California) they are known as *negros*. In Oaxaca, there is a redder, smaller, hotter, smoky-smelling chile called *pasilla* or *pasilla oaxaqueño* that is stuffed or used in salsas; it is very different from standard pasillas which, in Oaxaca, usually go by the name *pasilla mexicano*.

Stats: An average pasilla is almost black, about ⅓ ounce, about 7 inches long by 1 inch wide, the wrinkled-skin, long, straight body (with sloped shoulders) tapering to a blunted point just before the end.

dried pasilla chiles

Garlic and Onion on the Griddle: A Lesson in Roasting

Roasted garlic has become a modern cliché, though to most it means garlic roasted in oil by the radiant heat of an oven. Mexican roasted garlic differs: It is cooked on the direct heat of an ungreased griddle or open fire. While old-fashioned Mexican cooks recommend roasting a whole head directly in the coals, when cooking at home, I break the head into cloves and roast just a few at a time on a griddle. Direct dry-heat roasting browns the garlic a little, while the papery skin protects it from burning—all working together to yield a toasty sweetness, rather than the buttery sweetness of the oil-roasted garlic.

Roasted onions in Mexico are also done without oil and, especially in Yucatan, they're regularly roasted whole directly in the fire. For small quantities, I roast *slices* of onion, either directly on a seasoned charcoal or gas grill, or on a foil-lined griddle or skillet. Since foil is flexible, you can peel it off the sticky onion slices, rather than trying to scrape the onion from the bottom of a dry pan.

ESSENTIAL SIMMERED GUAJILLO SAUCE

Salsa de Chile Guajillo

THE BRIGHT AND sassy flavor of this slow-simmered guajillo sauce is, I think, what first enticed me into real Mexican cooking; I know it's what keeps me wedded to it. The simple, quick procedure of toasting these readily available dried chiles will fill the kitchen with warm, roasty redolence; skip that step and the brightness of guajillos tastes ungrounded.

Searing the sauce in a hot pan is the most unusual technique you'll encounter here, though after doing it several times it will be old hat. Skip it and move straight to the simple simmer? The sauce will be simple; it'll never lose that raw-chile harshness.

A perfectly made Guajillo Sauce is a harmonious, cherry-red beauty: spicy, rich and tangy, seasoned with a good dose of salt and enough sugar to balance the natural astringency of the chiles.

MAKES ABOUT 2 1/2 CUPS

6 garlic cloves, unpeeled

16 medium-large (about 4 ounces total) dried guajillo chiles

1 teaspoon dried oregano, preferably Mexican

1/4 teaspoon black pepper, whole or freshly ground

1/8 teaspoon cumin, whole or freshly ground

3 2/3 cups meat, poultry or fish broth, whichever is appropriate for the dish you're making, plus a little more if needed

1 1/2 tablespoons vegetable or olive oil

Salt, about 1 teaspoon, depending on the saltiness of the broth

Sugar, about 1 1/2 teaspoons

1. *The garlic and chiles.* Set a heavy ungreased skillet or griddle over medium heat. Lay the unpeeled garlic on the hot surface and let it roast to a sweet mellowness, turning occasionally, until soft when pressed between your fingers (you'll notice it has blackened in a few small spots), about 15 minutes. Cool, then slip off the papery skins and roughly chop.

While the garlic is roasting, break the stems off the chiles, tear the chiles open and remove the seeds; for the mildest sauce, remove all the stringy, light-colored veins. Toast the chiles a few at a time on your medium-hot skillet or griddle: Open them flat, lay them on the hot surface skin-side up, press flat for a few seconds with a metal spatula (if the temperature is right you'll hear a faint crackle), then flip them. (If you pressed them just long enough, they'll have changed to a mottled tan underneath. If you see a slight wisp of smoke, it's okay, but any more than that will mean burnt chiles.) Now, press down again to toast the other side. Transfer the toasted chiles to a bowl, cover with hot water and let rehydrate for 30 minutes, stirring regularly to ensure even soaking. Pour off all the water and discard.

2. *The puree.* If using whole spices, pulverize the oregano, pepper, and cumin in a mortar or spice grinder, then transfer to a food processor or blender along with the drained chiles and garlic. Measure in ⅔ *cup* of the broth and process to a smooth puree, scraping and stirring every few seconds. (If you're using a blender and the mixture won't move through the blades, add more broth a little at a time until everything is moving.) With a rubber spatula, work the puree through a medium-mesh strainer into a bowl; discard the skins and seeds that remain in the strainer.

3. *Cooking the sauce.* Heat the oil in a medium-size (4-quart) pot (like a Dutch oven or Mexican *cazuela*) over medium-high. When hot enough to make a drop of the puree sizzle sharply, add it all at once. Cook, stirring constantly, as the puree sears, reduces and darkens to an attractively earthy brick-red paste (usually about 7 minutes). Taste it: You'll know it's cooked enough when it has lost that harsh raw-chile edge.

Stir in the remaining 3 *cups* of the broth, partially cover and simmer, stirring occasionally, about 30 minutes. If the sauce has thickened past the consistency of a light cream soup, add more broth. Taste and season with salt and sugar—salt to brighten and focus the flavors, sugar to smooth any rough or bitter chile edges.

ADVANCE PREPARATION—Covered and refrigerated, the sauce will keep about a week; feel free to freeze it, though you'll need to boil it to get back the lovely texture.

OTHER CHILES YOU CAN USE—An equal amount of dried New Mexico chiles can replace the guajillos, although the sauce will not be as full-flavored; a chipotle or two adds complexity.

TRADITIONAL DISHES THAT USE THIS ESSENTIAL AS A STARTING POINT
Guajillo *Chilaquiles* (page 204); Guajillo-Sauced Shrimp (page 336); Hearty Seven Seas Soup (page 341); Grilled Steak with Spicy Guajillo Sauce (page 364)

SIMPLE IDEAS FROM MY AMERICAN HOME

Cheesy "Tex-Mex" Enchiladas—Set out about 4 cups of grated melting cheese, such as Chihuahua, and steam-heat a dozen tortillas (page 145). Coat a 13 x 9-inch baking dish with a little sauce, then roll ¼ cup cheese into each tortilla and fit them into the pan. Ladle a couple of cups of sauce over the top, sprinkle with more grated cheese, then bake at 425 degrees until bubbly and browned. Sprinkle with chopped white onion and cilantro and these oozy, delicious enchiladas are ready to eat.

Red Chile Vegetables for Tacos—In salted water, boil 1 cup *each* cubed potatoes and carrots until just tender; drain. Film a large skillet with oil and set over medium-high heat. Add 1 medium sliced onion; cook 3 minutes. Add 1½ cups sliced mushrooms (I prefer shiitakes here) and stir for 3 or 4 more minutes as the mushrooms wilt. Add the potatoes and carrots and stir frequently until everything starts to brown. Add enough guajillo sauce to moisten everything well (it shouldn't be soupy), let simmer a few minutes, taste for salt and serve with steaming tortillas and Mexican *queso fresco* or *queso añejo*.

DRIED GUAJILLO CHILES

· · · · ·

These are workhorse chiles with a lot of dazzle. Along with anchos, they're the most commonly used chiles in Mexico (and in my kitchen). What anchos are to "deep" and "rich," guajillos are to "spicy" and "dynamic." I can't remember ever seeing them fresh in the States. In West-Central Mexico, where they're primarily grown, I've seen fresh ones at times in the markets, called *mirasoles,* but the dried ones are easy to find here and practically anywhere in Mexico.

A puree of toasted, rehydrated guajillo sings with a chorus of bright flavors that combine spiciness, tanginess (like cranberry), a slight smokiness and the warm flavor of ripe, juicy, sweet tomato; the flavors go on and on. The puree is a deep, rich, red-orange—the color of good tomato paste.

Stats: A typical guajillo (its name, "little gourd," refers to its shape) is that same deep, dark-cherry red of New Mexico chiles, four to an ounce, about 5 inches by 1 to 1½ inches, with a smooth, leathery skin (smoother than most New Mexico chiles) and very sloping shoulders that give way to a body that bows out slightly in the middle, then tapers to a point.

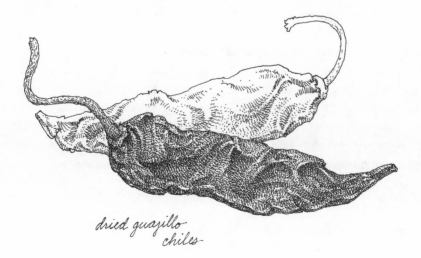

dried guajillo
chiles

Frying: The Key to Mexican Sauces

Though *frying* a sauce may sound strange, this unique technique develops the characteristics I associate with Mexico: deep, earthy colors; unctuous textures; and toasty, complex, thoroughly wedded flavors. Sauces made from rehydrated dried chiles become sweeter and lose their raw flavor during this frying step (taste a bit of the chile puree before and after the cooking); those made from tomatoes or tomatillos become more complex and richer, with all the flavors in harmony.

Since this technique is so important in creating attractive flavors, I'll spell out the details. In Mexico, sauces are fried in a wide earthenware *cazuela,* usually six to eight inches deep and shaped like a slope-sided bowl. The thick earthenware heats slowly (Mexican recipes often tell you to heat the *cazuela* half an hour before cooking) and holds the heat like nothing I've ever seen. In the States, I like to work in a wide, heavy, medium-deep pot—at the restaurant we use heavy stainless steel with an aluminum core; at home I work in enameled cast iron (such as Le Creuset).

To be sure your sauce base (the puree of chiles and/or tomatoes or tomatillos) fries properly, heat the empty pot for a few minutes over medium-high. Next, film the bottom with oil or lard, as your recipe directs; it'll immediately become very hot. Test the temperature of the oil with a drop of puree: If it sizzles sharply, the oil is ready. Now add the sauce base all at once. It'll crackle, spatter a bit (be prepared to grab a lid or spatter screen), and boil almost instantly; it should never lose that boil. Stir constantly (I like to use a long, wide, wooden spatula to reach all corners of the pan) until the sauce base has darkened and reduced to a thick mass, about 5 minutes. Nothing should stick or scorch; you don't want to char or burn anything here. (Be sure the sauce base you start with is quite thick; watery ones won't sizzle, sear and boil like the thick ones, and they never taste rich.) Finally, stir broth into this concentrated base—enough to give it a nice "saucy" consistency—and let the whole thing simmer for a few minutes to give the flavors time to come together.

A tip to those who are timid about frying a sauce: In the restaurant, where we do several-gallon batches, we use a method that needs less tending and causes a little less splashing, but takes a long time. We sear and stir for several minutes in the oily hot pan, then reduce the heat to low and let the sauce concentrate for a couple of hours. You can follow our restaurant procedure with smaller batches, though you'll need only a half hour, say, rather than two hours, to concentrate your sauce.

Why Strain a Sauce?

For centuries, Mexicans have strained things. They've made colanders from clay (I bought a beautiful and ancient-looking clay *tlachiquihuite* in Chilapa, Guerrero, years ago) and strainers from gourds (I found my favorite in Juichitan, Oaxaca), and they've counted them as essential equipment in their sparsely equipped kitchens.

A sauce made from soaked dried chiles really is much more appealing, most Mexicans will say, if the chile skins (and stray seeds) are strained out. A *mole* thickened with ground nuts and sesame or pumpkin seeds will be smoother—definitely more velvety and elegant, less seedy—if you pass it through a strainer. A medium-mesh strainer, the kind you find cheap at the grocery store, works perfectly.

To make straining simple, choose the right equipment (I suggest a medium size—about eight-inch diameter—strainer set over a large bowl and a rubber spatula for working the mixture) and do it often enough to feel comfortable. There's nothing tricky here. In fact, you'll quickly learn which chiles have the highest pulp-to-skin ratio (anchos), which have the most leathery skins (guajillos or New Mexicos). Chiles that have a low pulp-to-skin ratio, like árbol and cascabel, are the hotter chiles usually used for table salsas, and they rarely are strained.

If you've done your pureeing well, there should be no more than a few tablespoons of matter left in the strainer to throw out (especially if you are straining a mixture made with the pulpy, thin-skinned chiles like ancho; more will be left with thick-skinned guajillos), and what's there should be clearly all skin or seed or hull. If you're worried that you've strained out too much, put the strained-out matter back in the blender or processor, add a little more liquid, reblend and restrain.

But is all this straining really necessary? You'll have to make that call. I doubt you'll notice much change in flavor; it's really texture we're talking about here.

ESSENTIAL ROASTED POBLANO *RAJAS*
WITH SEARED WHITE ONIONS AND HERBS

Rajas Poblanas

*W*E'RE ALL DRAWN to the smell of roasting peppers, I think. And when the peppers are poblanos, with their deep, concentrated richness, and they're roasted over a charcoal fire, they tap into something primordial in us. This preparation is one of the easiest true-blooded Mexican classics for American cooks to master, since most of us are now familiar with roasting peppers. Finishing the peppers with quick-fried onion, garlic and herbs produces an expeditious basis for a great variety of authentically flavored dishes. If you're wondering about the word *rajas,* it's Spanish for "strips," and in the Mexican kitchen they're most generally strips of chile.

Choose your roasting method based on the destination of your *rajas:* poblanos done over an open fire or flame roast quickly (the flesh doesn't soften much)—perfect for salads, salsas, fillings, accompaniments, anywhere their texture and rich, roasty flavor are important. Poblanos done under the slower heat of the broiler are fine for soups and sauces.

MAKES ABOUT 2 1/4 CUPS

1 pound (6 medium-large) fresh poblano chiles

1 large (8-ounce) white onion

1 tablespoon vegetable or olive oil

3 garlic cloves, peeled and finely chopped

1/2 teaspoon dried oregano, preferably Mexican

1/4 teaspoon dried thyme

Salt, about 1/2 teaspoon

1. *Roasting the chiles.* **The open flame method:** Directly over a gas flame or on a hot gas or charcoal grill, roast the chiles, turning occasionally, until blistered and blackened on all sides, 5 to 6 minutes. **The broiler method:** Lay the chiles on a baking sheet and set about 4 inches below a very hot broiler. Roast, turning occasionally, until blistered and blackened on all sides, 10 to 15 minutes.

Collect the roasted chiles in a large bowl, cover with a kitchen towel and let stand about 5 minutes. With your hands (wear rubber gloves if your hands are sensitive to the heat of the chiles), peel and rub off the charred skin (if you roasted the chiles without either under- or overdoing it, the skin will come off evenly), then use a paring knife to cut out the cores and scrape out and discard the seeds. If you think it's necessary, very briefly rinse the peppers to remove clinging bits of skin and seeds, but you'll also be rinsing away some of that roasty flavor. Cut the peppers into 1/4-inch-wide slices.

2. *Finishing the* rajas. Cut the onion in half, then cut each half into ¼-inch-thick slices. In a large (10- to 12-inch) heavy skillet, heat the oil over medium-high. Scoop the onion into the hot oil and cook, stirring regularly, until nicely golden but still slightly crunchy, about 5 minutes. Toss in the garlic and herbs, stir for a minute, then mix in the chiles and heat through, about 1 minute. Taste and season with salt.

ADVANCE PREPARATION—The chiles may be roasted, peeled, covered and refrigerated a couple of days ahead, or the whole preparation can be done ahead, for that matter.

OTHER CHILES YOU CAN USE—Mexican cooking is very regional, so each area's cooks make this preparation with whatever large fresh chiles are popular or available. You can do the same with anything from red bells to hot Hungarian wax.

TRADITIONAL DISHES THAT USE THIS ESSENTIAL AS A STARTING POINT

Roasted Poblano Chile Salad (page 100); Roasted Tomato Soup (page 124); Roasted Poblano *Crema* (page 134); Tacos of Creamy Braised Chard, Potatoes and Poblanos (page 163); Crusty Griddle-Baked Quesadillas (page 194); Crusty Baked *Masa* Boats (page 186); Tomato-Rice Casserole (page 260); Crusty Chayote Casserole (page 224); Oaxacan Omelette (page 268); Chicken Breasts with Poblanos, Mushrooms and Cream (page 324)

SIMPLE IDEAS FROM MY AMERICAN HOME

Roasted Pepper **Rajas** *as a Sauce/Vegetable/Filling*—If you simmer about ¼ cup of heavy cream or Thick Cream (page 165) or *crème fraîche* with the roasted pepper strips until thickened, you'll have a chunky, creamy "sauce" that's fabulous with grilled fish or chicken. If you're looking for a little more on the plate, try wilting about 3 cups of spinach leaves in with the onions, or adding a cup of fresh corn kernels or boiled, cubed potatoes. That all-vegetable version makes a great taco filling or vegetarian main dish, especially when served with a steaming bowl of rice. Though they're quite rich, I love soft tacos of creamy *rajas* sprinkled with crumbled Mexican *queso fresco* or pressed salted farmer's cheese.

FRESH POBLANO CHILES

· · · · ·

Though poblanos grow most abundantly in West-Central Mexico, their complex, rich flavor is relied on through most of the Republic, save the Yucatan and some far northern sections. They're the all-purpose fresh chile in my kitchen and, from the looks of their easy availability in the States these days, in many kitchens. Since they add flavor, spiciness and texture to a wide variety of dishes, from salsas and soups to vegetable dishes and elegant cream sauces, I even add them to potato salad and baked beans.

Because of a quirk of migratory history, some Californians still refer to this chile, and its dried counterpart, as "pasilla," as they do in Michoacan. Otherwise, everyone else knows them as "poblano," or simply *"chile verde"* in Mexican regions where they're the only game in town. Occasionally it's their use that's featured in their name: *chile para rellenar* (stuffing chile) or *chile para deshebrar* (shredding chile). When dried, poblanos are called "anchos" (except, again, in California and Michoacan, where they're often referred to as "pasillas.")

The flesh of a raw poblano has a compact texture, usually a good amount of heat (though it can vary from mild to quite hot) and a full, green-bean green flavor; you'll notice herbal notes, too, reminiscent of flat-leaf parsley. Roasted, it softens into a lingering, near-sweet, harmonious richness—to me, the quintessential Mexican flavor and aroma—that makes you think it's been cooked with olive oil, rosemary or thyme. You can use long green chiles (Anaheims) anywhere that poblanos are called for, but I don't think your dish will be as flavorful.

Stats: An average poblano is a dark forest green (occasionally they're available in fully mature red), about 3 ounces, 4 to 5 inches long by 2½ inches wide (at the deeply indented shoulder), the sometimes gnarled or dimpled body tapering at the bottom to a point.

fresh poblano chiles

How to Roast Fresh Chiles

I prefer to roast large fresh chiles like poblanos over a charcoal or wood fire because I think that's the way they taste the best. However, I admit it's impractical on my seventeenth-story balcony in Chicago in January. My second choice is to roast them over the flame of a gas burner. Third choice is to roast them close up under a very hot broiler. With this last method, the flesh of the chile tends to cook more than

I like before the skin blisters, because most home broilers aren't nearly as hot as the grill or the flame.

The reason we roast chiles at all is to cook the flesh a little (cooked chiles taste less grassy), to rid them of their tough skins, and to add a touch of smokiness. Large fresh chiles require a bit of vigilance during the roasting process: You want to evenly char—really char—the skin without turning the flesh to mush. That means a very hot fire and frequent turning.

Many cooks tell you to put roasted chiles in a plastic bag and let them cool before peeling. Trapping all that heat means almost certain overcooking to me, so I prefer to put them in a bowl and cover them with a towel for a few minutes. The steam they release under the towel is enough to loosen the skin, making them easier to peel.

Most small chiles, like serranos and jalapeños, are roasted directly on a dry skillet or griddle until soft and irregularly charred. Small chiles are rarely peeled after roasting.

Don't hesitate to roast and peel fresh chiles a day or two ahead; they keep well in the refrigerator. Lots of cooks, especially in the American Southwest where large chiles are grown, like to roast a lot of chiles at once and freeze them; the practice in vogue seems to be freezing the roasted chiles with the skins on; peeling them when defrosted seems to preserve flavor and texture.

ESSENTIAL GARLICKY ACHIOTE
SEASONING PASTE
Adobo de Achiote

ACHIOTE IS THE SAFFRON of Mexico: If it's not fresh or if it's used in tiny pinches, the orangey color is all you notice. More than a pinch of fresh achiote gives any dish an exotic, earthy perfume that to me is as captivating as good, musky saffron; it's certainly less expensive. You'll know you've got fresh achiote when the little chalky-feeling seeds have a punchy aroma and a vibrant rusty color that's more red than orange.

Though in Oaxaca they make "pure" achiote paste (it has only a little salt, sugar and acid added), it is the Yucatecan garlic-flavored, spice-riddled achiote paste that most Mexicans use. Even in the States, Yucatecan achiote paste is available in most Mexican groceries.

Homemade achiote paste has the brightest, most concentrated flavors (some of the commercial brands contain fillers), and it's really very simple.

Smeared over fish before it's grilled, slathered on pork before it's braised or roasted, stirred in tamal dough before it's steamed—achiote reveals the genius of Mexican cooks. Not spicy-hot here, but spicy-complex without chile. My version nods more in that direction than some I've encountered. Silvio Campos, a Yucatecan who came to Frontera Grill to make his famous pork *pibil*, made his with double the achiote of mine and half the spices. Try that version for an even more true-to-achiote flavor.

MAKES ABOUT 1/3 CUP

2 tablespoons achiote seeds

2 teaspoons allspice, whole or freshly ground

1 teaspoon black pepper, whole or freshly ground

1 1/2 teaspoons dried oregano, preferably Mexican

3 tablespoons cider vinegar

6 garlic cloves, peeled

Generous teaspoon salt

The spice-grinder method: In a spice grinder, pulverize the achiote as finely as possible, then dump it into a small bowl. Pulverize the allspice and black pepper (if you're using whole) along with the oregano, and add to the achiote. Sprinkle in the cider vinegar and mix thoroughly (it'll be a damp powder at this point and won't hold together). Roughly chop the garlic, sprinkle it with salt, then, right on your cutting board, use the back of a spoon or the side of a knife to work it back and forth into a paste. Little by little, work in the spice mixture (it probably still won't hold together). Last, work in a tablespoon or two of water, if it's needed to give the mixture the consistency of a thick paste. **The minichopper method:** Pulverize the achiote, allspice, peppercorns and oregano together with the sharp blade. Add the vinegar to the spices, along with the garlic and salt. Pulse until the garlic is roughly chopped, then let the machine run until everything is as smooth as possible. Dribble in a tablespoon or two of water, if it's necessary, to bring everything together into a thick, pasty consistency.

ADVANCE PREPARATION—This seasoning will last for several months in the refrigerator, if tightly covered (I suggest a small jar).

TRADITIONAL DISHES THAT USE THIS ESSENTIAL AS A STARTING POINT

Yucatecan Grilled Fish Tacos (page 153); Achiote-Roasted Pork Tacos (page 170); Achiote Rice Supper with Pork *Carnitas* (page 258); Achiote-Grilled Turkey Breast (page 326); Tomato-Braised Grouper (page 354)

SIMPLE IDEAS FROM MY AMERICAN HOME

A Twist on Tomato Salad—When tomatoes are at their peak, slice them and arrange on a platter. Make a dressing from one part fruit or white-wine vinegar and three parts good olive oil. Stir in your seasoning a bit at a time until everything is beautifully orange and the achiote is nicely detectable; you may need to season the dressing with more salt. Drizzle over the tomatoes, then sprinkle with thinly sliced green onions or sliced green-tops-on white onion. Strew with chopped fresh herbs (anything from cilantro to chervil will be welcome), and you're ready to serve.

Baked Ham with Yucatecan Flavors—Roast a poblano or long green chile; peel, seed and slice. In a large skillet filmed with oil, quickly fry an onion over medium-high heat until it begins to brown, then add the chile. Cut 1 to 1¼ pounds ham steak into 4 portions and nestle them into the skillet. Mix together 1 cup of orange juice with 3 tablespoons of the seasoning, taste for salt, drizzle over the ham, cover, and cook over low heat for 15 minutes. Uncover and simmer over medium-high until the liquid is reduced to about ¼ cup (it'll start to look thick). Serve the ham topped with the vegetables and a drizzle of the pan juices. For a fruitier version, add 1 cup of chopped fresh pineapple along with the orange juice.

The Fragrance of Freshly Ground Spices

I know most of us take for granted that spices come powdered in little jars, but we're missing out on so much pleasure by not grinding them fresh ourselves. Not only do finished dishes taste livelier when made from freshly pulverized spices, but the aroma wafting from the mortar or grinder as you're reducing them to dust is downright exhilarating.

Since cooks in Mexico are used to working with whole spices (you'd be hard-pressed to find *ground* spices in a Mexican marketplace), I suggest you look for the freshest whole spices in a Mexican grocery here in the States. I keep a mortar and electric spice grinder within easy reach to encourage me to grind fresh, and, to make the whole process really easy, I store a small brush in the mortar to whisk out what I've ground.

Though an electric spice grinder (the kind that often doubles as a small electric coffee mill) works great for cinnamon sticks and larger quantities of spices, I prefer a medium (five- to seven-inch) mortar for small jobs. The lava-rock *molcajetes* from Mexico are ideal.

CORN TORTILLAS
Tortillas de Maíz

$\mathcal{I}$ ENCOURAGE YOU to make your own corn tortillas at least once, if for no other reason than to fill the kitchen with that alluring aroma and to relish the instant gratification of a toasty, pressed-baked-eaten tortilla. If you can buy fresh *masa* from a tortilla factory, I more than encourage you to make them, to feel that fluffy, puttylike dough between your fingers. If you've only tasted corn tortillas from the frozen-food counter case, you've tasted only Wonder bread in a world that can offer you a crusty sourdough loaf.

For centuries, this daily bread was rhythmically patted into discs between accomplished palms that flattened their first corn dough as toddlers; if not patted between palms, the *masa* was pat-pat-patted flat onto a large leaf. Today, many youngsters in Mexico learn only the pressing between the metal or wood plates of a tortilla press—certainly an efficient, but less artisanal, procedure. For the first timer, or even an old hand like me, it's the only manageable approach, so that's the way I've written this recipe.

Now, the recipe may look long, but that's not because tortilla making is difficult or time-consuming—compared to bread making, tortilla dough is ultrasimple, as the dough is very forgiving. I simply want to spell out all the nuances of the process, so you'll get the best tortillas. Once you've gotten a little practice, you'll refer to this page only for the proportions—which are very simple, since corn tortillas are nothing but lime-processed ground corn and water. No salt, no added fat, almost whole grain. Certainly among the healthiest breads in the world. So eat lots of good corn tortillas and go light on the fat-laden flour ones, if health issues are a concern.

Fresh *masa* versus *masa harina*: Fresh *masa* is hands-down the best, but it's close to impossible to make at home, it's an effort to find in most communities and it's easily perishable. To get the very best tortilla, the *masa* needs to have been ground that day and never refrigerated; the *masa* will spoil within a dozen hours, and if refrigerated (or frozen) will yield a tortilla that's more dense. Get fresh *masa* for special occasions. Dehydrated, powdered *masa* (what is sold as *masa harina*) works quite well for tortillas (I'd use it regularly if the fresh *masa* weren't so readily available to me in Chicago), especially since good varieties like Maseca brand are available these days. The texture of tortillas made from *masa harina* is a little less smooth and meaty (they're a little mealier), but the smell of the baking tortilla is still compelling.

ABOUT 15 TORTILLAS

1 pound fresh masa *for tortillas*

   OR *1¾ cups* masa harina *for tortillas*
   (such as Maseca brand) mixed with
   1 cup plus 2 tablespoons hot
   tap water

1. *The dough.* For fresh *masa,* knead the dough with a little cool water until soft and easily malleable (I think it feels like soft Play-Doh or cookie dough); add water a tablespoon at a time and stop before the dough becomes sticky. Cover with plastic wrap.

For reconstituted *masa harina,* cover the *masa harina*-water mixture and let stand 30 minutes, then work in cool water, a tablespoon at a time, until dough is as soft as you can get it without being sticky; it will feel a little grittier, less puttylike than fresh *masa,* and it should feel slightly softer than *masa* when the proper amount of water has been worked in. Cover with plastic wrap.

2. *Pressing and unmolding the tortillas.* Divide the dough into 15 balls and cover with plastic wrap. Heat an ungreased double-size griddle (one that fits over two burners) or 2 ungreased large skillets so that one end of the griddle (or one skillet) is between medium-low and medium, the other end (or other skillet) is at medium-high. (If you're using cast iron, the heat will build as you're making tortillas, so you'll likely have to adjust the temperatures downward as you work.)

Cut 2 squares of medium-heavy plastic (at our restaurant, we cut up a medium-weight garbage bag) to fit over the plates of your tortilla press (a little bigger than the plates is fine). Open the press (if you're right-handed, you'll want the opened top plate to your left, the pressure handle to your right) and lay 1 square of plastic on the bottom plate. Center a ball of dough on the plastic, flattening it a little with your hand to make it stick, and cover with the other square of plastic. Close the top plate, then fold the pressure handle over onto the top plate and press down somewhat firmly. (Knowing just how hard to press will take a little practice—too light and you'll have an uneven, thick tortilla; too heavy and it'll be too thin to get off the plastic.) You're looking for a round that is 5 to 6 inches in diameter and less than ⅛ inch thick.

Fold back the pressure handle, open the top plate, and, while the plastic-wrapped tortilla is still lying on the bottom plate, take hold of the top piece of plastic and quickly pull it off. Now, pick up the tortilla by the plastic with one hand, and flip it over, uncovered side down, onto the slightly separated fingers of your other hand—it'll cover your fingers and half your palm. (If you're right-handed, I suggest that you pick up the plastic and tortilla with your left hand and flip it onto your right. As you get good at all this, work to align the top of the tortilla with the top of your index finger, with the circle extending just slightly past the tip of your middle finger; this will leave an inch or two of tortilla hanging down below your little finger.)

Starting at one edge, quickly peel the remaining plastic off the tortilla (go too slowly and you'll risk ripping the tortilla), leaving the raw, flattened disc of *masa* on your hand. If the dough is too soft, you'll have difficulty peeling off the plastic; to correct the problem, work a little *masa harina* into the dough and continue.

3. *Baking the tortillas.* Lay the tortilla on the cooler end of the griddle (or cooler skillet). Now, the practiced hand of most Mexican *señoras* will get that tortilla on the griddle in a flash with a deft, swift move that seems just the opposite of what you'd expect. Rather than

turning her hand over to release the tortilla onto the griddle, she moves her hand (held at a 45-degree angle to the griddle) away from her, letting the overhanging portion of the tortilla go down first, then quickly rolling her hand out from underneath the tortilla (the movement looks as though she's brushing something off the griddle with the back of her hand), letting it smoothly fall flat. It looks easy, but practically all of us North Americans get to the "sweeping" part, think we're going to burn the backs of our hands (especially the backs of our little fingers), and jerk straight up rather than away from us, leaving behind a ripped or folded-over tortilla. You simply need to summon your courage—realize that feeling the heat on the back of your hand isn't the same thing as burning yourself—and just learn to do it. Turning your hand over to release a tortilla this size onto the griddle usually gives you a rippled tortilla that's impossible to cook evenly. (A word of advice: Try pressing, unmolding and laying the tortillas on your countertop before you start with the griddle. You can scrape up the dough, roll it back into a ball and do it all again. You'll notice that once you have that unmolded tortilla on your hand, you need to get it off and onto the counter or griddle quickly or it will start to stick to your fingers.)

When you lay the tortilla on the griddle, it will immediately stick. If you have your temperature right, it'll release itself within 15 seconds, at which point you should flip it (with your fingers *a la mexicana* or with a spatula) onto the hotter surface. (If the heat is too low, the tortilla will dry out before it releases itself; if too high, it'll blister. Both translate to "not great texture.")

In 30 to 45 seconds, the tortilla should be speckled brown underneath. (If it browns faster, the temperature's too hot.) Flip it over, still on the hotter surface, and brown the other side for another half minute or so. A perfect tortilla is one that balloons up like pita bread after this second flip—something you can encourage by lightly pressing on the tortilla with your fingertips or spatula. Or, you can encourage ballooning, as many Mexicans do, by stacking a finished tortilla or two onto one that's just been flipped.

Always taste your first tortilla: If the dough is too dry, the texture will be heavy (it'll probably have cracked around the edges when pressed, too).

As tortillas are finished, collect them in a cloth-lined basket. They're best after they've rested together for about 10 minutes (and steamed from their own heat), but still have the original heat of the griddle.

Tortilla Presses

Some writers will tell you that it's possible to press out the dough for tortillas between two flat plates or to roll it out with a pin, and I suppose either is feasible if you're determined and dexterous. Then again, Mexican cooks, for millennia, have been patting out tortillas by hand or on leaves, so why would I even suggest a press? Simply put, without years of hand-patting experience, the easiest way for most of us to get a consistently flat tortilla is to press it out between the plates of an inexpensive tortilla press.

Tortilla presses are generally made of cast iron or aluminum. I prefer the cast-iron ones simply because their weight makes them less likely to move around. Either will get the job done with ease, as will the massive wooden ones that you find around Mexico (18-inch-square ones are used in Oaxaca for making *tlayudas*), though the wooden are probably better suited to those whose production is high and relentless (like for every meal). In the States, tortilla presses are sold in many cookware stores and most all Mexican groceries.

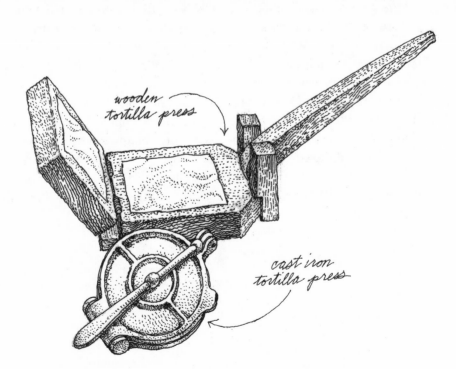

wooden
tortilla press

cast iron
tortilla press

Corn—Center of the Mexican Culinary Universe

Corn is used to make tortillas and tamales, of course, but first that corn has to be transformed into *masa*. And to understand what *masa* is, I think it best to talk first about what it is not. It is not "cornmeal dough," as so many American writers call it, since using the word "cornmeal" easily conjures up visions of a dry powdery something that's mixed with liquid.

And *masa* is not dough made from sweet corn, that delicious, tender vegetable that most Americans think of as the only corn. Rather, it is dough made from dried, starchy, decidedly unsweet *field* corn, the same that is used for cornmeal, hominy and grits.

To make *masa* from the dried field corn, you first have to boil the kernels briefly with calcium hydroxide (known as pickling or mason's lime, *cal* in Spanish), a process that dissolves the difficult-to-digest outer hull of the kernel and remarkably increases its nutritional potential. The boiled corn, which is called *nixtamal* in Mexican Spanish, is rinsed thoroughly.

At this point, the corn can be returned to the fire for several hours of gentle bobbing over the heat, until it becomes tender, puffy *pozole*—the Mexican word for what we call *hominy.*

Or, the briefly boiled, rinsed corn (the *nixtamal*) can be made into *masa*: the damp kernels—they're still chalky at the core—are stone-ground into a dryish paste. For eons, the stone grinder has consisted of the *metate* (the three-legged lava-rock grinding stone) and *mano* (the rolling-pin-like crusher), powered by a strong back and biceps. Since the mid-1800s, motorized mills have helped relieve the physical work of that chore, and what they turn out is very good because they all use stone burrs (metal ones, they tell me, heat up the corn too much, cooking their starches and yielding an unworkable dough). The finest ground *masa* makes what most people consider the best tortillas; coarse-ground *masa* is often preferred for tamales.

The fresh-ground *masa* is patted between palms (less common these days), pressed out between metal or wood, or squeezed out between metal rollers (then die-cut) to become the flat disc that's griddle-baked into a fragrant tortilla.

CHAPTER TWO

· · · · ·

SALADS AND OTHER STARTERS

WHO DOESN'T WELCOME A BOWL OF GUACAMOLE AT A GATHERING OF FRIENDS? AND NOT JUST we chip-and-dip Americans, either. Just the other night, I was at a birthday party at the home of some Mexican friends here in Chicago, and what did they serve? Guacamole, followed by a celebratory kettle of *pozole*—pork and hominy soup—and a lavishly decorated bakery cake. Yes, it's as popular among Mexicans as it is in the States, so that's where we're starting our starters. I've detailed the guacamole that's become our signature at Frontera Grill and Topolobampo, followed by an all-green version seasoned with tomatillos rather than tomatoes. Don't pass up the latter—it's uncommonly delicious. And don't limit yourselves to chips around your welcoming bowl of guacamole: Sliced raw vegetables (jícama, cucumber, radishes, fennel) are among my favorites.

One of the reasons we're drawn to Mexican food is its convivial informality. Many starters—as well as some of the main dishes—are perfect for setting out to share. Though my commitment to traditional Mexican cooking keeps me away from the Texan nachos, I can't stay away from cheese as a starter. If you share my penchant, try *queso frito,* seared slabs of fresh cheese doused with saucy tomatoes, chiles and herbs, a very Oaxacan take on the cheese-and-chile theme. Because the fresh cheese doesn't melt, the dish makes a very distinctive first mouthful.

Our American understanding of Mexican-style starters rarely includes Mexico's great seafood offerings. With more than three thousand miles of coastline, it's easy to imagine that the cuisine includes a large variety of fish and shellfish dishes. Perhaps the most classic as a starter or light meal is seviche, lime-cured raw fish mixed with the typical flavors of tomato, chile and cilantro and piled onto a crisp tortilla or into a "sundae" cup. If you're squeamish about the fact that the fish isn't cooked, be aware that lime marinating changes the fish's texture from squishy-raw to one that's similar to cooked. Very fresh fish from a very reputable purveyor is essential.

I've included a second seviche made from cooked shrimp marinated in lime—a less intimidating place to start if you haven't worked much with raw fish. I jazzed up this "safer" seviche with bits of exotic-sounding roasted cactus; they're a fun filip that has various easy substitutes. As you find yourself regularly turning to the recipe, you will be reminded of its neighbor, oysters baked in a shroud of tangy ancho chile, under a crust of crispy crumbs— perfect for an elegant dinner or any group of lusty eaters.

If you've wandered the byways of Mexico, you've doubtless seen sidewalk stands that sell jícama, cucumbers and oranges, sometimes mangoes and coconuts as well, drizzled with lime and dusted with hot powdered chile. Arrange them all on a platter, drizzle and dust, then sprinkle with chopped cilantro and you've got a wonderfully informal and healthy appetizer for a crowd. It's a perfect example of how to use tang, spice and herbs to make raw vegetables and fruits as exciting as melted cheese.

Though very traditional, the ever-present cactus salad may seem more like a relish than a salad, but it is a salad in the Mexican sense: crunchy raw things to eat alongside—or roll into a tortilla with—meat or cheese or fish. You can serve cactus like that, or focus it in the center of a small bed of greens, maybe even toss it with a little crab or smoked fish first, and make more of an American first-course salad. Dressed strips of roasted poblano can function as a salad in exactly the same way, and I think their flavor and texture are a little more familiar than cactus; when dressed up with shreds of something smoked and nestled in greens, poblanos become one of the most elegant salads from the Mexican kitchen.

At the request of loyal customers, I've included our Topolobampo house salad: a spin on the classic Caesar with green chile, cilantro and Mexican cheese. It's certainly not traditionally Mexican, though the flavor will be welcome at just about any Mexican meal. Perhaps it's the same loyal customers that are always requesting the recipe for plantain turnovers. I love these easy sweet-and-savory delectables made from cooking bananas and fresh cheese.

Stuffed chiles hadn't been thought of as "starters" in the States until some frozen food companies got hold of the Mexican idea of stuffing jalapeños. I've written up a really great rendition for those spicy little torpedos, one that can be turned into a lively beginning to an elegant dinner, when set amid lightly dressed salad greens.

Pickling dried chiles like chipotles, though common in Mexico, is little known outside the homeland. I heartily encourage you to expand your horizons to the wonderful mix of flavors. If you pickle anchos, you can also stuff them, resulting in an unusual combination of tastes and textures as in the traditional recipe I've included here: tangy marinated dried ancho chile, with its lovely melting texture and concentrated, dried-fruit flavor, wrapped around savory sausage and potatoes, and doused with a mellow, sweet-sour escabeche of red onions and carrots.

Crepes (*crepas* in Spanish) are one of the most sophisticated starters in the broad array of traditional, albeit traditionally fancy, Mexican dishes. Thinking you'll want to utilize these lacy corn-*masa* crepes for a nice dinner, I've given details for a delectable creamy filling of corn, poblanos and herbs, then included plenty of ideas for exotic, special-occasion fillings, like squash blossoms and the black corn mushrooms, *huitlacoche*. Burnish your crepes with Roasted Poblano Cream when you want to pull out all the stops.

GUACAMOLE

$\mathcal{W}$E'RE RIGHT HERE at the starting point for most people's exploration of Mexican cooking: a verdant, thick-textured bowl of festivity, ripe with the elusive flavor of avocado. (Has anyone ever adequately described the avocado's powerfully unctuous, near-herby, near-nutty subtlety in a way that really rings true?) Mash in a little lime, raw onion, cilantro, chile, perhaps tomato, and the avocado comes fully alive.

At Frontera, we carefully chop the tomatoes, serranos, cilantro and garlic (we use roasted garlic for more mellowness) up to a day ahead, then mix them with coarsely mashed avocado, rinsed chopped white onion, lime juice and salt just before we serve our guacamole. We use the dark, pebbly-skinned Hass avocados to ensure great texture. They have a good amount of oil, natural density and are slow to oxidize. Covered as I've described, the guacamole won't discolor for hours. We serve it with chips in Frontera, slices of jícama, cucumber and radish in Topolobampo, and we serve it to dollop on wood-grilled steak or to roll up with tender bits of pork *carnitas*. But I doubt you need ideas as to how to serve guacamole.

MAKES ABOUT 4 CUPS, SERVING 6 AS AN APPETIZER, UP TO 12 AS A NIBBLE

FOR 1½ CUPS ESSENTIAL CHOPPED TOMATO-SERRANO SALSA

1 large ripe, round tomato, cut into ⅛-inch dice

Fresh serrano chiles to taste (roughly 2 or 3), stemmed and finely chopped

1 garlic clove, peeled and very finely chopped (optional)

3 tablespoons chopped cilantro, plus a little additional for garnish

½ cup finely diced white onion, plus a little additional for garnish

3 large (about 1½ pounds) soft-ripe avocados

2 to 3 teaspoons fresh lime juice

Salt, about 1 teaspoon

Radish slices or roses, for garnish

1. *Making 1½ cups Essential Chopped Tomato-Serrano Salsa.* In a small bowl, mix together the tomato, chiles, optional garlic and cilantro. Scoop the onion into a strainer and rinse under cold water; shake to remove excess water and add to the mixture.

2. *Finishing the guacamole.* Cut the avocados in half, running your knife around the pit from stem to blossom end and back up again; twist the halves in opposite directions to free the pits and pull the halves apart. Either scoop out the pits with a spoon, or gently lodge your knife into them and twist to free. With a soup spoon, scoop out the avocado flesh (this is easiest with the thick-skinned Hass avocados, though with some practice, you'll learn to do it with most other varieties) and place in a medium-size bowl.

Mash the avocados with a large fork, a potato masher, or with your hand (don't resort to a food processor, which produces baby-food texture). Stir in the salsa, then taste and season with lime juice and salt. Cover with plastic wrap pressed directly on the surface of the guacamole and let stand a few minutes for the flavors to meld.

Serve in a Mexican *molcajete* (the rustic lava-rock mortar) or decorative bowl, sprinkled with a little chopped onion, cilantro and radish slices or roses.

ADVANCE PREPARATION—The guacamole can be made up to 4 or 5 hours ahead and stored tightly covered with thick plastic wrap such as Saran wrap in the refrigerator—any longer and the onion will overpower the delicate avocado flavor. Be forewarned that the flavors and textures fade quickly once the guacamole has warmed to room temperature.

VARIATIONS AND IMPROVISATIONS

For a simpler guacamole perfect for winter when good tomatoes aren't abundant, omit the tomatoes and, if you wish, replace the cilantro with a sprinkling of dried Mexican oregano.

Molcajete Guacamole—Make ½ recipe of the Essential Roasted Tomato-Jalapeño Salsa (page 21), omitting the water. Remove it from your mortar, coarsely mash 3 avocados in the mortar, then work in as much of the salsa as you think appropriate (it should take most of it). Season with salt and a little lime juice.

Avocados and Their Leaves

Of the three main strains of avocados (Mexican, Guatemalan and Caribbean), it was the Mexican variety that was hybridized into the very popular, pebbly-skinned Hass (the variety often labeled *California* in the stores). The flavor of the non-hybridized, tender-skinned little wild Mexican original, called *crillo* in most places, has an intense toasted-almond-and-fennel creaminess that is a bit diluted in the Hass, even less apparent in Fuerte avocados and others from the Guatemalan strain. Caribbean (what we usually call *Florida*) avocados are large, with lighter texture, lower oil content and wonderfully fruity sweetness.

The Mexican strain is the only one with aromatic leaves used for cooking. Since leaves from the U.S.-grown hybrids have little flavor, it's always a treat to run across leaves from Mexico (see Sources, page 425). When you're using the leaves in a dish they're usually toasted, then added as you'd add (the related) bay leaves. As a bed to nestle marinated meat in *barbacoa*-making, they're frequently left untoasted.

It's no wonder that guacamole developed in Mexico. The dense, oily flesh of Mexican avocados can be easily mashed into a thick and unctuous texture; they have the richness of flavor that welcomes tomatoes, cilantro, onion and the like. Avocados from other strains are better used when sliced and diced as garnishes.

Hass avocados are easiest to work with because they can be ripened on a countertop, in a paper bag to speed things along, then stored in the refrigerator for a few days to hold them at their prime. The mashed flesh darkens slowly, too. Don't let this deter you from buying other varieties, since the world of avocados offers a remarkable variety of flavors.

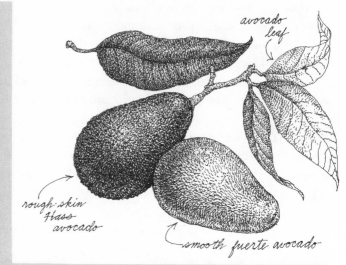

Unless I'm shopping in a Mexican market, I never expect to buy *ripe* avocados. Avocados are one of the few fruits that does not ripen on the tree. In fact, ripening won't start until you pick them and give them a warm environment. Produce purveyors and grocery store owners love this fact, because they can keep those hard green globes in their unripe state of suspended animation without risk of spoilage. We cooks, however, have to plan days ahead for a bowl of guacamole. If you do find ripe avocados, make sure they don't have any dents, which mean dark bruises underneath, and that the pit isn't shaking around inside, indicating over ripeness.

For garnishes, many Mexican cooks slice through the unpeeled avocado directly toward the pit, cut out wedges, then peel off the strip of skin. Alternatively, you can cut around the pit from stem to flower ends and back up again; then twist the two halves apart in different directions (the pit will stay attached to one half). Scoop out the pit, or carefully lodge a knife into the pit and twist the knife/pit until the pit is dislodged. Scoop the flesh from the skin with a large spoon.

Stats: A large Hass avocado weighs about ½ pound and yields about ¾ cup pulp.

TOMATILLO-GREEN GUACAMOLE

Guacamole de Tomate Verde

*T*HIS IS MY FAVORITE twist on guacamole—a little zippier than the tomato version, a little more unctuous because the tomatillos that replace the raw tomatoes are roasted. Don't overlook its possibilities as a spread for sandwiches or a flavorful dollop on charcoal-grilled fish.

MAKES 4 GENEROUS CUPS

FOR 1 CUP ESSENTIAL ROASTED TOMATILLO-SERRANO SALSA

8 ounces (5 to 6 medium) tomatillos, husked and rinsed

Fresh serrano chiles to taste (roughly 2 to 3)

1 large garlic clove, unpeeled

½ *small white onion, finely chopped*

¼ *cup roughly chopped cilantro*

4 *large ripe avocados*

Salt, about 1 teaspoon

1. *Making 1 cup Essential Roasted Tomatillo-Serrano Salsa.* Lay the tomatillos on a baking sheet and place 4 inches below a very hot broiler. When the tomatillos blister, blacken and soften on one side, about 5 minutes, turn them over and roast the other side. Cool.

Roast the chiles and garlic on an ungreased griddle or heavy skillet over medium heat, turning occasionally, until blackened in spots and soft, 5 to 10 minutes for the chiles, about 15 minutes for the garlic. Cool, then pull the stems from the chiles and peel the garlic.

Combine the tomatillos, chiles and garlic in a food processor or blender. Process to a coarse puree. Transfer to a medium-size bowl. Scoop the onion into a strainer, rinse under cold water, shake off the excess and stir into the tomatillo mixture along with the cilantro.

2. *Finishing the guacamole.* Cut the avocados in half, running your knife around the pit from stem to blossom end and back up again, twist the halves in opposite directions to free the pits and pull the halves apart. Scoop out the pits. With a soup spoon, scoop out the avocado flesh. Place in a medium-size bowl.

Mash the avocados with a large fork, a potato masher or with your hand. Stir in the salsa, then taste and season with salt. Cover with plastic wrap pressed directly on the surface of the guacamole.

ADVANCE PREPARATION—The salsa can be made 2 days ahead, but don't add onion and cilantro until using. Finished guacamole keeps, covered and refrigerated, up to 5 hours.

OAXACAN SEARED CHEESE
WITH TOMATO AND GREEN CHILE
Queso Frito Estilo Oaxaqueño

QUESO FRITO SHOWS the soul of ethnic Mexican cooking: roasted tomatoes and garlic worked together in a stone mortar, then warmed with green chile, pungent-smelling *epazote* and crusty iron skillet–seared slices of toothsome, slightly squeaky fresh cheese. Yes, the whole thing is perfectly easy in Oaxaca, where you can always buy a round of that morning's cheese (the tightly packed curds come wrapped in woven palm bands), the pointy *chile de agua* (it looks like a lighter green miniature version of a poblano) and big bunches of *epazote*. But I love it in the States as well, made with ripe tomatoes, poblano chiles, *epazote* or cilantro and the Mozzarella Company's very fresh, light-textured *queso blanco* (see Sources, page 425). When Mozzarella Company's cheese isn't available, I look for the slightly meatier *queso fresco* from Supremo (available widely in Chicago). Most any *queso fresco* made in the States will work (meaning it will crust without melting); if you try to sear Jack or brick this way, you'll end up with a skillet of melted cheese.

I've given directions for roasting everything on the griddle *a la oaxaqueña*, but feel free to roast tomatoes under a hot broiler as I've directed in many other recipes. No mortar? Chop the garlic in a food processor, then add the tomatoes and pulse to a coarse puree. Set out your cheese as a casual starter or light main dish, with a big salad, encouraging your guests to make dribbly soft tacos or to simply scoop it onto their plates to eat with a fork and tortillas on the side. *Queso frito* goes great with Bohemia and other Mexican beers.

SERVES 4 TO 6

A generous pound (6 to 8) *plum tomatoes*

1 thick slice white onion

2 large garlic cloves, unpeeled

2 or 3 fresh Oaxacan chiles de agua or 1 large poblano chile

½ cup chicken broth

Salt, about 1 teaspoon

1 large sprig epazote (or several sprigs cilantro), leaves removed and roughly chopped, plus a few leaves for garnish

1 tablespoon vegetable or olive oil, plus a little more if needed

1 pound Mexican queso fresco, sliced into ½-inch-thick slabs

1. *The sauce.* Set an ungreased griddle or heavy skillet over medium heat. Place a piece of foil over part of the hot surface and lay the tomatoes and onion slice on it; on the uncovered part, place the garlic. Roast everything, turning occasionally, until the tomatoes, onion and

garlic are all soft and blackened in spots, about 15 minutes. Meanwhile, roast the chile(s) directly over an open flame or 4 inches below a very hot broiler until blackened all over, about 5 minutes for an open flame, about 10 minutes for a broiler. Cool all the roasted vegetables until handleable, then peel the tomatoes (collecting the juices), chile(s) and garlic. Pull out the stem and seed pod from the chile(s), then rinse *briefly* to remove all seeds and bits of skin; slice into ⅛-inch strips.

In a large mortar or a food processor, make a coarse puree from the onion and garlic. Add the tomatoes and their juice, then crush or process into a thick, coarse, sauce. Transfer to a bowl and stir in the chile strips, broth, salt and chopped *epazote*.

2. *Finishing the dish.* Heat the oil in a large (10- to 12-inch) nonstick or well-seasoned skillet over medium-high. When very hot, lay in the cheese slices in a single layer (you will probably have to work in batches) and brown for a minute or so on one side, carefully flip over and brown on the other side. If you've chosen the right cheese, it will sear and get crispy but not melt. Remove to a warm, deep serving platter.

Immediately add the sauce to the pan and cook quickly, stirring constantly, for 2 to 3 minutes, to warm and reduce it slightly. Taste and season with salt, then spoon the sauce over the cheese, garnish with *epazote* or cilantro leaves, and serve right away.

ADVANCE PREPARATION—The sauce holds well in the refrigerator for several days, but do not fry the cheese until you are ready to serve the dish.

SHORTCUTS—Though the dish won't have the richer flavor of roasted tomatoes, ⅔ of a 28-ounce can of good-quality plum tomatoes makes a good dish.

VARIATIONS AND IMPROVISATIONS

Open-faced **Queso Frito** *Sandwich*—Make the recipe as directed, then give it a contemporary twist by broiling or grilling ½-inch-thick slices of crusty bread until richly browned. Then, spoon the cheese mixture over the top and garnish with a little more *epazote*. Fresh basil could be a contemporary American replacement for the *epazote*.

CLASSIC SEVICHE TOSTADAS
Tostadas de Seviche

*T*O MANY MEXICANS and Americans who have visited Mexico, crispy tortillas topped with limy fish and Mexican confetti (tomato, onion, green chiles and cilantro) means a vacation at the beach. There's a tender meatiness to the fish, and although it's not technically cooked, only "pickled" in lime, it does not resemble raw fish in texture. Choose fish from a place you trust and, if you're worried about potential health problems, freeze the fish solid for a couple of days, defrost it in the refrigerator overnight, then make your seviche.

Each fish has its own particular flavor and texture, but use what you can get—though the experts tell us ocean fish are much safer than fresh-water fish.

If passing these tostadas as nibbles doesn't fit my plans, I set out the seviche in an attractive bowl with chips (fried or baked, page 87) for guests to put together themselves. It's great margarita food, though it pairs well with a hoppy beer like Bohemia, too. Wine is difficult to pair with seviche because of all that tart lime, but a steely sparkling wine or very tart Sauvignon Blanc can be okay.

MAKES ABOUT 4 CUPS OF SEVICHE, SERVED ON 36 TOSTADITAS, ENOUGH FOR 8 AS AN APPETIZER

1 pound very fresh boneless, skinless, ocean fish fillets (I like tuna, marlin, snapper, grouper, salmon or one of the stronger fish such as mackerel or bluefish—but only if they're very, very fresh)

6 to 8 limes

FOR 1½ CUPS ESSENTIAL CHOPPED TOMATO-SERRANO SALSA

1 large round, ripe tomato, cut into small dice

Fresh serrano chiles to taste (roughly 3 or more), stemmed and finely chopped

3 tablespoons finely chopped cilantro, plus several dozen leaves for garnish

½ cup finely diced white onion

2 to 3 tablespoons olive oil

Salt, about ¾ teaspoon

Sugar, about 1 teaspoon (optional)

1 large ripe avocado, peeled, pitted and cut into ½-inch dice

36 crisp tortilla chips (preferably fairly large homemade ones, page 87)

1. *Marinating the fish.* Cut the fish into ¼-inch dice and scoop into a large bowl. Squeeze the juice from the limes, pour it over the fish, and stir well—the cup of juice you get should

be enough to generously cover the fish. Cover and refrigerate for several hours, until the pieces of fish are no longer pink and raw looking when broken apart. Drain in a colander, pressing gently on the fish to help remove excess lime juice.

2. *Making 1½ cups Essential Chopped Tomato-Serrano Salsa.* In a large bowl, mix together the tomato, chiles and cilantro. Scoop the onion into a strainer, rinse under cold water, shake off the excess, then add to the tomato mixture.

3. *Finishing the seviche.* Just before serving, mix the drained fish, salsa and enough olive oil to coat everything lightly. Taste and season with salt (and sugar if you'd like to take the edge off the tanginess), then stir in the diced avocado.

Spoon a generous tablespoon of the fish mixture onto each tortilla chip. Top with a leaf of cilantro, arrange on a decorative platter and your little tostadas are ready to pass.

ADVANCE PREPARATION—The fish can marinate in the lime juice in the refrigerator for up to six hours; after thoroughly draining off the juice, the fish can be refrigerated for up to 18 hours. Add the salsa and avocado just before serving.

VARIATIONS AND IMPROVISATIONS

Tangy Grilled Fish Tostadas—You can do a modern seviche-style preparation by grilling your fish (choose flaky fish that can be cooked all the way through without getting dry—snapper, mahimahi, sea bass), then breaking it up and mixing it with the salsa, a couple tablespoons of fresh lime juice and salt to taste.

Mexican Fresh and Aged Cheeses
(*Queso Fresco y Queso Añejo*)

Perhaps it's easiest to think of Mexican fresh cheese (*queso fresco*) as the cultural equivalent of our fresh goat cheese. *Queso fresco* is drier, crumblier and saltier than most fresh goat cheeses, but it's similarly fresh-tasting. And, like fresh goat cheese, most *quesos frescos* won't melt; they just soften when heated.

And consider Mexican aged cheese (*queso añejo*) as the cultural equivalent of Parmesan. It's likewise hard and pungent, perfect for grating over a dish.

In Mexico, fresh cheeses are a cottage industry (like cottage cheese used to be in the United States) and they vary a lot in consistency (from very finely ground compact curds to coarse, loosely packed ones) and in flavor (from simple to salty to tangy to richly complex from good milk and culturing). *Queso fresco* usually is sold in smallish cakes, meant to be crumbled or sliced and eaten within a few days.

There are many manufacturers of Mexican fresh cheese in the United States. If there weren't we'd have none at all; FDA regulations require cheese made from unpasteurized milk to be aged six months before entering the country, I've been told. And quite a few are good: my favorite is the *queso blanco* from Mozzarella Company (see Sources, page 425), followed by the commercially distributed Supremo Brand from Chicago. (Beware that some companies turn out a fresh-tasting *melting* cheese and label it *queso fresco*.) If I couldn't find *queso fresco*, I'd choose pressed, salted farmer's cheese (Andrulis brand looks like a flat pear-shaped cake), fresh goat cheese (it really doesn't crumble well), feta (it's very moist and should be soaked in cool water to leach out some salt), or dry cottage cheese (it will need a good amount of salt). If I've called for *queso fresco* to be sprinkled over something and you're having a problem getting it (or one of the substitutes), you could just use some grated brick or Jack, though the flavor will be very different

In some regions of Mexico, they simply let the *queso fresco* age until it's thoroughly dry: *Queso fresco* ("fresh cheese") becomes *queso añejo* ("aged cheese"). Because most *quesos frescos* are salty, tangy and pretty complex, the *añejos* are all that and more. In fact, we chose Parmesan as our everyday substitute throughout this book, thinking of its grateable pungency as being in the same ballpark; pecorino romano, though not as commonly available, is really closer. Asiago is welcome, too, as is dry Jack (see Sources, page 425). A commercial *añejo* from Cotija, Michoacan, Mexico, is being distributed widely in Mexican markets in the States; although it's not the best *añejo* I've ever tasted, I'm thrilled to have its authentic flavor in my cooking. Most of the *queso añejo* made in the United States has a rather disappointing flavor, so I'd probably choose one of the other substitutes.

Other names for *queso fresco* are *queso ranchero*, *queso del rancho*, *queso de metate* and just plain *queso*. *Queso añejo* goes by *queso Cotija*, *queso enchilado* (when it has been rubbed with powdered red chile), *queso oreado* and *queso seco*.

CRISPY TORTILLAS, FRIED OR BAKED

Tostadas y Tostaditas

*I*N MANY TRADITIONAL kitchens in Mexico, you'll see yesterday's tortillas basking on the griddle, wavy and toasty-crisp, in a rustic sort of way. They're not as tender as fried tortillas. But then again, Mexicans don't eat as many chips as we do.

If you fry chips tender in corn oil, they'll be delicious; freshly rendered pork lard produces a richer flavor that's unsurpassable. Frying, if done correctly and used judiciously, isn't something to apologize for, and choosing vegetable oil over lard doesn't make your fried foods holy. The bottom line: Don't fry very often, and when you do, make sure you've got hot oil or lard and a finished flavor that makes it all worthwhile.

For the crispiest, most tender chips or tostadas, choose thin factory-made tortillas (tortilla factories usually sell "chip" tortillas that are thin, dry and made from more coarsely ground corn; they fry up tender without puffing). Homemade tortillas absorb a lot of oil and brown excessively before they crisp—not really a mouthful that's worth the effort.

MAKES 12 TOSTADAS OR 8 CUPS (ABOUT 8 OUNCES) OF CHIPS

12 corn tortillas, preferably thin, factory-made

Vegetable oil or freshly rendered pork lard,
   to a depth of 1 inch, if frying

Salt, as desired

For chips, cut the tortillas into 6 wedges; for tostadas, leave them whole.

The frying method: Spread the wedges or whole tortillas in a single layer, cover lightly with a dry towel to keep them from curling, and let dry until leathery, about 30 minutes. Heat the oil or lard (there needs to be at least a 1-inch depth) in a large (9- to 10-inch) heavy skillet over medium to medium-high, until very hot—380 degrees on a deep-fry thermometer. For tostadas, lay the tortillas in the oil one at a time, flip them after about 30 seconds, then fry them until they are *lightly* browned and crisp, about 30 seconds longer. For chips, distribute a few wedges of tortilla over the oil and stir them nearly constantly to keep them separate for 45 seconds to 1 minute, until *lightly* browned and crisp. Tostadas and chips are not done until nearly all bubbling has stopped. Remove from the oil using a slotted spoon or skimmer, shake off the excess oil and drain on paper towels. While the chips are warm, sprinkle with salt, if you like.

The oven-crisped method: Turn on the oven to 350 degrees. Place a cooling rack on a baking sheet and lay out the tortillas or chips in a single layer; cover with a second, *inverted* cooling rack to keep the tortillas from curling as they bake. Toast the tortillas in the oven until thoroughly crisp, about 10 to 15 minutes.

SHRIMP SEVICHE WITH ROASTED CACTUS
Seviche de Camarón con Nopales

*T*HE REFRESHING, slightly chewy texture of this Shrimp Seviche has all the sunny flavors of the previous recipe, but may seem a little less intimidating. After all, the shrimp are simply cooked and dressed (for years I've used the foolproof shrimp-cooking method I adapted from *The Encyclopedia Fish Cookery*).

I've mixed in a little roasted cactus, which I hope won't dissuade you from heading to the kitchen with this recipe in hand. Cactus adds an unusual and enjoyable taste and texture, but easily could be omitted. Though I've outlined an elegant buffet presentation here, shrimp seviche looks dazzling on a crispy chip or tostada.

MAKES 5 CUPS, SERVING 6 AS A FIRST COURSE, MORE AS A BUFFET OR PASS-AROUND APPETIZER

1 lime, halved

1 pound medium-large (about 24 pieces) shrimp, unpeeled

7 medium (about 14 ounces total) fresh cactus paddles (nopales)

1 tablespoon vegetable oil for brushing cactus

Salt, about 1 teaspoon, plus some for sprinkling on the cactus

1 small red onion, finely diced

⅓ cup plus 2 tablespoons fresh lime juice

2 tablespoons cider vinegar

1 teaspoon finely chopped fresh thyme or ¼ teaspoon dried

½ teaspoon dried oregano, preferably Mexican

2 to 3 fresh serrano or jalapeño chiles, finely chopped

2 medium-large ripe round tomatoes, diced

3 tablespoons chopped cilantro

1 large ripe avocado, peeled, pitted and diced

Lettuce leaves, for lining your serving bowl

1. *The shrimp.* Squeeze the juice from the two lime halves into a medium-size (2- to 3-quart) saucepan, then add the squeezed rinds and 1 quart of water. Cover and simmer over medium-low heat for 10 minutes (this gives a nice limey flavor to your shrimp-poaching liquid).

Raise the heat to high, add the shrimp, cover and let the liquid return to a full boil. Immediately remove from the heat, hold the lid slightly askew and drain off the liquid. Set the pan of shrimp aside, tightly covered, for 15 minutes to finish the cooking, then spread them out on a tray to cool.

Peel the shrimp, then devein them by running a knife down the back and scraping out the (usually) dark intestinal tract. Cut the shrimp into ¼-inch bits.

2. *The cactus.* Turn on the oven to 375 degrees. Holding a cactus paddle gingerly between the nodes of the prickly spines, trim off the edge that outlines the paddle, including the blunt end where the paddle was severed from the plant. Slice or scrape off the spiny nodes from both sides. Cut into ¾-inch squares; there will be about 3 cups.

Transfer the cactus to a baking sheet, toss with the oil, sprinkle with a little salt and roast, stirring occasionally, until tender and all exuded liquid has evaporated, about 20 minutes. (After 5 minutes in the oven, the cactus will begin to leak its sticky liquid. As they roast, the liquid will evaporate.) Cool.

3. *Finishing the dish.* Mix the shrimp with the onion, lime juice, vinegar, thyme, oregano and chiles in a medium-size bowl. Cover and let stand at room temperature up to 1 hour.

Just before serving, stir in the cactus, tomatoes, cilantro and avocado, then season with salt, usually about 1 teaspoon. Line a decorative bowl with lettuce leaves, toss the seviche with its dressing, then scoop the mixture into the bowl and it's ready to serve.

ADVANCE PREPARATION—The shrimp and cactus can be cooked a day or two in advance and kept covered in the refrigerator until you are ready to finish the dish.

SHORTCUTS—A quicker version is made from store-bought cooked shrimp and no cactus.

VARIATIONS AND IMPROVISATIONS

Ways to move further from the original include replacing the fresh green chile with pickled jalapeños, replacing red onion with white that has been slowly cooked over the coals, replacing the cooked cactus with 1½ cups raw diced jícama, and replacing the tomatoes with another diced avocado. Make all the replacements and you have a very delicious, very different dish from the original.

Grilled Squid Seviche—One pound of squid grilled briefly on a hot fire, then sliced, can replace the shrimp.

SPICY CHILE-BAKED OYSTERS

Ostiones Adobados

$\mathcal{M}$Y FAVORITE WAY to eat oysters is cooked until just firm around the edges, but still soft and ethereal inside, bathed in a rich, smoky, piquant chile seasoning and nestled under crunchy crumbs and onions.

Oysters are relatively easy to find in reliable markets. They should be tightly closed (their closing muscle weakens as they die) and will last several days if kept flat-side up in an *unsealed* container in the refrigerator. Allow plenty of time if this is your first time shucking oysters (or buy shucked oysters and bake them in ramekins).

Set the salt-lined baking dish of oysters right on the table or buffet, have great bread at hand and enjoy a dry Riesling, Gewürztraminer or toasty Champagne.

SERVES 4 TO 6 AS AN APPETIZER

FOR ¾ CUP ESSENTIAL SWEET-AND-SPICY ANCHO SEASONING PASTE

6 garlic cloves, unpeeled

6 medium (about 3 ounces total) dried ancho chiles, stemmed and seeded

1 teaspoon dried oregano, preferably Mexican

½ teaspoon black pepper, preferably freshly ground

A pinch cumin seeds, preferably freshly ground

⅛ teaspoon cloves, preferably freshly ground

1¼ cups fish or chicken broth

Salt, about 1 teaspoon

3 tablespoons olive oil

1 medium white onion, finely diced

2 canned chipotle chiles en adobo, seeded and finely chopped

1 tablespoon fresh lime juice

20 to 24 oysters in the shell, scrubbed clean

3 to 4 cups rock salt or coarse salt to stabilize the oysters in the baking dish

¼ cup dry bread crumbs

2 tablespoons chopped cilantro, for garnish

2 limes, cut into 4 wedges each

1. *Making ¾ cup Essential Sweet-and-Spicy Ancho Seasoning Paste.* Roast the unpeeled garlic directly on an ungreased griddle or heavy skillet over medium heat, turning occasionally, until soft (they'll blacken in spots), about 15 minutes; cool and peel. While the garlic is roasting, toast the chiles on another side of the griddle or skillet: 1 or 2 at a time, open them

flat and press down firmly on the hot surface with a spatula; in a few seconds, when they crackle, even send up a wisp of smoke, flip them and press down to toast the other side. In a small bowl, cover the chiles with hot water and let rehydrate 30 minutes, stirring frequently to ensure even soaking. Drain and discard the water.

Combine the oregano, black pepper, cumin, cloves, chiles, garlic and ½ *cup* of the broth in a food processor or blender. Blend to a smooth puree, scraping and stirring every few seconds. If the mixture won't go through the blender blades, add a little more liquid. Press through a medium-mesh strainer into a bowl. Season with about ¾ *teaspoon* of the salt.

2. *The sauce.* In a medium-size (8- to 9-inch) skillet, heat 2 *tablespoons* of the olive oil over medium. Set aside 2 *tablespoons* of the onion for garnish and fry the rest until golden, about 7 minutes. Raise the heat to medium-high, and, when the oil is hot enough to make a drop of the ancho seasoning sizzle sharply, add it along with the chipotles. Cook, stirring until very thick and noticeably darker, about 8 minutes. Add the remaining ¾ cup broth and simmer, partially covered, over low, stirring often, until medium-thick, about 20 minutes. Taste and season with salt, usually ¼ teaspoon, and the lime juice. Cool.

3. *The oysters.* Shuck the oysters over a bowl to catch any juices: Working one at a time on a cutting board with oysters flat-side up and a towel to hold them steady, use a stubby oyster knife, bottle cap opener or flat-blade screwdriver to wedge in between the shells at the narrow end where the hinge is; pry the shells apart, revealing the oysters nestled in their delicious juice. Strain the juices into a small bowl, measure ½ cup (if there's not that much, add water to bring it to that level) and combine with the sauce and the oysters. Spread the rock or coarse salt into a decorative baking dish or a 17 x 11-inch baking sheet. Nestle the deep halves of the oyster shells in the salt. Divide oysters and sauce among the shells.

4. *Finishing the dish.* Turn on the oven to 450 degrees. In a small skillet, combine the bread crumbs and remaining 1 *tablespoon* olive oil. Set over medium heat and stir until toasted, about 2 minutes. Sprinkle the crumbs evenly over the oysters.

Bake 10 to 12 minutes, until the sauce bubbles and the oysters are beginning to firm up (when you lightly touch one, it won't feel squishy-raw). Sprinkle with the reserved onion and the cilantro. Carry the oysters to the table and serve with lime wedges.

ADVANCE PREPARATION—The recipe may be prepared through step 2 several days in advance. The oysters and sauce can be arranged in their shells 1 to 2 hours before serving and refrigerated. Top with the crumbs just before baking.

RUSTIC JÍCAMA APPETIZER
WITH RED CHILE AND LIME
Entremés de Jícama

A PLATE OF THIS elemental, full-flavored jícama appetizer is one of the best ways to experience Mexico: the gentle sweet crunch jazzed with a squeeze of tartness, a dusting of powdered heat and a sprinkling of perfume—in short, all the flavors and textures celebrated in Mexico's salsas and snacks.

I've tossed oranges, cucumbers and radishes into the mix to add even more variety. And why the pickled red onions? Though they're not part of most versions of this classic, which I've enjoyed most often in Yucatan and West-Central Mexico, these Yucatecan onions add a dramatic magenta topknot that's sweet-sour, crunchy and herby.

SERVES 8 OR SO AS A SNACK OR INFORMAL APPETIZER

1 medium (about 1 pound) jícama

2 small cucumbers

3 seedless oranges

6 radishes, thinly sliced

The juice of 2 limes (about ⅓ cup)

Salt, about ½ teaspoon

About 2 teaspoons powdered dried hot chile, preferably ancho or guajillo

About ⅔ cup Pickled Red Onions (optional) (page 172)

About ⅓ cup roughly chopped cilantro, plus a few sprigs for garnish

1. *The vegetables and fruit.* Peel away the brown skin and fibrous exterior layer of the jícama (a small knife works best for this), then cut in half. Lay each half on its cut side and slice ¼ inch thick; cut slices in half diagonally. Slice cucumbers lengthwise in half, scoop out the seeds (if there are a lot), and cut each half diagonally into ¼-inch-thick slices. Cut stem and blossom end off oranges, stand oranges on cutting board and, working close to the flesh, cut away the rind and all white pith. Cut oranges in half, then slice each half cross-wise into ¼-inch-thick slices.

2. *Finishing the salad.* Mix the jícama, cucumbers, oranges, radishes and lime juice in a large bowl. Let marinate about 20 minutes, then season with salt.

Pile the vegetables and fruit onto a serving platter and drizzle with any accumulated juices. Sprinkle liberally with the powdered chile, top with the optional pickled onions and strew with the chopped cilantro. Garnish with the cilantro sprigs and your simple crunchy appetizer is ready to set before your guests.

ADVANCE PREPARATION—This incredibly fresh, rustic appetizer should really be eaten moments after it's put together.

SHORTCUTS—Feel free to omit the pickled onions or replace them with thinly sliced red onion (I'd toss them into the mix, rather than strewing them on top).

VARIATIONS AND IMPROVISATIONS—This recipe is very flexible: It can be made with just jícama or just cucumber; sliced young raw turnips make an interesting addition, as does sliced raw fennel, apple or Asian pear. Oranges can easily be varied to grapefruit and tangerines, while the powdered chile may be replaced with bottled hot sauce.

Jícama

A crunchy mouthful of jícama is an excellent snack. It's slightly sweet, with a juicy, porous texture that's thoroughly refreshing, and with a taste that cries out for a squeeze of lime and the traditional sprinkle of hot powdered chile. If you've never had it, be ready for a bite that's less sweet, less tangy and more porous than an apple (and it won't be mealy). Unlike other tubers, jícama is rarely cooked.

The rough-looking, brown-skinned tuber is easily available these days, though in grocery stores where jícamas are not in demand, they may have sat on the shelves long enough to shrivel. Available most of the year (because they store well in refrigeration), fall jícamas frequently look as if they've been out of the ground too long. The small, fresh-dug "babies" of the new harvest are typical in piñatas at Christmas.

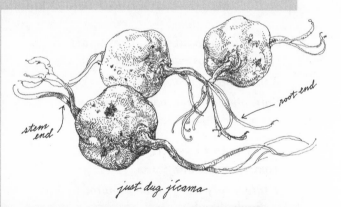

just dug jícama

Choose jícamas that feel solid and heavy, with no withered look to the skin. Pare off the skin and ⅛ inch or so of fibrous flesh just below, then slice or dice and go. An unwrapped jícama that's in good shape will keep for a week or two in the vegetable crisper of your refrigerator. If you find a bit of surface mold, cut it off; mold rarely means the whole jícama is bad. Brown spots in the flesh have an off taste and texture, so cut them out.

Stats: A medium jícama weighs 1 pound.

ROASTED CACTUS SALAD

Ensalada de Nopales Asados

THIS CHUNKY, RELISHY salad of slightly crunchy cactus stirred up with lively salsa would be considered by most a tasty novelty to include among a variety of soft taco fillings, to spoon on a lettuce leaf aside grilled chicken, or even to include on a buffet of salads. But fresh cactus (this is the fleshy, paddle-shaped "stem" of prickly pear cactus) shouldn't stay just a novelty; it's a great vegetable to add to your regular repertoire, especially in the winter when there are less attractive choices. I wouldn't blame you if you've tasted bottled cactus and vowed never again to repeat the experience. Those slithery-textured pieces have as little flavor as canned green beans. My method for *roasting* cactus, though, is easy and it minimizes what we'll call "textural challenges" (like okra, they exude a thickish substance when boiled) and maximizes flavor (their wonderfully tart flavor is concentrated rather than washed away).

All varieties of prickly pear cactus are edible, but some are more tender than others. What is available in U.S. markets is usually a commercial almost-spineless variety that's easy to work with. Cactus is very healthful, and you'll find cooking it simple once you've done it a time or two.

MAKES 4 CUPS, SERVING 8 OR MORE AS AN ACCOMPANIMENT

7 medium (about 14 ounces total) fresh cactus paddles (nopales)

2 tablespoons olive oil

Salt, about ½ teaspoon, plus some for sprinkling on the cactus

FOR 1½ CUPS ESSENTIAL CHOPPED TOMATO-SERRANO SALSA

1 large, very ripe, round tomato, finely diced

Fresh serrano chiles to taste (roughly 2 or 3), stemmed and finely chopped

1 garlic clove, peeled and very finely chopped

3 tablespoons chopped cilantro

½ cup finely diced white onion

1 teaspoon fresh lime juice

Several romaine lettuce leaves, for lining your serving bowl

2 tablespoons finely crumbled Mexican queso añejo, dry feta or Parmesan

Several radish slices or roses, for garnish

1. *The cactus.* Turn on the oven to 375 degrees. Holding a cactus paddle gingerly between the nodes of the prickly spines, trim off the edge that outlines the paddle, including the blunt end where the paddle was severed from the plant. Slice or scrape off the spiny nodes from both sides. Cut into ¾-inch squares; there will be about 3 cups.

Transfer the cactus to a baking sheet, toss with *1 tablespoon* of the oil, sprinkle with a little salt and roast, stirring occasionally, until tender and all exuded liquid has evaporated, about 20 minutes. After 5 minutes in the oven, the cactus will begin to leak its sticky liquid. As they roast, the liquid will evaporate. Cool.

2. *Making 1½ cups Essential Chopped Tomato-Serrano Salsa.* In a large bowl, mix the tomato, chiles, garlic and cilantro. Rinse the onion under cold water, shake to remove the excess and add to the mixture along with the lime juice.

3. *Finishing the salad.* Stir the cooled cactus and the remaining *tablespoon* of olive oil into the salsa. Taste and season with salt, usually about ½ teaspoon. Line a decorative serving bowl with romaine leaves and scoop in the salad mixture. Sprinkle with the cheese and radishes, and it's ready to set out for your guests to eat as is or use as a condiment.

ADVANCE PREPARATION—The roasted cactus keeps nicely in the refrigerator for a day or so; the salsa can be prepared several hours in advance, but do not assemble the salad until shortly before serving.

VARIATIONS AND IMPROVISATIONS

A Winter Cactus Salad—When good tomatoes aren't around, replace the salsa with one thinly sliced medium red onion, ½ cup chopped cilantro, 4 sliced pickled jalapeños (if you like it spicy) and 2 tablespoons fresh lime juice.

Roasted Potato-Cactus Salad—Prepare the recipe with half the cactus and 10 ounces red-skin boiling potatoes cut into ½-inch cubes. Toss the potatoes with a little olive oil and salt and roast on a separate baking sheet at the same time as the cactus (they should take about the same amount of time). Cool and finish the salad as directed.

Cactus Paddles

Eating cactus may sound like a desperate measure, but, in truth, cactus is deliciously flavored and textured, commonly available (*very* common in Mexico) and quite healthful. Scientists have recently discovered that it's a useful (in prescientific times, essential) part of the diet for combating diabetes among groups that are prone to it, and many Native American people *are* prone to it when they eat a European diet.

Nopales (or *nopalitos*) refers to the fleshy, oval "stems" (or paddles, as they're called) of some varieties of prickly pear cactus. Folks don't usually eat the thick-skinned, scrubby, low-growing varieties that are typical ornamentals throughout our Southwest (they're not tender or tasty); nor do they eat the tough paddles from the tree-size plants that are prized for their fruit. Rather, it's the somewhat thin paddles from roughly 4-foot-high plants (they're cultivated as a crop) that are most in demand, especially the spineless cultivars. This is what you'll likely find in Mexican markets or in the supermarket.

Look for *nopales* that are medium-size (large ones may be tough, small ones cook down to nothing). They should have a little rigidity; limp or withered *nopales* are old. Store cactus loosely wrapped in the refrigerator.

Nopales are best cleaned wearing gloves to protect your hands from tiny spines (even in the "spineless" varieties). Trim off the edge that outlines the paddle, including the blunt end where the paddle was severed from the plant. Slice or scrape off the spiny nodes from both sides, then cut the paddle up as your recipe directs. (Cactus may be cleaned and cut a day or two ahead; cover and refrigerate.)

Cactus paddles are customarily simmered in a large pot of water until thoroughly tender, then they're rinsed several times to wash away all of the mucilagenous substance (ever eaten boiled okra?) that has been exuded during cooking and will continue to be exuded as long as there is any appreciable moisture present.

When I saw street-side cooks in West-Central Mexico grilling cactus, I gave up boiling almost completely. If you slowly grill a salted, lightly oiled paddle until it's thoroughly limp, then cool and cut it, the cactus will be richly flavored and not sticky. I admit it's a little chewier than when it's boiled, but I like that chewiness. You can achieve the same effect by cutting up the cactus, tossing it in a little oil, spreading it on a baking sheet and roasting it at 375 degrees for about twenty minutes. The sticky juice seeps out but evaporates, leaving you with lovely, light cactus—more tender than the grilled, better flavored than the boiled.

Stats: A medium paddle measures about 8 by 4 inches and weighs a generous 2 ounces.

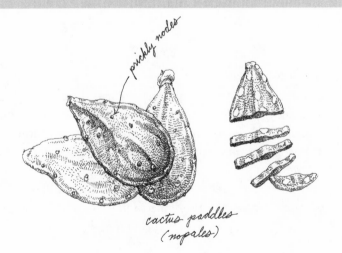

prickly nodes

cactus paddles
(nopales)

Corn Tortillas *(page 69)*

Classic Seviche Tostadas *(page 84)*

Roasted Poblano Chile Salad with smoked fish *(page 100)*   3

Ripe Plantain Turnovers with fresh cheese filling *(page 102)*

Sweet Pickled Chipotles (*page 107*)

CHORIZO-STUFFED ANCHO CHILES WITH SWEET-SOUR ESCABECHE *(page 108)*

CHILIED TORTILLA SOUP WITH SHREDDED CHARD *(page 117)*

SLOW-SIMMERED FAVA BEAN SOUP WITH MINT AND PASILLA CHILE *(page 132)*

TOPOLO "CAESAR" SALAD

Ensalada Estilo Topolobampo

THOUGH WE'RE SURE this was invented in Mexico (by Italian immigrant Caesar Cardini), I'd never call it traditionally Mexican. In Puebla or Chilpancingo or Oaxaca, its existence is still here-say. I've included it because I love the Mexicanized version I came up with for our restaurant, Topolobampo—green chile and lime, not lemon, in the dressing, cilantro with the greens and *queso añejo* or Vella's dry Jack cheese (see Sources, page 425), not Parmesan, over everything.

It seems there are numerous "original" versions of Caesar salad around, though for me truth always lies with Julia. How can you doubt the one who taught you to master hollandaise and puff pastry? *From Julia Child's Kitchen* details a very good original formula that was my starting point here. I've chosen to add a raw egg to the dressing, but to keep it from becoming too thick and mayonnaisy, I whisk in half the oil by hand. If using raw eggs bothers you, make a spicy vinaigrette without the egg for a very good, but different, salad.

SERVES 4 TO 6; ABOUT 1 1/2 CUPS DRESSING

FOR THE DRESSING (THIS IS THE MINIMUM QUANTITY MANAGEABLE, THOUGH IT MAKES ENOUGH FOR 4 ROUNDS OF THIS SALAD)

1 cup fruity olive oil

1 1/2 tablespoons vinegar, preferably sherry vinegar

4 teaspoons Worcestershire sauce

1 fresh serrano chile, stemmed and halved

The zest (colored part only) of 1 1/2 limes

1 egg

Salt, about 1/2 teaspoon

FOR THE CROUTONS

1/4 cup olive oil

4 garlic cloves, peeled and roughly chopped

2 cups firm bread (preferably sourdough) crusts removed, cut into 1/2-inch cubes

FOR FINISHING THE SALAD

2 medium-small heads romaine lettuce, tough outer leaves removed, inner leaves rinsed and dried

OR 8 ounces (about 8 cups moderately packed) mixed young greens, rinsed and dried

3/4 cup finely crumbled Mexican queso añejo, dry Jack or Parmesan cheese

1/2 cup roughly chopped cilantro

1. *The dressing.* Combine *1/2 cup* of the olive oil plus all other dressing ingredients in a food processor or blender and process one full minute. Scrape into a small bowl and slowly whisk in the remaining *1/2 cup* olive oil. Taste and add more salt if you think necessary.

2. *The croutons.* Turn on the oven to 350 degrees. In a small (1- to 1½-quart) saucepan, combine the ¼ cup olive oil and the garlic. Set over the lowest heat and stir every now and again until the garlic is very soft, about 20 minutes. While the garlic is cooking, spread the bread cubes on a baking sheet and bake, stirring occasionally, until completely crisp and dry, about 20 minutes. Gently mash the garlic in the oil to extract as much flavor as possible, then pour the oil through a fine mesh strainer into a small bowl. Toss the oil with the bread cubes to coat evenly, return to the oven and bake until nicely golden, about 5 more minutes.

3. *Finishing the salad.* In a large salad bowl, combine the lettuce, *⅓ cup* of the dressing, *half* of the cheese and all of the cilantro. Toss to coat thoroughly, then divide onto salad plates, top with the remaining cheese and the croutons and serve right away.

ADVANCE PREPARATION—The dressing will keep for several days in a closed jar in the refrigerator. The croutons may be prepared a day or two ahead.

SHORTCUTS—You can buy wonderful garlic oil these days, so feel free to use it. Plain, toasted bread croutons are available in lots of bakeries.

VARIATIONS AND IMPROVISATIONS

Tomato Salad—Replace the lettuce with sliced tomatoes. Drizzle them with some of the dressing and sprinkle with cilantro, cheese and croutons. An alternative to croutons is slices of grilled bread smeared with goat cheese.

Mexican-Flavored Bread Salad—Make the croutons using 6 to 8 cups of bread cubes (sourdough bread works well here) and then toss with enough of the dressing to moisten. There should be enough dressing to flavor them but not make them soggy. Stir in 3 or 4 diced tomatoes, ½ cup sliced green onions, a handful of chopped pitted calamata olives and the cheese and cilantro. Serve on crisp romaine leaves.

Cilantro

Cilantro is *the* Mexican herb, perfuming plates and markets everywhere with its pungency. We cookbook authors used to tread gingerly through recipes that celebrated its distinctive aroma, instructing Stateside cooks to sprinkle it on at their own discretion. Having served close to a million and a half diners in the last decade, I can confidently say, we've almost all been won over. We *love* cilantro . . . with very few exceptions.

Good-looking fresh cilantro is widely available. Formerly called fresh coriander or Chinese parsley, it's now cilantro practically everywhere and it's as cheap as parsley. While sprigs of the large-leafed variety are beautiful as a garnish, smaller cilantro seems to be tastier, with no soapy, bitter flavor.

If cilantro is sold with the roots, it will last a little longer in the refrigerator. At the restaurant, we refrigerate cilantro standing up in a tub with a little water at the bottom. At home, I've had good luck loosely rolling unwashed cilantro in *barely* damp paper towels and storing it in a plastic bag. Too much water will cause the leaves to deteriorate quickly; the dry air of a refrigerator is cilantro's worst enemy, so keep it covered. I like to soak my garnishing cilantro sprigs in cold water for an hour or so before their debut to perk them up to a just-picked crispness.

To chop cilantro, rinse and *thoroughly* dry it—pat it with paper towels or gently shake the bunch over the sink for a minute or two until the leaves have dried (chopping damp cilantro yields a

just-picked cilantro

wet, verdant mass rather than emerald fluff). Choose a sharp, thin-bladed knife so as not to bruise the delicate leaves, bunch the leafy ends of the sprigs together, fold under the top spray of leaves (this gives you a compact bunch), then very thinly *slice* across the cilantro, including the stems, all the way down the bunch until you run out of leaves (there'll be stems left). Now, fluff the thinly sliced cilantro a dozen times or so with your fingertips (this allows the stems, which are heavier, to fall to the bottom of the pile), then lift off the sliced leaves, leaving behind the bits of stems. Transfer the sliced leaves to a small dish. If the cilantro was dry and your knife was sharp, this fluffy "chopped" cilantro will last for 24 hours or so, tightly covered and refrigerated.

Stats: I'm not giving statistics for cilantro since the bunch sizes vary so much; bunches tend to be larger in Mexican groceries than in everyday supermarkets.

· ·

ROASTED POBLANO CHILE SALAD
WITH SMOKED FISH OR CHICKEN

Ensalada de Chile Poblano con Pescado (o Pollo) Ahumado

Across Central and West-Central Mexico bowls of chile strips, often roasted poblanos mixed with half-pickled onions, show up on tables to offer a spicy accent to a fried steak or soft taco. That wonderfully textured combination—soft, spicy chile against sharp, crunchy onion—makes an easy transition into an elegant first course or light main dish, especially when tossed with smoked chicken or fish and nestled in lettuce. In winter, I put the salad together with the chiles still warm. For casual summer entertaining, it's great as a cold buffet dish.

Though a crusty *bolillo* roll would be the typical accompaniment to a salad elegantly served in Mexico, I'd still choose warm corn tortillas. And a beer seems less appropriate to me here than does a chilled Hermitage blanc (or other Rhône or Rhône-style white—Viognier, Marsanne, Roussane) or full Sauvignon Blanc.

SERVES 4 AS AN APPETIZER

½ *small red onion, sliced into ¼-inch-thick rounds*

3 *tablespoons sherry vinegar*

   OR 4 ½ *tablespoons cider vinegar*

FOR 2 CUPS ESSENTIAL ROASTED POBLANO *RAJAS*

1 *pound (6 medium-large) fresh poblano chiles*

1 *tablespoon vegetable or olive oil*

1 *large white onion, sliced ¼ inch thick*

3 *garlic cloves, peeled and finely chopped*

½ **teaspoon dried oregano, preferably Mexican**

Salt, about ½ teaspoon

About 1 teaspoon chopped fresh thyme, plus 4 sprigs for garnish (optional)

¾ *cup coarsely shredded smoked fish (like whitefish or trout)*

   OR ¾ *cup coarsely shredded smoked chicken*

16 *small lettuce leaves, for lining the plates*

¼ *cup crumbled Mexican queso fresco or pressed, salted farmer's cheese*

1. *"Deflaming" the raw onion.* Separate the onion into rings, then mix with the vinegar in a small bowl and let stand for 15 to 20 minutes (this takes away some of their bite).

2. *Making 2 cups Essential Roasted Poblano* Rajas. Roast the chiles directly over a gas flame or 4 inches below a very hot broiler, turning until blackened on all sides, about 5 minutes for open flame, about 10 minutes for broiler. Cover with a kitchen towel and let stand

5 minutes. Peel, pull out the stem and seed pod, then rinse *briefly* to remove bits of skin and seeds. Slice into ¼-inch strips.

In a large (10-to 12-inch) skillet, heat the oil over medium to medium-high, add the white onion, and cook, stirring regularly, until nicely browned but still a little crunchy, about 5 minutes. Add the garlic and oregano, toss a minute longer, then stir in the chiles and just heat through. Taste and season with salt. Cool, if not planning to serve the salad warm.

3. *Finishing the salad.* Add the red onion mixture to the *rajas.* Stir in the optional chopped thyme and fish or chicken. Taste and season with a little more salt if needed.

Line 4 plates with the lettuce leaves. Spoon ¼ of your aromatic, spicy concoction in the center of each plate, sprinkle with cheese and garnish with sprigs of thyme if you have them. Set before your guests and pass warm tortillas.

ADVANCE PREPARATION—The onion can sit in the juice in the refrigerator for a day or so before using; the poblano *rajas* keep for several days when covered and refrigerated.

VARIATIONS AND IMPROVISATIONS—You can replace the chicken or fish with 4 cups of cubed potatoes and/or parsnips that have been tossed with a little oil and salt and roasted on a baking sheet in a 350-degree oven for 25 or 30 minutes, until tender and lightly browned. The smoked fish could be replaced with crab or smoked mussels, scallops, shrimp, turkey or sausage. Replace the bed of lettuce with sliced tomatoes (yellow ones are great here) and watercress. And all sorts of chiles and peppers, from cubanelle to bell, can stand in for the poblanos.

RIPE PLANTAIN TURNOVERS
WITH FRESH CHEESE FILLING
Empanadas de Plátano

*F*OLKS ALL ALONG the Gulf Coast of Mexico make these turnovers—gently sweet from plantains, salty from fresh cheese, fried to a crusty mahogany with lush softness inside. There is absolutely nothing tricky about making them and, luckily, plantains in varying stages of ripeness are available in many Latin markets. In this recipe, the ideal plantain is ripe enough so that it feels slightly soft but not mushy. Less ripe means less sweetness, more starchiness; very ripe means a dough that's soft and hard to work.

I love these as one of the choices at a party, where snacks are dinner. If you make them half-size, they are right for passing around.

MAKES 12 EMPANADAS, SERVING 4 TO 6 AS A SNACK

3 large (about 2 pounds total) yellow-ripe (not black and mushy-soft) plantains

1 cup all-purpose flour, plus a little more for forming the turnovers

¾ teaspoon salt

1½ cups (about 6 ounces) crumbled Mexican queso fresco or pressed, salted farmer's cheese

Vegetable oil to a depth of 1 inch, for frying

Coarse salt, for serving

1 cup salsa (such as Essential Roasted Tomatillo-Chipotle Salsa, page 45), for serving

1. *The dough.* Turn on the oven to 350 degrees. Cut the ends off the unpeeled plantains. Make a shallow incision down their length, then cut them crosswise in half. Bake the plantains on a baking sheet until very soft, about 40 minutes, then use 2 forks to peel back the skins to allow the steam to escape as they cool completely.

Scrape the cooled plantains into a food processor and puree; there will be about 2 cups. Add the flour and salt, and pulse the mixture until the flour is incorporated.

2. *Forming the empanadas.* Divide the cheese into 12 equal portions; press each portion into a flat oval and cover with plastic wrap. Divide the dough into 12 portions and roll into balls between your floured palms. Roll the balls lightly in flour. Cut 2 squares of medium-heavy plastic (a garbage bag works well) to cover the plates of your tortilla press. Lightly flour the plastic, then use the tortilla press to flatten a ball of dough between the plastic into a 4- to 5-inch disc about ⅛ inch thick. Place 1 portion of the cheese on one side, then use the plastic wrap to help fold the unfilled side over the cheese. Press the edges firmly

together with your fingertips to seal in the cheese. Gently remove from the plastic wrap, and lay the turnover on a clean towel that has been generously sprinkled with flour. Continue until you've made 12 empanadas.

3. *Frying the empanadas.* Turn the oven to the lowest setting and line a plate with paper towels. Heat the oil in a medium-to-large (9-to 10-inch) heavy skillet until hot—about 350 degrees on a deep-fry thermometer. Fry the empanadas 2 or 3 at a time, turning occasionally, until nicely golden, about 2 minutes total. Drain on paper towels; sprinkle with coarse salt and keep warm in a low oven until all are fried. Serve at once on a warm serving platter or a basket lined with a colorful cloth. Pass the salsa for guests to daub on as they like.

ADVANCE PREPARATION—The formed empanadas can be covered and refrigerated for up to several hours before frying. (When the dough or formed turnovers are held overnight, you will have a soft sticky mass on your hands.) The finished empanadas are best just hot out of the skillet, but they can be fried successfully early in the day, cooled, lightly covered, and refrigerated. Reheat in a 375-degree oven about 10 minutes.

VARIATIONS AND IMPROVISATIONS

Using the plantain dough as a casing, fillings can be as varied as your imagination is active. Smoky Shredded Pork (page 150) is typical, but goat cheese with a little canned chipotle and roasted garlic would be dynamite. This plantain dough is often made into a "torpedo" or croquette and called *plátanos rellenos* (see description on page 192).

Plaintain Turnovers with Crab Filling—Carmen Ramírez Degollado, a great Veracruzana cook, makes these regularly with shredded crab filling: Saute a little diced onion, garlic and jalapeño, add 1 diced medium tomato, simmer until reduced and thick, then stir in about a cup of crab meat and a small handful of chopped cilantro or a little *epazote,* if you have it. Serve the empanadas with Essential Roasted Tomato-Jalapeño Salsa (page 21).

PICADILLO-STUFFED JALAPEÑOS

Chiles Jalapeños Rellenos de Picadillo

*I*F WE WERE RAISED in the American Southwest or Mexico and anyone mentions *chiles rellenos,* our mouths water: Great green chiles stuffed with unctuous cheese (or savory minced meat) in a fluffy comforter of souffle batter. In the American Southwest, the chile is usually the long green (Anaheim); in Mexico, mostly poblano. Here, I use the Oaxacan and Veracruz variation: jalapeños packed with olive-studded, minced chicken or pork, shrouded in the classic coating—a much easier process than using the same batter on large chiles.

At the Hidalgo market in downtown Veracruz, these little pork-filled torpedos are wrapped in a double layer of tortilla, doused with salsa and eaten as tacos. In Oaxaca, our friend Ofelia Toledo blanches them with taming salt and sugar, stuffs them with chicken and serves them as an appetizer with an array of salsas on the side.

Though we've all been told (and told others) to serve *chiles rellenos* as soon as they're fried, I've decided I like them made several hours ahead and reheated on a parchment-lined or nonstick baking sheet at 450 degrees for about 8 minutes: They shed most of the oil they were harboring and sort of crisp up in a nice way. This makes the little jalapeños perfect party food, with an icy beer, Gewürztraminer, dry Muscat or full Sauvignon Blanc. For a dressier first course, serve a couple to each guest on a bed of lightly dressed frisee greens, sprinkled with *queso añejo,* chopped tomatoes and cilantro.

SERVES 8 OR 9 AS AN APPETIZER

18 large, fresh jalapeño chiles, stems intact

2 small cones (about 2 ounces) piloncillo (Mexican unrefined sugar), roughly chopped

OR ¼ cup dark brown sugar

Salt, about 1¼ teaspoons

8 ounces (1 medium-large round or 3 or 4 plum) ripe tomatoes, finely diced

1 small white onion, finely diced

½ cup finely chopped, pitted green olives, preferably manzanillos

2 large garlic cloves, peeled and finely chopped

1½ cups finely shredded, cooked chicken (see page 181) or pork

Oil to a depth of ¾ inch in a deep, medium-size skillet, for frying

¼ cup plus 1 tablespoon flour

3 eggs, preferably at room temperature

About 2 cups salsa (such as Essential Roasted Tomato-Jalapeño Salsa, page 21)

Sprigs of cilantro, for garnish

1. *The chiles.* Make a T-shaped slit in the side of each chile: the top of the T should be just below and parallel with the top of the chile (and no wider than ½ inch), the long part of the T should extend from the stem to the point. Fill a medium-large (3- to 4-quart) saucepan with about 3 inches of water, add the *piloncillo* (or brown sugar) and ½ *teaspoon* of the salt. Bring to boil, stir until the sugar is dissolved, add the chiles and simmer very gently over medium-low heat, stirring occasionally, until the chiles are almost tender, about 5 minutes. With a slotted spoon, remove the chiles from the liquid, drain for a minute or 2, cut-side down, then carefully scrape the seeds out with a small spoon.

2. *The* picadillo *filling.* In a medium-size (8- or 9-inch) skillet, combine the tomatoes, onion, olives and garlic, set over medium heat and stir until the tomatoes give up their juices, then let cook until the onions are nearly tender, stirring every once in a while (total cooking time will be 6 to 8 minutes). Stir in the shredded chicken or pork, reduce the heat to medium-low and cook until the mixture is reduced to a thick mass, about 5 minutes. Taste and season with salt, usually about ½ *teaspoon.* Cool completely.

3. *Stuffing the chiles.* Stuff the chiles with about a tablespoon of the *picadillo* (you'll likely have more filling than you need), pressing and molding them roughly into their original shape. I highly recommend that you freeze the chiles for at least half an hour to firm them up.

4. *Battering and frying the chiles.* Turn on the oven to its lowest setting. Heat the oil in a heavy, deep, medium-size (8-inch) skillet (you'll need a ¾-inch depth of oil) over medium to medium-high, until very hot—375 degrees on a deep-fry thermometer.

While the oil is heating, spread ¼ *cup* of the flour onto a shallow plate. Separate the eggs, letting the whites fall into your electric mixer bowl and collecting the yolks in a small dish. Measure ¼ *teaspoon* of salt into the whites, then begin to beat them at medium speed until they hold stiff peaks. With the mixer still going, add the remaining 1 *tablespoon* of flour, then the yolks, one at a time, letting each be fully incorporated before adding the next.

Working quickly (so that the batter won't deflate) and in groups of 3 or 4 (so the pan won't get crowded), dredge a chile through the plate of flour (it's easiest if you hold it by the stem), shake off the excess flour, then dip the chile into the egg batter to coat it evenly, and lay it in the hot oil. After about 2 minutes, use a spoon to very gently bathe the tops of the chiles with the hot oil. When they're golden underneath, about 1 more minute, use that same spoon to turn them over. Fry on the other side (no need to baste them this time), then use a slotted spoon to remove them to a baking sheet lined with several layers of paper towels. Keep the fried chiles warm in a low oven until all are done.

Spoon the salsa onto individual serving plates (or a platter, for family-style or buffet presentation), set the warm chiles on top, decorate with sprigs of cilantro and they're ready.

ADVANCE PREPARATION—The chiles can be simmered in the sugar water and the picadillo filling can be made several days in advance. The chiles can also be stuffed and fried several hours in advance; reheat them in a 450-degree oven for about 8 minutes.

SHORTCUTS—Canned pickled jalapeños can be used here; drain them well. The fresh tomatoes in the filling can be replaced with ⅔ of a 15-ounce can of tomatoes.

VARIATIONS AND IMPROVISATIONS

Larger **Chiles Rellenos**—Roast and peel (page 64) 6 good-size poblanos or 8 long green (Anaheim) chiles, and use them instead of the blanched jalapeños. You may replace the filling with 2 to 3 cups of shredded Mexican Chihuahua or other melting cheese; simply press it into the appropriate shape before fitting it into the chiles. For larger chiles, you'll need at least 1-inch depth of oil for frying, and they'll take a little longer to brown. Large *chiles rellenos* in Mexico are customarily doused with a brothy version of Essential Simmered Tomato-Jalapeño Sauce (page 18).

Stuffed **Chile Pasilla Oaxaqueño**—I wouldn't doubt that folks make expeditions to Oaxaca just to eat these chiles; not available elsewhere, these costly little wonders are one of the most delicious edibles on the planet. If you bring some dried *chile pasilla oaxaqueño* back from Oaxaca (or are cooking there), lightly toast 12 on an ungreased griddle or skillet over medium heat, pressing them flat, flipping and pressing again, until very fragrant, about 30 seconds. Soak in hot water for 10 to 20 minutes, just until pliable, drain and carefully slit and remove the seeds. Pack with the filling, coat with batter and fry as directed in the recipe. At Biche Pobre in Oaxaca, a great spot for snacks, they always serve these on a bed of soupy fried black beans sprinkled with crumbled fresh or aged cheese.

Tangy Unbattered Jalapeños—Blanch the jalapeños as directed, adding 3 tablespoons of cider vinegar to the water. Stuff with warm picadillo (a favorite of mine replaces chicken or pork with shredded smoked fish, replaces olives with raisins, and adds a little diced fried plantain) and serve sprinkled with crumbled *queso añejo* or Parmesan.

SWEET PICKLED CHIPOTLES
Chipotles en Escabeche

*T*HESE SWEET-HOT mouthfuls will become your treasure in the refrigerator. They can be made with either the light-brown or the black-red chipotles: Both work well when you set them out on the table as a condiment for nibbling or when you slice up these sweet-sour little firecrackers to enliven soups, eggs or snacks. Pickled chipotles also are famous on the crispy little *chalupitas* in Chilapa—this recipe was shared with me by a restaurant cook there—and on *cemita* sandwiches in Puebla.

MAKES ABOUT 4 CUPS

4 ounces (about 50) chipotle chiles (this recipe is traditionally made with the cranberry-red chiles called chipotle colorado *or* morita, *but the same weight of the sandy brown chipotle* meco *would work, too)*

1 cup cider vinegar

4 small cones (4 ounces total) pilon-cillo *(unrefined sugar)*

OR *1/2 cup packed dark brown sugar*

4 sprigs fresh thyme (or 1/2 teaspoon dried)

4 sprigs fresh marjoram (or 1/2 teaspoon dried)

3 bay leaves

1 medium white onion, sliced 1/4 inch thick

1 head garlic, cloves peeled and halved

Salt, about 2 teaspoons

1. *Soaking the chiles.* Place the chiles in a medium-size (2- to 3-quart) saucepan, cover with water and bring to a full rolling boil. Drain off all the water, cover with warm tap water, lay a small plate on top of the chiles to keep them submerged and let stand 10 minutes. Drain, cover once again with warm water, lay on the plate and let stand 10 more minutes. Drain off *most* of the water, then transfer to a jar (preferably one with a noncorrosive lid) large enough to comfortably hold all the chiles.

2. *Pickling the chiles.* In the saucepan, combine all the remaining ingredients with 1¼ cups of water. Bring to a gentle simmer and stir until the sugar is completely dissolved. Pour the hot liquid over the chiles and stir to mix the garlic and herbs down into the chiles as best you can. The chiles should be completely submerged, if there's not quite enough liquid to cover them, add equal parts cider vinegar and water. Taste the liquid for salt (it should be a little salty), cover and refrigerate a day or more before serving.

CHORIZO-STUFFED ANCHO CHILES
WITH *SWEET-SOUR ESCABECHE*

Chiles Anchos Rellenos en Escabeche

I OFTEN WONDER why such an unusual-sounding dish has such wide appeal. Is it the tenderness of the marinated ancho against the meaty, comforting potato-chorizo filling and crunchy vegetable garnish? The warmth of the inside against the cool of the topping? The dulcet tanginess of the escabeche against the dry-chile robustness of the ancho? I suppose it's this unexpected mix in perfect balance.

It was nine years ago now that Priscila Franco Satkoff, a co-worker at Frontera Grill, explained to me her family's delicious version of this Central Mexico specialty. Because all the parts can be prepared well in advance, this is a perfect party dish. It looks as stunning as a first course or light main dish as it does on a buffet-size platter.

SERVES 6 AS AN APPETIZER

1 medium carrot, peeled and cut into ⅛-inch dice

¼ cup olive oil

2 garlic cloves, peeled and halved

½ teaspoon ground allspice, preferably coarsely ground

2 bay leaves

½ cup cider vinegar

1 small cone (about 1 ounce) piloncillo (Mexican unrefined sugar)

OR 2 tablespoons dark brown sugar

1 small red onion, thinly sliced

½ teaspoon salt, plus a little more if needed

6 good-size, unblemished, dried ancho chiles with stems intact

4 medium-small boiling potatoes, cut into ⅜-inch cubes

1 tablespoon vegetable oil

8 ounces (1 cup) chorizo sausage, casing removed

Chopped or sprigs of cilantro, for garnish

1. *The escabeche.* Place the carrot into a large (10- to 12-inch) skillet, drizzle on the olive oil, cover and set over medium heat. Stir from time to time as the carrot cooks until crisp-tender, about 5 minutes. Add the garlic, allspice, bay, vinegar, ¾ cup water and *piloncillo*, bring to a simmer, stirring to dissolve the sugar, remove from the heat and add the onion and salt. Stir well and let cool. The flavors will improve if made a day ahead.

2. *The chiles.* Heat an ungreased griddle or heavy skillet over medium heat and toast the whole chiles one at a time, pressing them flat for 10 to 20 seconds with a spatula until they

become very aromatic, then flipping them and pressing down to lightly toast the other side. Slip them into escabeche, spooning the vegetables on top; let soak 30 minutes.

Remove the chiles from the escabeche, leaving behind as much liquid as possible, and, using a small knife, make a slit in the side of each one from stem to point. Now, with your fingers, carefully scrape out all the seeds that are clinging to the seed pod and attached to the veins. Set the chiles aside, covered. Reserve the escabeche and vegetables.

3. *The chorizo filling*. Boil the potatoes in salted water in a small saucepan, until tender, about 10 minutes; drain. Heat the oil in a large (10- to 12-inch), heavy skillet over medium-low, add the chorizo and cook, stirring to break up any clumps, until thoroughly done, about 10 minutes. Use a slotted spoon to scoop it out, leaving behind as much fat as possible. Pour off all but a thin coating of the fat and raise the temperature to medium.

Add the potatoes and fry, stirring and scraping the pan regularly, until well browned (they'll soften and mash up a bit), about 15 minutes. Add the chorizo and heat through. Taste and season with salt if necessary.

4. *Finishing the dish*. Just before serving, spoon about ⅓ cup of the warm potato-chorizo filling into each chile, press and mold them into a plump shape and set on individual serving plates. Spoon a portion of the escabeche and vegetables over each chile, garnish with cilantro and they're ready to serve.

ADVANCE PREPARATION—The escabeche and filling can be made and refrigerated several days in advance. Marinate chiles up to several hours ahead; stuff and serve.

VARIATIONS AND IMPROVISATIONS

Vegetarian Stuffed Anchos—In a large skillet filmed with oil, brown a sliced onion. Add 1 large diced tomato and cook until thick and reduced; stir in the potatoes and 1 cup cooked or canned garbanzos and cook, stirring, until everything comes together.

Chipotle-Baked Stuffed Anchos—Omit the escabeche in step 1. Rehydrate the chiles in hot water, but leave them only 15 minutes. Prepare 2 cups of the Essential Quick-Cooked Tomato-Chipotle Sauce (page 34) and the filling or the substitute outlined above. Stuff the chiles with the warm filling, lay in a large baking dish, spoon on the warm sauce and bake for 20 minutes at 375 degrees. Sprinkle with finely crumbled *queso añejo* or Parmesan and roughly chopped cilantro, and they're ready to serve.

CORN-MASA CREPAS WITH MEXICAN FLAVORS

Crepas a la Mexicana

*T*HESE LACY *CREPAS* offer the always-popular combination of roasted poblano chiles, corn and cream, flecked with zucchini, spinach and a hint of *epazote*. Yes, *crepas* have long played a role in Mexican cuisine, especially what's called *criollo* cooking: dishes that incorporate New World ingredients into classic European preparations.

At Topolobampo, we use this recipe as a springboard: When squash blossoms come our way, we use them in place of the spinach; when we're feeling exotic, we fill them with the black *huitlacoche* (corn mushroom) filling on page 158. If the menu needs something light, we fold them in triangles, bake them until crispy (see Variations and Improvisations) and serve them with a little watercress salad. And for a show-stopper, we gild them with Roasted Poblano Cream (page 113) instead of the cream, bake them in individual *cazuelas* (you can use little gratin dishes, too) and suggest folks have a glass of buttery Chardonnay or a voluptuous Viognier.

SERVES 6

FOR THE CREPES

3 large eggs

1¼ cups milk

¼ cup all purpose flour

¼ cup fresh masa *for tortillas*
    OR ⅓ cup masa harina, *mixed with ¼ cup hot water*

1 teaspoon sugar

¼ teaspoon salt

2½ tablespoons unsalted butter, *melted, plus a little more for brushing the skillet*

FOR THE VEGETABLE FILLING

2 fresh poblano chiles

1 small white onion, diced

2 tablespoons vegetable oil, unsalted butter or rich-tasting lard

2 ears corn, husked, kernels cut from cobs

2 medium zucchini, cut into ¼-inch dice

4 ounces (about 2¼ cups) loosely packed, chopped fresh spinach

½ cup chopped epazote leaves (or cilantro if epazote is *not available*)

⅓ cup milk

Salt, about 1 teaspoon

FOR FINISHING THE DISH

1 cup Thick Cream (page 165) or crème fraîche

¾ cup shredded Mexican Chihuahua cheese or other melting cheese, such as brick or Monterey Jack

3 tablespoons chopped cilantro, for garnish

1. *The crepe batter.* Place all the ingredients except the butter in a food processor or blender. Process until smooth, stopping the machine once to scrape down the sides. With the machine running, pour in the melted butter. Pour into a pitcher and set aside to rest for 2 hours.

2. *Making the crepes.* Set a 7-inch skillet (one that's well-seasoned or nonstick) or crepe pan over medium to medium-high heat and brush *very lightly* with butter. When quite hot, pour in about ¼ cup of the batter, quickly swirl it around to coat the bottom, then immediately pour the excess (what hasn't stuck) back into the pitcher.

   Cook until the edges begin to dry, 45 seconds to 1 minute. Loosen with a knife and trim off the irregular part (where you poured off the excess batter). Using your fingers or a narrow spatula, flip the crepe (it should be golden brown). Cook about a minute longer, until the underneath is golden, then remove to a plate. Continue making crepes in the same manner, buttering the pan from time to time and stacking the finished crepes on top of one another; cover with plastic wrap. You should have 12 to 14 crepes.

3. *The vegetable filling.* Roast the chiles directly over a gas flame or 4 inches below a very hot broiler, turning until blackened on all sides, about 5 minutes for open flame, about 10 minutes for broiler. Cover with a kitchen towel and let stand 5 minutes. Peel, pull out the stem and seed pod, then rinse *briefly* to remove bits of skin and seeds. Slice into ¼-inch strips.

   In a large (10- to 12-inch) skillet, cook the onion in the oil (or butter or lard) over medium heat until lightly browned, 5 to 7 minutes. Add the chiles, corn kernels, zucchini, spinach, *epazote* and milk. Cook, stirring frequently, until the zucchini is just tender and the milk has evaporated, about 7 minutes. Taste and season with salt, and let cool.

4. *Filling the crepes.* Lay out a crepe, prettiest-side down, and spoon about ¼ cup of the vegetable filling down the middle. Roll up to enclose the filling and place in a buttered 13 x 9-inch baking dish, preferably one that will look nice on a table. Continue spooning and rolling until all crepes are filled.

5. *Finishing the dish.* Turn on the oven to 400 degrees. Stir the Thick Cream until smooth (if it's very thick, stir in a little milk) and drizzle over the crepes. Sprinkle with the cheese. Bake until heated through and bubbling, about 15 minutes. Strew the cilantro over the crepes and they're ready to serve.

ADVANCE PREPARATION—The crepes can be made a couple of days in advance but you will need to put a piece of plastic wrap between each crepe so they don't stick together, then wrap them well and refrigerate. The filling can be made a few hours in advance but you will want to drain off any accumulated liquid from it. Fill the crepes and assemble the dish just before baking.

VARIATIONS AND IMPROVISATIONS

Squash Blossom Crepes—Use about 2 dozen squash blossoms instead of the spinach: Pull off the green sepals at the base of each blossom, break off the orange pistil inside, then slice the blossoms crosswise at ½-inch intervals.

Huitlacoche Crepes—Replace the vegetable filling in step 3 with the *huitlacoche* filling on page 158. Though they're excellent topped with cream as described above, replacing the cream with Roasted Poblano Cream (page 113) makes them even better.

Crispy Crepes—Instead of rolling the filling into the crepes, fold it in: Lay out a crepe, fold the top third down, spoon in a portion of filling in the middle, then fold the point at the upper right-hand side toward the bottom left-hand corner; fold the point at the upper left-hand side toward the bottom right-hand corner, creating a roughly triangular shape overall. Fill and fold the remainder of the crepes, lay on a parchment-lined or nonstick baking sheet, then bake in a 375-degree oven until crispy. Serve one per person as an elegant appetizer, accompanied by a little salad.

Roasted Poblano Cream

INSTEAD OF SPECIFYING one dish to enshrine this rich, special-occasion sauce, I've singled out the recipe here. It's far too versatile and extraordinary a combination to bury it in another dish; it's certainly a sauce that's inspired more sustained applause than practically any other we prepare at Frontera and Topolobampo. *Crema Poblana* is a perfect *mestizo* marriage of thick Spanish *crema* and roasted Mexican poblano chiles—wonderful with grilled fish, or chicken, or rice, or, well, most any of the lighter-flavored meats, fish, poultry, vegetables, legumes and grains. It's the classic nap for elegant Central-style crepes rolled around swarthy, earthy *huitlacoche* filling. Thin it with broth and you have a rich soup (page 134). Any way you serve Roasted Poblano Cream you'll have unwavering fans.

I've written out a not-too-rich version of the sauce here, similar to what they serve on the house-special enchiladas at Cafe de Tacuba in Mexico City. Sometimes, though, I omit the roux (the oil and flour mixture) and simply puree the poblano with a cup of warmed heavy cream, then simmer the mixture until it thickens lightly. *Crema Poblana* can become *crema de chilaca* by replacing the poblanos with chilaca chiles.

MAKES ABOUT 2 CUPS

1 fresh poblano chile, roasted, peeled (page 64), seeded and roughly chopped

1 cup milk

2 tablespoons olive or vegetable oil

1½ tablespoons flour

½ cup Thick Cream (page 165) or crème fraîche

¼ cup heavy (whipping) cream

Salt, about 1 teaspoon

Puree the roasted poblano and milk in a blender or food processor until smooth. Heat the mixture in a small (1- to 1½-quart) saucepan over medium-low. Blend oil and flour in another small saucepan; cook and stir over medium heat for 3 to 4 minutes. Gradually whisk in the hot milk mixture and cook until smooth and thickened, 3 to 4 more minutes.

Whisk in the Thick Cream and heavy cream until smooth. Taste and season with salt. Serve warm.

Vinegar

No wine vinegars, either red or white, are part of the typical Mexican pantry. Wine vinegar has a distinct, winey flavor that I love in French vinaigrettes, but not with Mexican dishes. Mexican cooking relies on fruit vinegars that are fresh and light, with an impression of sweetness. Whether made from apples, pineapples, bananas or other fruit, the local-made vinegars available in much of Mexico are mild enough that you can (almost) drink them. If you're making a recipe from a Mexican cookbook from Mexico and it calls for one cup of vinegar, assume they mean mild local vinegar; start with ½ cup of commercial American apple-cider vinegar (though soft, our vinegar is more potent), and work up from there. Occasionally I suggest you use balsamic or sherry vinegar in my variations. Though balsamic is a long-aged wine vinegar, I think that its sweet, almost molasses-like richness complements many Mexican flavors. Sherry vinegar is long-aged, too, equally mellow, but less sweet.

. . . .

Olives and Olive Oil

Almost without exception, only green manzanillo olives are used in Mexican cooking. Their tangy, crisp texture works well with typical Mexican flavors like cilantro and green chile. Olives are thought of as a special-occasion add-in to many dishes (Mexican "gourmet" cooking utilizes a preponderance of Spanish elements, and olives certainly are one of the most accessible). A good amount of olives in Mexico come from Spain; olive trees have been grown in Mexico since shortly after the Spaniards arrived, though they thrive only in the far northwest corner of the country.

I love olive oil and have listed it as an option in many recipes. Like olives, olive oil is thought of as a special (Spanish-gourmet) ingredient, though one that is readily available. Olive oil (both national and imported) is expensive in Mexico, but its flavor fits in well. When thought of as an alternative to rich-tasting pork lard, olive oil has considerably more to offer than neutral vegetable oils.

. . . .

CHAPTER THREE

· · · · ·

LIGHT
AND
HEARTY
SOUPS

SOUPS ARE AS INTEGRAL TO MEXICAN LIFE AS SALADS ARE THESE DAYS IN THE STATES. Perhaps it's the restorative quality they have, the comfort they bring as their warmth radiates through the body. Perhaps it's the natural healthiness of a long-simmered bowl of liquid refreshment, plus the fact that that liquid is welcoming to practically any flavor and texture a culture grabs onto. So when planning a dressy Mexican meal, plan on soup before the main dish; even for a casual gathering, plan on soup as the main dish itself or with some tacos, enchiladas or the like. I've offered you a wide range to choose from.

The most well known Mexican *sopa* (if you disqualify the stewlike *pozoles* and *menudos*) is probably tortilla soup. In *Authentic Mexican,* I presented the classic; here I offer a less complex version, Chilied Tortilla Soup, with wilted greens in a pasilla-flavored broth—traditional in flavor, modern in balance and vitality. The garlic soup I love so much from Spain is an essential part of the Mexican repertoire as well, though in *criollo* hands, this Mexican-Style Sweet Roasted Garlic Soup becomes gutsier, spicier, fuller in flavor. Hominess is the hallmark of Robust Red-Chile Beef Soup, an earthy-red puddle of rich broth chock full of Mexico's staple vegetables (corn, chayote, zucchini, green beans, carrots) and shreds of beef—just the kind of meal I like on a winter day. I'm offering two takes on tomatoes: long-simmered Roasted Tomato Soup, robust with poblano chiles, garlic and beef broth; and Rustic Ranch-Style Soup made quickly from chopped tomatoes, onions, green chile and a garlicky broth. Mushroom-Cactus Soup is one of the most easily likable, exotic-sounding dishes I've ever encountered. There's certainly a complexity to the mix of flavors and textures, but one that easily draws you in.

Bean soups aren't as common in Mexico as you'd expect them to be, simply because folks eat so many beans in other ways, I think. I love black bean soup, as I'm sure most of you do, so I've included a Oaxacan Black Bean Soup recipe which shows that cumin, sour cream and a dollop of sherry aren't the only flavorings the earthy potage enjoys. A specialty bean soup follows, Slow-Simmered Fava Bean Soup. It offers a remarkable contrast of textures: the coarse puree of the beans against the slightly chewy shreds of half-pickled pasilla chile.

The creamy soups I've saved for last, since they are my special-occasion offerings. Anyone I serve the classic Roasted Poblano *Crema* to just can't stop talking about it. The Golden Squash Blossom *Crema* is one of the crowning glories of Mexican cuisine, so I hope you'll use your ingenuity (including planting squash) to get the blossoms. It's a lovely, silky soup flecked with bit of fiery-golden blossom, verdant poblano and sunshiny corn; the leaves of pungent *epazote,* floating in the magic, bring quickly and thankfully to mind that the earth offers endless variety. We're blessed to be able to enjoy them.

CHILIED TORTILLA SOUP
WITH SHREDDED CHARD
Sopa de Tortilla y Acelgas

*T*ORTILLA SOUP is one of Mexico's most well known soups. I wrote a classic but flexible recipe for it in *Authentic Mexican,* but I still have more to say. At Frontera and Topolobampo, we work a little of the traditional toasted pasilla chile garnish into the tomato-flavored broth to deepen it. And I love to simmer in the satisfying complexity of chard—an unexpected addition for a soup this comforting. You can leave out the chard, of course, and serve the soup with diced avocado, even a spoonful of cream . . . but do try it with the greens, since it's a perfect opening to any meal.

MAKES ABOUT 6 CUPS, SERVING 4 TO 6

4 to 6 corn tortillas, preferably stale store-bought ones

⅓ cup plus 1 tablespoon vegetable oil

4 to 5 medium (about 1½ ounces total) dried pasilla chiles, stemmed and seeded

2 garlic cloves, unpeeled

1 medium-large round ripe tomato

1 medium white onion, sliced ⅛ inch thick

6 cups good broth, preferably chicken (page 137)

Salt, about ½ teaspoon, depending on saltiness of broth

2 cups (8 ounces) shredded Mexican Chihuahua cheese, or other melting cheese such as brick or Monterey Jack

1 large lime, cut into 6 wedges

4 cups loosely packed, thinly sliced (preferably red) chard leaves (you'll need about ⅔ of a 12-ounce bunch)

1. *Getting started.* Slice the tortillas into ⅛-inch-wide strips. Heat ⅓ *cup* of the vegetable oil in a medium-size (8- to 9-inch) skillet over medium-high. When hot, add about ⅓ of the tortilla strips and fry, turning frequently, until they are crisp on all sides. Remove with a slotted spoon and drain on paper towels. Fry the remaining strips in 2 batches.

Cut chiles into rough 1-inch squares using kitchen shears. Reduce the heat under the oil to medium-low, let cool a minute, then fry the squares very briefly to toast them, 3 or 4 seconds; immediately remove and drain on paper towels. Place ⅓ of the chiles in a small bowl, cover with hot water and let rehydrate for 30 minutes, stirring regularly to ensure even soaking. Drain and discard the water. Set aside the remaining fried chiles.

While the chiles are soaking, roast the unpeeled garlic on an ungreased griddle or heavy skillet over medium heat, turning occasionally, until blackened in spots and soft, about 15 minutes. Cool, then slip off the papery skins.

Roast the tomato on a baking sheet 4 inches below a very hot broiler until blackened and blistered on one side, about 6 minutes; flip and broil the other side. Cool, then peel, collecting any juices.

2. *Simmering the broth.* In a medium-size (4-quart) pot, heat the remaining *1 tablespoon* of oil over medium-low. Add the onion and fry until brown, about 10 minutes. Place the rehydrated chiles in a food processor or blender along with the roasted garlic, tomato and *1 cup* of the broth; puree until smooth. Raise the temperature under the pot to medium-high, and, when noticeably hotter, press the tomato-chile puree through a medium-mesh strainer into the fried onion. Stir for several minutes as the mixture thickens and darkens. Mix in the remaining 5 *cups* of broth, then simmer uncovered over medium-low, stirring occasionally, for 30 minutes. Season with salt.

3. *Finishing the soup.* Set out the garnishes: Make mounds of the fried tortilla strips, fried chiles, cheese and lime on a large platter. Just before serving, reheat the soup, add the sliced chard and simmer until the chard is tender, 5 or 6 minutes. Ladle into warm soup bowls and pass the garnishes for each guest to use *al gusto.*

ADVANCE PREPARATION—The soup itself can be prepared several days ahead. The fried tortillas will keep for a day wrapped in foil on the counter. Reheat the broth and set out the garnishes just before serving.

SHORTCUTS—You can purchase broth (I'd recommend one from the refrigerated or frozen case of a specialty shop rather than canned); if you can buy thickish tortilla chips, they could be broken and used in place of the fried strips.

VARIATIONS AND IMPROVISATIONS

A cup or so of shredded poached or rotisserie chicken makes this a main dish; vegetable stock and a couple cups of roasted or grilled vegetables makes it a vegetarian one.

Mexican Beans-and-Greens Soup—Simmer 8 ounces beans until tender (1½ hours or so) in 5 cups broth; add enough water or additional broth to bring it back to its original level. Prepare the soup as directed, adding the beans-and-broth mixture where the 5 cups of broth are called for.

Garlic

Except as a sweet, redolent bath for fish (*mojo de ajo*) and the focus of a soup (*sopa de ajo*), both dishes with Spanish roots, the role of garlic in the Mexican kitchen is to be an ever-present backdrop to more dominant flavors.

The garlic heads are smaller in Mexico, but the cloves have more concentrated flavor. The bigger cloves we've bred in the States are easier to peel, but they don't pack any more wallop of flavor than the tiny ones. Elephant garlic, the really enormous stuff, seems to have spread that same amount of garlic flavor over an even larger volume, as seems to be the case with the single clove *head* of garlic called *ajo macho* in Mexico (it's bulbous, looks like garlic, yet doesn't break into cloves). Red or white garlic? Each has its own followers, though I think in a cooked dish the differences start to blur.

A final note: Freshly dug garlic, the kind you buy at farmer's markets, will be quite "hot" until it's had time to cure. Garlic that's been out of the ground long enough to begin sprouting a green core is difficult to digest unless you cut out the green sprouts.

Stats: An average head of white garlic in the States has 12 large cloves.

· ·

MEXICAN-STYLE SWEET ROASTED GARLIC SOUP
Sopa de Ajo, Estilo Mexicano

*A*WARMING BOWL OF this quick-to-make brothy restorative shows a spirit that's both Spanish and Mexican: Spanish in substance (garlic soup with croutons and egg is one of Spain's standards), Mexican in vitality (avocado and tomato are the Mexican breath of life). Though Mexican kitchens commonly produce the simple Spanish-style soup, I've collected ideas for the elaborations spelled out here from several creative Mexican cooks.

Don't be put off by the large quantity of olive oil used to cook the garlic properly; only a little actually goes into the finished soup, leaving you with a wonderful treasure to use in salad dressings or for pan-searing fish. Whole eggs are frequently half-poached directly in each bowl of boiling broth in Mexico and in Spain. The whole egg idea is great if you want to serve *sopa de ajo* as a main dish with a salad and a loaf of good bread. For an appetizer, I've given directions for stirring in a little beaten egg, as you would for egg-drop soup, though here it's intended to make the broth creamy rather than filled with fully cooked threads. If less than fully cooked eggs bother you, simply omit them or drizzle in the beaten egg while the broth is simmering.

MAKES 4 CUPS, SERVING 4

1/2 cup fruity olive oil

1 large head of garlic, cloves peeled, chopped into rough 1/8-inch pieces

5 cups good chicken broth (page 137)

4 slices firm-textured bread, crusts removed

Salt, about 1 1/2 teaspoons, depending on the saltiness of the broth

1 ripe avocado, peeled, pitted and cut into 1/2-inch dice

3 ounces Mexican queso fresco or pressed, salted farmer's cheese, cut into 1/2-inch cubes, about 3/4 cup

1 large, ripe, round tomato, cored, seeded and cut into small dice (optional)

4 green onions, lightly brushed with olive oil, broiled or grilled on a gas or charcoal fire until soft, chopped (optional)

2 eggs, lightly beaten

4 canned chipotles en adobo, seeded and thinly sliced (optional)

1. *The garlic.* Heat the olive oil in a small heavy (1- to 1 1/2-quart) pot over medium-low. (A *heavy* pot is important—the garlic has a tendency to burn in a lightweight pot.) Add the garlic and cook, stirring frequently, until very soft and golden, 15 to 20 minutes. (The oil should never get hot enough to *fry* the garlic, but should look as though it is barely simmering; by the end of cooking, the garlic should be soft—almost gooey—not browned and crispy.)

Set a medium-mesh strainer over a small bowl and pour in the oil and garlic. Transfer the garlic into a medium-size (2- to 3-quart) saucepan and stir in the broth; partially cover and simmer over medium heat 30 minutes. (Set the garlic oil aside: you will need 3 tablespoons of it for the croutons; the remainder can be refrigerated for use in salad dressings, omelets, hash browns, etc.)

2. *The croutons.* Turn on the oven to 325 degrees. While the soup is simmering, cut the bread into ½-inch cubes and toast on a baking sheet in the oven until thoroughly dry but not brown, about 20 minutes. Drizzle with about 3 *tablespoons* of the garlic oil, toss to thoroughly coat and return to the oven for 5 minutes more, until the croutons are nicely golden.

3. *Finishing the soup.* When the soup is ready, taste and season with salt. Divide the avocado, fresh cheese and optional tomato and green onions among warm soup bowls. A couple of minutes before serving, remove the soup from the heat, let stand 30 seconds to cool a bit, stir in the eggs with a spoon (they give the broth body and creaminess), then ladle into the bowls. Top each portion with croutons and a few strips of chipotle (if you're using them), and carry directly to the table.

ADVANCE PREPARATION—The soup may be completed through step 2 up to half a week ahead (in fact, it gets better with a little age); cover and refrigerate. Just before serving, bring the soup to a simmer and continue with step 3.

SHORTCUTS—Good-quality canned broth, preferably low in sodium, or stock from the freezer or refrigerator of a specialty market can replace the homemade.

VARIATIONS AND IMPROVISATIONS—I love to use this garlicky broth as the base for other soups—especially vegetable soup (see Rustic Ranch-Style Soup, page 126). As is, it can be dressed up just before serving with shreds of smoked or rotisserie chicken, a little dollop of cream and a handful of spinach leaves; unless you've added cream, lime wedges are a welcome pass-around.

ROBUST RED-CHILE BEEF SOUP
WITH MEXICAN VEGETABLES

Mole de Olla

MEXICAN SOUPS HAVE become renowned, in my opinion, because they are enriched with strong, straightforward flavors and textures. And this simple *mole de olla,* with its pureed dried chiles, chunky vegetables, crunchy raw onion and lively squirt of lime, is, perhaps, the best beef-and-vegetable soup ever made. *Mole de olla* is such a way of life in Central Mexico that produce vendors sell piles or bags of "soup" vegetables. Sour prickly pears, by the way, show up regularly in Mexican markets in the United States. The fruit is a little more sour than an underripe plum, which, actually, could be an acceptable substitute.

MAKES ABOUT 12 CUPS, SERVING 12 AS A FIRST COURSE, 4 TO 6 AS A MAIN COURSE

12 ounces boneless, lean beef chuck, cut into 1½-inch cubes

12 ounces beef soup bones, oxtails or shank (*ask the butcher to cut them into 2-inch pieces*)

5 medium (*about 8 ounces total*) xoconostles (*also called* tunas ágrias *or sour prickly pear*) (*optional*)

1 teaspoon salt, plus a little more if needed

1 small white onion, diced, plus an additional ½ cup finely diced for garnish

3 garlic cloves, peeled and finely chopped

3 bay leaves

Big pinch cloves, preferably freshly ground

¼ teaspoon cumin, preferably freshly ground

¼ teaspoon black pepper, preferably freshly ground

2 small (*about ¾ ounce total*) dried ancho chiles, stemmed and seeded

3 medium (*about ¾ ounce total*) dried guajillo chiles, stemmed and seeded

1 medium-small, round, ripe tomato, cored and roughly chopped

3 to 5 large sprigs epazote (*or use a small bunch of cilantro if epazote is unavailable*)

2 large carrots, peeled and sliced ¼ inch thick

2 medium zucchini, cut into ½-inch dice

OR 1 large chayote, peeled, pitted, and cut into ½-inch dice

2 ears corn, husked, cut crosswise into 1-inch sections

1 cup (*about 4 ounces*) green beans, ends snipped, cut in half

2 limes, cut into wedges, for serving

1. *The meat and broth.* In a large (6-quart) pot, place the meat, bones and 3 quarts of water and bring to a boil. Reduce the heat to medium-low and skim off the grayish foam that rises during the first few minutes of simmering.

With a small knife, peel the optional *xoconostles*; cut in half, scoop out the seeds with a spoon, then slice into ¼-inch strips. To the pot, add the *xoconostles,* salt, onion, garlic, bay leaves, cloves, cumin and pepper, partially cover and simmer 1½ hours.

2. *The chiles and other flavorings.* Tear the chiles into flat pieces and toast on an ungreased griddle or heavy skillet over medium heat, pressing firmly down with a metal spatula for a few seconds until there is a crackle, then flip and press down to toast on the other side. In a small bowl, cover the chiles with hot water and let rehydrate 30 minutes, stirring frequently to ensure even soaking. Drain and discard the water.

Place the chiles in a food processor or blender with the tomato and 3 tablespoons water. Process until smooth, adding a little more water if necessary to keep everything moving through the blades, then press through a medium-mesh sieve into a bowl; set aside.

When the meat has cooked 1½ hours, take it off the heat. If using soup bones, pick off the meat and return to the pot. (Oxtails and shank can be served as is.) Spoon off the fat from the top of the broth, then stir in the chile puree and *epazote,* partially cover and simmer 30 minutes.

3. *Finishing the soup.* Uncover, raise the heat to medium-high and add the carrots; cook 10 minutes, then add the zucchini or chayote, corn and green beans. (If there isn't enough broth to cover them, add water to bring up the level.) Cook the vegetables about 10 minutes, until tender. Taste and add more salt if necessary.

Ladle the *mole de olla* into warm soup bowls, sprinkle on the chopped onion, and you're ready to go. Pass the lime wedges for everyone to squeeze on the soup as they like.

ADVANCE PREPARATION—The soup can be prepared through step 2, covered and refrigerated for several days; complete step 3 just before serving.

A Note on Nomenclature—There is none of the chile-and-nut thickening here that is characteristic of *moles* like *mole poblano* or *mole verde.* Of the dishes that carry *mole* in their name, this "pot" *mole,* as the name translates, perhaps comes closest to the use of *mole* in its broader, original Aztec meaning of stew/sauce.

ROASTED TOMATO SOUP
WITH POBLANOS, OREGANO AND FRESH CHEESE

Sopa de Jitomate y Rajas

*T*HOUGH IT'S POSSIBLE to make a good tomato soup at any time of the year, this is a wonderful summertime farmer's market recipe. Ripe tomatoes are roasted and coarsely pureed with good beef broth, then simmered with roasted chiles. It's fabulous served with thick slices of grilled bread, a salad of young greens, a plate of cheese and a bottle of young red wine. It's even good cold, drizzled with a little dark vinegar.

These are purely Mexican flavors that can be made even more distinctive by simmering the soup with a branch of *epazote*. Some perfectly ripe tomatoes will retain the intensity of fresh flavor all the way to the table; others may cry out for a sprinkling of fresh thyme or cilantro over the finished soup to create the lively flavor you're after.

MAKES ABOUT 8 CUPS, SERVING 4 TO 6

2½ pounds (5 medium-large round or 15 to 20 medium plum) ripe tomatoes

FOR 2 CUPS ESSENTIAL ROASTED POBLANO *RAJAS*

1 pound (6 medium-large) fresh poblano chiles

1 tablespoon vegetable or olive oil

1 large white onion, halved and sliced ¼ inch thick

3 garlic cloves, peeled and finely chopped

1 teaspoon dried oregano, preferably Mexican

6 cups good beef broth (page 137)

Salt, about 1 teaspoon, depending on the saltiness of the broth

8 ounces Mexican queso fresco or pressed, salted farmer's cheese, cut into ½-inch cubes, about 2 cups

1. *Roasting the tomatoes.* Roast the tomatoes on a baking sheet 4 inches below a very hot broiler until the skins are blackened on one side, about 6 minutes, then flip and broil the other side. Cool, then peel, collecting all the juices. Place the tomatoes and their juices in a food processor or blender, and process to a coarse puree.

2. *Making 2 cups Essential Roasted Poblano* Rajas. Roast the chiles directly over a gas flame or 4 inches below a very hot broiler, turning occasionally until blackened on all sides, about 5 minutes for open flame, about 10 minutes for broiler. Cover with a kitchen towel and let stand 5 minutes. Peel, pull out the stem and seed pod, then rinse *briefly* to remove bits of skin and seeds. Slice into ¼-inch-wide strips.

In a medium-size (4-quart) pot, heat the oil over medium to medium-high, then add the onion and cook, stirring regularly, until nicely browned but still a little crunchy, about 5 minutes. Add the garlic and oregano, toss a minute longer, then stir in the chiles and just heat through.

3. *Finishing the soup.* Add the tomato puree to the *rajas* and cook over medium-high, stirring frequently, until very thick and reduced, about 7 minutes. Stir in the broth, partially cover and simmer over medium-low for 30 minutes. Season with salt. Serve the soup in warm bowls, topped with cubes of the fresh cheese.

ADVANCE PREPARATION—The soup can be made a day or two in advance, but don't simmer it for the 30 minutes. When reheating, cook the soup enough to blend the flavors, season with salt and serve with the cheese.

SHORTCUTS—Though canned broth is an option, it wouldn't be terribly welcome in this soup; you're better off buying frozen or refrigerated broth from a specialty store that makes their own.

VARIATIONS AND IMPROVISATIONS

Fresh herbs like thyme and cilantro can be sprinkled over the soup; ¼-inch-thick rounds of goat cheese are delicious in place of the fresh cheese; and tomatoes roasted over a medium-low grill make the soup taste very fashionable, as do dried yellow tomatoes sprinkled on the soup. A good garlicky vegetable broth is an option for the beef broth.

Seafood Tomato Soup—Make the soup with chicken stock, and add 2 dozen clams and 8 ounces cubed fish fillets during the last 5 minutes of simmering. When the clams are open, ladle into bowls and sprinkle generously with chopped cilantro (or oregano). For a contemporary twist replace the fish with 8 to 12 ounces cleaned squid, quickly grill it, slice it into small pieces and add it just before serving.

RUSTIC RANCH-STYLE SOUP
WITH TOMATO, JALAPEÑO AND AVOCADO

Sopa Ranchera

*O*NCE THE GARLIC has concentrated and sweetened with the broth, this soup is ready in a flash. *Salsa mexicana* flavors (tomato, green chile, onion) bubble for a few minutes in the garlicky liquid before it is topped with avocado and cilantro to yield a satisfying bowl that is perfect everyday fare. Add shreds of chicken to make it a main dish or squash blossoms for a dressy starter before a special meal of Teloloapan Red *Mole*, page 277. Make *Sopa Ranchera* when you can get ripe tomatoes. Broth made from a good chicken will shine here.

MAKES 8 CUPS, SERVING 6 TO 8

3 quarts rich chicken broth
   (*page 137*)

1 large head of garlic, unpeeled

1 large sprig fresh epazote (*optional*)

2 fresh jalapeño chiles, stemmed

1 medium white onion, cut into
   ¼-inch dice

2 large ripe tomatoes, cored, seeded
   and cut into ¼-inch dice

Salt, about 1½ teaspoons depending
   on the saltiness of the broth

¾ cup loosely packed chopped
   cilantro

About 1 cup coarsely shredded cooked
   chicken (*optional*)

2 ripe avocados, peeled, pitted and cut
   into ½-inch dice

1 lime, cut into 6 to 8 wedges

1. *The broth.* Measure the broth into a large (6-quart) pot. Slice the unpeeled head of garlic in half widthwise and add both halves to the broth along with the optional *epazote.* Bring to a boil, then simmer over medium-low, partially covered, for about an hour. The liquid should have reduced to about 7 cups. Remove the garlic and *epazote,* and discard.

2. *Finishing the soup.* While the broth is simmering, cut the chiles in half lengthwise, and cut out the seed pod. Slice into very thin lengthwise strips, and set aside with the diced onion and tomatoes.

    Generously season the broth with salt, then add the chiles and onion, partially cover and simmer for 7 minutes. Add the tomatoes, cilantro and optional chicken and simmer another 3 minutes, then ladle into warm bowls. Garnish with avocados, serve to your guests and pass the lime separately for each to squeeze in to their liking.

ADVANCE PREPARATION—The seasoned broth in step 1 can be made several days ahead and refrigerated. Finish step 2 just before serving.

SHORTCUTS—Because the broth is critical, only purchase it if you can get good quality.

VARIATIONS AND IMPROVISATIONS

Smoked chicken or other poultry is delicious shredded into the soup. Drizzle in a little Thick Cream (page 165) or *crème fraîche* to make it richer. Or start with 6 cups chicken broth and 1 cup dry white wine, and add 2 pounds of clams with the tomatoes; when the clams open, garnish and serve.

Sopa Xochitl—To prepare this elegant soup named after the Aztec goddess of flowers, add 12 to 16 squash blossoms to the soup with the tomatoes. Before adding them, you'll need to pull off the thin green sepals at the base of each blossom, then twist out the pistil deep inside the petals. You may either wilt the blossoms whole in the simmering broth or, easier for serving, tear them into pieces before adding them.

MUSHROOM-CACTUS SOUP
WITH ROASTED TOMATILLOS

Sopa de Hongos y Nopales

$\mathscr{T}$HIS IS ONE of the most distinctive and widely applauded soups I know. Years ago, Alicia De'Angeli, of El Tajín Restaurant in Mexico City, taught me the interplay of slightly crunchy, tangy cactus with tender, woodsy-tasting mushrooms, both brought to life by tomatillos, herbs and a crumbling of spicy toasted pasilla chile. When Alicia prepared this for a dinner at Topolobampo, the parts magically come together into a delicious whole: exotic, but not strange tasting, a great first experience with cactus. All the main ingredients are roasted, so you'll learn how this classic technique translates into deep, rich flavor. And the traditional herbs (*epazote*, *hoja santa* and cilantro) play an important role here.

MAKES ABOUT 6 CUPS, SERVING 4 TO 6

- *4 ounces (2 to 3 medium) tomatillos, husked and rinsed*
- *12 ounces (2 medium-small round or 4 to 6 plum) ripe tomatoes*
- *4 garlic cloves, unpeeled*
- *1 small fresh hot green chile (such as serrano or jalapeño), stem removed*
- *1 small white onion, cut into 3 thick slices*
- *1 small sprig epazote (or substitute extra cilantro)*
- *½ small hoja santa leaf*
  - *OR ⅛ teaspoon anise seed, preferably freshly ground*
- *4 large sprigs cilantro*
- *4 cups good chicken broth (page 137)*
- *1½ tablespoons vegetable or olive oil*
- *½ pound fresh shiitake (or other full-flavored) mushrooms, stems removed, caps sliced*
- *Salt, about 1 teaspoon depending on saltiness of broth*
- *4 medium (about 8 ounces total) cactus paddles (nopales)*
- *2 dried pasilla chiles, stemmed, seeded and cut into ¼-inch strips*

1. *The soup.* Lay the tomatillos and tomatoes on a baking sheet and set 4 inches below a very hot broiler. When blackened in spots and soft, 5 to 6 minutes, flip and roast the other side. Cool; peel the tomatoes, collecting all the juice. On an ungreased griddle or heavy skillet set over medium heat, roast the garlic and chile: Turn the unpeeled garlic and the chile regularly until blackened in spots and soft, 10 to 15 minutes. While the garlic and chile are roasting, lay the onion out on a small piece of foil, set on the griddle or skillet, and dry-roast

until deeply browned and soft, about 5 minutes per side. Let garlic cool, then slip off the papery skins.

Combine all the roasted ingredients in a food processor or blender with the *epazote, hoja santa* (or anise seed), cilantro and *1 cup* of the broth. Process to a smooth puree.

In a medium-size (4-quart) pot, heat *1 tablespoon* of the oil over medium-high. When hot enough to make a drop of the puree sizzle sharply, add it all at once. Stir continually until darker and noticeably thicker, about 5 minutes. Add the remaining 3 *cups* of broth and the mushrooms, reduce the heat to medium-low and let gently simmer for 30 minutes, partially covered. Taste and season with salt.

2. The cactus and dried chile. While the soup is simmering, prepare the cactus: Holding a cactus paddle gingerly between the nodes of the prickly spines, trim off the edge that outlines the paddle, including the blunt end where the paddle was severed from the plant. Slice or scrape off the spiny nodes from both sides. Brush the paddles with the remaining ½ *tablespoon* oil and place them on a baking sheet. Set 4 inches below a very hot broiler or on a preheated gas grill and cook, turning the paddles occasionally, until limp, 10 to 15 minutes, depending on the heat of your fire. Cool, cut in half lengthwise, then cut each half crosswise into ¼-inch slices.

Turn on the oven to 325 degrees. Spread the chile strips on a small baking sheet and toast in the oven until fragrant and lightly crisp, 5 to 8 minutes.

3. Serving the soup. Just before serving, add the cactus to the soup and bring to a boil. Ladle into warm soup bowls and sprinkle with the toasted chile.

ADVANCE PREPARATION—The soup can be made through step 2 several days ahead and refrigerated, covered. Reheat it and finish step 3 to serve.

SHORTCUTS—Purchased broth can replace homemade and the cactus could be replaced by an additional ¼ pound of mushrooms.

VARIATIONS AND IMPROVISATIONS

Creamy Potato-Mushroom Soup with bacon and cilantro—Prepare the soup as described, omitting the herbs and adding 8 ounces diced Yukon Gold potatoes along with the mushrooms. Omit the cactus. Just before serving, stir in ⅔ cup chopped cilantro and ½ cup Thick Cream (page 165) or heavy cream. Serve each bowl topped with a sprinkling of crumbled cooked bacon, chopped cilantro and pasilla chile.

OAXACAN BLACK BEAN SOUP

Sopa de Frijoles Negros

*W*HEN WE MAKE this dish in Oaxaca, it tastes of the full-flavored little black beans from a nearby valley, of the anisey, herby avocado leaves from wild trees, of the inimitable rusty-red chorizo and the meaty, sweet-tasting dried shrimp.

So why include such a locally rooted recipe in a book for American cooks? Because everytime I make my simple Stateside equivalent, I love it. It is truly a wonderful black bean soup—scented with anise and tangy chorizo, lively with crunchy tortillas and fresh cheese.

I also love the unlikely sounding combination of shrimp with beans, so I've included a shrimp option. In Oaxaca, I buy 3 ounces of the large, not-too-dry dried shrimp, soak them for several hours, peel them, then simmer them for 20 to 30 minutes in the pureed soup; here I usually use fresh shrimp. One or two lightly toasted *chiles pasillas oaxaqueños,* the local favorite that bears a smoky resemblance to the smaller *chile chipotle colorado,* add a perfect spiciness if simmered in the pot from the beginning.

This is a meal in itself, though small cups of it can easily start a menu of Ancho-Marinated Whole Roast Fish (page 356) or Grilled Steak with Spicy Guajillo Sauce (page 364).

MAKES 7 CUPS, SERVING 6

12 ounces (about 2 cups) dry black beans, cleaned

4 avocado leaves

  OR 1 rib fresh fennel, roughly chopped

½ cup (4 ounces) chorizo sausage, casing removed

1 small white onion, diced

Salt, about 1 teaspoon

⅓ cup vegetable oil, for frying

4 to 6 corn tortillas (preferably stale store-bought ones), sliced into ⅛-inch-wide strips, for garnish

8 ounces (about 12) medium-large shrimp, peeled (optional)

About ½ cup crumbled Mexican queso fresco or pressed, salted farmer's cheese

1. **The beans.** Place the beans in a medium-size (4-quart) pot, cover with 6 cups water, remove any beans that float and heat slowly to a simmer.

If using avocado leaves, toast them briefly directly over a medium gas flame or on a hot griddle. Add the avocado leaves (or fennel), chorizo and onion to the beans, partially cover and simmer over medium-low heat, stirring occasionally, until the beans are fully tender, 1½ to 2 hours. If you see the beans peeking up through the liquid, add hot water to cover them by ½ inch.

2. *Finishing the soup.* Use an immersion blender to coarsely puree the soup, or puree in batches in a food processor or *loosely covered* blender. Return it to the pot. Add enough water to thin to a medium-thick consistency. Taste and season with salt.

Heat the oil in a medium-size (8- to 9-inch) skillet over medium-high. When hot, add about ⅓ of the tortilla strips and fry, turning frequently, until they are crisp. Drain on paper towels. Fry the remaining strips in 2 batches.

3. *Serving the soup.* If using the shrimp, devein each one by making a shallow incision down the back, exposing the (usually) dark intestinal track; scrape it out. Heat the soup to a boil, add the shrimp and cook until just done, about 2 minutes. Ladle into warm soup bowls, top with a few of the crisp tortilla strips and sprinkle with a little cheese.

ADVANCE PREPARATION—The soup can be made and refrigerated several days ahead through the pureeing in step 2; you'll likely need to thin the reheated soup before adding the (optional) shrimp. The tortilla strips keep a day or so wrapped in foil on the counter.

SHORTCUTS—Don't try it with canned beans—the result will be quite gray. Broken, good-quality chips could replace the fried tortilla strips.

VARIATIONS AND IMPROVISATIONS

A very good black bean soup can be made without avocado leaves and chorizo, using several chopped canned chipotles or a tablespoon or so of Essential Sweet-and-Smoky Chipotle Seasoning Salsa (page 52) added with the dry beans. I also love banana chips in place of tortilla strips.

Dressy Black Bean Soup—Prepare the soup without shrimp in any of the variations outlined above. Puree it fully. Serve each cup or bowl with a swirl of Thick Cream (page 165) or *crème fraîche* and a swirl of Roasted Tomatillo-Chipotle Salsa (page 45). Sprinkle with chopped grilled green onion rather than cheese.

SLOW-SIMMERED FAVA BEAN SOUP
WITH MINT AND PASILLA CHILE

Sopa de Habas

*T*HESE ARE FLAVORS from the pages of *Mexico en la cocina de Marichú,* one of the most well crafted cookbooks from Mexico earlier in this century. The soup is thick with that inimitable, rustic texture of slow-simmered fava beans, deepened with the flavors of roasted tomatoes, garlic and onions, and scented with mint and cilantro. Up to this point the soup is essentially a delicious Spanish concoction (favas originate in the Mediterranean, unlike pinto, kidney, navy and their ilk, which are from the New World). Adding the pasilla chile "condiment" makes this hearty bowlful Mexican. The tangy richness of the chile against the earthy, ripe fava flavor is one of my favorite combinations.

Dried favas are available in many specialty stores, though often with the brown hull still on. If that's all you can get, soak them several hours, then peel off the hulls, revealing a yellow bean below. Mexican markets sell the already-hulled yellow dry bean.

MAKES ABOUT 10 CUPS, SERVING 8 TO 10

1 pound (about 2⅔ cups) hulled
   dry (yellow) fava beans, cleaned

8 cups good chicken broth (page 137)
   or water

6 garlic cloves, unpeeled

1 large white onion, thickly sliced

1½ pounds (3 medium-large round
   or 9 to 12 plum) ripe tomatoes

6 medium (about 2 ounces total)
   dried pasilla chiles, stemmed
   and seeded

2 tablespoons olive oil, *plus extra for
   garnish*

2 tablespoons cider vinegar

¾ teaspoon dried oregano, preferably
   Mexican

Salt, about 2½ teaspoons

½ cup loosely packed chopped
   cilantro

1 to 2 tablespoons chopped fresh mint,
   preferably spearmint

About ½ cup finely crumbled
   Mexican queso añejo, *dry feta
   or Parmesan*

1. *The soup base.* Rinse the fava beans, place in a large (6-quart) pot, cover with 8 cups of broth or water, and simmer over medium-low heat, partially covered, until very tender (they will begin falling apart), about 1 hour.

While the beans are simmering, roast the garlic on an ungreased griddle or heavy skillet over medium heat, turning occasionally, until blackened in spots and soft, about 15 minutes. Cool, then slip off the papery skins and finely chop. On a piece of foil in the same skillet, roast the onion slices in a single layer, turning once, until richly browned and soft, 6 or 7 minutes per side; dice. Roast the tomatoes 4 inches below a very hot broiler or in the foil-lined skillet until blackened on one side, about 6 minutes, then flip and roast the other side. Cool, then peel and chop, saving all the juices.

Add the garlic, onion and tomatoes to the tender fava beans and simmer about 30 minutes more, until the beans are the consistency of a coarse, rough-looking puree.

2. *The chiles.* While the soup is simmering, cut the chiles into ⅛-inch slivers using kitchen shears. Heat the olive oil in a small (1- to 1½-quart) saucepan over medium heat. Add the chiles and stir for a minute. Remove from the heat and add the vinegar, 3 tablespoons water, oregano, and a scant ½ *teaspoon* of the salt. Let stand at least ½ hour, stirring occasionally.

3. *Finishing the soup.* Just before serving, add a little water (or broth), if necessary, to bring the soup to the consistency of medium-thick bean soup. Stir in the cilantro and mint, taste and season with salt, usually about 2 teaspoons. Ladle the soup into warm bowls, spoon about a tablespoon of chiles into the center, drizzle with a little olive oil (this traditional touch shows the soup's obvious Mediterranean roots) and sprinkle with the finely crumbled cheese.

ADVANCE PREPARATION—The recipe can be made several days ahead through step 2; refrigerate the soup and chile mixture separately.

SHORTCUTS—A simple version can be prepared without the chile "condiment"; serve bottled hot sauce on the side.

VARIATIONS AND IMPROVISATIONS

Though *fresh* favas aren't appropriate here, you can make a great soup substituting dry garbanzos (they will take several hours of simmering to become tender), lentils, navy beans, pintos, pinks or any number of "heirloom" beans available in specialty stores and catalogs.

Fava Soup with Moroccan Aspirations—Prepare the soup as directed, adding ½ to 1 teaspoon crumbled saffron threads and 1 teaspoon powdered ginger; skip the chile "condiment" and crumbled cheese garnish. Sprinkle bowls of the finished soup with crumbled toasted árbol chile or red pepper flakes.

Fava Soup with Huitlacoche—When you're lucky enough to have *huitlacoche,* prepare the soup without mint, replacing the chile "condiment" in each bowl with a tablespoon of *huitlacoche* filling (page 158) and crumbling toasted pasilla on top.

ROASTED POBLANO *CREMA*
WITH MEXICAN GREENS
Crema de Chile Poblano y Acelgas (o Espinacas)

*P*OBLANOS AND CREAM, when showcased together, become one of the undisputed crowd pleasers of the Mexican kitchen. Rich and roasty, unctuous and green-chile spicy, all against a background of sweet onion and garlic. My recipe here is rather robust, garnished with bits of ham and potatoes and topped with tiny tortilla strips. Serve it in small portions before a not-too-rich main dish like Campeche-Baked Fish Fillets (page 348) or Ancho-Marinated Whole Roast Fish (page 356).

MAKES 6 CUPS, SERVING 6

FOR 2 CUPS ESSENTIAL ROASTED POBLANO *RAJAS*

1 pound (6 medium-large) fresh poblano chiles

1 tablespoon vegetable or olive oil

1 large white onion, sliced ¼ inch thick

3 garlic cloves, peeled and finely chopped

½ teaspoon dried oregano, preferably Mexican

¼ teaspoon dried thyme

6 cups loosely packed, sliced chard leaves (½-inch-thick slices; you'll need a 12-ounce bunch)

OR 6 cups loosely packed, sliced, spinach leaves (½-inch-thick slices; start with about 10 ounces)

4½ cups good chicken broth (page 137)

½ cup Thick Cream (page 165), whipping cream or crème fraîche

⅓ cup fresh masa for tortillas OR ½ cup masa harina

Salt, about 1 teaspoon, depending on the saltiness of the broth

⅓ cup vegetable oil, for frying

4 to 6 corn tortillas (preferably stale store-bought ones), sliced into ⅛-inch-wide strips, for garnish

1 cup diced ham, for garnish

1 cup diced red-skin potatoes, boiled in salted water until tender, for garnish

3 tablespoons chopped epazote or cilantro (or 1 tablespoon chopped fresh thyme), for garnish

1. *Making 2 cups Essential Roasted Poblano* **Rajas.** Roast the chiles directly over a gas flame or on a baking sheet 4 inches below a very hot broiler, turning occasionally, until blackened on all sides, about 5 minutes for open flame, about 10 minutes for broiler. Cover

with a kitchen towel and let stand 5 minutes. Peel, pull out the stem and seed pod, then rinse *briefly* to remove bits of skin and seeds. Slice into ¼-inch-wide strips.

In a heavy, medium-size (4-quart) pot, heat 1 tablespoon oil over medium to medium-high, then add the onion and cook, stirring regularly, until nicely browned but still a little crunchy, about 5 minutes. Add the garlic and herbs, toss a minute longer, then stir in the chiles and just heat through.

2. *The soup base.* Add the sliced chard or spinach and *1 cup* of the broth to the *rajas*. Cover and simmer over medium heat, until the chard or spinach is thoroughly cooked but still vibrant green, 3 or 4 minutes for spinach, 5 or 6 for chard. Puree in batches in a food processor or *loosely covered* blender; push through a medium-mesh strainer into a bowl.

Return the pot to the heat. Pour in *3 cups* of the remaining broth, the vegetable puree and cream; bring to a simmer. Thoroughly mix the remaining ½ cup broth with the *masa* or *masa harina* in a small bowl, then strain the mixture into the simmering soup, whisking all the while. Continue whisking until the soup returns to a boil; it will thicken right away. Partially cover and simmer for 10 minutes, then taste and season with salt.

3. *Serving the soup.* Heat ⅓ cup vegetable oil in a medium (8- to 9-inch) skillet over medium-high. When hot, add about ⅓ of the tortilla strips and fry, turning frequently, until crisp, about 1 minute. Drain on paper towels. Fry the remaining strips in two batches.

Divide the ham and potatoes among warm soup bowls. Ladle in the soup, top with a portion of the tortilla strips and a sprinkling of *epazote* or cilantro. Serve right away.

ADVANCE PREPARATION—The *rajas* can be made several days ahead (they can even be frozen for this recipe since they will be pureed in the final soup). The soup can be finished through step 2 a day or so ahead and refrigerated. The tortilla strips keep a day or so wrapped in foil on the counter.

VARIATIONS AND IMPROVISATIONS—The ham could be replaced by other smoked meat (I love smoked chicken) and seafood (try smoked shrimp); parsnips, though not Mexican, are wonderful in the soup, as is a little corn.

Mexican Greens

Greens are a big part of the nonurban Mexican diet, especially the diets of those who are close to their native roots. In Mexico you find them as part of robust stews, blanched and fried with garlic for a taco filling or simmered with tortillas and a spicy sauce for memorable *chilaquiles*.

about 1½ inches long

lamb's quarters
(quelites)

In the language of the Aztecs, the word *quelitl* was used for edible leafy greens or herbs. Today, the Hispanicized version of the Aztec original, *quelite,* maintains a rather generic translation as *greens,* though most commonly lamb's quarters, a delectable, prolific, dark-green, jagged-edge leafy "weed" that grows easily without cultivation all through North and Central America. Lamb's quarters are cousins to the herb *epazote* and the green/vegetable called *huauzoncle* (dock). When you're walking through a park in the summer, you'll likely find lamb's quarters—the leaves have a gray-green underside that feels like they've been rubbed in ash, hence the Mexican name *quelites cenizos,* "ashen greens." Don't hesitate to harvest some, give them a good rinsing and cook them; they're sturdier than spinach, with a rich green flavor that's not at all strong—truly my favorite cooked green. Though difficult to find, look for these delicious greens in some farmer's markets; a cultivated French variety, known as magenta lamb's quarters, sometimes turns up.

A recent publication from Mexico, *Los quelites, un tesoro culinario,* done in conjunction with the National Autonomous University, provides pictures and descriptions of seventeen commonly eaten greens. Of them, besides *quelites cenizos,* the most widely seen varieties include *verdolagas* (purslane, tangy flavored with a succulent texture, most frequently cooked with tomato sauce and pork), *romeritos* (a rosemarylike green—no relation to rosemary, noted as a distant relative of *epazote*—that has a light flavor, nice texture and a place in the traditional fast-day dish with shrimp cakes and *mole*), *quintoniles* (amaranth greens, used as much as lamb's quarters, available widely in Asian markets), *chepil* (a light-flavored herb/green with small, thin leaves that's used mostly in southern Mexico as an addition to soups and rice), *chaya* (the large Yucatecan leaf with a delicious—not strong—dark-green flavor), *berros* (watercress, used as a salad or cooked in a dish) and the above-mentioned *huauzoncles.* Look for them in Mexico around the perimeter of the markets, where women set up mats to sell produce collected from the wild.

Chard is a European introduction to Mexico, and while it doesn't offer the varieties of texture and taste of the native greens, it is abundantly available on both sides of the border. Feel free to use it wherever native greens are appropriate. I like it much better than tender, mild spinach. In cooking, most of these greens are interchangeable—some take longer (*quelites,* for example) than the others (like chard), but most cook relatively quickly.

· ·

Chicken Broth

IT SEEMS THERE'S always a pot with chicken stewing in every Mexican kitchen—the meat for the main course, the broth for the sauce. The broth isn't stock, made from bones and simmered for hours until reduced and concentrated. Strong stock like that takes the focus off the chiles, tomatoes, tomatillos and so forth that are what Mexican sauces are all about. In fact, when I'm asked to cook Mexican food in other restaurants, I typically dilute their stock by half before using it to make a sauce. For Mexican sauce making, canned chicken broth is usually an okay substitute. When it comes to homemade soup, I prefer a richer broth like this. Not that it has more vegetables and herbs *per se* (those aren't really part of Mexican broths), just that it's cooked a little longer with a generous amount of a full-flavored chicken.

MAKES A GENEROUS 2 QUARTS

1 medium (2½- to 3-pound) whole chicken, quartered

OR 3 pounds chicken wings or bones (such as necks or carcasses)

1 medium white onion, thinly sliced

3 garlic cloves, peeled and halved

3 bay leaves

¾ teaspoon dried marjoram

¾ teaspoon dried thyme

½ teaspoon black peppercorns, very coarsely ground

Place the chicken quarters, wings or bones in a large (6-quart) pot. Add the onion, garlic and 4½ quarts water and heat slowly to a simmer. Skim off all the grayish foam that rises during the first few minutes of simmering, then add the remaining ingredients, partially cover and simmer gently over medium-low heat about 2 hours.

Strain the broth through a fine wire-mesh strainer into a large bowl; discard the solids. If time allows, refrigerate the broth until cold, then skim off the congealed fat. If you intend to use the broth right away use a wide shallow spoon to skim off the fat that rises to the top.

ADVANCE PREPARATION—Refrigerate for up to 5 days, or freeze.

VARIATIONS AND IMPROVISATIONS

Beef Broth—Replace the chicken with 3 pounds of meaty beef bones (marrow bones make a rich broth, neck bones give a meaty flavor). The bones usually are not roasted, though roasting them in a 400-degree oven for 1½ hours or so will add both richness and color.

GOLDEN SQUASH BLOSSOM *CREMA*

Crema de Flores de Calabaza

$\mathcal{A}$N ELEGANT GOLDEN squash blossom soup captures the freshness of the Mexican countryside. The blossoms offer leafy green flavors, a hint of yellow squash, a light herbal aroma. The little bit of potato blends in body, the dice of poblano adds smoky spice, the corn and zucchini underscore the just-picked blush and a light creaminess hums elegantly through every bite.

Huge bundles of squash blossoms pass hands every day in Mexican markets, so this soup is relatively inexpensive there. Unless you live near a farmer's market or harvest blossoms yourself, you'll have to search them out. My gardening guru, Jeff Dawson, conducted a tasting of day lilies for the Chefs Collaborative several years ago, and I found them to be a decent substitute; be sure the plants have not been sprayed. Otherwise, the squash-and-spinach version described below is an elegant alternative.

So don't skip this recipe just because you've never had a bunch of blossoms on your counter. Figure out which direction you want to take the recipe, then invite some friends for soup, Smoky Peanut *Mole* (page 286) or Smoky Braised Squab (page 328) and Yucatecan-Style Fresh Coconut Pie (page 402). It'll be a meal they never forget.

MAKES ABOUT 7 CUPS, ENOUGH FOR 6 GENEROUS SERVINGS

1 ½ tablespoons butter

1 large white onion, chopped into ¼-inch dice

3 cups good chicken broth (page 137)

1 small boiling potato (like the red-skin ones), peeled and roughly chopped

25 large (3- to 4-inch) squash blossoms (male blossoms with no squash attached)

2 fresh poblano chiles

1 cup milk

1 medium zucchini, cut into ¼-inch cubes

1 large ear of corn, husked, kernels cut from the cob

½ cup Thick Cream (page 165), whipping cream or crème fraîche

Salt, about 1 ½ teaspoons, depending on the saltiness of the broth

A little chopped epazote or parsley, for garnish

1. *The broth.* In a medium-size (4-quart) soup pot, melt the butter over medium heat. Add the onion and cook, stirring frequently, until lightly brown, about 5 minutes. Scoop out *half* of the onion and set aside. Add the broth and potato, partially cover and simmer over medium-low heat for 20 minutes.

2. *The blossoms.* While the broth is simmering, clean the squash blossoms: Break off the stems, then the little green sepals that come out from the base of the blossoms (they originally covered the buds). Use your fingers to break loose the long pistils in the center of each flower and discard. With a very sharp knife, cut the blossoms crosswise into ¼-inch strips, including the bulbous base.

Add *half* the blossoms to the broth and simmer 3 minutes. In a food processor or in batches in a *loosely covered* blender, puree the mixture; return to the pot.

3. *The chiles.* Roast the chiles directly over the gas flame, on a medium-hot gas grill or 4 inches below a very hot broiler. Turn occasionally until blistered and blackened on all sides, 5 to 6 minutes for the flame or grill, about 10 minutes for the broiler. Cover with a kitchen towel and let stand about 5 minutes. Peel off the charred skin, cut out the seed pod, then quickly rinse to remove straggling bits of skin and seeds. Cut into ¼-inch dice.

4. *Finishing the soup.* Add the chiles to the soup along with the milk and reserved onion; bring to a simmer and cook for 10 minutes. Add the zucchini and corn, simmer a couple of minutes, then add the remaining squash blossoms. Simmer a couple of minutes longer (the strips of blossom will soften into deep-golden "streamers"), remove from the heat, stir in the cream, taste and season with salt. Serve in warm bowls garnished with *epazote* or parsley.

ADVANCE PREPARATION—The soup can be prepared a day or so ahead through step 3; refrigerate all the parts covered. Complete the soup just before you plan to serve it.

VARIATIONS AND IMPROVISATIONS

"Squash Blossom" Soup with yellow squash and spinach—Replace the blossoms with 2 medium yellow squash cut into ¼-inch dice; add half to the soup in each of the two places the blossoms are called for. Add one cup thinly sliced spinach along with the zucchini and corn.

Exotic Soup of Blossoms and Wild Mushrooms—Prepare the soup as described, replacing the milk with an equal amount of broth. Add 2 cups sliced, not-too-strong wild mushrooms (I prefer fresh chanterelle, hedgehogs or cauliflower) to the pot along with the chiles. Omit the zucchini and corn; serve the soup as is, or add a little thinly sliced spinach along with the second batch of blossoms.

Squash Blossoms

Probably the most beautiful and thrilling bouquet you could bring an adventurous cook, especially in the States, is one of squash blossoms. Their daffodil-yellow luminescence floods the kitchen. If it's true that "the Earth laughs in flowers," as Emerson said, then I'd have to say that eating these giggles can make you giddy. Just think what it means to partake of all this jovial beauty.

Metaphysics aside, the blossoms are delicious and traditional—mostly used in quesadillas (wilted with fried onion and green chile, then griddle-baked in a corn *masa* turnover) and soups, though occasionally they're stuffed with cheese, soufflé-battered (like the jalapeños on page 104) and fried. The abundance of blossoms in Mexico makes it easily feasible to chop up great gobs of them to sauté or stew. The half dollar I often pay for each blossom in Chicago can buy a dozen or two in Mexico.

Though you may not detect it in a stuffed-blossom dish, squash blossoms have a distinctive, light-green flavor (I'm thinking here of Bibb lettuce) that somehow includes the flavor of yellow squash, too. They are not floral.

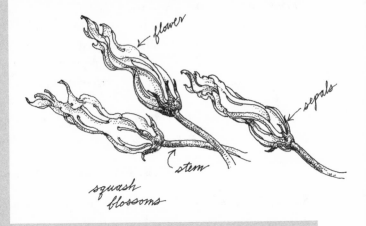

squash blossoms

The blossoms used in Mexico are only the males—the ones with the pistils in the center of the blossom and no evidence of developing squash at the base. Males never produce fruit. To clean a squash blossom, first break off the stem (unless you're stuffing it, in which case leave the stem to use as a "handle"), then pull off all the spiky green sepals around the base of the petals (these were originally the covering of the flower bud). Now, work a finger into the blossom, break off the pistil and discard it. Some cooks tell you to break off the bulbous base, leaving only the flower petals; I think the base has good flavor, so I leave it on.

There are varieties of squash planted solely for their big beautiful blossoms. But if you have zucchini, yellow squash, pumpkins or the like growing in the backyard, don't hesitate to pick the male blossoms (or even females, if you don't care about having less fruit) to cook with. They're best used the day they're picked, though if you lay them out on a paper towel–lined tray, lightly cover them with plastic and store in the warmest part of your refrigerator, they'll keep for a couple of days.

· ·

TACOS, ENCHILADAS AND OTHER CASUAL FARE

Antojitos Mexicanos

WHEN A FRIEND ASKS IF YOU WANT TO EAT MEXICAN FOOD, WHAT COMES TO MIND? Tacos, mostly, I would guess, and not squash-blossom soup, turkey in rich red *mole* and *cajeta*-flavored bread pudding. Yet our thinking of tacos as representing the breadth of Mexican food is as limited, say, as hamburgers delineating all there is to American cooking. "What about all the regional barbecues?" we would ask chauvinistically. "What about planked whitefish and salmon? Chicken and dumplings? Gumbo?"

That doesn't mean I'm turning my back on tacos, however, though I do want to get beyond those crisp-fried U-shaped shells that, in fact, are a north-of-the-border specialty. You see, in Mexico, most tacos aren't fried at all: They're warm tortillas wrapped around anything from a flavorful stew or grilled steak to scrambled eggs or salady stuff. And if you put out a bunch of fillings for guests to fold into tortillas as they choose, you're hosting a *taquisa,* a taco party. The first section of this chapter offers all the details about how to put on that taco party, including a wide variety of fillings for soft tacos and a couple of recipes for fried or knife-and-fork tacos.

The mass-market researchers tell us that enchiladas haven't ever really caught on in the States because, unlike "real" Mexican food (you can understand this to mean popular America-Mexican fare like tacos and burritos), they aren't as much fun: They can't be picked up and eaten. Or perhaps they haven't caught on because the enchiladas they're talking about are awash in a mediocre red sauce under a flow of melted cheese. Luckily for those of us interested in a variety of tastes and textures, truly Mexican dishes that are grouped nicely under the heading "enchiladas" have a lot to offer.

There are recipes here for elegant enchiladas filled with flaked fish, unfilled ones doused with robust tomato sauce, and *mole*-sauced enchiladas that don't take all day to make. If you've ever eaten the dip-and-sear street-style enchiladas in Mexico, you'll be happy I included a recipe for them here, topped with bright and crunchy delectables.

Tacos and enchiladas don't begin to cover all the ingenious Mexican preparations of tortillas and tortilla dough (*masa*). Because they're so common and delicious, I think everyone should at least know about *sopes* (the little *masa* boats that go by regional names like *picadas* and *memelas*), tostadas (crisp tortillas that support a variety of flavors) and *gorditas* (the little fat tortillas that often get split and filled). I've covered the most well known recipes in *Authentic Mexican,* so here I'm branching out to include a modern baked *sope* filled with roasted peppers and cheese (I've called it a *cazuelita*), and the Veracruz-style black bean–laced *gorditas* that are anointed with Sweet-and-Smoky Chipotle Seasoning Salsa. Very old-fashioned Central-Mexican oval *masa* cakes filled with black beans, plus Pueblan (or Veracruz or Oaxacan) potato-and-*masa* torpedos filled with cheese, complete the remaining regional classics I've pulled together.

Quesadillas, turnovers made from tortillas and cheese, are widely known Mexican snacks in the United States. Real Mexican versions are filled with a surprising diversity of ingredients. I've tried to offer snapshots of what's out there, including the classic, crusty, griddle-toasted quesadillas (made with fresh-baked corn tortillas) harboring fillings as simple as melted cheese with herbs and chiles, or as lusciously exotic as Oaxacan yellow *mole*.

Tortilla casseroles, whether the simmered type called *chilaquiles* or the layered *budines,* are some of my favorite homey dishes. Though in *Authentic Mexican* I included a recipe for the ubiquitous, restaurant-style *chilaquiles* made with crisp-fried tortillas simmered with tomato or tomatillo sauce, here I've expanded to an even more compelling version, crispy tortillas sauced with spicy red guajillo chile. Of the two layered tortilla casseroles I have here, one is the very typical, lasagnalike production of tortillas, vegetables, cheese and tomato sauce (it's often called *tamal azteca*). The other is a wondrously complex, black-and-white lamination of pale corn tortillas, pungent black pasilla sauce, white thick cream and black beans. And in case all this *masa* variety hasn't quite hit the spot, maybe a tamal casserole will. It's easy, it's crusty and it's got the texture of an authentically good tamal.

TACOS

Tacos are perfect party food. They're comfortable because you eat them with your hands, they're full of lively flavors, and they're welcoming because each guest can fill and sauce them to his or her own liking. Having a *taquisa,* a taco party, is an enjoyable way to entertain casually, as long as you think through all the details.

First, secure your supply of tortillas, five to eight per person if this is dinner. Since tacos in Mexico are as much about tortillas as they are about filling (this approach keeps everything in good nutritional balance), I suggest you search out good tortillas, preferably ones made by a local tortilla factory, available at Mexican groceries and in some grocery stores, rather than buy the ones in the refrigerated food counter or make them yourselves. On page 145, I've given directions for steam-heating factory-made tortillas; and these steam-heated tortillas will stay warm for an hour or two if you keep the whole steamer apparatus in a low oven or set the steamer over the fire for a couple of minutes every so often to keep the interior steamy. Make sure the baskets you use for the tortillas are lined with heavy towels.

Second, set out four fillings if your party is for six or fewer. Have about 2 cups of each filling (if it's appropriate to measure the filling that way) to ensure that your guests can have one or two tacos of each flavor with the appropriate scant 1/4 cup of filling in each. Add another filling for every two or three more guests you invite, but I'd never have more than six or seven choices, even for a huge party.

You'll likely want to include a meaty filling or two, so why not start with the distinctive Tomatillo Chicken: shreds of meatiness brightened with roasted tomatillos and fresh cheese. If beef appeals, shred it for the Spicy Yucatecan Beef "Salad," one of the many taco fillings you find in Mexico that are served at room temperature. Or shred pork to simmer with chipotles, tomatoes, almonds and raisins for Smoky Shredded Pork. In this section, I've included Yucatecan Grilled Fish, a versatile achiote-marinated fish taco filling that is dramatically wrapped in banana leaves, cooked over the coals, then sliced for your guests to roll into tortillas.

Spicy Pasilla Mushrooms have an exhilarating earthiness, and Inky Corn Mushrooms are exotic. Garlicky Mexican Greens shows a complex, deep-green side of Mexican cooking that will surprise some folks, while the Creamy Braised Chard, Potatoes and Poblanos envelopes the greens in flavors that will keep folks coming back time and again.

The cheese filling for Herby Ricotta-Poblano Tacos is delicious simply put out in a decorative bowl, though in that recipe I give instructions for how to dress up soft tacos to serve as a first course, in a pool of salsa with lovely fresh garnishes. One of my favorite recipes here is for Crispy Black Bean–Bacon Tacos, which you may or may not want to include in your *taquisa,* since these, too, are best served individually in their tangy bed of lettuce and tomato. Also served on individual plates with knives and forks are the traditional Yucatecan Achiote-Roasted Pork Tacos, doused with the incredibly luscious braising juices and crunchy pickled onions.

While you're serving guests at the *taquisa,* it's best to keep the fillings warm in chafing dishes or on a food-warming tray. Lacking either of those, mimic the Mexican market cooks do and serve your fillings in heavy, flameproof dishes (they use thick earthenware in Mexico because it holds heat for an hour) so you can reheat them on the stovetop from time to time.

There are two (maybe three) other elements I'd include in a *taquisa:* salsas, beans and perhaps a salad. I've listed what I think are good salsas to serve with each filling recipe (if one is appropriate). As a general guide, I like to include a chopped fresh tomato salsa (Essential Chopped Tomato-Serrano Salsa, page 25, or Essential Chopped Tomato-Habanero Salsa, page 28), a tomatillo salsa (like Essential Roasted Tomatillo-Serrano Salsa, page 42) and a dried chile salsa (like Essential Roasted Tomatillo-Chipotle Salsa, page 45). I'd also make a pot of beans to serve in small bowls (coffee cups or mugs work well if you don't have small bowls); take a look at the recipe for "Drunken" Pintos (page 239), if you'd like something a little unusual. And last, if salad is a must, toss together some crunchy lettuce like romaine (it contrasts nicely with the softness of the tortillas and beans) with a light dressing, sprinkle it with sliced radishes, chopped fresh cilantro and slivered green onion, and you're ready for the party.

Ready, that is, if you've got your drinks together. Margaritas are legend in this country and I've given you my three favorites (pages 422 through 424). A variety of beers would be welcome, too, from the light Corona, to the sweet-and-malty Dos Equis, the hoppy Bohemia and the rich and slightly bitter Negra Modelo.

REHEATING CORN TORTILLAS

· · · · ·

The best corn tortillas are those that still retain the heat of their original griddle-baking: supple, toasty-smelling, earthy tasting. These (almost) whole-grain goodies have no added fat, which makes them very healthy. Once cooked, though, they dry out quickly, like real French bread.

Making tortillas for every meal isn't practical for most of us, however; neither is running to the local tortilla shop just before sitting down to dine, as many do in Mexico. So that brings us to the method of reheating cold, factory-made corn tortillas. Realize, first, that the quality of tortillas from small local factories (those often sold on unrefrigerated supermarket shelves) is generally better than that of ones from huge, far-off companies (usually found in the refrigerated or frozen counters). Though when cold, any corn tortilla is like dry meal in your mouth; steam-heating is an effective way of bringing back suppleness.

Steam-Heating Tortillas—Set up a steamer (a small vegetable steamer for a dozen or so tortillas; a large Chinese steamer or roasting rack in a covered roasting pan for larger amounts); pour in ½ inch of water, cover and bring to a boil. Wrap each dozen tortillas (you can push it to 14, but no more) in a heavy, preferably terrycloth, kitchen towel. Place in the steaming steamer, cover tightly with a lid, time 1 minute, turn off the heat, let stand without opening for 15 minutes and they're ready. If you place the steamer in a low (200-degree) oven, you can keep them warm for an hour or so. Plan to heat a few more tortillas than you need, since the top and bottom ones tend to get so soft they fall apart.

Other Reheating Methods—Tortillas packed in paper wrappers (they may have a thin plasticlike coating inside) may be successfully reheated in a microwave oven: Make a tiny hole in the package to release steam, then microwave for 30 to 60 seconds on high (depending on the power of your oven). Wrap in a heavy cloth and let stand a few minutes before serving.

For just a few tortillas, moisten your hands with water, rub those damp hands across the tortillas, then lay a stack of four on a griddle heated over medium. Flip them every few seconds, shuffling the deck from time to time, until all four are soft and hot. The water creates a little steam, the stack keeps the steam from evaporating quickly.

If your tortillas are moist and fresh, heat them one at a time on a hot griddle or over a medium gas flame, turning every few seconds until hot and a toasty (total time on griddle or flame is about 15 seconds).

Keeping Tortillas Warm for Serving—Tradition dictates an uncovered basket, called a *chiquihuite,* lined with a cloth. Right off the griddle, a stack of 20 can stay warm for an hour if the cloth is heavy and the basket tightly woven. A Styrofoam-like, covered tortilla warmer, though perhaps not environmentally sound, does a great job of keeping tortillas warm for an hour, as do a number of other insulated containers that have appeared on the market.

TACOS OF TOMATILLO CHICKEN
WITH WILTED GREENS AND FRESH CHEESE

Tacos de Pollo en Salsa Verde

*T*HE CLASSIC COMBINATION of chicken with bracing roasted tomatillos, spicy green chile and fragrant cilantro is beloved in the cuisine of Mexico. Braise some greens in the pot with the chicken (I've given a wide range of options, from substantial lamb's quarters to tangy purslane to easy-to-find chard and spinach), sprinkle the whole with a little fresh cheese (this helps to balance the natural tanginess of the dish) and you've got the cornerstone of a very satisfying, nutritious and Mexican-tasting meal. If you buy a rotisserie chicken, the recipe is quick to make—a wonderful everyday supper dish. I encourage you to make a double or triple batch of sauce, so you can freeze the extra for another meal. For a special but still very informal meal, simmer up a pot of Oaxacan Black Bean Soup (page 130) and finish off with Chocolate Pecan Pie (page 404).

MAKES ABOUT 3 CUPS OF FILLING, ENOUGH FOR 12 TACOS

FOR 1¼ CUPS ESSENTIAL SIMMERED TOMATILLO-SERRANO SAUCE

8 ounces (5 to 6 medium) tomatillos, husked and rinsed

Fresh serrano chiles to taste (roughly 2), stemmed

1½ tablespoons olive or vegetable oil

½ medium white onion, roughly chopped

1 garlic clove, peeled and roughly chopped

1 cup chicken broth

3 tablespoons roughly chopped cilantro

Salt, ¼ to ½ teaspoon, depending on the saltiness of the broth

12 corn tortillas (plus a few extra, in case some break)

2 cups firmly packed sliced chard leaves, lamb's quarters (quelites), sliced amaranth greens (quintoniles), purslane (verdolagas) or spinach (all pieces should be about ½ inch wide and 2 inches long)

1⅓ cups coarsely shredded cooked chicken (you'll need, for instance, 1 very large chicken breast for this amount; see page 181 for details)

½ to ¾ cup crumbled Mexican queso fresco or pressed, salted farmer's cheese

1. *Making 1¼ cups of Essential Simmered Tomatillo-Serrano Sauce.* Roast the tomatillos and chiles on a baking sheet 4 inches below a very hot broiler until blackened and soft on one side, 5 to 6 minutes, then turn them over and roast the other side. Transfer (including all juices) to a food processor or blender.

Heat *1 tablespoon* of the oil in a large (10- to 12-inch) heavy skillet over medium, add the onion and cook, stirring regularly, until deep golden, about 8 minutes. Stir in the garlic, cook 1 minute, then scrape into the food processor or blender. Process to a medium-coarse puree.

Heat the remaining ½ *tablespoon* of the oil in the skillet and set over medium-high. Add the puree all at once and stir for about 5 minutes, until noticeably darker and thick. Stir in the broth, partially cover and simmer over medium-low for 10 minutes. (The sauce will be a little soupy.) Stir in the cilantro and generously season with salt.

2. *Finishing the dish.* Set up a steamer (a vegetable steamer in a large saucepan filled with ½ inch of water works well); heat to a boil. Wrap the tortillas in a heavy kitchen towel, lay in the steamer and cover with a tight lid. Boil 1 minute, turn off the heat and let stand without opening the steamer for 15 minutes.

Bring the sauce to a boil and add the greens. When the mixture returns to a boil, stir in the cooked chicken and simmer until the greens are done (lamb's quarters will take the longest, about 5 minutes; spinach, the least amount of time, about 2 minutes). Taste and season with additional salt, if necessary.

The moment you're ready to serve, make the tacos one at a time, spooning a portion of the filling into a warm tortilla, sprinkling on the cheese and folding it over. As with all tacos, they are informal morsels intended to be filled, folded and eaten on the spot.

ADVANCE PREPARATION—The Tomatillo-Serrano Sauce will keep nicely for several days in the refrigerator, covered; reheat it, then finish step 2.

VARIATIONS AND IMPROVISATIONS—The same approach can be taken replacing the tomatillo sauce with Essential Quick-Cooked Tomato-Chipotle Sauce (page 34) or Essential Roasted Tomato-Jalapeño Salsa (page 21—the latter will need to be simmered a little bit; both of these replacements may need the addition of a little broth or water to give you the right sauciness). Essential Simmered Guajillo Sauce (page 57) can be used, too; I like it best when a few grilled onions—maybe even a few boiled potatoes—are added.

SPICY YUCATECAN BEEF "SALAD" TACOS

Tacos de Dzik

THE CHARACTERISTICS OF most Yucatecan flavors—sharp, spicy and light—offer perfect relief from the near-constant heat of the place. Most taco fillings there typify that refreshing theme since they're served at room temperature and seasoned simply with lime or sour orange. A bowl of incendiary habanero salsa is usually within reach.

Through the whole peninsula, you'll find some version of *dzik* (also called *salpicón*), usually quite plain with the flavors of fresh vegetables and shredded beef; in decades past it incorporated shredded, pit-cooked venison. Some cooks serve limes or sour oranges on the side, for each eater to add *al gusto;* I prefer to mix everything in the kitchen. I've called for cooking the meat using a stovetop "re-creation" of the pit-cooking (save the delicious steaming juices for rice or soup); if you have leftover roast beef (or other meat), use it here.

Think of *dzik* as a "salad" taco filling, similar to the meat-and-vegetable salads in Thai and Vietnamese cooking. Or present *dzik* at an informal summer meal with hot tortillas, guacamole, black beans and a big salad.

MAKES 4 CUPS OF FILLING, ENOUGH FOR 16 TO 18 TACOS

1 pound boneless beef brisket, flank or skirt steak

2 tablespoons vegetable oil

½ small white onion, roughly chopped

2 garlic cloves, peeled and roughly chopped

Salt, a scant 2 teaspoons

One 18-inch piece of banana leaf (if you can get it), defrosted if frozen

FOR 1 CUP ESSENTIAL CHOPPED TOMATO-HABANERO SALSA

½ small red onion

5 tablespoons fresh sour orange juice

  OR 3 tablespoons fresh lime juice plus 2 tablespoons fresh orange juice

6 ounces (1 medium-small or 2 to 3 medium plum) red ripe tomatoes

3 radishes

About ½ fresh habanero chile, depending on your preference for heat

6 large sprigs cilantro

16 to 18 corn tortillas (plus a few extra, in case some break)

3 or 4 leaves of curly leaf lettuce, for garnish

1. *The shredded beef.* Dry the meat on paper towels. In a medium-size (8- to 9-inch) heavy skillet over medium, heat the vegetable oil. When very hot, add the meat and brown it thoroughly on all sides, 10 to 15 minutes.

Set up a steamer with about 1 inch of water in the bottom of a pot. Add the white onion, garlic and *1 teaspoon* of the salt to the water, then set the steamer in place.

Loosely wrap the browned meat in the banana leaf (if you have it), place it in the steamer, cover tightly and steam over medium-low until fork-tender, 1 to 2 hours, depending on the cut of meat. Check the water often; dribble in more if it gets low.

Remove the meat from the steamer, cool until handleable, unwrap if shrouded in banana leaf, then shred into *thin* strands. You will have 2½ to 3 cups of meat.

2. *Making 1 cup Essential Chopped Tomato-Habanero Salsa.* Very finely mince the red onion, scoop it into a strainer and rinse under cold water; shake off as much water as possible. Transfer to a small bowl and stir in *1 tablespoon* of the juice.

Core the tomatoes and cut crosswise in half, scrape out seeds, finely chop and put into a large bowl. Slice the radishes ¹⁄₁₆ inch thick, then chop into small dice. Add to the tomato. Carefully cut out the seed pod from the chile, then mince the chile into tiny bits. Add to the tomato. Carefully bunch up the cilantro sprigs and, with a very sharp knife, slice them ¹⁄₁₆ inch thick, beginning at the leafy end, stems and all, until you've run out of leaves. Add the cilantro to the tomato mixture along with the onion.

3. *Finishing the filling.* Stir the beef into the salsa along with the remaining *4 tablespoons* juice. Taste and season with salt, usually about a scant teaspoon. Cover and let stand at room temperature until serving time, but preferably no more than about an hour.

4. *Serving the dzik.* Set up a steamer (you'll need 2 vegetable steamers in saucepans or a big Chinese steamer) with ½ inch of water in the bottom; heat to a boil. Wrap the tortillas in 2 stacks in heavy kitchen towels, lay in the steamer(s) and cover tightly. Boil 1 minute, turn off the heat and let stand without opening the steamer for 15 minutes.

Line a decorative bowl with lettuce leaves, toss the *dzik* with its dressing, then scoop into the bowl. Pass with warm tortillas for making soft tacos.

ADVANCE PREPARATION—The beef may be cooked several days ahead, but shred it the day you serve. The tomato-habanero salsa can be made 2 hours ahead.

VARIATIONS AND IMPROVISATIONS—Make *dzik* a main-course salad by nestling the finished mixture into dressed greens. You may want to substitute smoked meat or poultry for the beef.

SMOKY SHREDDED PORK TACOS

Tacos de Picadillo Oaxaqueño

MINCED PORK *picadillo* is Mexico's answer to practically any question about what to use as a filling. Frankly, I find most versions uninteresting because of their reliance on ground meat stewed with a little tomato and hint of chile. I prefer the texture of hand-chopped or shredded pork, well browned and simmered with roasted tomatoes and the smoky sting of chipotle—the *picadillo* you find in Veracruz and in Oaxaca where smoky *chile pasilla oaxaqueño* is the standard. Though this filling's name derives from *picar* ("to chop," not "to grind"), I've chosen a boiled and shredded version here. The hint of sweet and spice is very appealing, very comfortable.

This is an easy recipe and you'll think of many uses for it. I often include it on a soft taco buffet, but just as frequently I rely on it to fill tamales, chiles (poblanos, jalapeños, chipotles, *chiles pasillas oaxaqueños*), *molotes*, quesadillas and so forth.

MAKES ABOUT 4 CUPS OF FILLING, ENOUGH FOR 16 TO 18 TACOS

1 1/2 *pounds boneless pork shoulder, trimmed of fat and cut into 2-inch cubes*

5 *garlic cloves, unpeeled*

1 *large white onion, diced*

FOR 1 1/2 CUPS ESSENTIAL QUICK-COOKED TOMATO-CHIPOTLE SAUCE

2 to 3 *dried, stemmed chipotle chiles (or canned chipotle chiles en adobo)*

OR 1 to 2 *stemmed* chiles pasillas oaxaqueños

A generous pound (2 large round or 7 to 8 plum) ripe tomatoes

2 1/2 *tablespoons olive or vegetable oil, or rich-tasting lard*

Salt, about a scant 1/2 teaspoon

1/2 *teaspoon cinnamon, preferably freshly ground Mexican* canela

1/4 *teaspoon black pepper, preferably freshly ground*

1/8 *teaspoon cloves, preferably freshly ground*

1/2 *cup raisins*

1/2 *cup slivered almonds*

16 to 18 *corn tortillas (plus a few extra, in case some break)*

A little hot sauce, if you and your guests like it really picante

1. *The meat.* In a medium-size (2- to 3-quart) saucepan, cover meat with heavily salted water. Peel and roughly chop 2 *cloves* of the garlic and add along with *half* of the onion. Bring to a gentle boil, skim off any grayish foam that rises during the first few minutes, partially cover and simmer over medium-low until thoroughly tender, about 1 1/2 hours.

If time permits, cool the meat in the broth. Shred it between your fingers or with two forks held back to back. (There will be about 4 cups meat; reserve the broth for soup or sauce.)

2. *Making 1½ cups Essential Quick-Cooked Tomato-Chipotle Sauce.* For dried chiles, toast them on an ungreased griddle or heavy skillet over medium heat, turning regularly and pressing flat, until very aromatic, about 30 seconds. In a small bowl, cover chiles with hot water and let rehydrate 30 minutes, stirring to ensure even soaking. Drain and discard the water. (Canned chiles need only be removed from their canning sauce.)

Roast the remaining 3 *cloves* of the unpeeled garlic on the griddle or skillet, turning occasionally, until soft, about 15 minutes; cool and peel. Roast the tomatoes on a baking sheet 4 inches below a very hot broiler until blackened on one side, about 6 minutes; flip and roast the other side. Cool, then peel, collecting all the juices with the tomatoes.

In a food processor or blender, pulse the tomatoes, rehydrated or canned chiles and garlic to a medium-fine puree. Heat *1 tablespoon* of the oil or lard in a heavy, medium-size (2- to 3-quart) saucepan over medium-high. Add the puree and stir for about 5 minutes as it sears and thickens. Taste and season with salt.

3. *The* picadillo. In a large (10- to 12-inch) heavy, well-seasoned or nonstick skillet, heat the remaining 1½ *tablespoons* oil or lard over medium-high. When hot, add the shredded meat and remaining *half* of the onion. Fry, regularly stirring and scraping up browned bits from the bottom, until the whole mixture is crispy and golden, 12 to 14 minutes.

Sprinkle the cinnamon, pepper, cloves and raisins over the meat, then pour on the tomato-chipotle sauce. Reduce the heat to medium and simmer briskly, stirring occasionally, until nearly all the liquid has evaporated, 4 to 5 minutes.

Turn on the oven to 350 degrees. Toast the almonds in the oven in a small baking pan until fragrant and lightly browned, 6 to 8 minutes, then stir them into the *picadillo.* Taste and season with a little more salt if necessary.

4. *Finishing the dish.* Set up a steamer (with this many tortillas, you'll need 2 vegetable steamers set up in saucepans or a big Chinese steamer—either choice with ½ inch of water under the steamer basket); heat to a boil. Wrap the tortillas in 2 stacks in heavy kitchen towels, lay in the steamer(s) and cover tightly. Boil 1 minute, turn off the heat and let stand without opening the steamer for 15 minutes.

You can prepare the tacos in the kitchen by scooping a couple of heaping tablespoons of filling into each warm tortilla, rolling or folding them and nestling them into a cloth-lined basket. Or scoop the filling into a warm bowl and set out with a cloth-lined basket of steaming tortillas for your guests to construct their own tacos. In either case, pass the hot sauce separately if you have it.

ADVANCE PREPARATION—The pork can be simmered several days in advance (refrigerate it in a covered container with its broth, then strain and shred before continuing with the dish) or finish the *picadillo* a day or two ahead, cover it and refrigerate.

SHORTCUTS—Two-thirds of a 28-ounce can of tomatoes can replace the fresh roasted ones; 4 cups shredded roast pork, if you have it leftover, can replace the boiled and shredded pork.

VARIATIONS AND IMPROVISATIONS

Try mixing leftover *picadillo* with shredded cheese, baking it to heat through, then serving it as a communal appetizer or light main dish with tortillas—a variation on *queso fundido*.

Shredded Pork Enchiladas—Prepare the recipe tripling the sauce; set the extra ⅔ of the sauce aside. Roll the filling in the tortillas, fit them into a baking dish, pour the reserved sauce over them and bake at 375 degrees to warm through. Sprinkle with *queso añejo* or Parmesan and chopped cilantro; serve immediately.

Chiles Rellenos for a Buffet—Roast and peel six poblanos, make a slit in their sides, remove the seeds, then fill each with about ⅓ cup of the filling (you'll only need ½ the batch) and fit into a decorative baking dish. Slowly cook 2 large sliced onions in a little olive oil until nicely browned, soft and caramelized. Strew over the chiles and bake the whole assembly to heat through. Sprinkle liberally with *queso añejo* or Parmesan and set out on the buffet.

YUCATECAN GRILLED FISH TACOS

Tacos de Pescado Tikin Xik

PERHAPS YOU'VE GONE FISHING in the Yucatan and, upon returning, had your Mexican guide split open some of your catch, smear it with achiote and grill your *tikin xik* on a banana leaf over a wood fire. With a little blazing habanero salsa and some fresh tortillas, there is simply no better eating. I love the perfume that wafts from a grill full of banana leaves, and I'm sold on the flavor it imparts to the fish. Don't be afraid the leaves will burn: If your fire is only medium hot, the leaves will crisp slightly, but still be pliable.

MAKES ABOUT 12 TO 16 TACOS

FOR ⅓ CUP ESSENTIAL GARLICKY
ACHIOTE SEASONING PASTE

2 tablespoons achiote seeds

*2 teaspoons whole allspice, preferably
freshly ground*

*1 teaspoon black pepper, preferably
freshly ground*

*1½ teaspoons dried oregano,
preferably Mexican*

3 tablespoons cider vinegar

6 garlic cloves, peeled

Salt, about 1 generous teaspoon

*3 tablespoons fresh sour orange or
lime juice*

*1 to 1½ pounds skinless fish fillets
(such as sea bass, snapper, grouper,
halibut, mahimahi),
cut into 4 pieces*

*1 banana leaf (you'll need a piece at
least 2 feet long, 10 to 12 inches
wide), plus extra for garnish if you
wish, defrosted if frozen*

*12 to 16 corn tortillas (plus a few
extra, in case some break)*

*About 1 cup salsa (the classic here is
Essential Chopped Tomato-
Habanero Salsa, page 28),
for serving*

1. *Making ⅓ cup of Essential Garlicky Achiote Seasoning Paste.* Very finely pulverize the achiote in a spice grinder, then transfer it to a small bowl and mix in the allspice, pepper, oregano and vinegar (you'll have a crumbly, very thick mixture at this point). Roughly chop the garlic, sprinkle with the salt, then on your cutting board work the two into a smooth paste with a spoon or the flat side of a knife. Scoop the achiote mixture onto the garlic, work the two together, then dribble on and work in enough water (about a tablespoon or 2) to give it all the consistency of a thick but spreadable paste.

2. *Marinating the fish.* Stir together 3 *tablespoons* of the achiote seasoning (cover and refrigerate the rest to use as a seasoning for rice or marinade for chicken or pork) and the sour orange or lime juice in a shallow dish. Lay in the fish fillets and turn to coat well with the marinade. Cover and refrigerate about an hour but not longer than 3 hours.

3. *Finishing the dish.* Light a gas grill or prepare a charcoal fire, letting the coals burn until they are covered with a gray ash and medium-hot. Position the grill grate about 8 inches above the coals and lightly oil.

While the grill is heating, tear off eight ½-inch strips of banana leaf (tear with the grain—each strip will be about 12 inches long). Cut the remaining leaf into 4 sections—they should be about twice as wide as your fillets.

Lay out one section of leaf, center a fillet on it, spoon on a little of the marinade that's still in the dish, then fold the leaf over to enclose the fillet and fold both ends up. Tie each direction with one of the banana-leaf strips. Wrap the other fillets in the same manner.

Set up a steamer (a vegetable steamer in a large saucepan filled with ½ inch of water works well); heat to a boil. Wrap the tortillas in a heavy kitchen towel, lay in the steamer and cover. Boil 1 minute, turn off the heat and let stand without opening for 15 minutes.

Lay the fish packets on the medium-hot grill. Cover the grill and cook for about 10 minutes, a little longer for large fillets—there's really no way to tell if the fish is done enough to flake without opening a package, though 10 minutes is about average.

You have two choices for serving: Either remove the fish from the packages, slice into ½-inch strips and serve on a small warm platter (be sure to drizzle on all the juices from the packets) with salsa and warm tortillas passed separately; or carefully open the packets, fold the leaves back and under, creating a little nest for the fish, and serve each guest a packet to pick at, flaking off fish to dollop with salsa, wrap in warm tortillas and enjoy immensely.

ADVANCE PREPARATION—The achiote seasoning paste can be made a week or more in advance of marinating the fish. The fish can marinate as long as 3 hours before grilling.

SHORTCUTS—Commercial achiote paste can replace homemade, and the banana leaves may be omitted (make sure your grill grates are well oiled to ensure that the fish won't stick).

VARIATIONS AND IMPROVISATIONS—Perhaps you'll want to make extra to have leftovers to flake into pasta (penne would be nice); top the dish with a chopped tomato salsa and Parmesan, if you want, and you'll be ready to eat. You can prepare the same dish with 4 boneless, skinless chicken breasts (you'll have a hurry-up *pollo pibil*); simply increase the grilling time to about 15 minutes.

Mushrooms

When enjoying a Tex-Mex–style plate of cheese-and-onion enchiladas covered with red chile gravy, it's hard to imagine that wild mushrooms play any role in Mexican cooking. Wild mushroom broth with *epazote;* wild mushroom–stuffed fish roasted in banana leaves; crusty, griddle-baked wild mushroom quesadillas—they all probably sound like modern American inventions if you don't know their important place in the traditional cuisine of Mexico. In fact, I've got four cookbooks from Mexico devoted entirely to wild mushrooms.

In the central part of Mexico, from coast to coast and dipping down south into Oaxaca, a place well known for a mushroom of a more psychotropic variety, the mountains offer an abundance of wild mushrooms during rainy season. If you visit the massive Merced market in Mexico City, the southeast corner is usually filled with vendors of seasonal mushrooms—everything from morels and fresh porcini to oyster and coral. Driving the heights from Mexico City to Toluca, there's a bank of roadside stands at about the halfway point that sells broth and quesadillas made from the local mushroom harvest. The women that collect provisions from the wild to sell will lay out wild mushrooms on their mats at the edges of markets in Michoacan, Puebla and Veracruz.

Though in Mexico cultivated button mushrooms (usually called *champiñones* rather than *hongos,* which is reserved for wild ones) have that "gourmet" appeal, local wild mushrooms are often equal in price and have better flavor and texture. Wild mushrooms everywhere are subject to larvae infestation (you may have to discard some or briefly blanch them to force the larvae out). But wild mushrooms are definitely more interesting to work with. Because wild ones are so expensive in the United States, I often use the flavorful, but less expensive, cultivated shiitakes in their place.

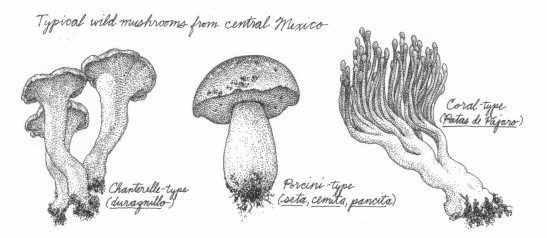

Typical wild mushrooms from central Mexico

Chanterelle-type (duraznillo)

Porcini-type (seta, cemita, pancita)

Coral-type (Patas de Pájaro)

SPICY PASILLA-MUSHROOM TACOS

Tacos de Hongos al Pasilla

$\mathcal{I}$T TOOK ME YEARS to settle in with pasillas, perhaps because they're so bold: none of the sweetness of anchos or the smokiness of chipotles, but a rich, earthy spice that hints at flavors of chocolate and tomato. Through the years I've grown very fond of how their woodsy flavor complements the earthiness of mushrooms. A little *epazote,* if you have it, sharpens everything into a uniquely Mexican focus. The pureed pasillas have an unctuous, creamlike quality (though the dish is low in fat), and, when handled properly (this is true of any chile), they have that magnetism that captures you.

MAKES ABOUT 3 CUPS OF FILLING, ENOUGH FOR 12 TACOS

FOR ⅔ CUP ESSENTIAL BOLD PASILLA SEASONING PASTE

8 garlic cloves, unpeeled

6 large (about 2 ounces total) dried pasilla chiles, stemmed and seeded

1 teaspoon dried oregano, preferably Mexican

¼ teaspoon black pepper, preferably freshly ground

⅛ teaspoon cumin, preferably freshly ground

1 tablespoon vegetable or olive oil

About ½ cup chicken or beef broth

4 cups (about 8 ounces) sliced woodland mushrooms (such as shiitakes or portobellos, or wild morels, porcini or chanterelles)

¼ cup thinly sliced epazote (or cilantro), plus a few leaves for garnish

12 corn tortillas (plus a few extra in case some break)

Salt, about ¾ teaspoon

½ cup finely diced white onion

⅓ cup finely crumbled Mexican queso añejo, dry feta or Parmesan

1. *Making ⅔ cup Essential Bold Pasilla Seasoning Paste.* Roast the unpeeled garlic on an ungreased griddle or heavy skillet over medium heat, turning occasionally, until soft (they will blacken in spots), about 15 minutes; cool and peel. While the garlic is roasting, toast the chiles on another side of the griddle or skillet: 1 or 2 at a time, open them flat and press down firmly on the hot surface with a spatula; in a few seconds, when they crackle, even send up a wisp of smoke, flip them and press down to toast the other side. In a small bowl, cover the chiles with hot water and let rehydrate 30 minutes, stirring frequently to ensure even soaking. Drain, *reserving ⅓ cup of the soaking water.*

In a food processor or blender, combine the chiles and soaking liquid, garlic, oregano, pepper and cumin. Blend to a smooth puree, scraping down and stirring frequently. (If the mixture won't move through the blender blades, stir in a tablespoon or two of water.) With a rubber spatula, work the chile mixture through a medium-mesh strainer into a bowl.

2. *The mushrooms.* Heat the oil in a medium-size (4-quart) pot (preferably a Dutch oven or Mexican *cazuela*) over medium-high heat. When hot enough to make a drop of the seasoning sizzle sharply, add it all at once. Stir for about 5 minutes as the mixture thickens and concentrates all those rich, pungent flavors. Stir in the broth, then add mushrooms and *epazote* (or cilantro). Partially cover and simmer gently over medium-low, stirring frequently, until mushrooms are soft and the sauce has reduced to coat them rather thickly (too thin will mean messy tacos), about 15 minutes.

3. *Warming the tortillas.* While the mushrooms are cooking, set up a steamer (a vegetable steamer in a large saucepan filled with ½ inch of water works well); heat to a boil. Wrap the tortillas in a heavy kitchen towel, lay in the steamer and cover with a tight lid. Boil 1 minute, turn off the heat and let stand without opening the steamer for 15 minutes.

4. *Finishing the dish.* Taste the mushrooms and season with salt. Scoop into a warm serving dish, sprinkle with onion and cheese, garnish with *epazote* (or cilantro) leaves and serve with a basket of the steaming hot tortillas for your guests to use in making their tacos.

ADVANCE PREPARATION—The pasilla seasoning can be made several days in advance and refrigerated (it can also be frozen). The mushroom mixture can be made a day ahead, covered and refrigerated; reheat before serving.

VARIATIONS AND IMPROVISATIONS

Lamb and Mushrooms al Pasilla—Brown 1 pound cubed boneless lamb for stew in a hot oiled skillet. Prepare the recipe, doubling the pasilla seasoning, adding the lamb with the mushrooms and increasing the broth to 1 cup; simmer until the meat is tender, about 1 hour.

Grilled Eggplant al Pasilla—Brush 2 large sliced eggplants with oil, sprinkle with salt and grill until just softening; transfer to a baking dish. Prepare the pasilla-mushroom mixture, but simmer it only 5 minutes. Spoon over the eggplant and bake until bubbly and the sauce is reduced a little.

TACOS OF INKY "CORN MUSHROOM"

Tacos de Huitlacoche

*W*HAT WORDS can ready you for the flavors and textures that will fill your mouth with each bite of a *huitlacoche* taco? Earthy? Herby? Sweet? Delicious? Can words capture a unique flavor, or do they simply send you in search of comparisons that distract from the singularity of the experience? There simply is nothing like *huitlacoche,* and if you've never tasted it, I doubt there's anything I can say that will make it easier or more thrilling for you to take that first bite of black fungus. At Topolobampo, where we nearly always feature a *huitlacoche* dish, folks clamor for the stuff—something I certainly never predicted.

There are those of you who will search out *huitlacoche* at all costs (from local farmers or mail order); others will carry this recipe to Mexico, get a place with a kitchen and cook some from the market. You're the gastronomical adventurers and I applaud you.

MAKES A GENEROUS 2 CUPS FILLING, ENOUGH FOR 12 TACOS

2 fresh poblano chiles

2 tablespoons olive or vegetable oil

1 medium white onion, finely diced

4 cloves garlic, peeled and finely chopped

1 medium tomato, diced

2 cups packed, roughly chopped lobes of huitlacoche

Salt, about 1 teaspoon

2 to 3 tablespoons chopped epazote leaves (or cilantro, if no epazote is available)

12 corn tortillas (plus a few extra, in case some break)

1. *The corn-mushroom filling.* Roast the chiles directly over a gas flame or 4 inches below a very hot broiler until blackened on all sides, about 5 minutes for open flame, about 10 minutes for broiler. Cover with a kitchen towel and let stand 5 minutes. Peel, remove stem and seeds, then rinse *briefly.* Chop into ¼-inch bits.

In a medium-size (8- to 9-inch) skillet, heat the oil over medium. Add the onion and fry, stirring regularly, until lightly browned, 7 to 10 minutes. Stir in the garlic and cook about 2 minutes more. Increase the heat to medium-high, add the tomato and cook, stirring occasionally, until the juices have reduced, about 4 minutes.

Add the poblanos to the tomato mixture along with the *huitlacoche* and simmer, stirring often, until reduced and quite thick, about 10 minutes. Season with salt and *epazote.*

2. *Warming the tortillas.* Set up a steamer (a vegetable steamer in a large saucepan filled with ½ inch of water works well); heat to a boil. Wrap the tortillas in a heavy kitchen towel, lay in the steamer and cover with a tight lid. Boil 1 minute, turn off the heat and let stand without opening the steamer for 15 minutes.

3. *Finishing the tacos.* Just before serving, reheat the filling. Make the tacos one at a time, spooning a portion of the filling into a warm tortilla and folding it over. As with all tacos, these are informal morsels and should be enjoyed with your guests as soon as they're made.

ADVANCE PREPARATION—The filling can be prepared several days ahead, covered and refrigerated.

VARIATIONS AND IMPROVISATIONS—It is common to make *huitlacoche* quesadillas (follow the directions for Crusty Griddle-Baked Quesadillas, page 194) with or without a little cheese in with the filling. A dollop of this filling is delicious in the Slow-Simmered Fava Bean Soup (page 132) if you leave out the mint and simply crumble toasted pasilla chiles over the top. My very favorite *huitlacoche* dish, however, is crepes bathed with poblano cream (page 110).

Huitlacoche

This mysterious-looking "mushroom" that grows right out from the ear of corn is pure luxury to some, anathema to others. Treasured since pre-Columbian times, most ardently in Central Mexico, *huitlacoche* is thought of as a blight in the United States, referred to delicately as *corn smut*. Rather than being a mushroom that grows into a distinctive shape all its own, *huitlacoche* spores grow right in kernels of corn, causing the kernels to balloon up into amorphous shapes that, frankly, look like something's gone wrong.

In Mexican markets, mostly during rainy season, it's common to buy cobs with the *huitlacoche* attached; the lobes break up fairly easily once detached. The lobes will keep several days, well covered, in the refrigerator; they freeze successfully, though there will be some liquid lost as they defrost; just add the liquid to the pot and simmer until reduced.

While scientists in the United States have developed a method for innoculating corn with *huitlacoche* spores (for years the same group worked to get rid of it), only a few specialty farmers have been farsighted enough to perceive that there is a market for the stuff (see Sources, page 425). If harvested immature, the lobes will be tight and bitter, if picked too mature, they'll crumble into an overripe mess. *Huitlacoche* is available canned from Mexico, though I think it has about as much appeal as canned asparagus.

Stats: Because the amount on each cob varies, *huitlacoche* usually is measured by weight or volume of the removed lobes.

huitlacoche
on cob

huitlacoche
lobe

GOLDEN SQUASH BLOSSOM *CREMA* (*page 138*)

Yucatecan Grilled Fish Tacos (*page 153*)

Street-Style Red Chile Enchiladas with zucchini, aged cheese and crunchy garnishes (*page 182*)   3

Oval *Masa* Cakes with Black Bean Filling (*page 190*)

"Drunken" Pintos with cilantro and bacon (*page 239*)

SMOKY PEANUT *MOLE* WITH GRILLED QUAIL (*Page 286*)

Spicy Mushroom Tamales *(page 294)*

TACOS OF GARLICKY MEXICAN GREENS
WITH SEARED ONION AND FRESH CHEESE

Tacos de Quelites

EVER SINCE I FIRST ate *quelites* tacos at a market stall in Toluca, they've been high on my list. I know a taco of Mexican greens sounds trendy or made-up, so I encourage you to go to Toluca on a Friday morning (market day) and taste handmade, just-baked blue-corn tortillas wrapped around emerald-green *quelites* (lamb's quarters) dashed with red chile salsa. There they think of this rustic earthy taco as old-fashioned (poor people's) food. I think of it as some of the best food on the face of the earth.

Chard makes a nice substitute for lamb's quarters, though it doesn't have as much body or richness and won't hold the green color as well. Don't use these greens only as a taco filling; they make a wonderful accompaniment to *moles* and such.

Be sure to have all your ingredients ready before you warm the tortillas; the cooking of the filling goes very quickly.

MAKES A GENEROUS 2 CUPS OF FILLING, ENOUGH FOR 8 TO 10 SOFT TACOS

8 to 10 corn tortillas (plus a few extra, in case some break)

9 cups (about 1 pound) loosely packed, stemmed lamb's quarters (quelites)

OR 6 cups loosely packed, sliced green or red chard leaves (slice them ½ inch thick; you'll need a 12-ounce bunch)

1 tablespoon olive or vegetable oil

1 medium white onion, sliced ¼ inch thick

3 garlic cloves, peeled and finely chopped

Salt, about ½ teaspoon

¼ cup finely crumbled Mexican queso fresco, queso añejo, *dry feta, pressed, salted farmer's cheese or Parmesan*

About ¾ cup salsa (I love the Essential Roasted Tomatillo-Chipotle Salsa, page 45, with these greens), for serving

1. *Warming the tortillas.* Set up a steamer (a vegetable steamer in a large saucepan filled with ½ inch of water works well); heat to a boil. Wrap the tortillas in a heavy kitchen towel, lay in the steamer and cover with a tight lid. Boil 1 minute, turn off the heat and let stand without opening the steamer for about 15 minutes.

2. *The greens-and-onion filling.* While the tortillas are steaming, prepare the filling. Bring 3 quarts of salted water to a boil in a large pot. Add the greens and cook until barely tender,

about 2 to 3 minutes for the lamb's quarters, 1 to 2 minutes for the chard. Pour into a colander, then spread out on a large plate or baking sheet to cool. When cool enough to handle, roughly chop.

Heat the oil in a large (10- to 12-inch) skillet over medium-high. Add the onion and cook, stirring frequently, until golden brown, about 10 minutes. Add the garlic, stir for 1 minute, then add the greens, and stir for a minute or so longer, just enough to heat them through. Taste and season with salt.

3. *The tacos.* Scoop the mixture into a deep warm serving dish, sprinkle with the cheese if you're using it, and carry to the table along with the warm tortillas in a cloth-lined basket for each of your guests to assemble tacos *al gusto.* For a sit-down appetizer, you may want to roll the tortillas around the filling, arranging them by twos on each plate, then spoon the salsa in a strip across their middles, sprinkle with cheese and top with sprigs of cilantro.

ADVANCE PREPARATION—The greens can be blanched a few hours in advance.

VARIATIONS AND IMPROVISATIONS

A variety of greens, from collards to spinach, is good here, though each has a slightly different cooking time. At times it seems appropriate to put a few diced boiled potatoes in the mix, sometimes I add a few spoons of cream along with the blanched greens, other times I use grilled onions in place of the fried ones. Another approach to cooking the greens is to combine *raw* greens with the fried onions and garlic in a very large skillet, add ⅔ cup salted broth (plus a tablespoon of olive oil if you like), and boil over high heat, stirring very frequently, until all liquid has evaporated.

Tangy Quelite Enchiladas—Roll the greens in the tortillas and lay in a baking dish. Douse with about 2½ cups of warm Essential Simmered Tomatillo-Serrano Sauce (page 38), sprinkle with 1½ cups shredded Chihuahua or other melting cheese and bake at 400 degrees until the cheese has melted.

TACOS OF CREAMY BRAISED CHARD, POTATOES AND POBLANOS

Tacos de Acelgas Guisadas con Crema

*T*HERE IS SOMETHING about this creamy combination of greens and green chile that I want to taste time and again. Cream and poblanos are meant for each other, while the greens give the mix a grown-up flavor, and the potatoes make it more substantial. The preparation is rich and simple, a great vegetarian starter or light main dish. You may want to accompany it with some Classic Mexican Fried Beans (page 237), or even start off with Spicy Chile-Baked Oysters (page 90).

MAKES ABOUT 4 CUPS OF FILLING, ENOUGH FOR 16 TO 18 SOFT TACOS

FOR 1 1/2 CUPS ESSENTIAL ROASTED POBLANO *RAJAS*

12 ounces (4 medium-large) fresh poblano chiles

A scant 1 tablespoon vegetable or olive oil

1 medium white onion, sliced 1/4 inch thick

2 garlic cloves, peeled and finely chopped

A generous 1/4 teaspoon dried oregano, preferably Mexican

A generous 1/8 teaspoon dried thyme

16 to 18 corn tortillas (plus a few extra, in case some break)

3/4 cup chicken broth

3 medium (about 10 ounces total) red-skin boiling potatoes, cut into 1/2-inch cubes

6 cups loosely packed, sliced red or white chard leaves (slice them 1/2 inch thick; you'll need a 12-ounce bunch)

1/2 to 3/4 cup Thick Cream (page 165), whipping cream or crème fraîche

Salt, about 1/2 teaspoon

1/2 to 3/4 cup crumbled Mexican queso fresco or pressed, salted farmer's cheese (optional)

1. *Making 1 1/2 cups of the Essential Roasted Poblano* **Rajas.** Roast the chiles directly over a gas flame or 4 inches below a very hot broiler until blackened on all sides, about 5 minutes for open flame, about 10 minutes for broiler. Cover with a kitchen towel and let stand 5 minutes. Peel, pull out the stem and seed pod, then rinse *briefly* to remove bits of skin and seeds. Slice into 1/4-inch strips.

In a large (10- to 12-inch) skillet heat the oil over medium, then add the onion and cook, stirring regularly, until nicely browned but still a little crunchy, about 5 minutes. Add the garlic and herbs, toss a minute longer, then stir in the chiles.

2. *Warming the tortillas*. Set up a steamer (with this many tortillas, you'll need 2 vegetable steamers set up in saucepans or a big Chinese steamer—either choice with ½ inch of water under the steamer basket); heat to a boil. Wrap the tortillas in 2 stacks in heavy kitchen towels, lay in the steamer(s) and cover tightly. Boil 1 minute, turn off the heat and let stand without opening the steamer(s) for about 15 minutes.

3. *The filling*. While the tortillas are steaming, prepare the filling. In a small saucepan, combine the broth and potatoes, cover and simmer over medium-low heat until nearly tender, about 15 minutes.

Pour the potatoes and broth into the *rajas* pan, mix in the chard, and boil over medium-high heat until the broth has evaporated, about 4 minutes. Mix in the cream and continue to boil, stirring regularly, until the cream is reduced enough to coat the mixture nicely. Taste and season with salt.

Scoop the mixture into a warm, deep serving dish, sprinkle with the cheese if you're using it and carry to the table along with the warm tortillas in a cloth-lined basket for each of your guests to assemble tacos *al gusto*.

ADVANCE PREPARATION—The poblano *rajas* can be made several days ahead, but it is best to finish the filling shortly before serving.

VARIATIONS AND IMPROVISATIONS—As you might expect, a simple dish like this can be varied in many ways: Serve it over grilled chicken (or dice the grilled chicken and stir it in); replace the cream with ¼ to ⅓ cup yogurt (just heat it through, but don't boil; it'll curdle); or don't reduce the cream, stir in a little chopped ham and toss with cooked egg noodles or bow-tie pasta and sprinkle with lots of chopped cilantro before serving.

Thick Cream

THOUGH NUTRITIONISTS have frightened us away from all cream and encouraged what I consider the development of such questionable products as fat-free sour cream, I have to champion Mexican thick cream—rich, ripe and slightly sour. It plays an important role in the cuisine, though it's used sparingly. Which is as it should be. On those special dishes, its nutty, well-developed flavor and glorious texture are relished with great gusto.

Much of the cream in Mexican markets is allowed to ripen, thicken and sour naturally, utilizing whatever natural-culturing bacteria are around. Simply setting out cream doesn't do much but encourage spoilage in urban America, replete as we are with (ultra-)pasteurized cream. So we add an active "starter" from buttermilk, yogurt, *crème fraîche* or sour cream, then allow the warmish cream to culture and set. I prefer the flavor of cream set with buttermilk or *crème fraîche*, though if dolloped on something warm, this cream will thin out quickly. For use in our restaurants, we culture sweet cream with sour cream, adding it in a high proportion (one part sour cream to four parts heavy [whipping] cream); the cream sets a little more rapidly and holds its body when warmed a bit.

Important details: Smaller amounts of active culture mean a longer setting time, but more developed flavor. Always check to make sure whatever starter you're using has *active* cultures (the label usually says so). Chill your set cream before using it for a thicker texture; chilled cream will need to be stirred, perhaps thinned with a little cream or milk, to bring back that luscious texture. I've tried to give as many cream options as I think workable in the recipes.

ABOUT 1 CUP

1 cup heavy (whipping) cream

2 teaspoons active culture such as buttermilk,
  crème fraîche, *sour cream or plain yogurt*

POUR THE CREAM into a small saucepan, set over low heat and stir just until the chill is off; do not heat above 100 degrees (lukewarm). Remove from the heat, stir in the buttermilk (or one of its substitutes) and pour into a clean glass jar.

Place the lid on the jar, but don't tighten it, and put in a warm (80- to 90-degree) spot. Let the cream develop for 12 to 24 hours, until noticeably thicker. Stir gently and refrigerate at least 4 hours or overnight to chill and complete the thickening.

ADVANCE PREPARATION—Covered and refrigerated, the cream will keep 10 days or so.

HERBY RICOTTA-POBLANO TACOS

Tacos de Requesón y Chile Poblano

*I*F YOUR ONLY TASTE of ricotta has been in lasagna or ravioli, I'd love to put a simple ricotta taco in your hand—herby, green chile–studded, fresh-made ricotta rolled into a toasty tortilla, splashed with a little spicy salsa. You can have this delicious experience in Mexico just about anywhere there is dairying. I ate my first at a street stall in Patzcuaro, Michoacan.

Ricotta tacos are great party food: just put out a bowl of filling, warm tortillas (or crispy tostadas) in a colorful cloth-lined basket, and some salsa, so everyone can put together their own little tacos. Or dress them up for a first course or light main dish as I've suggested here, presenting them in a pool of luscious avocado salsa and strewing them with fresh, crunchy garnishes. They're a wonderful special-occasion starter before Grilled Steak with Spicy Guajillo Sauce (page 364). I recommend Mango-Lime Ice (page 393) and cookies to finish that boldly flavored meal.

The filling is easily adaptable. I use it often in the middle of crisp-fried tacos (*flautas*) and as part of a layered tortilla casserole with Essential Simmered Tomato-Jalapeño Sauce (page 18), steamed chard and a little Chihuahua cheese.

MAKES A GENEROUS CUP OF FILLING, ENOUGH FOR 8 TACOS

4 garlic cloves, unpeeled

2 fresh poblano chiles

1 cup ricotta cheese (the freshest you can find)

4 teaspoons chopped fresh herbs (such as cilantro, epazote, thyme, marjoram)

Salt, about ¼ teaspoon

About ⅛ teaspoon black pepper, preferably freshly ground

8 corn tortillas (plus a few extra, in case some break)

1¼ cups Tomatillo-Green Guacamole (page 81)

3 or 4 radishes, thinly sliced or cut into matchsticks

A few tablespoons chopped white onion, for garnish

Big, beautiful sprigs of cilantro, for garnish

1. *The filling.* On an ungreased griddle or small, heavy skillet set over medium heat, roast the garlic, turning frequently, until blackened in spots and soft to the touch, about 15 minutes. Cool, peel off the papery skins, then finely chop.

Roast the chiles directly over a gas flame or 4 inches below a very hot broiler until blackened on all sides, about 5 minutes for open flame, about 10 minutes for broiler. Cover with a kitchen towel and let stand 5 minutes. Peel, pull out the stem and seed pod, then rinse *briefly* to remove bits of seeds and stray bits of skin. Chop the chiles into ¼-inch bits.

In a medium-size bowl, mix together the garlic, ricotta, fresh herbs and *half* the chopped chiles. Taste and season with the salt and pepper. Cover and set aside.

2. *The tortillas.* Set up a steamer (a vegetable steamer in a large saucepan filled with ½ inch of water works well); heat to a boil. Wrap the tortillas in a heavy kitchen towel, lay in the steamer and cover with a tight lid. Boil 1 minute, turn off the heat and let stand without opening the steamer for 15 minutes.

3. *Finishing the dish.* Just before serving, mix the remaining *half* of the chopped chiles into the guacamole (plus enough water to make it easily spoonable), and spoon a portion of it onto each of 4 serving plates. One at a time, spread a generous 2 tablespoons of the ricotta filling over each of 8 hot tortillas, roll up and divide among your individual serving plates. Sprinkle with the radishes and onion, lay on a sprig of cilantro and you're ready for some light, zesty flavors.

ADVANCE PREPARATION—The filling will hold well for a couple of days in the refrigerator, but is best served at room temperature. Assemble the tacos at the last moment.

SHORTCUTS—You can replace the roasted poblano with well-drained canned pickled jalapeños or canned chipotle chiles *en adobo.*

VARIATIONS AND IMPROVISATIONS

I'm sure you'll come up with your own variations on this easily adaptable filling, but what comes to my mind is to replace the ricotta with fresh goat cheese or moist farmer's cheese, replace the poblano with chopped, oil-packed sun-dried tomatoes; use fresh basil as the herb, and mix in 1 cup chopped, grilled vegetables (I'm partial to grilled mushrooms here).

Very Spicy Bruschetta—Grill thick slabs of lightly oiled bread, then spread with ricotta mixture made with half of a fresh habanero (finely chopped). Warm under a broiler and top with Essential Chopped Tomato-Habanero Salsa (page 28).

CRISPY BLACK BEAN- BACON TACOS
WITH TANGY ROMAINE SALAD

Taquitos de Frijol y Tocino con Ensalada

FILLED WITH THE COMFORTING mash of black beans and bacon, these cylindrical, crisp-fried tacos or *taquitos* (some would call them *flautas*) find a perfect match in the freshness of lettuce and tomato. (Dare I call this a Mexican version of a bacon-lettuce-and-tomato sandwich?) Though you'd expect such a dish on American Southwest menus, I learned these tacos from Josephina Velázquez de León's 1950s classic *Antojitos mexicanos*.

The method used here is classic for most fried tacos: quick-fry thin tortillas to soften them, blot them dry, fill and roll them, then pan-fry until crisp. With oil that is hot enough, they will come out greaseless; the sprightly vinegar dressing on the lettuce and tomato is just the right foil to the crisp-fried taco.

MAKES 12 TACOS, SERVING 4 TO 6 AS A HEFTY SNACK OR SIMPLE MEAL

6 slices bacon

1 small white onion, finely chopped

1½ cups seasoned, cooked black beans (either canned or homemade, page 234), drained of most of their cooking liquid

2 to 3 pickled jalapeños or canned chipotle chiles en adobo, *stemmed, seeded and finely chopped*

A sprinkling of salt

Vegetable oil to a depth of ½ inch for frying

12 very thin factory-made corn tortillas

⅔ cup crumbled Mexican queso fresco or pressed, salted farmer's cheese

6 good-size romaine leaves

1½ tablespoons cider vinegar

1 large tomato, cored and chopped into ¼-inch dice

1. *The beans.* In a large (10- to 12-inch) heavy skillet, lay out the bacon and fry over medium heat, turning when browned underneath, until thoroughly crisp, about 10 minutes. Remove to a paper towel–lined plate. Pour off all but a thin coating of the drippings.

Add the onion to the pan and cook, stirring regularly, until deep golden, about 10 minutes. Stir in the beans, then coarsely mash with a bean or potato masher or the back of a wooden spoon. Crumble the bacon and add *half* of it to the beans along with the chiles; stir over the heat until quite thick, about 5 minutes. Taste and season with salt. Cool.

2. *The* **taquitos.** Clean the skillet, pour in the oil and heat over medium-high. When hot, one by one, quick-fry the tortillas for several seconds to soften, then remove them with tongs and pat thoroughly dry on paper towels. Stack the blotted tortillas together, and remove the oil from the heat.

Spoon 2 tablespoons of the black-bean mixture down the center of each tortilla, sprinkle each with about ½ tablespoon of the cheese, and roll up. Cover with plastic wrap.

3. *Finishing the dish.* Return the oil to between medium and medium-high heat; you should still have at least ¼ inch of it in your skillet. Slice the romaine crosswise into ⅜-inch ribbons and toss with the vinegar and a little salt.

When the oil is very hot (it shouldn't be smoking; 375 degrees on a deep-fry thermometer is just right), fry the *taquitos* 4 at a time, being sure to lay them into the hot oil *flap-side down.* When crispy underneath, about 2 minutes, flip them over and fry the other side, 1 to 2 minutes more. Remove from the oil with tongs or a slotted spatula, drain on paper towels and tip them to ensure no oil is inside. Keep warm in a low oven until all are fried.

Spread the lettuce onto a serving platter (or divide it between individual plates) and top with the *taquitos.* Spoon the chopped tomato down the center of the tacos, sprinkle with the remaining cheese and bacon and carry the whole assembly to the table.

ADVANCE PREPARATION—The bean filling can be made several days ahead; refrigerate, covered. *Taquitos* can be rolled 2 hours ahead; keep at room temperature.

SHORTCUTS—You can make black bean–bacon tacos with steaming hot tortillas just as you are ready to serve them, skipping the frying. I'd spoon a little salsa over them (try the Essential Roasted Tomatillo-Chipotle Salsa, page 45) before serving.

VARIATIONS AND IMPROVISATIONS—You can use about 1½ cups of other fillings, like the potato-chorizo filling outlined for the Chorizo-Stuffed Ancho Chiles (page 108), or the one from Herby Ricotta-Poblano Tacos (page 166), or simply mashed boiled potatoes with a little roasted garlic and *queso añejo* or Parmesan. In all these variations, I'd omit the chile and *queso fresco* called for here.

ACHIOTE-ROASTED PORK TACOS
WITH PICKLED RED ONIONS

Tacos de Cochinita Pibil

*T*HE BEST PLACE to eat these little tacos is in small-town markets throughout the Yucatan where folks still achiote-marinate the pork, wrap it in the banana leaves, then bury it in wood-fired pits in the ground. The smoky slow cooking gives the meat a succulence (partly due to the great pigs they use) that you find only at that spot on the globe.

My simpler pot-roasted version calls for slow-cooking the meat, shredding it, mixing it with some of the juices, rolling it in soft tortillas, then dousing it all with the cooking juices and topping it with fuchsia-colored pickled onions. These are knife-and-fork tacos—perfect for a special supper with a bowl of black beans, a platter of Rustic Jícama Appetizer (page 92) and a finish of Yucatecan-Style Fresh Coconut Pie (page 402).

MAKES ABOUT 4 CUPS OF FILLING, ENOUGH FOR 16 TO 18 TACOS, SERVING 6 TO 8 AS AN INFORMAL MAIN DISH

FOR ⅓ CUP ESSENTIAL GARLICKY ACHIOTE SEASONING PASTE

2 tablespoons achiote seeds

2 teaspoons allspice, preferably freshly ground

1 teaspoon black pepper, preferably freshly ground

1½ teaspoons dried oregano, preferably Mexican

3 tablespoons cider vinegar

6 garlic cloves, peeled

1 generous teaspoon salt

6 tablespoons sour orange juice OR ¼ cup fresh lime juice plus 2 tablespoons fresh orange juice

A 2-pound piece lean boneless pork shoulder (Boston butt) or a 3-pound bone-in pork blade roast

Two 12-by-18-inch pieces of banana leaf (if you can find them), defrosted if frozen

16 to 18 fresh corn tortillas (plus a few extra, in case some break)

1½ cups Pickled Red Onions (page 172)

Beautiful sprigs of cilantro, for garnish

1. *Making ⅓ cup of Essential Garlicky Achiote Seasoning Paste.* Very finely pulverize the achiote in a spice grinder, then transfer it to a small bowl and mix in the allspice, pepper, oregano and vinegar (you'll have a crumbly, very thick mixture at this point). Roughly chop

the garlic, sprinkle with the salt, then, on your cutting board, work the two into a smooth paste with a spoon or the side of a knife. Scoop the achiote mixture onto the garlic, work the two together, then dribble on and work in enough water, usually about a tablespoon or 2, to give it the consistency of a thick, but spreadable, paste.

2. *Marinating the meat.* In a large bowl, mix together the achiote seasoning and juice. Lay in the meat, then flip it over, smearing or spooning the marinade into every crevice. Cover the bowl and refrigerate for at least 2 hours (preferably overnight).

3. *Pot-roasting the meat.* Turn on the oven to 325 degrees. Set out a large (6-quart) pot (preferably a Dutch oven). If you're using banana leaves, drape the 2 pieces over the bottom and up the sides of the pot in the form of a cross. Set the meat in the middle, scraping all the marinating juices on top. Fold the banana leaves over the meat to enclose it. If you are not using banana leaves, just set the meat in the pot and scrape all the marinade over it.

Drizzle 1 cup of water around the meat, cover tightly and roast in the oven until fall-apart tender, about 3 hours. Occasionally check the liquid level in the pot, adding water if all has evaporated. With spatulas or meat forks, remove the meat to a cutting board; then pour the juices into a large measuring cup or gravy separator. Let both meat and juices cool slightly.

Roughly chop or shred the meat (there will be about 4 cups), sprinkle with a little salt and return it to the pot in which it was roasted. Spoon off the fat that has risen to the top of the juices, then pour a little into the meat to moisten it; cover and keep warm over low heat. Transfer the remaining juices to a small saucepan, cover and keep warm. (There should be a cup or less of juice; if you've got more, boil it until reduced to that amount.)

4. *Serving the tacos.* Set up a steamer (with this many tortillas, you'll need 2 vegetable steamers set up in saucepans or a big Chinese steamer—either choice with ½ inch of water under the steamer basket); heat to a boil. Wrap the tortillas in 2 stacks in heavy kitchen towels, lay in the steamer(s) and cover tightly. Boil 1 minute, turn off the heat and let stand without opening the steamer(s) for 15 minutes.

Roll 2 generous tablespoons of meat into each soft tortilla, lay on warm plates, ladle on a portion of the juices and top with pickled onions. Sprigs of cilantro make a beautiful garnish.

ADVANCE PREPARATION—The recipe can be made 2 or 3 days ahead through step 3; cover and refrigerate meat separately from the juice. Reheat the pork and juice before heating tortillas.

SHORTCUTS—Buying prepared achiote seasoning will save time.

Pickled Red Onions

THESE LIVELY FLAVORED, crunchy, fuchsia-colored lovelies are the perfect condiment on everything from Achiote-Roasted Pork Tacos (page 170) to roast beef sandwiches. Throughout the Yucatan, they're left out on most tables for everyone to enjoy on whatever's at hand.

MAKES A GENEROUS 1 CUP

*1 small red onion, peeled and sliced
   1/8 inch thick*

1/4 teaspoon black peppercorns

1/4 teaspoon cumin seeds

*1/2 teaspoon dried oregano,
   preferably Mexican*

2 garlic cloves, peeled and halved

1/4 teaspoon salt

1/3 cup cider vinegar

1. *Parboiling the onion.* Blanch the onion slices in boiling salted water for 45 seconds, then drain and place in a medium-size bowl.

2. *The pickling.* Coarsely grind the peppercorns and cumin in a mortar or spice grinder, and add to the onions. Add the remaining ingredients plus enough water to barely cover. Stir well and let stand for several hours until the onions turn bright pink.

ADVANCE PREPARATION—Covered and refrigerated, the onions last several weeks.

ENCHILADAS

. . . . .

I really do enjoy a plate of enchiladas, but let's face it: They *can* be rather heavy fare, especially if they're covered in melted cheese. And when you come to the step in the recipe where you're instructed to quick-fry each tortilla to make it rollable, you may stop right in your tracks, living as we all do in the nutritional climate of "fat-free." To simply throw out the enchilada baby with its bath water would be ridiculous, though, and I have two reasons.

First, fat plays a roll in the diet of developing countries and it's important to understand that fact when exploring traditional cooking around the world. True, we live in a world of superabundance and tend to look down on any country that celebrates fat in its special-occasion dishes. That's not only disrespectful but very poorly informed: In a subsistence diet of corn tortillas, beans, vegetable soup and salsas (the diet many have survived on in Mexico for millennia), everyday, nearly fat-free eating is jubilantly thrown off at any possible occasion in favor of a high-fat alternative. Why? Because anything with fat has wonderful texture (why do you think Proctor and Gamble spent billions of dollars developing Olestra?) and because the calories are so concentrated that one feels full and more satisfied for a longer time. If you factor into this Mexican nutritional equation both the physical activity required to live in a rural area and the physiological interaction of fat, especially saturated fat, with beans and corn tortillas, the health concerns aren't many—even with regular high-fat splurges.

But I'm cooking in America for my (usually) American guests, so should I only make enchiladas on those rare occasions when I'm doing a historical-theme dinner and trying to make museum-quality reproductions of dishes that don't play any role on the contemporary table? My answer is no. Definitively no. Though enchiladas are a great way to utilize leftover cold tortillas in a Mexican household, and frying is the easiest way to soften them into suppleness, most versions don't have to be made with quick-fried tortillas. I've been served enchiladas made from steaming-hot, fresh (unfried) tortillas many times in Mexico and that's how I choose to make most versions in the States. I've started off my enchilada recipes here with one that does just that, filling them with flakes of fish and squares of potato, splashed with a roasted tomatillo sauce and dusted with aged cheese.

For a simple meal, Spicy Tomato-Sauced Enchiladas show how delectable roasted tomatoes, green chiles, tortillas and cheese can be. For special occasions, on the other hand, *Mole* Enchiladas will evoke enthusiasm. I've put together the simplest recipe for a good-tasting *mole* here.

I wouldn't touch a thing in the traditional recipe called Street-Style Red Chile Enchiladas. They're made in the "other" style of enchilada preparation: a cold tortilla is dipped in a robust red chile sauce, then seared quickly on an oiled surface. One taste and you'll understand why they're a favorite street food (spicy, a little oily, fun to eat).

TANGY TOMATILLO-SAUCED FISH ENCHILADAS

Enchiladas Verdes de Pescado

*T*HESE SHREDDED-FISH enchiladas offer a wonderful combination of flavors and textures. Flakes of fish play against the sustenance of a warm tortilla seasoned with the creamy sharpness of a tomatillo sauce. I know fish enchiladas must sound trendy, but like good cooks everywhere, those on Mexico's coasts take advantage of their local ingredients.

I find myself drawn to this kind of enchilada regularly, because the tortillas, sauce and garnishes are happy wrapped around a variety of fillings, from leftover shredded chicken or pork, to shrimp, smoked fish or a combination of steamed, sauteed or roasted vegetables; you need 1½ cups of filling. The potatoes are my addition; they add another texture and keep these light enough to serve as a first course. A great dinner can be made by serving these enchiladas before Grilled Steak with Spicy Guajillo Sauce (page 364).

SERVES 8 AS AN APPETIZER, 4 AS A LIGHT MAIN DISH

FOR 2 CUPS ESSENTIAL SIMMERED TOMATILLO-SERRANO SAUCE

12 ounces (7 to 8 medium) tomatillos, husked and rinsed

Fresh serrano chiles to taste (about 2), stemmed

1 tablespoon olive or vegetable oil

1 large white onion, chopped into ¼-inch dice

2 garlic cloves, peeled and roughly chopped

1½ cups fish or chicken broth

8 ounces boneless, skinless fish fillets (such as grouper, snapper, sea bass, mahimahi—skate, if you can get it, is particularly good)

2 medium-small boiling potatoes, peeled and cut into ½-inch cubes

8 corn tortillas (plus a few extra, in case some break)

¼ cup Thick Cream (page 165), crème fraîche or sour cream

A generous ⅓ cup chopped cilantro, plus 8 sprigs for garnish

Salt, about ½ teaspoon, depending on the saltiness of the broth

3 tablespoons finely crumbled Mexican queso añejo, dry feta or Parmesan

4 radishes, finely diced or cut into matchsticks

1. *Making 2 cups Essential Simmered Tomatillo-Serrano Sauce.* Lay the tomatillos and chiles on a baking sheet and place about 4 inches below a very hot broiler. When the tomatillos and chiles blister, darken and soften on one side, about 5 minutes, turn them

over and roast on the other side. Transfer tomatillos, chiles and any accumulated juices to a food processor or blender.

Heat ½ *tablespoon* of the oil in a medium-large (9-to 10-inch) heavy skillet over medium. Add *half* of the onion and cook, stirring often, until richly browned, about 10 minutes. Stir in garlic and cook 1 minute more. Add to the chile mixture in the food processor or blender and process to a medium-fine puree.

Wipe the skillet clean, set it over medium-high and add the remaining ½ *tablespoon* oil. When hot enough to make a drop of the puree sizzle sharply, pour it all in at once and stir for about 5 minutes, until darker and thicker. Add the broth, let return to a boil, reduce the heat to medium, and simmer briskly until thick enough to coat a spoon, about 10 minutes.

2. *The filling.* Place the fish in a small (1- to 2-quart) saucepan, cover with salted water, set over medium heat and simmer until the fish flakes easily, 5 to 10 minutes, depending on the thickness of the fillets. Transfer the fillets to a plate with a slotted spoon, then scoop the potatoes into the fish's broth and simmer until tender, about 5 minutes; drain off the liquid, leaving the potatoes in the pan. Flake the fish into the saucepan and gently mix with the potatoes and ½ *cup* of the tomatillo sauce; cover and set aside.

3. *Warming the tortillas.* Set up a steamer (a vegetable steamer in a large saucepan filled with ½ inch of water works well); heat to a boil. Wrap the tortillas in a heavy kitchen towel, lay in the steamer and cover with a tight lid. Boil 1 minute, turn off the heat and let stand without opening the steamer for 15 minutes.

4. *Finishing the dish.* Turn the oven on to the lowest setting and warm 4 to 8 plates in it. Bring the remaining tomatillo sauce to a simmer over low heat, add the Thick Cream (or one of its stand-ins) and ¼ *cup* of the chopped cilantro. Taste, season with salt and keep warm; warm up the fish and potato filling. Mix the remaining *half* of the onion with the remaining 2 *tablespoons* of the chopped cilantro.

One serving at a time, finish the enchiladas: Lay a warm tortilla on an individual plate (2 tortillas if you're serving these as a light main dish), spoon a portion of filling across one side of the tortilla(s), fold over, ladle on a portion of sauce and sprinkle with cheese, the onion-cilantro mixture and radishes. Garnish with a sprig(s) of cilantro and serve.

ADVANCE PREPARATION—The sauce will keep several days, the filling 1 day; refrigerate both tightly covered. Complete steps 3 and 4 just before serving.

SHORTCUTS—A time-saver here would be to buy about 12 ounces of smoked fish or cooked shrimp and eliminate the potatoes.

SPICY TOMATO-SAUCED ENCHILADAS
WITH JALAPEÑOS AND AGED CHEESE

Enjitomatadas

I ALWAYS THINK of these spicy, roasty, tomato-sauced "enchiladas" as a great brunch dish, not only because they're served at that late morning breakfast/lunch called *almuerzo* in Mexico, but because they're light and packed with invigorating flavor. It's a simple, comfortable recipe for any American cook, perfect when meat is not your focus (though I must say they are wonderful with seared pieces of *cecina*—the half-cured or chilied meat they sell in Mexican butcher shops—or chorizo, grilled fish, steak or scrambled eggs).

The word *enjitomatadas* is Spanish for "covered with tomato," short for "tortilla covered with tomato." And to make them you simply dip the tortillas in the sauce, fold them over and splash with a little more sauce. Here they are unfilled as is common with many enchiladas in Mexico where the feature is tortilla and sauce, not filling. Served with chile slivers, cheese, cilantro and a spoon of black beans, you have a nutritiously balanced and delicious lunch or supper.

SERVES 6 AS AN APPETIZER, 4 AS A CASUAL MAIN COURSE

FOR 4 CUPS ESSENTIAL SIMMERED TOMATO-JALAPEÑO SAUCE

2¼ pounds (about 4 medium-large to large round, 14 to 18 plum) tomatoes

3 to 4 fresh jalapeño chiles, stemmed

2 tablespoons vegetable oil or rich-tasting pork lard

1 large white onion, thinly sliced

1½ cups chicken broth

Salt, about 1½ teaspoons, depending on the saltiness of the broth

12 corn tortillas (plus a few extra, in case some break)

⅔ cup finely crumbled Mexican queso añejo, dry feta or Parmesan

Thin strips of pickled jalapeño, for garnish

12 good-size sprigs of cilantro

1. *Making 4 cups of Essential Simmered Tomato-Jalapeño Sauce.* Roast the tomatoes and chiles on a baking sheet 4 inches below a very hot broiler until blackened on one side, about 6 minutes, then flip and roast the other side. Cool, then peel the tomatoes, collecting all the juices. Roughly chop the jalapeños. Coarsely puree the tomatoes (with their juices) and chiles in a food processor or blender.

In a medium-size (4-quart) pot (like a Dutch oven or Mexican *cazuela*), heat the oil or lard over medium. Add *half* of the onion and fry, stirring often, until browned, about 8 minutes. Increase the heat to medium-high, and when very hot, add the tomato-chile puree mixture. Stir for about 5 minutes as the mixture sears and thickens, then reduce the heat to medium-low, stir in the broth and simmer about 20 minutes, until just beginning to thicken again. Taste and season with salt. Cover and keep warm.

2. *Warming the tortillas.* Set up a steamer (a vegetable steamer in a large saucepan filled with ½ inch of water works well); heat to a boil. Wrap the tortillas in a heavy kitchen towel, lay in the steamer and cover with a tight lid. Boil 1 minute, turn off the heat and let stand without opening the steamer for 15 minutes.

3. *Making the* enjitomatadas. Turn on the oven to the lowest setting and warm 4 to 6 plates in it. Bring the tomato sauce to a boil and pour ½ cup into a deep dish. Then, one by one, dip both sides of the warm tortillas into the sauce, fold over and use a spatula to transfer them to the warm plates. Arrange 2 or 3 of the dipped, folded tortillas, slightly overlapping, on each plate and keep warm in the oven.

Scrape any remaining sauce from the dipping dish back into the sauce pot. Reheat the sauce, then ladle a portion of it over each serving. Sprinkle with the cheese and strew with the remaining sliced onion and pickled jalapeño. Decorate each plate with a sprig or two of cilantro, and carry them right to the table.

ADVANCE PREPARATION—The sauce will keep, covered in the refrigerator, for several days; it also freezes well. Finish steps 2 and 3 just before serving.

SHORTCUTS—One-and-a-half 28-ounce cans of tomatoes can replace the fresh ones.

VARIATIONS AND IMPROVISATIONS—You can make *enjitomatadas* more substantial by spooning a little ricotta or soft goat cheese into them before folding; or use shredded smoked or poached fish or poultry. For either one you'll need between 1 and 1½ cups. A delicious variation on the sauce is to replace the jalapeños with canned chipotle *en adobo*.

SIMPLE RED MOLE ENCHILADAS
WITH SHREDDED CHICKEN

Enchiladas de Mole Rojo

$\mathcal{M}$OLE IS THE SOUL of the Mexican kitchen and, when it's lovingly made, it is uncontestably one of the wonders of the culinary world: thick with an unctuous puree of nuts or seeds, rich with chile and complex with a multitude of spices. *Mole* is a dish with pre-Columbian roots, though as Sophie Coe explains in *The True History of Chocolate*, the *mole* most of us know came into its own during the seventeenth century, *after* the Spanish conquest, at a time when experimentation with chocolate as a cooking spice was popular.

When you read the lengthy lists of ingredients and consider the countless hours of grinding, straining, frying and simmering, it's no wonder that few of the uninitiated ever attempt it. This simple version is my recommendation for first timers.

Serve these impressive enchiladas with Classic Mexican Fried Beans (page 237).

SERVES 6 TO 9, WITH ABOUT 6 CUPS OF SAUCE

FOR 1 CUP ESSENTIAL SWEET-AND-SPICY ANCHO SEASONING PASTE

8 garlic cloves, unpeeled

8 medium (about 4 ounces total) dried ancho chiles, stemmed and seeded

1½ teaspoons dried oregano, preferably Mexican

½ teaspoon black pepper, preferably freshly ground

A big pinch cumin, preferably freshly ground

A scant ¼ teaspoon cloves, preferably freshly ground

About 6 cups chicken broth

3 tablespoons vegetable oil or rich-tasting pork lard, plus a little more if needed

2 ounces (about ½ cup) whole almonds (with or without skins)

1 medium white onion, sliced ⅛ inch thick

¼ cup raisins

5 ounces (1 small round or 2 to 3 plum) ripe tomatoes

A scant ½ teaspoon cinnamon, preferably freshly ground Mexican canela

¼ cup (about 1½ ounces) roughly chopped Mexican chocolate

2 slices firm white bread (or ½ Mexican bolillo), toasted

Salt, about 2½ teaspoons, depending on saltiness of the broth

Sugar, about 1 tablespoon

18 corn tortillas (plus a few extra, in case some break)

A spoonful or two of sesame seeds, for garnish

3 cups cooked, coarsely shredded chicken (page 181)

1. *Making 1 cup Essential Sweet-and-Spicy Ancho Seasoning Paste.* Roast the unpeeled garlic directly on an ungreased griddle or heavy skillet over medium heat until soft (they'll blacken in spots), about 15 minutes; cool and peel. While the garlic is roasting, toast the chiles on another side of the griddle or skillet: 1 or 2 at a time, open them flat and press down firmly on the hot surface with a spatula; in a few seconds, when they crackle, even send up a wisp of smoke, flip them and press down to toast the other side. In a small bowl, cover the chiles with hot water and let rehydrate 30 minutes, stirring frequently to ensure even soaking. Drain and discard the water.

Combine the oregano, black pepper, cumin and cloves in a food processor or blender, along with the chiles, garlic and ⅔ *cup* of the broth. Process to a smooth puree, scraping and stirring every few seconds. If the mixture won't go through the blender blades, add a little more liquid. Press through a medium-mesh strainer into a bowl.

2. *From ancho seasoning to* mole. In a medium-size (4-quart) pot (preferably a Dutch oven or Mexican *cazuela*), heat 1½ *tablespoons* of the oil or lard over medium. Add the almonds and cook, stirring regularly, until lightly toasted, about 3 minutes. Using a slotted spoon, remove the almonds to a blender or food processor. Add *half* of the onion to the pan and cook, stirring frequently, until richly browned, about 10 minutes. Use the slotted spoon to scoop the onions in with the almonds, leaving behind as much oil as possible. (If needed, add a little more oil or lard to the pan, let heat, then continue.) Add the raisins, stir for a minute as they puff, then use the slotted spoon to scoop them in with the almonds.

Roast the tomatoes on a baking sheet 4 inches below a very hot broiler until blackened on one side, about 6 minutes, then flip them over and roast the other side. Cool, peel and add to the almond mixture in the blender, along with the cinnamon, chocolate and bread. Add *1 cup* of the broth and blend to a smooth puree, scraping and stirring every few seconds.

Return the pot to medium-high heat and, if necessary, add a little more oil or lard to coat the bottom lightly. When very hot, add the ancho mixture and cook, stirring almost constantly, until darker and very thick, about 5 minutes. Add the pureed almond mixture and cook, stirring constantly for another few minutes, until very thick once again. Stir in the remaining 4⅓ *cups* of the broth, partially cover and simmer, stirring occasionally, over medium-low for 45 minutes. Taste and season with salt and sugar. (If you have never made *mole* before, season it until it's slightly sweet—the sugar balances the strong flavors.)

3. *Warming the tortillas.* Set up a steamer (with this many tortillas, you'll need 2 vegetable steamers set up in saucepans or a big Chinese steamer—either choice with ½ inch of water under the steamer basket); heat to a boil. Wrap the tortillas in 2 stacks in heavy kitchen towels, lay in the steamer, and cover tightly. Boil 1 minute, turn off the heat and let stand without opening the steamer for 15 minutes.

4. *Finishing the enchiladas.* Turn on the oven to the lowest setting and warm 6 to 9 plates in it. Toast the sesame seeds in a small skillet, stirring frequently, over medium heat until golden, 2 to 3 minutes. In a medium-size saucepan, combine the chicken with 1½ cups of the *mole* and warm over medium heat. Bring the remaining *mole* to a simmer.

When you're ready to serve, quickly make the enchiladas by scooping 2 generous tablespoons of chicken onto a tortilla, rolling it up and placing it on a warm dinner plate. Continue making enchiladas, arranging 2 or 3 per plate, then douse them liberally with the hot *mole.* Strew with the remaining sliced onion and sesame seeds.

ADVANCE PREPARATION—The finished *mole* will keep several days, covered and refrigerated; it also freezes well. Reheat, taste and adjust the seasonings before finishing steps 3 and 4.

VARIATIONS AND IMPROVISATIONS

The filling needn't be kept to chicken (though that's most common); pork is good (leftover shredded roast or a more complicated preparation like Smoky Shredded Pork, page 150), as is turkey or more contemporary options like slivered, grilled steak or duck breast. To go a modern vegetable route, use roasted pumpkin or sweet potato mixed with grilled or sauteed onion and a little blanched chard. Just keep in mind that you need about 3 cups total filling.

Chicken in Simple Red Mole—For an informal, but very special, dinner for 8 people, poach 4 split (bone in, skin on) chicken breasts as described on page 181. Use the broth to make the *mole,* then reheat the cooked chicken breasts in the sauce just before serving. Transfer to a deep serving platter, garnish with sesame seeds and pass among your guests along with a big bowl of Classic Red Tomato Rice (page 250).

Poached Chicken

WHEN I COOK in Mexico, I keep in mind that the range chickens do best with a good, long simmer in aromatic broth. The breast doesn't turn to sawdust; in fact, the texture seems to enjoy the extended hot bath. That long bath would ruin our leaner, less-developed American birds. Here, I've done a recipe for *American* chicken that cooks them slowly to a perfect, succulent doneness—just right to use in tacos, enchiladas and the like.

**MAKES ABOUT 1 1/2 POUNDS POACHED CHICKEN,
ABOUT 3 CUPS SHREDDED**

1 medium white onion, sliced

2 garlic cloves, peeled and roughly chopped

1 large carrot, peeled and thinly sliced

1 teaspoon salt

1 good-size (3-pound) chicken, cut into quarters

2 bay leaves

1/4 teaspoon dried marjoram

IN A LARGE (6-quart) pot, bring 8 cups of water to a boil. Add the onion, garlic, carrot, the salt and the chicken back (if you're lucky enough to have a separated one), neck, heart and giblets. Skim off any foam that rises after a minute or two, partially cover and simmer over medium-low for 20 minutes. Add the dark meat quarters, skim again after a couple of minutes, then add the bay, marjoram and thyme; partially cover and cook over medium heat for 10 minutes. Add the breast quarters, skim when the liquid returns to the simmer; partially cover and cook 13 minutes. Remove the pot from the heat and let the chicken cool for a few minutes in the broth.

Remove the breast and leg quarters from the broth and set aside. Strain the broth, discarding the solids and spoon off any fat that rises to the top. (Refrigerate the broth, covered, for up to 5 days or freeze it for up to 3 months.) When the chicken quarters are cool, pull the meat off the bones in coarse shreds. (Discard the skin and bones.) The meat will keep covered and refrigerated for several days or frozen for a few weeks.

STREET-STYLE RED CHILE ENCHILADAS
WITH ZUCCHINI, AGED CHEESE AND CRUNCHY GARNISHES

Enchiladas Callejeras

*J*UST THE THOUGHT of these spicy little snacks gets mouths watering practically everywhere in Mexico, especially in West-Central Mexico. They're street food and as gutsy as street food should be. You even see them at Mexican street fairs in Chicago, where cooks set up those Mexican frying tables—the ones that look like big rolled steel trays with a flame-heated, wok-sized depression in the center—and go on all night dipping tortillas in the spicy red chile puree, searing them on the oily surface, folding them and sprinkling with crumbled cheese. They're not saucy, though they perfectly live up to their name, since "enchilada" literally means "(tortilla) covered in chile."

Potatoes and carrots, fried along with the tortillas, are typical West-Central accompaniments. Here I've taken the lead of the Sinaloa-style *enchiladas del suelo* and used zucchini. The tangy romaine and jalapeño and the crunchy radish and onion give all the contrasting flavors and textures that make everything sing in harmony.

SERVES 4 AS A CASUAL MAIN COURSE (OR YOU MIGHT WANT TO SERVE THEM AS AN APPETIZER FOR 6)

FOR ¾ CUP ESSENTIAL SWEET-AND-SPICY ANCHO SEASONING PASTE

6 garlic cloves, unpeeled

6 medium (about 3 ounces total) dried ancho chiles, stemmed and seeded

A generous teaspoon dried oregano, preferably Mexican

A scant ½ teaspoon black pepper, preferably freshly ground

A big pinch cumin seeds, preferably freshly ground

⅛ teaspoon cloves, preferably freshly ground

½ cup chicken broth, plus a little more if needed

Salt, a generous ¾ teaspoon

2 tablespoons cider vinegar

¼ cup finely crumbled Mexican queso añejo, dry feta or Parmesan

3 small romaine lettuce leaves, sliced crosswise into ⅛-inch strips

4 radishes, thinly sliced

¼ cup finely chopped white onion

2 tablespoons chopped cilantro

2 pickled jalapeños, stemmed, seeded and cut into thin strips

2 medium zucchini

2 to 3 tablespoons vegetable oil

12 corn tortillas

1. *For ¾ cup Essential Sweet-and-Spicy Ancho Seasoning Paste.* Roast the unpeeled garlic directly on an ungreased griddle or heavy skillet over medium heat, turning occasionally, until soft (they'll blacken in spots), about 15 minutes; cool and peel. While the garlic is roasting, toast the chiles on another side of the griddle or skillet: 1 or 2 at a time, open them flat and press down firmly on the hot surface with a spatula; in a few seconds, when they crackle, even send up a wisp of smoke, flip them and press down to toast the other side. In a small bowl, cover the chiles with hot water and let rehydrate 30 minutes, stirring frequently to ensure even soaking. Drain and discard the water.

Combine the oregano, black pepper, cumin and cloves in a food processor or blender along with the chiles, garlic and broth. Process to a smooth puree, scraping and stirring every few seconds. If the mixture won't go through the blender blades, add a little more broth. Press through a medium-mesh strainer into a bowl. Taste and season liberally with salt; it should taste salty and will have a trace of bitterness.

2. *The sauce.* In a wide, shallow bowl, combine the ancho seasoning paste with 1 tablespoon of the vinegar and enough water (it can take up to 4 or 5 tablespoons) to bring the mixture to the consistency of canned tomato sauce.

3. *Other preliminaries.* Turn on the oven to your lowest setting and warm 4 plates in it. Set out the garnishes: crumbled cheese, sliced lettuce and radishes, chopped onion, cilantro and pickled jalapeños. Cut the zucchini lengthwise into ¼-inch-thick slices, cut each slice into ¼-inch-wide sticks about 2 inches long.

4. *Finishing the enchiladas.* Heat a wok or large (12-inch) heavy skillet over medium heat. Add *1 tablespoon* of the oil and start making the first plate of the enchiladas: one at a time, dip both sides of 3 tortillas into the sauce, immediately laying each one in the hot pan, overlapping as little as possible. After about 10 seconds, flip them with a spatula and sear the sauce into the other side for a few seconds, then fold in half; use your spatula to remove them, draining as much oil as possible back into the pan. Line them up on a warm dinner plate, slightly overlapping them. Set the plate in the warm oven while you prepare the remaining 3 servings in the same way; you will need to add a little more oil for each trio of tortillas (don't let the pan get too hot or the sauce that clings to the pan after each round will begin to burn).

With the pan still over medium heat, measure in *½ tablespoon* of oil, then add the zucchini and stir-fry until it begins to soften, 2 to 3 minutes. Stir in any remaining sauce and cook about a minute longer. Spoon a portion of zucchini over each serving of enchiladas, then sprinkle with cheese. Toss the lettuce with the remaining *1 tablespoon* of vinegar. Arrange a quarter of the lettuce, radishes, onion, cilantro and jalapeño across the middle of each serving and carry to the table without hesitation.

ADVANCE PREPARATION—Step 1 can be completed several days ahead (refrigerate the seasoning paste); step 2 several hours ahead (again, refrigerate everything); the cooking and assembly just before serving.

VARIATIONS AND IMPROVISATIONS—Think of the core of this recipe as the seasoning paste and tortillas, then improvise to suit your taste. Add a little chipotle to the seasoning or make it with all or half guajillos. Corn kernels and/or diced chayote can be added to the zucchini, as can cooked chorizo, flaked fish or shredded meat or poultry.

More Classics from Corn Masa

· · · · ·

Masa *made from* ground corn is a wonderfully malleable, thoroughly adaptable dough, and it's the basis of most *antojitos*. You can press it out and bake it plain to make tortillas. Leave the tortillas on the griddle a little longer and they crisp to tostadas. Fry them and you have chips (*totopos* or *tostaditas*). Beat the dough with solid shortening and a little broth and it steams up light and tender as corn husk– or banana leaf–wrapped tamales. Having eaten these and dozens of variations on their native soil, I know that each *antojito* has its own beguiling charm.

Sopes are probably the most well-known *antojito* after tacos, enchiladas and tostadas (I'm leaving out the mostly American burritos). They're generally small fat tortillas with a pinched border, crisped a little on an oily griddle, then splashed with biting salsa and sprinkled with crumbled cheese and onion. Finding them hard to turn out well in large quantities for a party, I developed my own *baked* version that I call *cazuelitas*. Filled with roasted poblanos and melted cheese, *cazuelitas* are always a hit.

Pressed-out, unbaked tortillas are slid into hot oil through the Gulf region, and, whether they're called *gorditas, salbutes* or *panuchos,* they are wonderful snacks. I've included here the very classic black bean–*masa* cakes that fry up puffed like sopapillas.

Tlacoyos—crusty, bean-filled oval *masa* cakes—are a regional *antojito* found in Central Mexico. Sometimes you'll see unfilled versions called *memelas* or *huaraches* around Mexico City; sometimes they're made like turnovers in Tlaxcala (called *tlatlaoyos*). My favorites are made from blue corn with a little yellow fava bean filling showing.

The last recipe in this section is for a potato-*masa* croquette that's a little tapered on the ends so it resembles a torpedo or cigar, an example of the special touches regional cooks give to their *antojitos*. A little-known specialty of South-Central Mexico, these *molotes* are not difficult to prepare and can even be fried a little ahead and rewarmed. They are a crowd pleaser, and they welcome practically any salsa. Good reasons to keep them in mind if you're planning an array of *antojitos* for a party.

Turnovers made from tortillas are a natural for the Mexican kitchen. If the filling is cheese, I'm sure you'll recognize the turnover as a quesadilla, the best being when the thickish corn tortilla's just been laid on the griddle to bake, the cheese or other filling is spooned across it, then it's folded over, the edges pressed together to hold everything inside. After a few minutes of toasting on the griddle, that crusty quesadilla is one of the best mouthfuls our planet has to offer. My recipe shows you how to make quesadillas in an American kitchen, and it's a good way to practice your tortilla making skills. Try them with fresh *masa* or with *masa harina*. You'll like the results with either.

When you have time, prepare the very Oaxacan-tasting yellow *mole* filling for *Empanadas de Amarillo*. Though these griddle-baked quesadillas are called empanadas in Oaxaca, the procedure for making them is very much like the one used for the quesadillas described above.

CRUSTY BAKED MASA BOATS
WITH ROASTED POBLANOS AND MELTED CHEESE

Cazuelitas de Queso y Rajas

Sopes, MEMELAS, PICADAS—they are all little boats of *masa* (corn tortilla dough) shaped to hold savory fillings, as are the *cazuelitas* in this recipe. Though classic *sopes* and their cousins are made from thick, griddle-baked tortillas pinched up to form a border, then griddle-fried to a crisp, I designed these *masa* boats to be baked in the oven. Baked until crispy, melting and oozy, topped with a little chorizo or salsa—they are a fabulous mouthful. I thank Alicia De'Angeli for suggesting the name "little casserole dish" in her book *Epazote y Molcajete*. This recipe is a fine place to start for those using *masa* for the first time. The dough is easy to work with and shaped without a tortilla press and it's very good made with widely available dehydrated *masa harina*.

**MAKES 8 "BOATS," ENOUGH FOR 8 AS AN APPETIZER
OR 4 AS A CASUAL MAIN DISH**

FOR 1 CUP ESSENTIAL ROASTED POBLANO *RAJAS*

8 ounces (3 medium-large) fresh poblano chiles

1 tablespoon vegetable or olive oil

1 small white onion, sliced ¼ inch thick

2 garlic cloves, peeled and finely chopped

1¼ teaspoons dried oregano, preferably Mexican

⅛ teaspoon dried thyme

Salt, about ¾ teaspoon, plus a little for sprinkling on the lettuce

½ pound (1 cup) fresh masa for tortillas

OR 1 cup masa harina *mixed with* ½ cup plus 2 tablespoons hot water

2 tablespoons rich-tasting lard or vegetable shortening

1½ cups (6 ounces) shredded Mexican Chihuahua cheese or other melting cheese, such as brick or Monterey Jack

¼ cup finely crumbled Mexican queso añejo, *dry feta or Parmesan*

1 egg yolk

1 teaspoon baking powder

⅔ cup (a generous 5 ounces) chorizo sausage, casing removed

OR *about* ½ cup Essential Chopped Tomato-Serrano Salsa (page 25)

4 cups sliced romaine lettuce (¼-inch pieces), about 8 large leaves

4 radishes, thinly sliced

2 tablespoons cider vinegar

1. *Making 1 cup Essential Roasted Poblano* **Rajas.** Roast the chiles directly over a gas flame or 4 inches below a very hot broiler until blackened on all sides, about 5 minutes for open flame, about 10 minutes for broiler. Cover with a kitchen towel and let stand 5 minutes. Peel, pull out the stem and seed pod, then rinse *briefly* to remove bits of skin and seeds. Slice into ¼-inch strips.

In a medium-size skillet, heat the oil over medium to medium-high, then add the onion and cook, stirring regularly, until nicely browned but still a little crunchy, about 5 minutes. Add the garlic, ¼ *teaspoon* of the oregano and the thyme, toss a minute longer, then stir in the chiles. Taste and season with salt, usually about ¼ teaspoon, and cool.

2. *Forming the* **cazuelitas.** Turn the oven on to 350 degrees. In a large bowl, combine the *masa* (fresh or reconstituted) with the lard or vegetable shortening, ½ *cup* of the Chihuahua cheese, the *queso añejo,* egg yolk, baking powder and ½ *teaspoon* of the salt, working everything together with your hands until you have a smooth dough. If necessary, add a little water to give it the consistency of *soft* (but not sticky) cookie dough. Divide into 8 balls, then, with your fingers, flatten each into a 3-inch disc, taking care to make the edges neat. Place on a greased or parchment-lined baking sheet, and bake in the upper third of the oven until *barely* set and just beginning to brown, about 15 minutes.

Cool slightly (but don't let cool completely), then pinch a ½-inch-high border of the still-soft *masa* around the edge of each *cazuelita*. Press down the centers to flatten evenly. Cover with plastic wrap if not finishing immediately.

3. *Finishing the* **cazuelitas.** Combine the poblano *rajas* with the remaining *1 cup* Chihuahua cheese and divide among the *cazuelitas*. Bake until the cheese melts, 10 minutes.

While they are baking, cook the chorizo, if you're using it, in a small skillet over medium heat, stirring from time to time to break up any lumps, until thoroughly done, about 10 minutes. Drain on paper toweling.

In a large bowl, toss the lettuce with the radishes, vinegar and a little salt. Divide between your serving plates. Nestle the *cazuelitas* into the lettuce, then top each one with a spoonful of chorizo, or with a spoonful of the salsa, and a sprinkling of the remaining *1 teaspoon* of the oregano. Serve without delay.

ADVANCE PREPARATION—The *rajas* can be made several days ahead; refrigerate covered. The *cazuelitas* may be made 2 days in advance through step 2; refrigerate covered.

PUFFED BLACK BEAN–MASA CAKES
WITH SMOKY CHIPOTLE

Gorditas Infladas de Frijol con salsa negra

I'M A PUSHOVER for fried dough of any kind. Street-fare *churros*, elephant ears, funnel cakes—they all make my pulse quicken. So it is predictable that these *gorditas infladas* are among my favorites: puffy, chocolate-brown fried tortillas (*gordita* means "fat tortilla"), earthy with beans and corn, and just waiting for the sweet-and-hot smear of chipotle salsa.

I got my first fill of this Veracruz style of *gorditas* at a popular little snack place called Samborcito in Veracruz about fifteen years ago. When I got to know Veracruzana Carmen Ramírez Degallado, the generous and charming owner of Mexico City's El Bajío Restaurant, I learned to make them myself. Though the chipotle salsa seems a little involved (really, any red chile salsa would be delicious here), do make Carmen's version of the traditional favorite for an unforgettable experience.

MAKES 24 CAKES, ENOUGH TO SERVE 8 TO 12 AS AN APPETIZER OR SNACK

FOR 1¼ CUPS ESSENTIAL SWEET-AND-SMOKY CHIPOTLE SEASONING SALSA

2½ ounces (2½ small cones) piloncillo (Mexican unrefined sugar)

OR ⅓ cup dark brown sugar plus 2 teaspoons molasses

Vegetable oil to a depth of ¼ inch for frying

4 ounces (about 50) dried chipotle chiles (the cranberry-red colorados or moritas, *not the sandy brown* mecos), stemmed

3 garlic cloves, peeled

Salt, about 1½ teaspoons

1 cup drained, seasoned, cooked black beans (either canned or homemade, page 234)

1 avocado leaf (if available)

1 pound (2 cups) fresh masa for tortillas

OR 1¾ cups masa harina *mixed with 1 cup plus 2 tablespoons hot tap water*

Vegetable oil or rich-tasting lard to a depth of ¾ inch, for frying

A few tablespoons finely crumbled Mexican queso añejo, *dry feta or Parmesan*

1. *Making 1¼ cups of Essential Sweet-and-Smoky Chipotle Seasoning Salsa.* Into a medium-size saucepan, measure 1¼ cups of water and the *piloncillo* (or brown sugar and molasses), bring to a boil, remove from the heat and stir until the sugar is dissolved.

Set a medium-size (8- to 9-inch) skillet with its ¼ inch of oil over medium heat. When quite hot, add *half* the chiles. Stir with a slotted spoon as they toast to a spicy-smelling, mahogany brown, about 2 minutes. Scoop out, leaving as much oil as possible behind, and drop them directly into the sweet water. Repeat with the remaining chiles.

Pour off all but a thin coating of oil in the skillet and return to medium heat. Add the garlic and cook, stirring regularly, until golden, 3 to 4 minutes. Scoop in with the chiles.

Pour the chile mixture, water and all, into a food processor or blender, and puree.

Set the same well-oiled skillet over medium-high heat. When quite hot, add the puree all at once. Stir for a minute or so, then reduce the heat to medium-low and cook for about 20 minutes, until thick and nearly black. (If you've left a generous coating of oil in the skillet, you'll know the sauce is sufficiently reduced when the oil begins to shine on top.) Taste gingerly and season with salt, usually about ½ teaspoon.

2. The dough. Place the drained beans in a food processor. Toast the avocado leaf (if you're using it) on a skillet over medium heat until aromatic and lightly browned, 15 or 20 seconds per side. Crumble into the beans and process to a very smooth puree. The bean puree should be quite thick. Scrape into a bowl and mix thoroughly with the *masa* (fresh or reconstituted) and remaining *1 teaspoon* of the salt. The consistency of the dough is important: It should not be soft and sticky, nor unworkably firm—about like a medium cookie dough, a little softer than Play-Doh. Divide the dough into 24 balls, and cover with plastic wrap.

3. Finishing the gorditas. Turn on the oven to the lowest setting. Cut two squares of medium-heavy plastic (a garbage bag works well) to fit over the plates of your tortilla press. Heat the oil in a large (9- to 10-inch) heavy skillet (there needs to be at least a ¾-inch depth) over medium to medium-high heat until very hot—375 degrees on a deep-fry thermometer (temperature is important in getting *gorditas* to puff).

Between the two sheets of plastic, press out a ball of dough in the tortilla press into a circle about 4 inches in diameter, ⅛ inch thick. Pull off the top sheet of plastic, flip the uncovered side of the "tortilla" over onto your hand (the top of the tortilla should align with your index finger; fingers should be slightly spread), then gently peel off the plastic.

Now, carefully slide the tortilla into the hot oil. As it rises to the top, use a spoon to lightly bathe it with oil so that it will begin to puff. (At this point you can press out another ball of dough to have ready when this *gordita* is fried.) After 30 seconds, flip the *gordita* and fry for 15 to 20 seconds. Use a skimmer or slotted spoon to transfer the *gordita* to a tray lined with paper towels; keep warm in the oven while you fry the remaining *gorditas*.

Serve the *gorditas* without hesitation on warm plates dolloped with a little of the chipotle seasoning salsa and a liberal dusting of the crumbled cheese.

ADVANCE PREPARATION—The salsa will keep several weeks, covered and refrigerated. The dough can be mixed several hours ahead.

OVAL *MASA* CAKES WITH BLACK BEAN FILLING

Tlacoyos

$\mathcal{T}$HE NATIVES OF mile-and-a-half-high Toluca in Central Mexico, having successfully ducked the original campaign of the *conquistadores,* became known as a traditional, conservative lot. So it's not too surprising that the old Aztec *tlacoyo* (*masa*-cased turnover) has survived in the city marketplace's culinary repertoire. Besides, it's the perfect example of an earthy, elementally nourishing combination of the *frijoles* and *maíz* that kept Mexico going through centuries of a practically meatless existence. The recipe that follows is based on what I learned from a Tolucan market vendor that we've visited several times over the years. There, the market vendors don't work with tortilla presses, but hand-pat a tortilla, drape it over one hand, spread in a stripe of filling, then work the two edges over, moving it from hand to hand until they've formed the proper-looking oval cakes. I've developed a plastic-wrapped way of forming them for those of us who weren't raised patting tortillas.

MAKES 12 *TLACOYOS,* SERVING 4 AS A MAIN DISH

1 pound (2 cups) fresh masa *for tortillas*

OR *1¾ cups* masa harina *mixed with 1 cup plus 2 tablespoons water*

2 tablespoons rich-tasting lard or vegetable shortening

1 teaspoon salt

¾ cup seasoned, cooked, black beans (either canned or homemade, page 234)

⅓ cup vegetable oil, plus a little more if necessary

1¼ cups (10 ounces) chorizo sausage, casing removed

About 1 cup Essential Roasted Tomatillo-Serrano Salsa (page 42)

½ cup (about 2 ounces) crumbled Mexican queso fresco, queso añejo, pressed, salted farmer's cheese, dry feta or Parmesan

¼ cup finely chopped white onion

3 or 4 tablespoons chopped cilantro

Handful of sliced radishes, for garnish

1. *The dough.* Mix *masa* (fresh or reconstituted), lard or shortening and salt in a large bowl, kneading it to combine the ingredients thoroughly. If necessary, add a little water to give the *masa* mixture the consistency of soft cookie dough.

2. *Forming the* masa *cakes.* Divide the dough into 12 portions; lay them on a small plate and cover with plastic. Drain the beans (reserving the liquid), then coarsely mash them with a bean or potato masher or the back of a wooden spoon; if they are very thick (almost dry-looking), stir in a little of the reserved bean broth. You want them thick but spreadable.

Cut two squares of medium-heavy plastic (a garbage bag works well) to cover the plates of your tortilla press. Between the two sheets of plastic, use the tortilla press to press out a ball of dough into a circle about 4 inches in diameter, ⅛ inch thick. Pull off the top sheet of plastic. Spread 1 tablespoon of the cold mashed beans in a 1-inch strip down the center of the tortilla, leaving a ½-inch border at the top and bottom. Slip your two hands under the plastic beneath the tortilla, paralleling the strip of filling. Fold in the two sides of the tortillas to meet in the center and roughly cover the filling. Now, working the two ends (with plastic between you and the dough), lift and mold the *masa* from both sides up over the filling to completely cover it at the ends, creating an oval cake. Peel the plastic open to expose the *tlacoyo,* lay another piece of plastic over it and pat it gently with your fingers to flatten the top. Unmold the *tlacoyo* from the plastic.

3. *Griddle-baking.* As the *tlacoyos* are formed, lay them on an ungreased griddle or heavy skillet heated to medium-low. Cook about 10 minutes, turning periodically. When they are done, the sides will have lost their soft, moist feel and the tops and bottoms will be nicely browned. Remove to a wire rack; when cool, cover with plastic wrap.

4. *Finishing the* tlacoyos. Turn on the oven to the lowest setting. Heat the vegetable oil in a medium-size skillet over medium. When the oil is hot enough to make the edge of the *tlacoyo* sizzle, begin frying them, a batch at a time, for about 2 minutes per side to heat them through and make them more tender. Add more oil if necessary between batches. Drain on paper towels and keep warm on a baking sheet in the oven while frying the rest.

While the *tlacoyos* are frying, cook the chorizo in a small skillet over medium heat, stirring regularly and breaking up any lumps, until thoroughly done, about 10 minutes; drain. Line the *tlacoyos* on a decorative serving platter. Spoon the salsa over the top, letting it dribble down to fill the plate. Sprinkle with crumbled cheese, chopped onion, warm chorizo, cilantro and radish slices. Serve right away.

ADVANCE PREPARATION—The *tlacoyos* can be shaped and griddle-baked a day ahead; fry them just before serving (or at least within an hour or so; reheat in a 400-degree oven).

VARIATIONS AND IMPROVISATIONS— Little *tlacoyos* (made about half size) are perfect finger food to pass at parties; serve salsa on the side. Any kind of bean makes a good filling, or be creative and use things like black olive paste (or a good *anchoïade*), Spicy Pasilla Mushrooms (page 156), shredded pork (page 150) or even goat cheese mixed with herbs and green chile.

POTATO-MASA "TORPEDOES"
WITH FRESH CHEESE
Molotes de Papa y Queso

*T*HESE CRUSTY, cheese-filled "torpedoes" are lively party fare—in fact, they're a must if you are putting together a selection of Mexican snacks (sort of tapas-style) that includes dishes like Guacamole (page 78), Classic Seviche Tostadas (page 84), *Picadillo*-Stuffed Jalapeños (page 104) and Spicy Pasilla-Mushroom Tacos (page 156). Or, make them the centerpiece of an informal meatless meal—just add a big romaine salad and bowls of long-simmered black beans.

Molotes are easy to make, hold well (can even be fried a little ahead of time), and are a very tasty vehicle for salsa. I love the potato-*masa* dough (it has a moister, cakier texture than straight *masa*), and I find myself using the same dough to make quesadillas and *sopes*.

Molotes come into their own in South-Central Mexico (I've seen them most in Puebla, as well as parts of Veracruz and Oaxaca). Sometimes they're unfilled, sometimes filled with other fillings (minced pork *picadillo* is popular)—so the precedent for variation is built in. Often they're a little roughly shaped, so don't worry if yours aren't perfect-looking.

MAKES 2 DOZEN MOLOTES, 4 TO 6 SERVINGS AS A CASUAL MEAL

2 medium-large (8 ounces total)
   boiling potatoes, peeled and
   quartered

1 pound Mexican queso fresco or
   pressed salted farmer's cheese

1 pound (2 cups) fresh masa for tortillas
   OR 1¾ cups masa harina mixed with
   1 cup plus 2 tablespoons hot water

1 teaspoon salt

Vegetable oil to a depth of 1 inch,
   for frying

About 1½ cups salsa (such as Essential
   Roasted Tomatillo-Serrano Salsa,
   page 42), for serving

Sprigs of cilantro, for garnish

1. **The dough.** In a small saucepan, boil the potatoes in salted water to cover until completely tender, about 15 minutes. Remove from the water, use a fork to break them apart (this helps release steam), and let cool to room temperature.

Slice off ⅕ (*about 3 ounces*) of the cheese, break it up into your food processor, and pulse to finely crumble; you should have about ¾ cup. Add the potato and continue pulsing until the potato is smooth and thoroughly mixed with the cheese. Roughly crumble the *masa* (either fresh or reconstituted) into the processor, add the salt and pulse until everything is thoroughly combined. If the mixture is stiffer than soft cookie dough, you'll need to work in some water, a tablespoon at a time.

2. *Making the* **molotes.** Turn on the oven to the lowest setting and have ready a paper-towel–lined tray. Cut the remaining cheese into 24 sticks, each 2-inches long by ½ inch square. Divide the dough into 24 balls the size of walnuts and cover with plastic wrap. One by one, form the *molotes:* on your work surface, use your fingers to press out a ball of dough into a 3-inch circle, lay a stick of cheese across the center, and fold the two sides up, overlapping them, to enclose the cheese. Pick up the package, and roll it between your palms, tapering and sealing the ends into a torpedo shape. Lay on a plate or tray and cover with plastic wrap.

Heat the oil in a large (9- to 10-inch) heavy skillet (there needs to be at least a 1-inch depth) over medium to medium-high until very hot—375 degrees on a deep-fry thermometer. A few at a time, fry the *molotes,* turning regularly until golden and crusty, about 2 minutes total. Remove to the tray lined with paper towels and keep warm in the oven until all are fried.

Lay the *molotes* out on a warm platter, spoon the salsa across them, decorate with the sprigs of cilantro, and serve immediately.

ADVANCE PREPARATION—The *molotes* can be shaped early in the day you're serving them; store them, covered, in the refrigerator. They can be fried up to 2 hours ahead, then reheated for 7 to 8 minutes in a 400-degree oven.

VARIATIONS AND IMPROVISATIONS— If I'm cooking in Mexico, I often follow Mexican cooks who replace the 3 ounces of cheese that goes into the dough with ground *chicharrón prensado* (bought from those big cakes of cooked, pressed pigskin—there are bits of meat in there, too). In the States, I crumble up about ¾ cup of crunchy *chicharrón* (fried pork rind) to give a similar flavor. The Smoky Shredded Pork (page 150) is a substantial replacement for the fresh cheese, as is smoked fish or chicken or practically any melting cheese.

CRUSTY GRIDDLE-BAKED QUESADILLAS

Quesadillas Asadas

*Q*UESADILLAS ARE THE grilled cheese sandwiches of Mexico, so they should become part of your quick-to-prepare repertoire. Though you can make quesadillas with ready-made corn tortillas folded over melting cheese and toasted on a griddle, I prefer making them with homemade tortillas as they do throughout Central and Southern Mexico. Cooks simply lay a thin circle of dough onto the griddle, spread on the filling, fold it over and bake until crusty. It is a wonder of texture, from the remarkable chewy crust, to the soft *masa* inside, to the velvety cheese, sweet onion and spicy chile filling. Lace it all with a spoonful of tangy salsa and you've got a dish that truly captures the imagination.

MAKES 12 QUESADILLAS, SERVING 4 TO 6 AS A CASUAL MAIN DISH OR SNACK

FOR 2 CUPS ESSENTIAL ROASTED-POBLANO *RAJAS*

1 pound (6 medium-large) fresh poblano chiles

1 tablespoon vegetable or olive oil

1 large white onion, sliced ¼ inch thick

3 garlic cloves, peeled and finely chopped

1 teaspoon dried oregano, preferably Mexican

Salt, about ½ teaspoon

1 pound (2 cups) fresh masa *for tortillas*

OR 1¾ cups masa harina mixed with 1 cup plus 2 tablespoons hot water

2½ cups (about 10 ounces) shredded Mexican Chihuahua cheese, or other melting cheese such as brick or Monterey Jack

About 1 cup salsa (such as Essential Chopped Tomato-Serrano Salsa, page 25, or Essential Roasted Tomatillo-Serrano Salsa, page 42), for serving

1. *Making about 2 cups of the Essential Roasted-Poblano* **Rajas.** Roast the chiles directly over a gas flame or 4 inches below a very hot broiler until blackened on all sides, about 5 minutes for open flame, about 10 minutes for broiler. Cover with a kitchen towel and let stand 5 minutes. Peel, pull out the stem and seed pod, then rinse *briefly* to remove bits of skin and seeds. Slice into ¼-inch strips.

In a medium-size (8- to 9-inch) skillet, heat the oil over medium to medium-high, then add the onion and cook, stirring regularly, until nicely browned but still a little crunchy, about 5 minutes. Add the garlic and oregano, toss a minute longer, then stir in the chiles and just heat through. Taste and season with salt.

2. The quesadillas. Cut two squares of medium-heavy plastic (a garbage bag works well) to cover the plates of your tortilla press. If necessary, knead a few drops more water into the *masa* to give it the consistency of a soft cookie dough, then roll it into 12 balls. Cover with plastic. Divide the cheese into 12 equal portions; cover with plastic.

Turn on the oven to the lowest setting. Heat a large griddle or heavy skillet over medium. One by one, use the tortilla press to press out the dough between the two sheets of plastic, peel off the top sheet, then flip the uncovered side of the tortilla onto your hand (the top of the tortilla should align with your index finger, and fingers should be slightly spread to give support). Carefully peel off the plastic, then, with a gentle, swift motion, lay the tortilla on the hot griddle. Evenly sprinkle on a portion of the cheese, leaving a ½-inch border all around so cheese doesn't run out onto the griddle, then lay a portion of the *rajas* down the center. When the tortilla comes free from the griddle (it will take about 20 seconds), use a spatula to fold it in half, and gently press the edges together, more or less sealing them. Move the quesadilla to the side to continue baking as you begin the next one. Continue making and folding quesadillas, letting them bake on the griddle until crispy/crunchy and nicely browned (the *masa* on the inside will still be a little soft), 2 or 3 minutes in all. Keep finished quesadillas warm on a rack set on a baking pan in the oven.

When all are made, immediately line them up on a warm serving platter or wooden board or a basket lined with colored paper or a napkin, and serve with the salsa.

ADVANCE PREPARATION—*Rajas* can be made 2 days ahead; cover and refrigerate.

SHORTCUTS—The simplest quesadilla is made from a fresh store-bought corn or flour tortilla. A few slices of pickled jalapeño will spice it up. (If the corn tortilla is stale, it will toast up pretty hard.) Here's JeanMarie's method: Toast a store-bought tortilla on an open flame until warmed through, sprinkle on the cheese and *rajas,* fold over and microwave on high on a plate for 10 to 20 seconds, just to melt the cheese. They have to be served right away.

VARIATIONS AND IMPROVISATIONS—Of course, quesadillas can take practically any filling you are drawn to. For lunch at the restaurant we serve them filled with shredded duck and *rajas,* with grilled shrimp dashed with chopped canned chipotles, with grilled chicken dolloped with guacamole, and with braised wild mushrooms, poblano and *epazote.* At night, we make little appetizer ones from time to time, filled with *huitlacoche* or squash blossoms (that's very, very Mexico City).

OAXACAN GRIDDLE-BAKED TURNOVERS OF YELLOW *MOLE*

Empanadas de Mole Amarillo

*T*HESE EMPANADAS ARE probably *the* favorite, certainly *my* favorite, holiday street food in Oaxaca. They are made like the crusty, griddle-baked quesadillas of the previous recipe, which means they've got an earthy crustiness on the outside. Inside there's a wondrous filling of Oaxaca's yellow *mole* (*amarillo*), shredded chicken and anisey *hoja santa*—classic here, though lacking it, these empanadas are very good with sprigs of cilantro.

MAKES 12 EMPANADAS, SERVING 4 TO 6 AS A CASUAL MAIN DISH OR SNACK (YOU'LL HAVE ENOUGH LEFTOVER *MOLE* TO MAKE ANOTHER ROUND)

1 large garlic clove, unpeeled

4 dried guajillo chiles, stemmed and seeded

1 small ripe tomato

2 medium tomatillos, husked and rinsed

1 thick slice of white onion

A small pinch cloves, preferably freshly ground

1/4 teaspoon black pepper, preferably freshly ground

1 tablespoon vegetable oil or rich-tasting lard

1 cup chicken broth

1 pound (2 cups) plus 2 tablespoons fresh masa *for tortillas*

OR 1 3/4 cups plus 2 tablespoons masa harina

Salt, about 1 teaspoon, depending on the saltiness of the broth

Sugar, about 3/4 teaspoon

1 cup cooked, coarsely shredded chicken (page 181)

1 leaf hoja santa, *cut into twelve 2 x 1-inch pieces (or 24 cilantro sprigs)*

1. *Making 2 cups yellow* mole. Roast the unpeeled garlic on an ungreased griddle or heavy skillet over medium heat until soft (it will blacken in spots), about 15 minutes; cool and peel. While the garlic is roasting, toast the chiles on another side of the griddle or skillet: 1 or 2 at a time, open them flat and press down firmly on the hot surface with a spatula; in a few seconds, when they start to crackle, even send up a faint wisp of smoke, flip them and press down to toast the other side. In a small bowl, cover the chiles with hot water and let rehydrate 30 minutes, stirring frequently. Drain and discard the water.

Lay the tomato, tomatillos and onion on a baking sheet and place about 4 inches below a very hot broiler. When they blister, darken and soften on one side, 5 or 6 minutes, turn them and roast the other side. When cool enough to handle, peel the tomato and transfer to a food processor or blender, along with the tomatillos, onion and any juices on the baking sheet. Add the garlic, chiles, cloves and pepper, then process to a smooth puree, scraping and stirring every few seconds. If the mixture won't move through the blades, add a little water. Press the puree through a medium-mesh strainer into a bowl.

Heat the oil or lard in a small (1- to 2-quart) heavy saucepan over medium-high. When hot enough to make a drop of the puree sizzle fiercely, add it all at once and stir for about 5 minutes as the puree sears, concentrates and darkens. Stir in ¾ *cup* of the broth, partially cover and simmer over medium-low for 30 minutes, stirring occasionally.

Thoroughly combine the remaining ¼ *cup* of the broth with the 2 tablespoons fresh or dried *masa,* then strain it through a small strainer into the simmering *mole.* Whisk vigorously to keep any lumps from forming. Taste and season with salt and sugar; cool.

2. *The empanadas.* If using *masa harina,* mix the remaining 1¾ *cups* with 1 cup plus 2 tablespoons hot water in a large bowl and let stand 20 minutes. Cut 2 pieces of plastic (preferably the weight of a plastic garbage bag) to cover the plates of your tortilla press. If necessary, knead a few drops of water into the *masa* (fresh or the reconstituted) to give it the consistency of a soft cookie dough, then roll into 12 balls. Cover with plastic. Set the *mole,* shredded chicken, and *hoja santa* pieces (or cilantro sprigs) near the cooking surface.

Turn on the oven to the lowest setting. Heat a large griddle or heavy skillet, over medium. One by one, use the tortilla press to press out the dough between the two sheets of plastic, peel off the top sheet, then flip the tortilla onto your hand, exposed side down. Carefully peel off the plastic, then, with a gentle, swift motion, lay the tortilla on the hot griddle. Evenly sprinkle on a generous tablespoon of the *mole,* a few shreds of chicken and a piece of *hoja santa* or 2 cilantro sprigs. Work quickly so that before the top surface of the tortilla has dried out, you can fold it over to encase the filling. With seasoned fingers or the back of a spoon, press the edges together to seal as best you can (it won't seal completely).

Move the empanada to the side to finish baking as you begin another one. Continue making empanadas, letting them bake on the griddle, turning regularly, until nicely crispy/crunchy and lightly browned (the *masa* on the inside will still be a little soft), 2 to 3 minutes total. Keep the finished empanadas warm on a rack set on a baking sheet in the oven. When all are done, serve the empanadas in a basket or on a warm platter lined with bright tissue paper or a napkin.

ADVANCE PREPARATION—Yellow *mole* keeps, refrigerated and covered, several days.

SHORTCUTS—You may choose to simply warm the *mole,* chicken and herbs together and use them to make soft tacos with fresh tortillas (steam-heat them, page 145)

VARIATIONS AND IMPROVISATIONS—This thick version of *amarillo* (as well as its beef-and-vegetable soupy cousin) can be made with the classic combination of *chile chilhuacle amarillo* and *chile costeño amarillo*, though these exotic yellowish dried chiles are expensive, even in Oaxaca. I've only very rarely seen either in the United States. Their nutty complexity and remarkable heat, of course, can't be easily replicated, but in Oaxaca a redder version of *amarillo* is often made with straight guajillo. Many call this version *amarillo rojo*, "yellow-red *mole*." Three or 4 *chilhuacles amarillos* and 3 or 4 *costeños amarillos* can replace the guajillos I've called for in this recipe. As with the griddle-baked quesadillas of the previous recipe, you may elect to vary the fillings: 2 cups Brick Red *Mole* (page 247) or the Simple Red *Mole* (page 178), plus other cooked, shredded meats, pork in particular. I love yellow mole with fish, so I'd replace the chicken in the main recipe with flaked smoked fish.

Mexican Melting Cheese

Stateside we often think of Mexican food as the stuff under an oozing blanket of cheese. But most dishes in Mexico are cheeseless, or simply sprinkled with some crumbled fresh or aged cheese—neither of which melt. Their predominance is understandable for two reasons: In developing Mexico, fresh and aged crumbly cheese is a simple cottage industry, and the traditional cuisine doesn't rely on ovens or broilers needed to melt cheese.

Mexico's most famous melting cheese is Chihuahua, a Cheshire-style cheese that resembles a mild cheddar, a flavorful brick or Monterey Jack. In the state of Chihuahua it is called *queso menonita*, because the cheese was introduced by Mennonites who immigrated there just over half a century ago. Chihuahua is the cheese used in the very popular Northern *queso fundido* or *enchiladas suizas* (Swiss enchiladas). To get that same gooey melt, try Sonoma Jack; see Sources, page 425.

There are rich melting cheeses called *asaderos* in Northern Mexico. A particularly unctuous one in Sinaloa is called *quesadilla;* it makes tortilla turnovers (quesadillas) famous.

Among my other favorite melting cheeses are the real Edam cheese you can buy in Yucatan (its availabil-

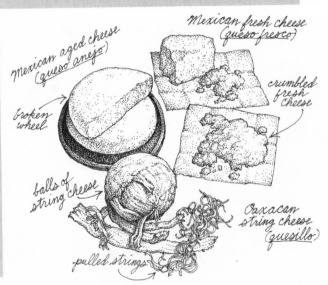

mexican aged cheese (queso añejo)

Mexican fresh cheese (queso fresco)

crumbled fresh cheese

broken wheel

balls of string cheese

Oaxacan string cheese (quesillo)

pulled strings

ity is an international trade quirk of fate) and an aged mozzarellalike cheese with a rich butter center made in Chiapas. Two great cheeses that are sold very fresh and won't melt much (though both are used to make quesadillas) are the *panela* from West-Central Mexico (try some if you go to Guadalajara or San Miguel de Allende) and the oh-so-popular, rich and tangy *quesillo* (string cheese) from Oaxaca.

· ·

Epazote

I could never understand this pungent (some say "stinky") herb until it moved in, quite literally, to a garden near my apartment in Los Angeles years ago. I rubbed my hands in it daily, a sort of culinary wrestling match I guess, until I thought I had it pegged.

Now *epazote* is part of the family, so I don't notice its brash ways as much. If it were gone, I'd miss it in my black beans, *Mole de Olla* (page 122) and Oaxacan Green *Mole* (page 290). But this native Mexican herb speaks only Spanish (maybe a little Aztec), so you'll have to work a little to understand it.

If this is your first time using *epazote,* think that you're holding an herb with the aggressiveness of fresh rosemary, the pungent assertiveness of cilantro and the tenacity of anise. First encountering it as a fresh garnish won't be as comfortable as encountering it in a long-simmered pot of beans, where its more subtle side shines.

Many Mexican markets carry either the green or purple varieties, but I don't detect a lot of difference in their flavors. Because *epazote* is a sturdy leaf that's generally cooked into a dish, don't worry if it is slightly wilted. *Epazote* is very easy to grow (see Sources, page 425). Whole sprigs can be frozen for use in cooked dishes; you'll need to double the quantity of fresh that's called for, because the flavor dissipates.

In my opinion, dried *epazote* is right for medicinal tea, not for cooking.

Stats: A large sprig of *epazote* is about 12 inches long and an average leaf is 2½ inches long.

· ·

about 2½ inches long.

epazote

TORTILLA CASSEROLES

. . . . .

Layered tortilla casseroles are made like lasagna, with tortillas replacing the noodles. But being Mexican, they sport a completely different array of flavors and textures. Most commonly, cold tortillas are quick-fried, blotted dry and layered with tomato or tomatillo sauce, vegetables, greens, meat, cheese—basically whatever you like and whatever's on hand.

My two layered casseroles here couldn't be more different. The first, *Tamal Azteca*, is the most lasagnalike (I've chosen an all-vegetable filling layered with Essential Quick-Cooked Tomato-Chipotle Sauce). You can vary the recipe to suit a spice-loving crowd or tone it down to the point hardly anyone will recognize it as Mexican.

My second casserole, *Budín al Pasilla*, is as stunning in its flavor as it is in appearance. Warm tortillas are layered with a reverberatingly rich and spicy pasilla chile sauce that's almost black. Spread black beans and white soured cream into the construction and you'll have a dramatic, though casual, dish that will really impress folks that enjoy full-flavored food. The overall texture will seem a bit more puddinglike (because the tortillas aren't fried) than that of the more sturdy *Tamal Azteca*.

Chilaquiles sounded strange to me before I ate them. Crispy tortilla chips simmered with a sauce? Damp and mushy, no? When they're done right, the tortillas soften nicely and take on the personality of the sauce. With a drizzle of cream, a sprinkling of cheese and a dollop of black beans to the side, they make me a very happy eater.

Chilaquiles are the most common tortilla casserole in Mexico, since they're simple and quick. They are typically served for *almuerzo* (that late-morning breakfast-brunch-lunch) and for supper, mostly made with tomato or tomatillo sauce. Here I give a spicy, red chile version to suit my readers who like that side of life (these are without a doubt my very favorite *chilaquiles*), plus a soulfully satisfying black bean version that's got bits of smoky chipotle and *epazote* simmered with the tortillas. Because *chilaquiles* are rich by nature, I suggest saving them for a special supper or brunch.

Though it's not exactly a tortilla casserole, the Crusty Baked Tamal is made with tortilla dough and it is a casserole. It offers a spicy, meaty filling encased in a tender, corny dough. If you haven't made tamales before, at least get started by learning this dough. It's exactly the one used for steamed tamales, though in this recipe, you simply pile it into a casserole dish or pie pan and bake.

LAYERED TORTILLA-TOMATO CASSEROLE
WITH GREENS AND MELTED CHEESE

Tamal Azteca

A SQUARE OF THIS cheesy, vegetable-laden casserole is a welcome lunch or supper dish. It has flavors and textures that draw you back time and again—a fact I know since it seems we have to make double at the restaurant to have enough for staff orders.

This dish is a classic that goes by names from *budín de tortillas* (tortilla pudding) to *budín Moctezuma* (Montezuma's pudding) to my favorite, *Tamal Azteca*. You can be sure that it's of fairly recent invention (pre-Columbian nomenclature notwithstanding), because home baking ovens didn't start becoming common until the 1940s. It's lasagnalike in its layerings and I suggest you serve it just in the same way—with a green salad as a main dish for an informal meal or in smaller squares with extra sauce dribbled around it as a first course.

The essentials here are the tortillas (quick-fried to make them pliable, yet keep them from disintegrating into the sauce), the sauce and the cheese. Everything else is up to you.

SERVES 8 AS A MAIN DISH, 12 TO 16 AS AN ACCOMPANIMENT

FOR 6 CUPS ESSENTIAL QUICK-COOKED TOMATO-CHIPOTLE SAUCE

9 to 12 (about ¾ ounce total) stemmed, dried chipotle chiles (or canned chipotle chiles en adobo)

12 garlic cloves, unpeeled

4½ pounds (9 medium-large round or 28 to 34 plum) ripe tomatoes

2 tablespoons plus ½ cup vegetable oil

Salt, about 1¾ teaspoons

4 cups (about 6 ounces) loosely packed, stemmed lamb's quarters (quelites)

OR *6 cups loosely packed spinach or ½-inch-long sliced chard leaves (you'll need a 12-ounce bunch)*

2 medium (12 ounces total) zucchini, cut into ¼-inch dice

2 medium ears corn, husked, kernels cut from the cob

OR *1½ cups frozen corn kernels, defrosted*

1 pound (about 4 cups) shredded Mexican Chihuahua cheese or other melting cheese such as brick or Monterey Jack

16 corn tortillas, preferably slightly stale factory-made ones

About ⅓ cup chopped fresh cilantro, for garnish

1. *Making 6 cups of Essential Quick-Cooked Tomato-Chipotle Sauce.* For dried chiles, toast them on an ungreased griddle or skillet over medium heat, turning regularly and pressing flat with a spatula, until very aromatic, about 30 seconds. In a small bowl, cover the chiles with hot water and let rehydrate 30 minutes, stirring frequently to ensure even soaking. Drain and discard the water. (Simply remove canned chiles from their canning sauce.)

While the chiles are soaking, roast the unpeeled garlic on the griddle or skillet, turning occasionally, until soft (they will blacken in spots), about 15 minutes; cool and peel. Roast the tomatoes on a baking sheet 4 inches below a very hot broiler until blackened on one side, about 6 minutes, then turn and roast the other side. Cool, then peel, collecting all the juices with the tomatoes.

Working in batches, in a food processor or blender, process the tomatoes with their juices, rehydrated or canned chiles and garlic to a medium-fine puree. Heat 2 *tablespoons* of the oil in a medium-size (4-quart) heavy pot (such as a Dutch oven or a Mexican *cazuela*) over medium-high heat. Add the tomato puree and stir nearly constantly for 8 to 10 minutes as it sears and thickens. Taste and season with salt, usually about 1½ teaspoons.

2. *The vegetables.* In a vegetable steamer, steam the lamb's quarters (or other greens), covered, until tender, 3 to 5 minutes for the lamb's quarters, 2 to 3 minutes for the spinach or chard. Immediately spread out on a baking sheet to cool, then roughly chop. Steam the diced zucchini until just tender, 2 to 3 minutes, then spread out to cool. Sprinkle the vegetables with ¼ teaspoon of the salt. Set out the corn, tomato sauce and shredded cheese.

3. *The tortillas.* Pour the remaining ½ *cup* of the oil into a small skillet and set over medium heat. Line a baking sheet with several layers of paper towels. When the oil is hot, quick-fry the tortillas one at a time for a few seconds per side, just to soften them. Drain the tortillas in a single layer on the paper towels, blotting them dry. Cut them in half.

4. *Making the casserole.* Turn on the oven to 350 degrees. Lightly grease a 13 x 9-inch baking dish. Spread a thin layer of the sauce over the bottom, then lay out 8 tortilla halves in a single layer, arranging them to cover as much sauce as possible. Evenly spread on the greens, a scant 1½ *cups* of the remaining sauce and 1 *cup* of the cheese. Top with another layer of 8 tortilla halves. Spread on the corn and the same amount of sauce and cheese. Top with a third layer of 8 tortilla halves, the zucchini and another round of sauce (1½ cups) and cheese (1 cup). Top with the remaining tortilla halves, sauce and cheese.

Cover lightly with foil and bake for 25 minutes. Uncover and bake for an additional 10 to 15 minutes, until bubbling and lightly browned. Let stand a few minutes before cutting into squares. Sprinkle with the chopped cilantro, then use a spatula (a squared-off metal one works best) to transfer the pieces to warm serving plates.

ADVANCE PREPARATION—The recipe can be made a couple of days ahead through step 2; refrigerate all the parts in separate covered containers. If baked a day ahead and rewarmed, it will have a more solid texture.

Shortcuts—The sauce can be prepared with three 28-ounce cans of good-quality plum tomatoes without losing much quality (only a little roasty flavor). About 1½ (10-ounce) packages of frozen chopped spinach (defrosted and well-drained) could replace the greens.

Variations and Improvisations—When it comes to sauce, 6 cups of practically any sauce fits here; I like Essential Simmered Tomatillo-Serrano Sauce (page 38) and Essential Simmered Tomato-Jalapeño Sauce (page 18). You may even find a bottled sauce you like (most you'll have to thin a little to get the right consistency). A cup or so of quick-fried mushrooms can be added in place of or in addition to other vegetables. And meat (anything from cooked, coarse-ground beef to chorizo and chicken) can always be worked in.

GUAJILLO *CHILAQUILES*
WITH THICK CREAM, AGED CHEESE AND WHITE ONION
Chilaquiles al Guajillo

*I*F YOU'VE NEVER had *chilaquiles,* you're in for a treat. They are my favorite Mexican soul food—a homey pot of slightly chewy tortillas simmered up with forthright flavors. Think of them as the Mexican equivalent of a rustic pasta dish (they have that same elemental ability to satisfy), but served more for *almuerzo* (the late morning breakfast or brunch) than at a special dinner.

Guajillo-sauced *chilaquiles* are not as common as tomatillo- or tomato-sauced ones in Mexico. Personally, I like the concentrated pungency of this version's red-chile sauce, though you can feel free to substitute another sauce. Classic Mexican Fried Beans (page 237) are the traditional accompaniment to *chilaquiles.* In some places in Mexico, scrambled or fried eggs are part of the mix, and in many places, shredded chicken is added along with the chips.

SERVES 4 AS A MAIN DISH, 6 AS A SIDE DISH

FOR 2 1/2 CUPS ESSENTIAL SIMMERED GUAJILLO SAUCE

6 garlic cloves, unpeeled

16 medium-large (about 4 ounces total) dried guajillo chiles, stemmed and seeded

1 teaspoon dried oregano, preferably Mexican

1/4 teaspoon black pepper, preferably freshly ground

1/8 teaspoon cumin, preferably freshly ground

5 1/3 cups chicken or beef broth

1 1/2 tablespoons vegetable oil or rich-tasting pork lard

Salt, about 1 teaspoon, depending on the saltiness of the broth

Sugar, about 1 1/2 teaspoons

8 ounces (about 8 loosely packed cups) tortilla chips (store-bought or homemade, page 87), preferably ones that are not too thin

1/4 cup Thick Cream (page 165), crème fraîche or sour cream thinned with a little milk for garnish

1/4 cup finely crumbled Mexican queso añejo, dry feta or Parmesan

1 small white onion, thinly sliced, for garnish

About 1/2 cup cilantro leaves, for garnish

1. *Making 2 1/2 cups of Essential Guajillo Sauce.* Roast the unpeeled garlic directly on an ungreased griddle or heavy skillet over medium heat until soft (they'll blacken in spots),

about 15 minutes; cool and peel. While the garlic is roasting, toast the chiles on another side of the griddle or skillet: 1 or 2 at a time, open them flat and press down firmly on the hot surface with a spatula; when they crackle, even send up a wisp of smoke, flip them and press down to toast the other side. In a small bowl, cover the chiles with hot water and let rehydrate 30 minutes, stirring frequently. Drain and discard the water.

Combine the oregano, black pepper and cumin in a food processor or blender, along with the drained chiles, garlic and ⅔ *cup* of the broth. Blend to a smooth puree, scraping and stirring every few seconds. (If the mixture won't go through the blender blades, add a little more liquid.) Press through a medium-mesh strainer into a small bowl.

Heat the oil in a heavy, medium-size (4-quart) pot (such as a Dutch oven or Mexican *cazuela*) over medium-high heat. When hot enough to make a drop of the puree sizzle sharply, add the puree all at once, and stir constantly until it reduces into a thick paste, 5 to 7 minutes. Stir in 3 *cups* of the broth, partially cover, and simmer over medium-low heat, stirring occasionally, for 45 minutes. If necessary, add more broth to bring the sauce to a medium consistency. Taste and season with salt and sugar.

2. The chilaquiles. Add the remaining 1⅔ *cups* of broth to the guajillo sauce, heat to a boil, then add the tortilla chips. Stir to coat the chips well, then rapidly boil over medium-high heat, stirring frequently, until the chips have softened (but still retain a little chewiness), and the sauce has reduced to a medium consistency, 2 to 3 minutes for thinner chips, 4 to 5 minutes for thicker chips.

Spoon the *chilaquiles* into a warm, deep serving platter (there should be enough sauce to pool around them), drizzle with the cream, sprinkle with the cheese and strew with the onion and cilantro leaves. Serve right away, since *chilaquiles* loose their texture quickly.

ADVANCE PREPARATION—The guajillo sauce keeps nicely, covered and refrigerated, for several days.

SHORTCUTS—Buying 8 ounces packaged chips is a time saver; choose thick ones for the best texture. Using 2½ cups of leftover or purchased sauce or salsa is an option, though you may have to adjust the broth to suit the thickness of what you're using.

VARIATIONS AND IMPROVISATIONS—The guajillo sauce is commonly replaced with 2½ cups of Essential Simmered Tomatillo-Serrano Sauce (page 38) or Essential Simmered Tomato-Jalapeño Sauce (page 18). Whole *epazote* leaves are typical in both the tomatillo and tomato versions, but I like to add 2 cups (packed) sliced chard or lamb's quarter (*quelites*) to the mix as well. Flaking grilled or smoked fish over the dish is delicious, as are shreds of grilled or poached chicken.

BLACK BEAN CHILAQUILES
WITH SMOKY CHIPOTLE

Chilaquiles de Frijol Negro

*I*F CHILAQUILES ARE Mexican soul food, then black bean *chilaquiles* are the most soulful of all. Black bean *chilaquiles,* which are most commonly featured in Veracruz, served with a hearty green salad and a dark beer or limeade, make a memorable meatless meal. Or simmer up a batch to put out as a family-style accompaniment at your next barbecue.

SERVES 4 AS A MAIN DISH, 6 AS A SIDE DISH

1¼ cups (about 8 ounces) dried black beans, cleaned

About 6 cups chicken or beef broth or water

½ medium white onion, roughly chopped

4 garlic cloves, peeled and roughly chopped

4 sprigs of epazote, *if you can get them*

3 canned chipotle chiles en adobo, plus 2 teaspoons tomatoey adobo from the can

Salt, about 1 teaspoon, depending on the saltiness of the broth

8 ounces (about 8 loosely packed cups) tortilla chips (store-bought or homemade, page 87), preferably ones that are not too thin

½ cup Thick Cream (page 165), crème fraîche *or sour cream thinned with a little milk*

¼ cup finely crumbled Mexican queso añejo, *dry feta or Parmesan*

1 small ripe avocado, peeled, pitted and cut into ½-inch cubes, for garnish

1. *The beans.* Rinse the beans, then scoop into a medium (4-quart) pot. Measure in 5 *cups* of the broth or water, the onion, garlic and *1 sprig* of the *epazote.* Cut the chipotle chiles lengthwise in half, scrape out the seeds and slice into thin strips. Add ⅓ of the chiles to the beans; set aside the remainder. Bring beans to a boil, then simmer, partially covered, over medium to medium-low heat, until the beans are thoroughly tender, about 2 hours. (If necessary, add a little extra water during the cooking to keep the beans completely submerged.)

In batches in a food processor or *loosely covered* blender, puree the bean mixture and all the liquid; transfer to a large (10- to 12-inch) skillet. Stir in enough broth or water (it may take an extra cup or so) to bring the bean sauce to the consistency of a *thin* cream soup. Taste and season with salt.

2. *The* chilaquiles. Bring the black bean sauce to a boil over medium heat. Add the tortilla chips, 8 good-size leaves plucked from *2 sprigs* of the *epazote* and another *third* of the chipotle chiles. Stir to coat the chips well, then rapidly boil over medium-high heat, stirring frequently, until the chips have softened (but still retain a little chewiness), and the sauce has reduced to a medium consistency, 2 to 3 minutes for thinner chips and 4 to 5 minutes for thicker chips.

Scoop the *chilaquiles* onto a warm, deep serving platter (a 10-inch deep-dish pie plate or small Mexican *cazuela* works well). Drizzle with the cream, sprinkle with cheese, and the remaining chipotle chiles, dot with the avocado and lastly strew with a few roughly chopped *epazote* leaves. Serve without hesitation.

ADVANCE PREPARATION—The beans may be cooked several days in advance.

SHORTCUTS—Although the finished dish will not be as dramatcally black, you can substitute two 16-ounce cans black beans (with their liquid) for the dried beans; puree as directed in step 1 along with a third of the chiles and broth or water as needed. Taste and season with salt, then proceed with step 2.

VARIATIONS AND IMPROVISATIONS

The family of Geno Bahena, one of our longtime chefs at Frontera Grill and Topolobampo, makes these *chilaquiles* by first softly scrambling an egg with the chips (don't let it completely set), then adding the sauce and continuing. I like to vary the chile flavor to pasilla or guajillo, simmering some with the beans, then crumbling a little crisply toasted chile on top. Because of my passion for shrimp and black beans, I love black bean *chilaquiles* strewn with coarsely chopped grilled shrimp.

***Dressed-up* Chilaquiles de Frijol Negro**—Slice 12 tortillas into ¼-inch strips, fry them as directed on page 117 and use these fried strips to prepare the *chilaquiles* through step 2. When the *chilaquiles* are ready, set four 3-inch metal rings (tuna cans with both ends cut out work well) onto 4 warm dinner plates. Spoon into the rings, packing them in lightly. Ladle ½ cup Essential Quick-Cooked Tomato-Chipotle Sauce (page 34) around each ring; remove the rings. Garnish with sour cream, chiles, avocado and *epazote*.

LAYERED PASILLA-TORTILLA CASSEROLE
WITH BLACK BEANS AND THICK CREAM

Budín al Pasilla

*T*HIS GUTSY, SPICY, layered tortilla casserole is my spin on some delectable *chilaquiles* my former assistant, *michoacana* Priscila Franco Satkoff, made for me. I've transformed them and their black bean accompaniment into a layering of hot tortillas, beans, sauce and garnishes. The result is what I'd call a near perfect balance of jubilant (or is it raucous?) flavors. Most tortilla casserole recipes call for the tortillas to be quick-fried, as they are in my *Tamal Azteca* (page 201), to make them less likely to fall apart. I chose quick-heating them on a flame or griddle because I want a lighter, almost puddinglike dish with a lilting texture.

SERVES 4 TO 6 AS A CASUAL MAIN DISH

FOR ⅔ CUP ESSENTIAL BOLD PASILLA
SEASONING PASTE

½ *small head of garlic, broken apart but not peeled*

6 *medium (about 2 ounces) dried pasilla chiles, stemmed and seeded*

1 *teaspoon dried oregano, preferably Mexican*

¼ *teaspoon black pepper, preferably freshly ground*

⅛ *teaspoon cumin, preferably freshly ground*

2 *tablespoons vegetable or olive oil*

1½ *cups chicken or beef broth*

Salt, *about 1½ teaspoons*

1 *small white onion, diced*

2 *cups seasoned, cooked black beans (either canned or homemade, page 234)*

6 *corn tortillas*

½ *cup Thick Cream (page 165), crème fraîche or sour cream thinned with a little milk*

½ *cup shredded Mexican Chihuahua cheese or other melting cheese such as brick or Monterey Jack*

A *few cilantro leaves, thinly sliced white onion and thinly sliced radishes, for garnish*

1. *Making ⅔ cup Essential Bold Pasilla Seasoning Paste.* Roast the unpeeled garlic on an ungreased griddle or heavy skillet over medium heat, turning occasionally, until soft (they will blacken in spots), about 15 minutes; cool and peel. While the garlic is roasting, toast the chiles on another side of the griddle or skillet: 1 or 2 at a time, open them flat and press down firmly on the hot surface with a spatula; in a few seconds, when they crackle, even send up a wisp of smoke, flip them and press down to toast the other side. In a small bowl,

cover the chiles with hot water and let rehydrate 30 minutes, stirring frequently to ensure even soaking. Drain, *reserving ⅓ cup of the soaking water.*

In a food processor or blender, combine the chiles, garlic, oregano, pepper and cumin and the reserved soaking water. Blend to a smooth puree, scraping down and stirring frequently. (If necessary, add a little water to get the mixture moving.)

2. *The sauce.* With a rubber spatula, work the pasilla seasoning through a medium-mesh strainer into a bowl. Heat *1 tablespoon* of the oil in a large (4-quart) heavy saucepan over medium-high. When hot enough to make a drop of the seasoning sizzle, add it all at once. Cook, stirring constantly, until dark and very thick, about 5 minutes. Stir in the broth and simmer, partially covered, for 30 minutes. Taste and season with salt, usually ½ to 1 teaspoon, depending on the saltiness of the broth. Keep warm over low heat.

3. *The beans.* While the sauce is simmering, in a medium-size skillet over medium heat, cook the onion in the remaining *1 tablespoon* of the oil until browned, about 8 minutes. Add beans and, using a bean or potato masher or the back of a large spoon, mash to a coarse puree. Add water or bean broth to thin beans, if necessary, to an easily spoonable (but not at all runny) consistency. Taste and season with salt (if the beans weren't seasoned at the end of cooking). Cover and keep warm.

4. *The tortillas.* One at a time, lightly toast the tortillas directly over a gas flame or on a heated griddle or skillet until warmed through, about 10 seconds per side. Stack the tortillas as they are heated, wrapping them in a thick towel to keep warm.

5. *Making the casserole.* Turn the oven to 350 degrees. Cut the tortillas in half. Spoon about ⅓ cup of the sauce over the bottom of a lightly oiled 8 x 8-inch baking dish. Cover with 4 tortilla halves, fitting them in to cover as much of the sauce as possible (while overlapping as little as possible). Top with the beans, another layer of tortilla halves, ⅔ cup of the sauce, *half* of the cream and *half* of the cheese. Make a final layer with the remaining tortilla halves, remaining sauce, cream and cheese. Bake, uncovered, until bubbly, about 20 minutes. Let stand for a few minutes to firm up, then cut into squares. Strew with cilantro leaves, onion slices and radish slices. Scoop out pieces onto warm plates (using a squared-off metal spatula makes the job easy) and they're ready to serve.

ADVANCE PREPARATION—The sauce can be made several days ahead; cover and refrigerate. If the *budín* is baked ahead, the texture will be compact and homogeneous.

CRUSTY BAKED TAMAL

Tamal de Cazuela

*I*F YOU LIKE the tender texture and rich, corny flavor of good tamales, but you can't imagine spending all the time forming, filling and wrapping them in cornhusks or banana leaves, a baked tamal, cut into wedges, may entice you into the kitchen. It has the rich moistness of a traditional tamal but with a crusty exterior; it goes together quickly and welcomes just about any filling. Serve with Mushroom-Cactus Soup (page 128) and Chicken in Pueblan Green Pumpkin Seed Sauce (page 316). Or serve it as the focal point of a light meal with a simple soup (Rustic Ranch-Style Soup, page 126, would be a good choice) and a green salad.

I'd suggest you try to find fresh *masa* and specify that it be coarse-ground if possible. If finding the *masa* doesn't coincide with your plans to make this tamal, freeze the *masa* until you're ready. Made from *masa harina,* the tamal will be very good, just a little less light. Lard is not only traditional, but it's the most delicious option (and healthier for you than butter). Vegetable shortening has no cholesterol, though it turns out a rather bland tamal and one that, according to some nutritionists, may not really be much better for you than the lard.

SERVES 8 AS A FIRST COURSE, 4 TO 5 AS A CASUAL MAIN DISH

6 ounces (about ¾) cup rich-tasting lard (or vegetable shortening if you want to), chilled

1½ teaspoons baking powder

1½ pounds (about 3 cups) cool, coarse-ground masa for tamales

OR 3 cups masa harina for tamales mixed with 1¾ cups hot water

About 1 cup cool chicken broth

Salt, about 1 generous teaspoon

2 cups of practically any Mexican sauce or mole—I especially like Simmered Tomatillo-Serrano Sauce (page 38), Simmered Guajillo Sauce (page 57) and Brick-Red Mole (page 247)

1 generous cup coarsely shredded, cooked chicken, pork or beef

1. *The batter.* With an electric mixer, beat the lard or other shortening with the baking powder in a large bowl until light in texture, about 1 minute. Continue beating as you add the *masa* (fresh or reconstituted) in three additions. Slowly beat in a generous ¾ *cup* of the broth. Continue beating for another minute or so, until a ½-teaspoon dollop of the dough floats in a cup of cold water.

Beat in enough additional broth to give the mixture the consistency of soft (not runny) cake batter (it should hold its shape in a spoon). Season with salt (which, yes, will involve tasting a little of the raw batter), usually a generous teaspoon, depending on the saltiness of the broth.

2. *Finishing the tamal.* Turn on the oven to 400 degrees. Combine ¾ *cup* of the sauce with the shredded chicken or meat in a small dish. Spread half of the batter into a greased earthenware *cazuela* or a 10-inch pie plate. Spoon the meat mixture evenly over the batter, then spoon on the remaining batter to cover the filling.

Bake in the upper third of the oven for 25 minutes. Then reduce the oven temperature to 300 degrees. Cover the top of the tamal lightly with foil and continue baking until the center springs back when pressed lightly and the top is golden brown, about 20 minutes. (If you'd like the top of the tamal a little browner, increase the oven temperature to 450 degrees and brown, uncovered, in the hot oven for a few minutes.) Let stand a few minutes before cutting into wedges and serving with a spoon or two of the remaining sauce.

ADVANCE PREPARATION—The finished tamal can be made several hours in advance. Reheat in a 400-degree oven before serving.

VARIATIONS AND IMPROVISATIONS—This skeleton of a recipe encourages you to flesh out the details to suit your own taste. Don't overlook layering in wild mushrooms or wilted greens, or even popular ingredients like olives, arugula, dried tomatoes and fresh herbs. Occasionally, I bake these in small *cazuelas,* soufflé cups or straight-sided gratin dishes and serve them directly in the dish. Reduce the cooking time to about 30 minutes.

CHAPTER FIVE

. . . . .

VEGETABLE, BEAN, RICE AND EGG DISHES

A MEXICAN DINNER PLATE ISN'T COMPOSED OF A MEAT, A GREEN VEGETABLE AND A STARCH, which, admittedly, is hard for most of us Americans to deal with. How do we plan a menu when there's no list of potato dishes, no broccoli, asparagus or greenbean dishes to choose from? Besides, do we really want to eat from a cuisine that's lacking in vegetables?

Let's think a little deeper. Maybe you have walked through those markets in Mexico and seen the thrilling displays of dead-ripe tomatoes; piles of tomatillos, green chiles, white onions and purple garlic; huge bundles of vibrant greens; bins of potatoes and carrots; stacks of unblemished zucchini and just-harvested cactus. Why is it all there? What becomes of all these vegetables in a cuisine that doesn't feature vegetables?

The simple answer is that they wind up right on that dinner plate, though not in forms that we easily recognize. Add the fact that Mexico is a developing country, and, as is true in most developing countries, a diet of vegetables, grains and legumes is the focus of private everyday rural eating, while meat is celebrated on special occasions such as baptisms, birthdays, Sundays and in special-occasion places like restaurants (which is where most tourists eat). It's no wonder most of us don't understand vegetables in the Mexican kitchen.

Two places where vegetables are used most in the Mexican kitchen, in my experience, are hearty soups (what we'd call brothy stews) and sauces (including salsa and relishy condiments). The soups are a meal in a bowl; many are so simple, they don't even show up in cookbooks. The sauces (salsas and so forth) are Mexico's expression of its national culinary identity, and so fill many cookbook pages and endless hours of impassioned discussion. They are made almost entirely of vegetables, plus nuts and seeds, rather than stocks, cream and butter as in much of European cooking. They're served generously. In Mexico, there's more emphasis on sauce than on meat in many dishes.

Vegetables are also the focus of many simple meals, where they're rolled into tortillas to make soft tacos. Sometimes these vegetable taco fillings contain a little meat, which, again, makes them hard for us Americans to categorize. Are they meat dishes or vegetable dishes? Accompaniments or main courses? When you read Mexican cookbooks, it's clear that our categories just don't fit. Mexican cooks are used to homey dishes that are mostly vegetables and served as main dishes (nutritionists have been trying to teach us how to eat like this for the last decade in the United States).

Now, the ways in which Mexican cooks serve rice and beans are easier for us Americans to understand. Both are starches and we have a sense of their usefulness as accompaniments as well as the foundation of main dishes. Egg dishes, while certainly not completely focused on vegetables, grains or legumes, fit nicely, I think, with the other meatless or little-meat main dishes we've grouped together here.

So this is a chapter of possibilities. You certainly won't *just* find accompaniments here. Rather, you have starters, main dishes, accompaniments and snacks, all with a focus that isn't meat, all that celebrate the bounty of Mexican soil.

VEGETABLES

· · · · ·

I've chosen to start out this collection of recipes with the vegetable-plus-a-little-meat main dishes; each has a special flavor and is pretty much a complete meal, if you add a stack of warm corn tortillas. First there's a *tinga,* that delicious simmering of toasted tomatoes, chile and chorizo—here flavoring zucchini rather than the typical pork or chicken. Pumpkin is native to Mexico, and its flavor and texture are perfect braised with a little pork and chipotle chiles.

If you simply like Mexican flavors and are looking for a vegetable to serve with roast beef, pork or chicken, you'll be happy choosing from the Roasted Vegetables in Green Sesame *Pipián* (an herby traditional sauce over a mix of vegetables), Crusty Chayote Casserole (it's spicy with roasted poblanos and rich with cheese) or Chile-Glazed Sweet Potatoes (they'll make you think of Thanksgiving dinner, if your Thanksgiving includes ancho chiles and roasted garlic). Though these dishes are perfect accompaniments, most would also be welcome as a main dish.

I definitely think of the Browned Vermicelli with Roasted Tomato, Zucchini and Aged Cheese as a delicious main dish, though in Mexico it is served commonly as a first course in place of soup. Here I've chosen a typical version that simmers the browned noodles with roasted tomatoes and smoky chiles, but I've included some special-occasion garnishes like cream, cheese and chorizo; I think you'll just love it. The final recipe, Crusty Lentil Cakes, are always served as a main dish, to my knowledge. They are thought of as being different from most Mexican bean preparations, so I've grouped them with other vegetable main dishes. The lentils are cooked until completely tender (hence moldable), mixed with cilantro and grilled onion, then coated with the classic Mexican egg-and-crumb breading, crisped in olive oil and served with spoonfuls of salsa.

SEARED ZUCCHINI WITH ROASTED TOMATO, CHIPOTLE AND CHORIZO

Tinga de Calabacitas

*I*N CENTRAL MEXICO, especially Puebla, this full-flavored stew of roasted tomatoes, chipotles and garlic flavors everything from pork and chicken to mushrooms and vegetables. In short, it seems you can make a *tinga* of practically everything. Though the chicken and pork versions are most common, I'm taken with this vegetable one I came across in *La cocina mexicana Océano*, a three-volume encyclopedia of Mexican cooking; its recipe has bits of pork rather than the chorizo I prefer here. This *tinga* makes an attractive main dish to serve with tortillas for soft tacos, on pasta or with roast chicken. Perhaps you'd like to start with a warming bowl of Mexican-Style Sweet Roasted Garlic Soup (page 120).

**MAKES 3 CUPS, 6 SERVINGS AS AN APPETIZER OR SIDE DISH,
4 SERVINGS AS A SMALL MAIN COURSE**

FOR 1 CUP ESSENTIAL QUICK-COOKED TOMATO-CHIPOTLE SAUCE BASE

1 to 2 stemmed, dried chipotle chiles (or canned chipotle chiles en adobo)

2 garlic cloves, unpeeled

12 ounces (2 medium-small round or 4 to 5 plum) ripe tomatoes

Salt, about ¼ teaspoon

2 tablespoons olive or vegetable oil

4 medium zucchini, chopped into ⅜-inch dice

1 medium white onion, sliced

½ cup (4 ounces) chorizo sausage, casing removed

1 teaspoon dried oregano, preferably Mexican

⅓ cup crumbled Mexican queso fresco, queso añejo, mild feta, pressed, salted farmer's cheese or Parmesan

1. *Making 1 cup Essential Quick-Cooked Tomato-Chipotle Sauce base.* Toast the dried chipotles on an ungreased griddle or heavy skillet over medium heat, turning regularly and pressing flat with a spatula, until they fully release their aroma into the kitchen, about 30 seconds. In a small bowl, cover chiles with hot water and let rehydrate 30 minutes, stirring occasionally to ensure even soaking. Drain and discard the water. (Canned chiles need only be removed from their sauce.)

While the chiles are soaking, roast the unpeeled garlic on the griddle or skillet turning occasionally, until soft and blackened in spots, about 15 minutes; cool and peel. Roast the tomatoes on a baking sheet 4 inches below a very hot broiler until blackened on one side, about 6 minutes, then flip and roast the other side. Cool, then peel, collecting all the juices.

In a food processor or blender, process the tomatoes, rehydrated or canned chiles and garlic until almost completely pureed (there should still be a little texture left to give the dish an attractive presentation). Taste and season with salt.

2. *Finishing the dish.* Measure *1 tablespoon* of the oil into a large (10- to 12-inch) heavy skillet and set over medium-high. When very hot, add the zucchini (the pieces should fit comfortably in a single layer), and stir regularly until nicely browned, about 5 minutes. With a slotted spoon, remove to a plate, spreading them into a single layer to stop the cooking.

Return the skillet to the heat, add the remaining *1 tablespoon* of oil, and scoop in the onion and chorizo. Cook, stirring frequently, until the onion is very soft and golden (and the chorizo is nearly cooked), about 7 minutes. Drain off all excess fat, and return the pan to the heat.

Add the tomato-chipotle sauce and the oregano, and stir for about 5 minutes as the sauce sears and thickens. Add the zucchini and heat through. Scoop into a warm serving bowl, sprinkle with the cheese and your *tinga* is ready to eat.

ADVANCE PREPARATION—The sauce in step 1 can be made several days ahead; cover and refrigerate. The dish may be completed a couple of hours ahead, then reheated before sprinkling with the cheese.

SHORTCUTS—One 15-ounce can of tomatoes can replace the roasted ones.

VARIATIONS AND IMPROVISATIONS—Zucchini can be replaced with any tender summer squash, or, for that matter, 3 or 4 cups of practically any vegetable cut into small pieces. Some quick-fried vegetables will need to simmer considerably longer once added to the sauce, so be prepared to cover the pot, reduce the temperature and simmer until tender. If you have a favorite lasagna recipe, this mixture can replace your sauce (you'll want to make at least a double recipe); it also can replace the sauce and greens in Layered Tortilla-Tomato Casserole (page 201). Stirring 1½ to 2 cups cooked rice or orzo pasta into the cooled dish will give you a nice salad. You'll probably want to sprinkle it with a little vinegar to brighten the saladlike flavors. A *tinga* of 2 cups cubed, oven-roasted potatoes and 2 cups of sliced shiitake mushrooms (both replacing the zucchini) is wonderful.

Zucchini and Chayote

Markets from Mazatlan to Merida are piled high with zucchini, but not exactly the zucchini we know. The vegetable, called *calabacita* there, has a pale-green complexion, and it is either tennis ball–size and shaped or it resembles a slender pear. The texture is compact, not porous or watery, and the flavor is slightly sweet.

Luckily I've been seeing zucchinilike squash that they call *tatume* or *ronde de nice* in my farmer's market, so our options are growing. Without them, I use small green zucchini. If they taste bitter, I salt the cut pieces and let them drain 20 minutes in a colander to extract the unpleasantness before cooking.

Chayote, a relative of zucchini, is pear-shaped, light green and smooth or dark green and spiny. Its crisp, juicy flesh can seem watery when boiled in water, so I either steam it, simmer it in a sauce or, better yet, roast or sauté it. The smooth variety can be eaten skin, seed and all, though most Mexican cooks peel it and remove the thin pit. The spiny chayote is hard to peel unless you boil the whole thing first until tender. Don't be alarmed that cut chayote will leave behind a slippery residue that will dry like a very thin second skin on your hands—you just need to scrub your hands a little when you wash up.

SMOKY BRAISED MEXICAN PUMPKIN
WITH SEARED WHITE ONION

Calabaza Guisada al Chipotle

CALABAZA, THE GREAT BIG tan or greenish pumpkin, knows its homeland to be Mexico. Though its flesh and seeds supplied nourishment to the locals for millennia, not too many savory *calabaza* recipes show up in cookbooks or restaurants or on special-occasion tables. Yet heavy slices hacked from big pumpkins are always for sale in my local Mexican grocery. Perhaps pumpkin has been relegated to the indigenous backroom stews that trace their history directly to times before the Spaniards brought "civilization" to Mexico.

I like pumpkin's texture and flavor, especially when braised with the classic Essential Roasted Tomatillo-Chipotle Salsa and pork. Add a scoop of Classic Mexican Fried Beans (page 237) or Classic Red Tomato Rice (page 250) and hot corn tortillas, and I've got a great meal.

SERVES 4 AS A SMALL ENTREE, 6 AS A HEARTY SIDEDISH

FOR 1¼ CUPS ESSENTIAL ROASTED TOMATILLO-CHIPOTLE SALSA

3 to 6 (¼ to ½ ounce) stemmed, dried chipotle chiles (or canned chipotle chiles en adobo)

3 large garlic cloves, unpeeled

8 ounces (about 5 medium) tomatillos, husked and rinsed

12 ounces (2 medium-small round or 4 to 5 plum) ripe tomatoes

1 tablespoon olive oil or rich-flavored lard

½ pound lean boneless pork shoulder, cut into ½-inch pieces (optional)

1 medium white onion, thinly sliced

¼ cup chicken broth or water

Salt, about 1 teaspoon

Sugar, about ¼ teaspoon

4 cups peeled, seeded and cubed (¾-inch pieces) fresh pumpkin, preferably from a 1½-pound wedge cut from a tan or green Mexican pumpkin (a 2-pound pie pumpkin will give you about the right amount, too)

1. *Making 1¼ cups Essential Roasted Tomatillo-Chipotle Salsa.* For dried chiles, toast them on an ungreased griddle or skillet over medium heat, turning regularly and pressing flat with a spatula, until very aromatic, about 30 seconds. In a small bowl, cover the chiles with hot water and let rehydrate 30 minutes, stirring frequently to ensure even soaking. Drain and discard the water. (Canned chiles need only be removed from their sauce.)

While chiles are soaking, roast the unpeeled garlic on the griddle or skillet, turning occasionally, until soft (they will blacken in spots), about 15 minutes; cool and peel. Roast the tomatillos on a baking sheet 4 inches below a very hot broiler until blackened on one side, about 5 minutes, then flip and roast the other side. (For the sake of efficiency, you can roast the tomatoes from step 2 while you're roasting the tomatillos.)

Scrape the tomatillos (and their juices), rehydrated or canned chiles and garlic into a food processor or blender, and process to a rather fine-textured puree. Transfer to a bowl and stir in enough water (3 to 4 tablespoons) to give the salsa a medium consistency.

2. *The braising sauce.* Roast the tomatoes on a baking sheet 4 inches below a very hot broiler until blackened on one side, about 6 minutes, then flip and roast the other side. Cool, then peel and roughly chop, collecting any juices with the tomatoes.

In a large (10- to 12-inch) heavy skillet, heat the oil or lard over medium-high. If using the cubed pork, fry it now, turning and scraping up bits of browned meat, until golden all over, about 10 minutes; scrape into a small bowl, leaving behind as much oil as possible.

In the same skillet, fry the onion, stirring regularly, until well browned, about 10 minutes. Add the tomatillo salsa and the tomatoes to the skillet, stir for several minutes as it all thickens and reduces, then stir in the broth or water. Taste and season with salt and sugar.

3. *Finishing the dish.* Turn on the oven to 350 degrees. Place the pumpkin cubes in an oven-proof baking/serving dish just big enough to hold them in about an inch-thick layer (a 9 x 9-inch Pyrex dish works well). Mix in the browned pork if using it. Pour the sauce over everything, cover with foil or a lid and bake until the pumpkin is tender, 40 to 45 minutes.

Uncover, raise the oven temperature to 400 degrees, bake until the sauce has reduced a little and the top is crusty, about 15 minutes longer, and it's ready to carry to the table.

ADVANCE PREPARATION—The braising sauce can be prepared through step 2 several days in advance; cover and refrigerate. The dish can be baked for 40 or 45 minutes, cooled and refrigerated; finish baking just before serving at 400 degrees for 15 or 20 minutes.

VARIATIONS AND IMPROVISATIONS—You can, of course, make this dish with other pumpkins and squash: Butternut squash offers a dense texture and rich taste; hubbard is lighter with a soft texture, pie pumpkins are very good all around—use what you can get your hands on. Also, to add a green balance of flavor, stir in 1 to 1½ cups of sliced chard, cleaned lamb's quarters (*quelites*) or amaranth greens (*quintoniles*) before baking.

ROASTED MEXICAN VEGETABLES IN GREEN SESAME *PIPIÁN*

Pipián Verde de Verduras

ANYONE WHO HAS TASTED tahini, the Middle Eastern sesame "butter," knows that it offers a voluptuously creamy texture without cream. That's the same texture that rolls across your tongue in this *pipián*, together with the inimitable Mexican mark of toasting and roasting, citrusy tomatillos and biting serranos. This modern vegetable main dish offers a twist (I roast the vegetables instead of boil them) on a Lenten dish of cactus and potatoes in *pipián verde*.

Serve it simply with white rice or as a taco filling, or divide it among individual casseroles, ramekins or gratin dishes, top with toasted bread crumbs (as called for in the Crusty Chayote Casserole, page 224) and bake until bubbling.

MAKES ABOUT 6 CUPS, SERVING 4 TO 6 AS A CASUAL ENTREE

FOR 2½ CUPS ESSENTIAL SIMMERED TOMATILLO-SERRANO SAUCE

1 pound (11 medium total) tomatillos, husked and rinsed

Fresh serrano chiles to taste (roughly 3), stemmed

4½ tablespoons olive or vegetable oil

1 medium white onion, roughly chopped

2 large garlic cloves, peeled and roughly chopped

2 cups chicken broth or water, plus a little more if needed

⅓ cup roughly chopped cilantro

½ cup (about 2½ ounces) hulled sesame seeds, plus a few extra for garnish

1 sprig epazote, plus a few extra leaves for garnish (or 8 or 10 sprigs of cilantro)

1 leaf hoja santa

   OR *½ cup roughly chopped green tops of fresh fennel bulb*

   OR *½ teaspoon aniseed, preferably freshly ground*

Salt, a generous teaspoon, plus a sprinkling for the vegetables

3 medium (6 to 7 ounces total) fresh cactus paddles

4 medium red-skin boiling potatoes, cut into ¾-inch dice

1 large chayote, peeled, pitted and cut into ¾-inch dice

2 medium zucchini, cut into ¾-inch dice

2 cups stemmed quelites (lamb's quarters)

   OR *3 cups stemmed verdolagas (purslane) or sliced green chard leaves (½-inch slices)*

1. *Making about 2½ cups Essential Simmered Tomatillo-Serrano Sauce.* Lay the tomatillos and chiles on a baking sheet and place about 4 inches below a very hot broiler. When the tomatillos and chiles blister, darken and soften on one side, about 5 minutes, turn them over and roast the other side. Transfer tomatillos and chiles (along with any accumulated juices) to a blender.

Heat *1 tablespoon* of the oil or lard in a large (10- to 12-inch) heavy skillet over medium. Add the onion and cook, stirring often, until deep golden, about 10 minutes. Stir in the garlic and cook 1 minute more. Scrape the onion mixture into the blender, cover *loosely* and blend until smooth.

Wipe the skillet clean, add another *½ tablespoon* oil and set over medium-high. When hot enough to make a drop of the puree sizzle sharply, pour it in all at once and stir constantly for about 5 minutes as it darkens and thickens. (Set the blender aside unwashed.) Add the broth, let return to a boil, reduce the heat to medium and simmer briskly, stirring frequently, until thick enough to coat a spoon, about 10 minutes. Stir in the cilantro.

2. *From tomatillo sauce to green* pipián. In a small (7- to 8-inch), ungreased skillet set over medium heat, toast the sesame seeds, stirring regularly until golden, about 5 minutes. Scoop them into the sauce, then add the *epazote* (or cilantro) and *hoja santa* (or one of its stand-ins). Partially cover and simmer 30 minutes, stirring frequently.

Ladle the sauce into your blender, cover *loosely* and blend for a good minute or so, until the sauce is smooth. (If you'd like an even smoother sauce, pass it through a medium-mesh strainer into a bowl.) Return the sauce to the pan, taste, and season with salt, usually a generous teaspoon. If necessary, thin with a little broth to bring the sauce to the consistency of a rather thick cream soup.

3. *The vegetables.* Turn on the oven to 375 degrees. Clean and roast the cactus: Holding a cactus paddle gingerly between the nodes of the prickly spines, trim off the edge that outlines the paddle. Slice or scrape off the spines from both sides, then cut into ¾-inch squares. Scoop the cactus onto a baking sheet, toss with *1 tablespoon* of the oil, sprinkle with a little salt, and bake, stirring occasionally, until tender and all exuded liquid has evaporated, 15 to 20 minutes. (After 5 minutes in the oven, the cactus pieces will begin to leak sticky liquid; as they roast, the liquid will evaporate.)

Meanwhile, roast the remaining vegetables: Scatter the potatoes on a baking sheet, drizzle with the remaining *2 tablespoons* of the oil, sprinkle with salt and toss to coat the potatoes well. Roast in the oven for 10 minutes. Sprinkle the chayote with salt, scatter it over the potatoes, then use a spatula to turn the potatoes and coat the chayote with oil. Return to the oven for another 5 minutes. Lastly, salt the zucchini, stir it into the potato mixture, and roast until everything is tender (but not overly soft), 8 to 10 more minutes.

4. *Finishing the dish.* Just before serving, reheat the sauce to a simmer over medium. Stir in the *quelites* (or one of the alternatives) and simmer until tender, 2 to 5 minutes. Use a slotted spoon or spatula to scoop all the roasted vegetables into the sauce, leaving behind as much oil as possible. When everything is heated through in a few minutes, scoop the mixture into a warm serving dish, sprinkle with sesame seeds, garnish with a few *epazote* or cilantro leaves and carry to table.

ADVANCE PREPARATION—The sauce can be prepared several days ahead through step 2; refrigerate, covered. The vegetables can be combined with the sauce several hours ahead if that helps, though the closer to serving the better.

SHORTCUTS—Cactus will be the time consumer here, and it can be replaced with more chayote (use 2 chayotes). Half of a 10-ounce package of spinach (defrosted, squeezed and roughly chopped) can replace the greens.

VARIATIONS AND IMPROVISATIONS—The sauce (there is about 3 cups) will serve 6 with chicken (bake 6 large boneless, skinless chicken breasts in the sauce for about 15 minutes) or with roasted pork or grilled pork chops. It can replace the tomatillo sauce in the Tomatillo-Braised Pork Country Ribs (page 382) or the *mole* in the Simple Red *Mole* Enchiladas (page 178). I could go on and on, but once you taste the sauce, you'll think of your own variations.

CRUSTY CHAYOTE CASSEROLE
WITH POBLANOS, CORN AND TWO CHEESES

Chayote con Rajas y Elote

*I*F YOU'VE ONLY HAD watery, bland, boiled chayote, you're in for a treat here. Cubes of steamed chayote are mixed with meaty roasted chiles and crisp-tender golden onions, and baked with melted cheese under a topping of crispy crumbs. I can't say I've eaten anything exactly like this in Mexico, but who can resist this combination? Beautifully cooked chayote is a very underrated vegetable simply because we don't yet understand its subtleties.

I'd put this chayote out on a brunch buffet with French toast, honey-baked ham and fruit salad. Or I'd serve it at a casual dinner with Chile-Glazed Country Ribs (page 380), Achiote Grilled Turkey Breast (page 326) or slices of the Great Big Tamal Roll with Chard (page 306).

SERVES 8 AS A SIDE DISH

3 1/2 pounds (5 medium) chayotes

FOR 1 CUP ESSENTIAL ROASTED POBLANO *RAJAS*

8 ounces (3 medium-large) fresh poblano chiles

2 1/2 tablespoons butter, vegetable or olive oil, plus a little more for the baking dish

1 small white onion, sliced 1/8 inch thick

2 garlic cloves, peeled and minced

1/4 teaspoon dried oregano, preferably Mexican

1/8 teaspoon dried thyme

2 ears corn, husked, kernels cut from the cobs (about a generous 1 1/2 cups)

2/3 cup milk

Salt, about 1 teaspoon

1 heaping cup (about 5 ounces) grated Mexican Chihuahua cheese or other melting cheese such as brick or Monterey Jack

3/4 cup coarse dry bread crumbs

1/3 cup finely crumbled Mexican queso añejo or Parmesan

Chopped cilantro, for garnish

1. *The chayotes.* Use a vegetable peeler to peel the chayotes, then cut them in half through the stem end, and use a small knife or spoon to wedge out the pit from each piece. Cut into 3/4-inch cubes. In a vegetable steamer, steam the chayote until crisp-tender, about 15 minutes. Stir the chayote around every 3 or 4 minutes so the pieces will steam evenly.

2. *Making 1 cup of Essential Roasted Poblano* **Rajas.** Roast the chiles directly over a gas flame or on a baking sheet 4 inches below a very hot broiler until blackened on all sides, about 5 minutes for open flame, about 10 minutes for broiler. Cover with a kitchen towel and let stand 5 minutes. Peel, pull out the stem and seed pod, then rinse briefly to remove bits of skin and seeds. Slice ⅛-inch thick; cut slices crosswise in half.

In a large (10- to 12-inch) skillet, melt *1 tablespoon* of the butter or oil over medium to medium-high. Scoop in the onion and cook, stirring regularly, until nicely browned but still a little crunchy, about 5 minutes. Add the garlic, herbs and chiles and mix thoroughly.

3. *Finishing the casserole.* Turn on the oven to 350 degrees. Add the corn, milk, and cooked chayote to the skillet with the *rajas* and bring to a boil. Taste and add salt. Spoon *half* of the mixture into a well-buttered 9 x 9-inch or 11 x 7-inch baking dish. Top with *half* of the Chihuahua cheese, the remaining chayote mixture, then the remaining cheese. Bake until bubbling nicely and beginning to brown, about 20 minutes.

While the chayote is baking, melt the remaining *1½ tablespoons* of the butter (no need to warm the oil, if that's what you are using) and stir it into the crumbs. Mix with the *queso añejo*, sprinkle over the casserole and return to the oven for 10 to 15 minutes more, until crusty and browned. Let stand 5 minutes before sprinkling with the cilantro and digging in.

ADVANCE PREPARATION—The casserole can be assembled (minus the crumbs) covered and refrigerated several hours ahead. Increase the first baking time slightly if the casserole is cold, then add the crumb mixture and finish baking.

VARIATIONS AND IMPROVISATIONS—Feel free to use about the same weight of zucchini (or other summer squash) or a mixture of zucchini and chayote (zucchini will need only about 6 minutes in the steamer). To turn your chayote into a main-dish casserole, add coarsely shredded cooked chicken or turkey or pork (preferably from the shoulder, so it won't come out dry) or ham. If you're wondering what to do with those kohlrabis you see at the market, this is a good preparation for them.

CHILE-GLAZED SWEET POTATOES
WITH CINNAMON AND ORANGE
Camote Adobado

*T*HIS CASSEROLE has all the homey appeal of the sweet, crusty, orange-scented sweet potatoes most of us put on our Thanksgiving tables. That's why I've included them, knowing
you'd have great ideas for putting them out. But keep in mind that these are Mexican—
robust with chile, tempered with honey, perfumed with herbs and spices.

Vegetables stewed in a rich and robust red-chile sauce, either as a taco filling dusted with
crumbled aged cheese or as a vegetable main course (customary for fast days on the Church
calendar), are deeply rooted in Mexican cuisine. Occasionally, I'll serve zucchini or chayote
simmered in a sauce similar to what I've given here (*calabacitas en adobillo*, a specialty of
Northwestern Mexico, for example), to lay beneath a roasted quail, guinea hen or young
chicken, even a piece of grilled tuna.

Here I've chosen a baked vegetable *adobado* dish (which works best with starchy tubers),
the idea for which came from the volume on celebration foods from the series of books
titled . . . *y la comida se hizo*.

SERVES 6 TO 8 AS AN ACCOMPANIMENT

**FOR ⅔ CUP ESSENTIAL SWEET-AND-
SPICY ANCHO CHILE SEASONING PASTE**

5 garlic cloves, unpeeled

*6 medium-to-small (a scant 3 ounces
   total) dried ancho chiles, stemmed
   and seeded*

*1 teaspoon dried oregano, preferably
   Mexican*

*½ teaspoon cinnamon, preferably
   freshly ground Mexican* canela

*A generous ¼ teaspoon black pepper,
   preferably freshly ground*

*A generous ⅛ teaspoon cloves, prefer-
   ably freshly ground*

½ cup chicken broth or water

*3 pounds (about 5 medium) sweet
   potatoes, unpeeled*

*1 tablespoon finely chopped
   orange zest (orange rind only), plus
   some thinly slivered zest
   for garnish*

½ cup fresh orange juice

2 tablespoons honey

Salt, a generous teaspoon

*2 tablespoons melted butter or olive
   oil (optional), plus a little
   extra for the pan*

*A few tablespoons chopped cilantro,
   for garnish*

*1 or 2 tablespoons Thick Cream
   (page 165), crème fraîche
   or sour cream thinned with
   a little milk, for garnish*

1. *Making ⅔ cup Essential Sweet-and-Spicy Ancho Chile Seasoning Paste.* Roast the unpeeled garlic on an ungreased griddle or heavy skillet over medium heat, turning occasionally, until soft (they'll blacken in spots), about 15 minutes; cool and peel. While the garlic is roasting, toast the chiles on another side of the griddle or skillet: 1 or 2 at a time, open them flat and press down firmly on the hot surface with a spatula; in a few seconds, when they crackle, even send up a wisp of smoke, flip them and press down to toast the other side. In a small bowl, cover the chiles with hot water and let rehydrate for 30 minutes, stirring regularly to ensure even soaking. Drain and discard the water.

Combine the oregano, cinnamon, black pepper and cloves in a food processor or blender, along with the chiles, garlic and broth or water. Process to a smooth puree, scraping and stirring every few seconds. (If the mixture won't go through the blender blades, add a little more liquid.) Press through a medium-mesh strainer into a small bowl.

2. *Assembling the dish.* Slice each of the sweet potatoes into 4 lengthwise wedges. Lightly butter or oil a 13 x 9-inch baking dish, and lay in the sweet potatoes in a single layer. Combine the chile seasoning paste with the orange zest, orange juice and honey. Taste and season with salt (it should taste salty, since this is the seasoning for the potatoes). Spoon evenly over the sweet potatoes.

3. *Baking the potatoes.* Turn on the oven to 350 degrees. Drizzle the sweet potatoes with the (optional) butter or oil, cover with aluminum foil and bake for 45 minutes or until the potatoes are almost fork-tender.

Raise the oven temperature to 425 degrees, uncover the potatoes, baste with the juices and bake until the potatoes are nicely glazed and the sauce reduced to a medium thickness, about 10 minutes. Sprinkle with slivers of orange zest, chopped cilantro and a drizzle of cream if you wish, and it's ready to serve.

ADVANCE PREPARATION—The seasoning paste may be made a week or so ahead. The potatoes can be assembled through step 2 several hours in advance, or the whole can even be baked and reheated. Garnish just before serving.

BROWNED VERMICELLI WITH ROASTED TOMATO, ZUCCHINI AND AGED CHEESE

Sopa Seca de Fideos

*B*ROWNING STRANDS of dried vermicelli to make these classic *fideos* adds a deep, rich nuttiness. Simmer the vermicelli with roasted tomatoes, smoky chipotles and zucchini, then enrich them with the complexity of a good aged cheese, and you've put together some very good eating. In my experience in Mexico this preparation (called *sopa seca,* "dry soup") is served as a first course in place of "wet soup" (there is also a brothy version of *fideos*).

Pasta as standard Mexican fare? Yes, though not as varied as Italian preparations (and usually starting with dried spaghetti and vermicelli). When my daughter returns from dinner with Mexican friends, she frequently reports they ate *sopa de fideos,* a kids' favorite.

The addition of zucchini, chorizo and cream turns this *fideos* into a special-occasion dish. I have Lula Bertrán, a Mexico City cooking authority and friend, to thank for opening my eyes to these luxurious additions to the standard.

SERVES 4 AS A CASUAL ENTREE, 6 AS A FIRST COURSE OR SIDE DISH

FOR 2 CUPS ESSENTIAL QUICK-COOKED TOMATO-CHIPOTLE SAUCE

3 to 4 *(about ¼ ounce total) stemmed, dried chipotle chiles (or canned chipotle chiles en adobo)*

4 *garlic cloves, unpeeled*

2½ *pounds (5 medium-large round, 15 to 17 plum) ripe tomatoes*

About ½ *cup vegetable oil*

¾ *cup (about 6 ounces) chorizo sausage, casing removed (optional)*

One 10-ounce *package dried* fideo *(vermicelli) noodles, preferably the thinnest ones called "angel hair" and sold in nest shapes*

1 *cup beef or chicken broth*

1 *teaspoon dried oregano, preferably Mexican*

½ *teaspoon black pepper, preferably freshly ground*

Salt, *about a scant teaspoon*

2 *medium zucchini, cut into ¼-inch dice*

¼ to ½ *cup Thick Cream (page 165), whipping cream or* crème fraîche *(optional)*

⅔ *cup finely grated Mexican queso añejo or Parmesan*

A few *tablespoons roughly chopped cilantro, for garnish*

1. *Making 2 cups of Essential Quick-Cooked Chipotle-Tomato Sauce.* For dried chiles, toast them on an ungreased griddle or heavy skillet over medium heat, turning regularly and pressing flat with a spatula, until very aromatic, about 30 seconds. In a small bowl, cover the chiles with hot water and rehydrate 30 minutes, stirring frequently to ensure even soaking. Drain and discard the water. (Canned chiles need only be removed from their sauce.)

Roast the unpeeled garlic on the griddle or skillet, turning occasionally, until soft, about 15 minutes; cool and peel. Roast *1½ pounds* of the tomatoes on a baking sheet 4 inches below a very hot broiler until blackened on one side, about 6 minutes, then flip and roast the other side. Cool, then peel, collecting all the juices with the tomatoes.

In a food processor or blender, process the tomatoes, rehydrated or canned chiles and garlic to a medium-fine puree. Heat *1 tablespoon* of the oil in medium-size (4-quart) pot (such as a Dutch oven or Mexican *cazuela*) over medium-high. Add the puree and stir for about 5 minutes as it sears and thickens. Set aside.

2. *Browning the chorizo and noodles.* If using chorizo, cook in a little oil over medium heat, breaking up large lumps as you go, until thoroughly cooked, about 10 minutes. Scoop it out with a slotted spoon, draining as much oil as possible back into the skillet.

Pour 6 *tablespoons* of the remaining oil into the skillet and return to the heat. When quite hot (drop a stray noodle in—it should sizzle but not brown immediately), lay in about ⅓ of the noodle nests to fry until noticeably browned, about 1 minute, then flip and brown the other side. Remove with a slotted spoon, draining as much oil as possible back into the skillet, and drain on paper towels. Continue until all have been browned.

3. *Finishing the dish.* Add the broth, oregano and pepper to the tomato sauce. Core the remaining *1 pound* of tomatoes and chop into ¼-inch bits. Add and simmer briskly until the sauce thickens to the consistency of a juicy tomato sauce, about 5 minutes. Taste and season with salt.

Add the noodles. In about 2 minutes pull the "nests" apart (they'll have softened enough to do it at this point), then add the zucchini and the chorizo (if you're using it). Simmer, stirring occasionally, until the noodles are tender but still firm, about 2 minutes.

If using the cream, add it now, raise the heat to medium-high and boil quickly until the sauce returns to its previous consistency. Taste again and readjust the salt, if necessary.

Stir in *half* of the grated cheese, scoop into a warm serving dish, sprinkle on the remaining cheese and the cilantro garnish, and it's ready to serve.

ADVANCE PREPARATION—The dish can be prepared a day or two ahead through step 2. Refrigerate the sauce and chorizo, covered, and leave the noodles at room temperature.

CRUSTY LENTIL CAKES WITH GARLIC AND HERBS

Tortas de Lentejas

I CAN'T TELL YOU how I look forward to eating these crusty cakes of tender lentils flecked with roasted garlic, aged cheese and cilantro! A bite that combines the crunchy outside with the steaming, soft variety within—all slathered in spicy salsa—is really memorable.

This very traditional Mexican Lenten dish (to which I've added a little grilled onion) is delicious paired with Essential Roasted Tomatillo-Chipotle Salsa (page 45) and Red Chile Rice (page 252). Add a salad and a cold beer and you have a casual dinner you'll want to make regularly.

MAKES 12 TO 14 LENTIL CAKES, SERVING 4 TO 6

1¾ cups (10 ounces) brown lentils (red lentils will work here, too, though the cooking time may be different, and they will fall apart more quickly than the brown ones)

1 medium white onion

About ½ cup vegetable or olive oil, for brushing the onions and for pan-frying

6 large garlic cloves, unpeeled

¼ cup finely crumbled Mexican queso añejo, dry feta or Parmesan

½ cup finely chopped cilantro, plus some sprigs for garnish

½ teaspoon black pepper, preferably freshly ground

Salt, about ¾ teaspoon

2 eggs

3 tablespoons milk

About 2 cups dry bread crumbs

About 3 cups salsa (like Essential Roasted Tomato-Jalapeño Salsa, page 21) or warm sauce (like Essential Quick-Cooked Tomato-Chipotle Sauce, page 34), for serving

1. *The lentil mixture.* In a large (4-quart) saucepan, bring 2 quarts heavily salted water to a boil. Add the lentils and simmer over medium heat until they are fully tender but most are still holding their shape, 30 to 35 minutes (too little cooking and the cakes won't hold together, too much and the texture will be a bit mushy). Drain, then spread the lentils in a thin layer on a baking sheet to cool completely.

Either slice the onion into ⅜-inch-thick rounds, brush with a little oil and grill on a medium-hot charcoal or gas grill until browned and tender (about 10 minutes), then chop after cooking; or, chop the onion and brown it in a little oil in a medium-size skillet over medium heat for about 10 minutes.

Roast the unpeeled garlic in a dry pan, turning occasionally, until soft and blackened in spots, about 15 minutes. Cool, peel and finely chop.

In a large bowl, mix the lentils, onion, garlic, cheese, cilantro and pepper. Taste and season with salt, usually about ½ teaspoon.

2. *Forming and breading the cakes*. Form the lentil mixture into 12 to 14 2-inch discs, each about ½ inch thick (packing the mixture into a ¼-cup measuring cup is an easy way to do this; gently tap the cake out of the measuring cup to dislodge it). Transfer the cakes to a baking sheet lined with foil. Freeze for a half hour or so, to firm for easier breading.

Beat the eggs, milk and remaining ¼ *teaspoon* salt in a flat dish, and spread out the bread crumbs on a plate. Dip both sides of each lentil cake in the egg mixture, then dredge in the crumbs, pressing the crumbs into a firm coating completely covering the cake. Refrigerate covered if not frying immediately.

3. *Frying the cakes*. Turn on the oven to the lowest setting. Heat a ⅛-inch coating of oil in a large (10- to 12-inch), well-seasoned or nonstick skillet over medium. In batches, fry the cakes in an uncrowded single layer until brown and crusty, about 3 minutes per side. Remove and drain on paper towels, keeping the fried cakes warm in a single layer in a low oven while finishing the others. Serve each portion of your crusty cakes on a warm dinner plate in a pool of spicy salsa or sauce, decorated with cilantro sprigs.

ADVANCE PREPARATION—The cakes can be shaped (as directed in step 2) and frozen (well wrapped) several weeks ahead. Bread them while frozen, then let them defrost for several hours in a single layer in the refrigerator. Fry, then serve right away (though they'll hold for a few minutes in a low oven).

VARIATIONS AND IMPROVISATIONS

These cakes can be made with about 4 cups of any cooked beans, though the texture will be heavier because most beans are creamier and denser than lentils. Dried hulled favas work well, as long as you cook them until falling apart, pour off the water, mix in the other ingredients and form the cakes while everything is still warm (they firm as they cool).

Lentil Salad with Identical Flavors—For a lentil salad, reduce the initial lentil cooking time in step 1 to 25 minutes (so they are just tender not falling apart). Season as directed in step 1, omit the shaping, breading and frying, and simply serve as a salad or room-temperature side dish, sprinkled with additional cheese and chopped cilantro.

SEARED CORN
WITH GREEN CHILE AND MEXICAN HERBS

Esquites Dorados

DOTTED ALL AROUND Central and Southern Mexico are street vendors' pushcarts loaded with big pots of soupy, field-corn kernels (the slightly chewy, nonsweet corn), boiled with chiles and branches of *epazote,* to be ladled into little plastic cups, sprinkled with crushed red chile and enlivened with lime. The snack is *esquites,* a healthy, delicious mouthful to anyone raised in Mexico. There's another version, less commonly made, that works well with our American sweet corn: fresh corn kernels seared quickly in a hot pan with chile, *epazote* and lime. You can serve them as a snack after a trip to the farmer's market as part of a summer menu that includes grilled fish with Essential Roasted Tomatillo-Serrano Salsa (page 42) or any of your favorites.

MAKES A GENEROUS 3 CUPS, SERVING 6 AS AN ACCOMPANIMENT OR SNACK

5 large ears fresh sweet corn, husked

Hot green chiles to taste (roughly 3 serranos or 2 small jalapeños), stemmed and sliced crosswise into rings, seeds and all

Generous ½ teaspoon salt

1 tablespoon fresh lime juice

3 tablespoons chopped epazote *(or about ¼ cup chopped cilantro)*

Several wedges of lime, for serving

1. *Cutting the corn from the cobs.* Cut the kernels from the corn cobs: Stand one ear on end in a shallow dish, then, using a sharp knife, slice down the length of the ear staying as close to the cob as you can get. Rotate the cob and continue until all of the kernels have been cut from the cob.

2. *Cooking the corn.* Heat a large (10- to 12-inch), well-seasoned or nonstick skillet (you'll need a lid) over medium-high. (Lacking a large skillet, work in a wok, in 2 smaller skillets, or in batches.) When hot, add the corn and chiles to the dry pan and stir for 5 to 10 minutes, until most of the corn kernels have browned a bit.

In a cup, combine ¼ cup water, the salt and lime juice, stirring until the salt is dissolved. Sprinkle the *epazote* (or cilantro) over the corn, then drizzle on the liquid, cover and remove from the heat. Let stand several minutes, then taste and add a little more salt if the *esquites* need it. Serve with wedges of lime to squirt on the corn, if you choose.

BEANS

. . . . .

Beans are a primary staple of the Mexican diet. And like tortillas, the other staple, they are mostly eaten quite plain—either soupy (*frijoles de la olla*) or mashed and fried (*frijoles refritos*). Though beans are omnipresent in the Mexican kitchen and a standard accompaniment to the snacks served at *almuerzo* (late morning breakfast/lunch) and *cena* (supper), they have a place in the now somewhat old-fashioned formal main meal as well. They're offered, although not necessarily taken or eaten by everyone, after the main dish, which attests, I think, to the fact either that the portions were much smaller (which, from older cookbooks, you can tell may be the case) or that folks ate a lot more than we do now (which may also be true, since folks used to be more physically active than we are). Either way, beans are not likely to play much of a role in your formal dinners, so I've concentrated on teaching the basics you'll need for more casual dining.

I start here with all the details for making the Classic Mexican "Pot" Beans—boiling beans is simple, though there are some pointers I can offer that will ensure the perfect pot. And Classic Mexican Fried Beans, the "refries" everyone expects in Mexican-American restaurants, are a mash of those long-simmered legumes seasoned with onions and garlic. If you've only tasted the run-of-the-mill restaurant versions or the canned ones, you'll be very pleasantly surprised by their enticing texture and distinctly just-cooked flavor.

Next comes alternatives on both those classics: the "Drunken" Pintos are a variation on "pot" beans, seasoned with green chile, cilantro, bacon and tequila; and Sonoran Fried Beans are, yes, a variation on fried beans, but one that includes a good dollop of red chile and rich melted cheese.

Veracruz cooks use black beans as the focal point of their Greens and Beans, definitely a homey option, though one whose red-chile seasoning makes it very attractive. And Oaxacan cooks focus on beans for their meatless Lenten dish of Runner Beans in Brick-Red *Mole,* a dish that shows beautifully the complex spicing so prized in that part of Mexico.

CLASSIC MEXICAN "POT" BEANS

Frijoles de la Olla

*T*HE COMFORTING AROMA of bubbling bean pots has, along with the toastiness of baking corn tortillas, accompanied the life of Mexicans for millennia. Beans and tortillas have nourished Mexican spirits and bones; they've become, in fact, the chorus that backs up each of the remarkably flavored soloists in the Mexican kitchen.

Yet, north of the border, we often turn our backs on beans, perhaps because they are thought of as filler, perhaps because they are cheap. I'm thankful that lately they're becoming fashionable, even if only the "heirloom" varieties.

Whatever type of bean you choose, cook enough of it to have for several meals (this recipe doubles easily). Not only will the beans cook more evenly in a good-size amount, but they'll have better texture and you'll be encouraged to enjoy them frequently and in different ways. However you plan to use your slow-simmered beans, they've got to be boiled first, which is really very straightforward; I've spelled out the classic Mexican approach in detail here.

Though few of you will think of these "pot" beans as the finished dish (you may be planning to turn them into Crispy Black Bean–Bacon Tacos, page 168, or simply Classic Mexican Fried Beans, page 237), one of my favorite suppers is a fragrant bowl of black beans, hot tortillas, fresh salsa and a salad.

MAKES 7 TO 8 CUPS, SERVING 8 TO 10 AS A SIDE DISH

1 pound (about 2½ cups) dry beans (black, pinto, pink, kidney or navy)

3 tablespoons vegetable oil or rich-tasting lard, bacon drippings or fat rendered from chorizo sausage

1 medium white onion, diced

1 large sprig epazote (optional, but highly recommended with black beans)

Salt, about 1½ teaspoons

1. *Cooking the beans.* Rinse the beans thoroughly. If you are using vegetable oil, measure it into a large (5- to 6-quart) pot (preferably a Dutch oven or Mexican earthenware *olla*) and set over medium heat. Add the onion and cook, stirring regularly, until deep golden, about 10 minutes (this gives a roasty flavor to the beans, reminiscent of what you'd find from pork fat). If you are using one of the pork fats, simply measure it into the large pot and add the onion. Scoop in the beans, measure in 2 quarts of water, and remove any beans that float.

Add the optional *epazote,* bring to a boil, then reduce the heat to medium-low and simmer, partially covered, until the beans are thoroughly tender, about 2 hours (there should be no chalkiness at all when you break a bean open), depending on the type and freshness of your beans. You'll need to gently stir the beans regularly and add water as necessary to keep the liquid a generous ½ inch above the level of the beans.

2. *Finishing the beans.* Season with salt, simmer another 10 to 15 minutes for the beans to absorb the seasoning, then remove from the heat, and they're ready to serve (to serve a bowl of beans, there should be just enough of the slightly creamy broth to cover the beans; for the best texture in both beans and broth, let the pot cool completely, then reheat before serving).

ADVANCE PREPARATION—Covered and refrigerated, beans keep for at least 4 days. Reheat slowly, stirring often to prevent sticking.

SHORTCUTS—If time is of the essence, beans may be cooked in a pressure cooker, though their texture won't be as nice and they won't have time to develop as much flavor. Put 2 cups (13 ounces) rinsed beans in a 4-quart pressure cooker (you can use 2½ cups [1 pound] beans if you have a 6-quart pressure cooker) along with 4½ cups water (6 cups if using the larger cooker and 1 pound beans), the oil or lard, the onion and *epazote*. Cook according to your manufacturer's directions for 30 minutes. Release the pressure and check the beans: If they're not quite tender, add a little more water to them and simmer (under pressure or not) until tender. Then season with salt and simmer a few minutes more.

VARIATIONS AND IMPROVISATIONS—Though beans in Mexico are cooked fairly plainly, you can simmer your pot beans with a little fresh jalapeño, serrano or poblano (I'd roast them first—and peel the poblano) or a toasted dried chile like chipotle, árbol or pequín (though fresh or dried chiles are frequently just eaten along with the beans). Take the stems off the chiles, shake seeds from dried ones or cut them from the fresh, cut in half and add to the pot with the dried beans. That's the appropriate time, too, to add chorizo, ham, bacon or smoked hocks, or turkey drumsticks. Just before serving, stir in a little Essential Sweet-and-Smoky Chipotle Seasoning Salsa (page 52).

Beans

If I knew where you grew up I could likely predict what you think about beans. In the South and Southwest, I grew to love the bowls of beans we had as a part of everyday eating. Living farther north, as I do now, I sense that folks aren't always comfortable putting beans on the table, either because they're not accustomed to cooking and eating them or, perhaps, they're a little embarrassed. Beans, of course, have the reputation for being hard to digest as well as, shall we say, not being very classy.

Beans, to most non-Southerners, are one of three kinds: canned pork and beans heated for a fast meal or doctored up for baked beans; canned kidneys for three-bean salad or, maybe, for chili; and small packages of white beans for soup. Nowadays, though, there seems to be some change afoot. Fashionable Mediterranean and modern Southwestern cooking have turned beans (at least white beans, garbanzos, favas and black beans) into something the trend-setters want on their dinner tables. Surround their modern appeal with nutritionists chanting the virtues of beans (do you know that eating ⅔ cup of cooked beans a day is one of the most effective ways of reducing cholesterol?), then pile on the availability of great-sounding heirloom beans (Jacob's cattle, soldier, speckled trout and Anasazi) and you've got beans in the mainstream.

Phaseolus beans, the ones native to Mexico, are the ones most of us think of as "beans." Though they come in all the imaginable earthy colors, Mexico boasts what I call a black-bean belt that runs pretty much across its middle. Below that line, everyday beans are black; above, they're light—usually the pinkish-brown *bayo* or *flor de mayo*—until you reach the far northern reaches near Texas, where pintos come into their own. Regionally you find the specialty *Phaseolus* beans like runners (Central, Eastern and Southern Mexico) and teparies (Northwestern Mexico), plus any number of colorful "regular" beans that are eaten in big enough quantities to be called a staple. Served in big bowls as an accompaniment or the main attraction, or served fried, mashed and dolloped alongside a snack or main dish, beans have been part of most meals in Mexico for eons. Simmered with *mole* or greens or *pozole* corn, made into soup or sauce for enchiladas or used as a filling for innumerable snacks, beans have been worked into practically every part of the menu.

All these *Phaseolus* beans have a similar taste and are more or less interchangeable. There's an earthiness to black beans and a sweetness to the redder varieties. Pintos are simple with a touch of earth, while white beans are a tiny bit vegetal. More than flavor, though, it's texture that distinguishes beans: from creamy to dry, tough-skinned to tender.

Though *Phaseolus* beans are native to Mexico, the European-brought garbanzos, lentils and favas were quickly adopted; it's my impression that the latter are seen more as specialty beans (often used for celebration dishes for European-oriented religious holidays).

Buy beans where there's a lot of turnover, since those that stay on the shelf for more than 6 to 8 months will be so dried out they won't cook evenly.

Stats: One pound of dried beans fills about 2½ cups, yielding 7 or 8 cups.

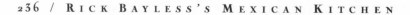

CLASSIC MEXICAN FRIED BEANS
WITH ONIONS AND GARLIC
Frijoles Refritos

*H*ARDLY A SOUL will cook from this book without visiting this page. What would a supper of soft tacos or *mole* enchiladas be without a forkful of thick-textured, homey fried beans? Fried beans are, shall we say, the mortar that holds together the Mexican kitchen.

There are many styles of fried beans in Mexico, but my favorite is a less rich, coarse textured (some whole beans left) version flavored with lots of onions and garlic. On the other end of the scale are the *frijoles chinitos*—the smooth-textured beans usually pureed in a blender, fried long enough and with enough lard or oil to make them shiny and rich. Both versions fall into the category of *frijoles refritos,* though the latter probably qualifies more as *re-fritos* since that "*re-*" in Spanish means "well" or "intensely," not "again and again."

You can make fried beans from any color bean, though common are black beans (from middle Mexico on south) and those that cook up brown (*bayo, flor de mayo, pinto, pink* and so on). For fun, I've made them from white beans and kidneys (or red beans); each has a unique flavor. And whether you choose oil or pork fat (lard, bacon fat or chorizo drippings) is up to you, though this is one place where pork fat makes an enormous flavor difference.

Two cooking notes: It's easier to mash warm beans than cold ones. And don't let the beans get too stiff (take them off the stove a little softer than you want them; they'll thicken up on the way to the table). Hold beans warm in a double boiler rather than over direct heat; check the consistency and stir in a little water if necessary, before serving.

MAKES ABOUT 3 1/2 CUPS, 6 GENEROUS SERVINGS

- 2 tablespoons vegetable oil, rich-tasting lard, bacon or chorizo drippings
- 1 medium white onion, chopped
- 4 garlic cloves, peeled and finely chopped
- 4 cups undrained, seasoned cooked beans (you can use practically any variety here, either canned or homemade, page 234), preferably slightly warm for easy mashing
- Salt, if necessary
- About 1/2 cup (2 ounces) crumbled Mexican queso fresco, queso añejo, pressed, salted farmer's cheese, dry feta or Parmesan, for garnish
- Handful of tortilla chips, for garnish

1. *Frying and mashing the beans.* In a large (10- to 12-inch), well-seasoned or nonstick skillet, heat the oil or pork fat over medium heat. Add the onion and cook, stirring frequently, until deep golden, about 10 minutes. Stir in the garlic, cook for a minute or so, then use a slotted spoon to scoop in about ¼ of the beans, leaving most of the liquid behind. With a bean (or potato) masher or the back of a large spoon, mash the beans into a coarse puree. Add another portion of the beans, mash them in, and continue until all of the beans have been added and coarsely mashed.

Add about a cup of bean liquid (or water if you have no liquid) and stir frequently over the heat until the beans are still a little soupier than you'd like to serve them (they'll thicken as they sit—I like my finished beans the consistency of soft mashed potatoes). The total cooking and mashing will take 10 to 15 minutes. Taste and season with salt, if necessary.

2. *Serving the beans.* Spoon the beans onto a warm serving platter (or onto individual plates), sprinkle with the crumbled cheese, decorate with the tortilla chips, and they're ready.

ADVANCE PREPARATION—The finished beans can be covered and refrigerated for several days. Add more water or bean liquid, as needed, to thin them while reheating.

VARIATIONS AND IMPROVISATIONS

Frijoles Chinitos—These are the shinier, smoother, richer beans that are prized in much of Mexico. Increase the oil or pork lard to ½ cup. Fry the onion and garlic as directed, but scoop it out with a slotted spoon or skimmer and transfer it to a blender or food processor. Puree with the beans. Return the oil or lard to the heat and add the bean puree. Cook, stirring very frequently, over medium-low for about 20 minutes, until the beans are quite thick and have a nice sheen to them. When you shake the pan back and forth, they should actually come free from the pan, as an omelette would (the way the beans come free in a single mass, leaving a film on the bottom of the skillet may remind you of making cream-puff dough). Season with salt if necessary. Turn them out (omelette-style) onto a warm plate, sprinkle with the cheese, decorate with the chips and serve.

"DRUNKEN" PINTOS WITH CILANTRO AND BACON

Frijoles Borrachos

I LOVE TO SERVE a cup of beans at a barbecue. The smoke and fire and the ripeness of the air seem the right accompaniment to beans, especially beans with tequila and cilantro.

Other than the alcoholic baptism these beans receive just before serving, they are similar to *frijoles charros,* the brothy beans (half soup, half accompaniment) so beloved in Mexico's North and indispensable at a meal of wood-grilled *tacos al carbón.* This version is my take on a recipe shared with me by the well-known cooking authority María Dolores Torres Yzábal of Mexico City. It's a loose combination of her recipe and my favorite version of *charro* beans. I like the interplay between the tequila, green chile, bacon and cilantro.

MAKES 4 CUPS, SERVING 4 TO 6 AS A SIDE DISH

8 ounces (about 1 ¼ cups) dry pinto beans

½ cup (about 2 ounces) cubed pork shoulder (or extra chopped bacon, if you wish)

4 thick slices bacon, cut into ½-inch pieces

1 small white onion, diced into ¼-inch pieces

Hot fresh green chile to taste (roughly 2 serranos or 1 jalapeño), stemmed, seeded and sliced

Salt, about ¾ teaspoon

1 ½ tablespoons tequila (plus a little more if you like)

¼ cup roughly chopped cilantro

1. *The beans.* Rinse the beans thoroughly and scoop into a medium-size (4-quart) pot (preferably a Dutch oven or Mexican earthenware *olla*). Add 5 cups water, remove any beans that float, then add the pork shoulder (or extra chopped bacon) and bring to a boil. Reduce the heat to medium-low, and very gently simmer, partially covered, until the beans are thoroughly tender, about 2 hours. You'll need to gently stir the beans regularly and add water as necessary to keep the liquid a generous ½ inch above the level of the beans.

2. *The flavorings.* In a medium-size skillet, fry the bacon (that is, the remaining bacon if you used some for the simmering), stirring regularly, until crisp, about 10 minutes. With a slotted spoon, remove the bacon, leaving behind as much of the drippings as possible. Pour off all but about 2 tablespoons of the drippings and return the pan to medium heat. Add the onion and chiles and fry until deep golden brown, about 10 minutes. Scrape the onion mixture into the beans, then taste and season it all with salt. Continue simmering, stirring occasionally, for 20 to 30 minutes to blend the flavors.

3. *Finishing the dish.* If the beans seem quite soupy, boil over medium-high heat, stirring frequently, until the consistency of a nice, brothy bean soup. (An alternative here is to puree ¼ of the beans in a food processor or blender, returning them to the pot to thicken the broth.)

Just before serving, stir in the tequila and cilantro, then serve in warm bowls topped with the crumbled bacon.

ADVANCE PREPARATION—The beans can be cooked through step 2 several days ahead; refrigerate, covered.

SHORTCUTS—Two 16-ounce cans of pinto beans can replace the beans in step 1.

VARIATIONS AND IMPROVISATIONS—A more rustic touch yet is to simmer the beans with a 2- to 3-ounce piece of beef jerky (cook it with the beans, then take it out, tear it into short shreds and return to the pot) instead of the pork. To make this more like the *frijoles charros,* replace the serrano with 2 roasted, peeled and diced poblanos and add 8 ounces of chopped tomatoes (roasted and peeled, preferably). As with most bean dishes, use any bean you like or can find easily.

Soaking and Cooking Beans

After having cooked almost 12,000 pounds of beans a year for most of the nearly ten years we've had Frontera and Topolobampo, I've learned quite a few things. Many are simple confirmations of what we've been taught all along—except one thing: I was taught to soak beans and I no longer do. Never having seen Mexican cooks soak beans, I've come to the conclusion that they know what is right. Soaking does practically nothing but reduce cooking time. Soaking doesn't really make the beans much more digestible, which is what we were all told. Yes, soaking and throwing out the soaking water does have *some* effect, the scientists now tell us, but nothing we should count on. What makes beans more digestible is a steady diet of beans, the diet nutritionists tell us we should have anyway.

Before you put the beans in the pot, give them a quick once-over. Though beans are cleaner than ever before, you'll still find an occasional stone or dirt clod. Next, rinse them, cover them with a good amount of water (roughly three times the volume of beans), bring them to a boil, then reduce the heat to the point that the water gently rolls up from the center. (Some Mexican cooks say to add baking soda to make beans more tender, though I don't see much point in it—some say it destroys some of their nutritional value.)

Here's where you can make choices: If the beans are covered during cooking, they come out creamier (though more likely to stick on the bottom); when uncovered, they're more separate and nicely intact (especially if you use lots of water). The more beans you cook at once, the more evenly cooked and better textured they'll be. (I know this because we cook 33 pounds of black beans a day, all in one pot.) When you simmer beans in an earthenware pot (like a traditional Mexican *olla*), they take on a distinctly earthy flavor.

After 1½ to 2½ hours the beans will be tender: Fish one out of the pot and blow on it to cool slightly (the skin should burst and roll back), then eat it. The interior of the bean should be thoroughly soft without a hint of chalkiness—we're not talking *al dente* here. (Personally, I think the current fad for undercooking beans—so that they are pretty and slightly crunchy—is silly; undercooked beans are terribly indigestible.) Timing can vary depending on the type of bean and, mostly, its freshness.

Only when the beans are completely tender should you add salt or anything acidic such as vinegar or tomatoes. I know there are folks who salt beans from the beginning, but I've found that an unreliable practice; sometimes the beans come out with an irregular texture, tough and mealy outside, soft within.

. . . .

SONORAN FRIED BEANS
WITH CHORIZO AND CHEESE

Frijoles Maneados

*T*HESE LUXURIOUSLY RICH BEANS—spicy with red chile and chorizo—are a terrific spread for steamy corn tortillas when you're rolling up slices of grilled skirt steak or chicken breast into soft tacos. I love to mash the beans coarsely and use the mixture as a filling for enchiladas, doused with Essential Simmered Tomatillo-Serrano Sauce (page 38) and sprinkled with *queso añejo.*

For years I flagged recipes for this Sonoran specialty in my cookbooks from Mexico, though I've never found a Sonoran to make it for me. I've included this version (based on one from *Cocina Sonorense,* published by *Instituto Sonorense de Cultura*) because I find it delicious and welcome at many special occasions. I haven't called for garnishes, though a sprinkle of ground chile, chopped onion or cilantro would be appropriate.

Since they are made like Classic Mexican Fried Beans (page 237), I suggest that you read the introduction to that recipe for more details.

MAKES 5 GENEROUS CUPS, 8 TO 10 SERVINGS AS AN ACCOMPANIMENT

1 pound (about 2½ cups) dry beans (preferably pinto or another light-skin bean)

Salt, about 1½ teaspoons

2 tablespoons butter or vegetable oil

½ cup (4 ounces) chorizo sausage, casing removed

2 tablespoons pure ground dried New Mexico, guajillo or ancho chile

2 cups (8 ounces) shredded Mexican Chihuahua cheese or other melting cheese such as brick or Monterey Jack

1. *The beans.* Rinse the beans thoroughly and scoop into a large (5- to 6-quart) pot (preferably a Dutch oven or Mexican earthenware *olla*), add 2 quarts of water and remove any beans that float. Bring to a boil, then reduce the heat to medium-low and very gently simmer, partially covered, until the beans are thoroughly tender (they should be creamy inside), about 2 hours, depending on the type and freshness of your beans. You'll need to gently stir the beans regularly and add water as necessary to keep the liquid a generous ½ inch above the level of the beans. Season with salt and simmer another 10 to 15 minutes to allow the beans to absorb the seasoning. Drain the beans, reserving their cooking liquid, and coarsely puree the beans in a food processor or blender, or by hand with a bean (or potato) masher, adding some of the reserved liquid, if needed, to bring them together into a very thick puree.

2. *The seasonings.* In a large (10- to 12-inch) skillet, preferably cast iron or nonstick, melt the butter or oil over medium heat, add the chorizo and cook, stirring to break up all the lumps, until thoroughly done, about 10 minutes. With a slotted spoon, scoop out the chorizo, leaving behind as much of the drippings as possible; add the chorizo to the beans.

In the rendered chorizo drippings, fry the ground chile over medium-low heat for a couple of minutes, stirring constantly, until very aromatic and roasty smelling (this really deepens the flavor). Scrape the bean mixture in with the chile, stir well and bring to a brisk simmer over medium heat. Season lightly with salt (the cheese you add later will impart its own saltiness) and let simmer, stirring and scraping nearly constantly, for a few minutes. The mixture should be very thick at this point.

3. *Finishing the dish.* Stir the warm beans to loosen them up. (You may want to add a few tablespoons of the bean cooking liquid at this point, but don't go overboard: They'll soften a lot when you add the cheese.) By handfuls, stir in the cheese, letting one handful melt before incorporating the next. The beans should have just enough body to hold their shape nicely in a spoon—if they're too stiff, stir in a little bean broth; if soft, simmer for a few more minutes until thicker. Taste the beans, add more salt if necessary, and they're ready to serve.

ADVANCE PREPARATION—The recipe can be made through step 2 several days in advance, covered and refrigerated. Complete step 3 shortly before serving, thinning as needed with water. (Finished beans *can* be reheated, though the texture won't be as nice.)

VARIATIONS AND IMPROVISATIONS—Feel free to make these without chorizo (we often do at Frontera); add another tablespoon or two of chile to replace the sausage's spiciness.

Mexican Earthenware Cooking Pots

When you bring home an earthenware pot from Mexico, be it the slope-sided *cazuela* for sauces or stews or the taller *olla* for beans, it will fill your kitchen with the smell of wet earth the first time you use it. Though *cazuelas* and *ollas* are hefty cooking vessels, they are surprisingly light because the clay is porous. Like clay cooking pots the world around, they're glazed on the inside only. (Pots glazed on the bottom are meant for decoration or serving, not direct heat.)

Many Mexican recipe writers instruct you to heat an empty *cazuela* for a long time before adding food (clay is a poor conductor of heat, so it heats slowly)—but only after the pot is cured. Cure by washing well, rubbing the exterior with a cut clove of raw garlic (they say this diminishes the raw earth smell), filling with water, setting over a medium heat (yes, they're made for direct heat, though gas is gentler than electric and a flame-tamer is a good idea) and bringing to a boil. Let simmer about half an hour, then remove from the heat. (A seasoned pot will need to be reboiled to temper the drying earthenware if it has not been used recently.) Earthenware holds heat so well that I've often taken a gurgling *cazuela* of *mole* off the stove and 10 minutes later found the liquid still gently simmering.

I like to partially cover sauces as they simmer to reduce evaporation. Since *cazuelas* and some *ollas* don't have lids, you'll have to fashion a lid of foil, borrow a lid from another pot or simply add a little water to adjust for evaporation. *Cazuelas* and *ollas* are very inexpensive in Mexico, and they have a simple beauty that's attractively irregular, almost accidental. But always choose a pot with no chips or cracks and one that's thoroughly glazed inside. What is the best stand-in for a *cazuela* or *olla*? Enameled cast iron, I'd say, since the enameled exterior is reminiscent of the earthenware's glaze and the iron holds heat like clay.

And the lead glazes? Yes, most Mexican earthenware pots have lead glazes. You'll have to make up your own mind, but let me tell you the essentials: It takes time and acid to leach lead from glazes. So stay away from very acidic food, don't store foods in them or simply boil vinegar-water in them until all has evaporated to a lead-filled residue, then scrub the residue out (this affects the color). Other than that, I encourage you to enjoy your *cazuela* from time to time—they have been a traditional and integral part of the Mexican kitchen for centuries.

. . . .

cazuelas

bean pots

earthenware cooking vessels

VERACRUZ-STYLE GREENS AND BEANS
WITH RED CHILE AND DUMPLINGS
Quelites con Frijoles, Estilo Veracruzano

A RICHLY SPICY STEW, this braise of black beans, greens and corny dumplings in red-chile sauce is the kind of delicious dish most of us stopped eating in America back in the 50s. Beans and greens, no matter what culture it was from, reminded us of the old-fashioned ways; steak and French fries were on every horizon. Today they tell us that beans and greens are what we should have been eating all along, if health is our concern.

This recipe is based on one I got in Veracruz, where the dish is made with a wild green (a heart-shaped tender leaf) called *xonequi*. It's for a cold afternoon when you're going to be around the house to monitor the simmering, and you want to fill the place with an enticing aroma. If you've invited guests, put together a bowl of Guacamole (page 78), toss together a romaine salad, and make a rich dessert like Chocolate Pecan Pie (page 404).

MAKES ABOUT 10 CUPS, SERVING 6 AS A MAIN COURSE

1 pound (about 2½ cups) dry black beans

4 stemmed, dried chipotle chiles (or canned chipotle chiles en adobo)

3 medium (1½ ounces total) dried ancho chiles, stemmed and seeded

3 garlic cloves, peeled and roughly chopped

½ small white onion, sliced

4 tablespoons olive or vegetable oil or rich-tasting lard

1 cup (8 ounces) fresh masa for tortillas

   OR *a generous ¾ cup dried masa* harina *mixed with ⅔ cup hot water*

Salt, about 2½ teaspoons

¾ cup chopped cilantro

1½ cups (6 ounces) crumbled Mexican queso fresco or pressed, salted farmer's cheese

6 cups stemmed, thickly sliced, sturdy greens (such as lamb's quarters [quelites], chard, collard or practically any other; if you're cooking in Mexico, try the Veracruz xonequi or quintoniles or Yucatecan chaya)

1. *The beans.* Rinse the beans, then scoop them into a large (6-quart) pot (preferably a Dutch oven or Mexican earthenware *olla*), add 2 quarts of water and remove any beans that float. Bring to a boil, reduce heat to medium-low and simmer, partially covered, until the

beans are tender (they will taste creamy, not chalky), about 2 hours. Stir regularly and add water to keep the level of the liquid a generous ½ inch above the beans.

2. *The chiles.* On an ungreased griddle or heavy skillet over medium heat, toast the dried chipotles, turning regularly, and pressing flat with a spatula, until they are very aromatic and a little toasty smelling, about 30 seconds. (Canned chipotles need no preparation.) Open the anchos flat and, 1 or 2 at a time, press flat for a few seconds with a metal spatula until they start to crackle, even send up a faint wisp of smoke, then flip and press down to toast the other side. In a small bowl, cover chiles with hot water and let rehydrate 30 minutes, stirring frequently to ensure even soaking. Drain and discard the water.

In a food processor or blender, puree the chiles with the garlic, onion and about ½ cup water (you may need a little more to get everything moving). Press through a medium-mesh strainer into a bowl. In a large saucepan, heat 2 *tablespoons* of the oil or lard over medium-high. Add the puree all at once and stir nearly constantly as it sears and thickens for about 5 minutes. When the beans are tender, add chile puree and simmer 30 minutes longer.

3. *The* masa *dumplings.* In a large bowl, knead together the fresh or reconstituted *masa* with the remaining 2 *tablespoons* of oil or lard, ½ *teaspoon* of the salt, ¼ *cup* of the chopped cilantro and the cheese. Form into about 48 balls. Cover and set aside.

4. *Finishing the dish.* There should be a good amount of broth in the beans (you have to add the dumplings and greens and still come out with a stewlike consistency, so add water if necessary), and the broth should be as thick as a light sauce (if it's not as thick as you'd like, puree a cup of the beans in a food processor or blender and return to the pot to thicken them). Liberally season the stew with salt, usually about 2 teaspoons.

With the pot simmering over medium, add the dumplings one at a time, nestling them into the gurgling broth. Simmer 5 minutes, then add the greens, stir *gently* so as not to break up the dumplings, and simmer until the greens are fully cooked (about 7 minutes for tender greens like chard, 10 to 12 minutes for collard and lamb's quarters).

Ladle into warm bowls, sprinkle with chopped cilantro and serve with steaming tortillas.

ADVANCE PREPARATION—The beans can be cooked through step 2 several days ahead; cover and refrigerate. The dumplings can be formed a day ahead; cover them, too, and refrigerate. Reheat the beans slowly before adding the dumplings and greens.

VARIATIONS AND IMPROVISATIONS—For a smoky taste, cook the beans with a ham hock. Or, add ½ pound of peeled shrimp just before adding the dumplings. Or, ladle a cup of stew into a pasta bowl, then lay a grilled pork chop on top.

RUNNER BEANS IN BRICK-RED *MOLE*

Ayocotes en Coloradito

$\mathcal{T}$HIS TRADITIONAL Oaxacan specialty that pairs runner beans with one of the famous seven *moles,* may seem like a lot of work for a pot of beans. Alone this simple *mole* has many uses: It makes a great sauce for enchiladas, tamales, grilled chicken, braised pork loin and so forth. But in combination with the great big lima-shaped runner beans (related to kidney, not limas, they're beautiful and extra creamy inside), the dish is classically brilliant.

A meatless Lenten dish, really, the beans in *mole* make a good taco filling if you simmer the sauce until thick—shredded pork or chicken would make it more substantial. Or serve as a meatless main dish with a good cheese, hot tortillas and a salad.

If you haven't worked with runner beans before, these heirlooms come in several colors and are easy to grow in the States. In Oaxaca, the variety is a deep purple; here a very similar one called *scarlet* is available. Expect them to take a full 3 hours to cook. If runner beans are unavailable, others will work fine.

MAKES 7 GENEROUS CUPS, 6 TO 8 SERVINGS AS AN ACCOMPANIMENT

12 ounces (about 2 cups) dry scarlet runner beans (or try black or kidney beans)

Salt, about 2½ teaspoons

6 medium (about 3 ounces total) dried ancho chiles, stemmed and seeded

3 medium (¾ ounce total) dried guajillo chiles, stemmed and seeded

6 ounces (1 medium-small round or 3 small plum) ripe tomatoes

4 garlic cloves, unpeeled

2 tablespoons sesame seeds

½ teaspoon cinnamon, preferably

freshly ground Mexican canela

1 generous teaspoon dried oregano, preferably Mexican

Scant ½ teaspoon black pepper, preferably freshly ground

3 tablespoons (about ¾ ounce) coarsely chopped Mexican chocolate

3 to 3½ cups chicken broth

1½ tablespoons vegetable or olive oil or rich-tasting pork lard

Sugar, about 2½ teaspoons

1. *The beans.* Rinse the beans, then scoop into a large (6-quart) pot (preferably Dutch oven or Mexican earthenware *olla*). Add 1½ quarts of water and remove any beans that float. Bring to a boil, then reduce the heat to medium-low and very gently simmer, partially covered, until tender (creamy, not chalky), 2 to 3 hours for scarlet runner beans, about 2 hours

for black or kidney. Stir the beans regularly and add water as necessary to keep the liquid a generous ½ inch above the beans. Season with about *1 teaspoon* of the salt, simmer for 20 minutes or so, then drain.

2. *Making 3 cups of* **Mole Coloradito.** While the beans are cooking, make the *mole*. On a ungreased griddle or heavy skillet heated over medium, toast the chiles a few at a time: open chiles flat, lay on the hot surface, press flat for a few seconds with a metal spatula (until they start to crackle, even send up a faint wisp of smoke), then flip and press down to toast the other side. In a medium-size bowl, cover the chiles with hot water and let rehydrate 30 minutes, stirring frequently to ensure even soaking. Drain and discard the water.

While the chiles are soaking, lay a piece of foil over part of your hot griddle or skillet and lay the tomatoes on it; on the uncovered part, place the garlic. Roast, turning everything occasionally, until blackened in spots and soft, 10 to 15 minutes. Cool slightly, then peel off the tomato and garlic skins. On the hot surface, toast the sesame seeds for a minute or so (they'll pop around), then scrape them into a blender along with the tomatoes and garlic. Add the chiles, cinnamon, oregano, pepper, chocolate and *1½ cups* of the broth. Blend to a smooth puree, then press through a medium-mesh strainer into a bowl.

Heat the oil or lard in a heavy, medium-size (2- to 3-quart) saucepan over medium-high. When hot enough to make a drop of the puree sizzle fiercely, add the puree all at once and stir for several minutes as it sears and thickens. Stir in another *1½ cups* of the broth, partially cover and simmer for about 1 hour, stirring occasionally. Taste and season highly with the salt, usually about 1½ teaspoons, and the sugar.

3. *Finishing the dish.* Stir the drained beans into the *mole*. Simmer about 20 minutes for the beans to absorb the flavors. Add a little more broth if needed to give the mixture a stew-like consistency. Taste for salt and they're ready to ladle into warm bowls.

ADVANCE PREPARATION—Covered and refrigerated, the dish keeps several days.

VARIATIONS AND IMPROVISATIONS—In Oaxaca, this has traditionally been made with other chiles. My favorite version is Panchita's (the best chile seller in the downtown market): 2 ounces each ancho and *chile chilhuacle rojo,* though she says ancho and guajillo are just about as good.

RICE

· · · · ·

Rice has two roles in the Mexican kitchen. Casually, it's an accompaniment to many main dishes (beans are considerably more "down home"). And in the framework of a formal meal, rice becomes a second course—what's called the *dry soup,* served after the first course *wet soup,* to translate Mexican culinary parlance. If you watch rice being made, it starts off soupy then becomes dry, which helps me logically understand the concept.

If anyone says *arroz* at a Mexican table, they probably mean the Classic Red Tomato Rice, made by frying raw rice, then simmering it with tomatoes, chiles, garlic and broth. That's the first recipe here.

Also made in this same pilaf style, other Mexican rices offer many unique colors and flavors to choose from. Dried chiles turn it a deep, burnished cranberry red; poblano chiles color it emerald and black bean broth makes the rice, not surprisingly, dark black-brown. They're all so distinctively good, I often want to make them the focal point of the meal.

One of my all-time favorite rices in Mexico is flavored with achiote, so it comes out orangey-yellow. Here I've turned that rice into a homey meal with bits of pork and vegetables. Still in the homey vein, I'm offering a comforting rice casserole, made from plain boiled rice (what's sometimes called *morisqueta*) and a tomato base with poblanos and melted cheese. My final rice recipe is probably the homiest of all, a one-pot meal of pilaf-style rice flecked with tomato, green chile, chorizo, zucchini and corn.

CLASSIC RED TOMATO RICE

Arroz a la Mexicana

*T*HIS IS MEXICAN RICE to most people; red with bits of tomato, sweet with onions and garlic. You'll notice that the flavorings are simply a salsa, my Essential Roasted-Tomato Jalapeño Salsa, so that'll help you to imagine the flavors: good rice, classically made in the fluffy pilaf (fried raw rice) style, shot through with the pure essence of Mexican flavor—even down to the sprinkling of chopped cilantro just before serving. It will be delicious with practically any Mexican main dish.

I've given a recipe that makes a large amount of rice for a big gathering or simply to enjoy over several days. Besides, we all thought, who would want to make so little of such a great rice? The method here calls for baking the rice to doneness. If you are planning to double or triple any of the other rices in this chapter, I recommend you follow this procedure.

MAKES ABOUT 6 CUPS, SERVING 6 TO 8

FOR 2 CUPS ESSENTIAL ROASTED TOMATO-JALAPEÑO SALSA

1 pound (2 medium-large round or 6 to 8 plum) ripe tomatoes

2 to 3 fresh jalapeño chiles

3 garlic cloves, unpeeled

Salt, about 1 1/2 teaspoons

1/2 small white onion, finely chopped

1 cup loosely packed chopped cilantro

2 tablespoons vegetable or olive oil

2 cups rice, preferably medium grain

1 1/2 cups chicken broth or water

1. *Making 2 cups Essential Roasted Tomato-Jalapeño Salsa.* Roast the tomatoes on a baking sheet 4 inches below a very hot broiler until blackened on 1 side, about 6 minutes, then flip and roast the other side. Cool and peel, collecting all the juices with the tomatoes. While the tomatoes are roasting, roast the chiles and unpeeled garlic directly on an ungreased griddle or heavy skillet over medium heat, turning occasionally, until soft (they'll blacken in spots: 5 to 10 minutes for the chiles, about 15 minutes for the garlic). Cool, then pull the stems from the chiles and peel the garlic.

In a large mortar (or food processor—the small ones work best here), pound (or whir) the chiles, garlic and *1/2 teaspoon* of the salt into a coarse-textured puree. Add the juicy tomatoes (a few at a time, if using a mortar) and work them into a coarse, rich-textured salsa. Rinse the onion in a strainer under cold water, shake off the excess and add to the tomato mixture along with *1/2 cup* of the cilantro.

2. *The rice.* Turn on the oven to 350 degrees. In a 3-quart, ovenproof saucepan or small Dutch oven (with a lid), heat the oil over medium. Add the rice and cook, stirring regularly, until the rice turns chalky looking, about 5 minutes. If some kernels brown, it's fine.

Add the salsa and stir for a minute as the salsa sears, releases its aroma and reduces a little, then add the broth or water and the remaining *1 teaspoon* of the salt. Bring to a boil, stir once, scrape down any rice kernels clinging to the sides of the pan, cover tightly and bake for 25 minutes; uncover and bite into a grain of rice: It should be nearly cooked through. If the rice is just about ready, re-cover and let stand out of the oven for 5 to 10 minutes longer to complete the cooking. If the rice seems far from done, re-cover and continue baking for 5 minutes or so, retest, then let stand out of the oven for a few more minutes.

Sprinkle the remaining *½ cup* of the cilantro over the rice, then use a fork to fluff the mixture and fold in the cilantro.

ADVANCE PREPARATION—The rice can be made several days ahead. Turn the fluffed rice out onto a baking sheet to cool, transfer to a storage container, then cover and refrigerate. Reheat the rice in a steamer over boiling water. Add cilantro just before serving.

SHORTCUTS—You can replace the tomatoes with ⅔ of a 28-ounce can.

VARIATIONS AND IMPROVISATIONS

You may vary the chile to serrano, manzano, habanero, roasted and peeled poblano—practically any fresh chile that suits your taste. Any broth may be used, from rich beef to fish. Blanched vegetables can be added during the last few minutes of cooking (classic are peas and carrots, though I like zucchini, chayote and chopped spinach or chard). And shreds of cooked meat, poultry or fish can be added to make it a one-pot meal.

Classic White Rice—Replace the salsa with 1 diced large white onion. Fry the onion with the raw rice for 5 minutes, then add 2½ cups of chicken broth and 1½ teaspoons salt, stir once and bake in a preheated 350-degree oven as described at the end of step 2.

Arroz con Bacalao—Soak ½ pound of salt cod in water for 24 hours, changing the water at least 3 times. Bring the cod to a boil in fresh water, simmer until the fish barely flakes, remove it from the broth, flake it and add to the rice as it browns. If the poaching liquid isn't too salty, use it for the rice-cooking liquid, otherwise use fish or chicken broth.

RED CHILE RICE

Arroz Rojo

As a guy who is perpetually drawn to the deep and complex flavor of chiles, I find this red-chile rice to be one of my favorites. Its stunning, deep rusty-red color and completely satisfying flavor make the additional effort of preparing the chile paste worthwhile.

Red Chile Rice is so flavorful that it easily becomes the star of dinner. Serve it with the Great Big Tamal Roll with Chard (page 306) and a little Essential Roasted Tomatillo-Chipotle Salsa (page 45) for a special meatless meal. Most will want to serve it with broiled or grilled steak, chicken or turkey, and with Classic Mexican Fried Beans (page 237). (Turkey? Just imagine Red Chile Rice on the Thanksgiving table with a smoked turkey.)

MAKES ABOUT 3 CUPS, SERVING 4

FOR 1 CUP ESSENTIAL SWEET-AND-SPICY ANCHO SEASONING PASTE

8 garlic cloves, unpeeled

8 medium (about 4 ounces total) dried ancho chiles, stemmed and seeded

1½ teaspoons dried oregano, preferably Mexican

½ teaspoon black pepper, preferably freshly ground

⅛ teaspoon cumin seeds, preferably freshly ground

A scant ¼ teaspoon cloves, preferably freshly ground

Salt, about 1½ teaspoons if using salted broth, 2 teaspoons for unsalted broth or water

1 tablespoon vegetable or olive oil

1 cup rice, preferably medium grain

1 small white onion, diced into ¼-inch pieces

1⅔ cups chicken broth or water

Chopped cilantro, for garnish

1. *Making about 1 cup Essential Sweet-and-Spicy Ancho Seasoning Paste.* Roast the unpeeled garlic on an ungreased griddle or heavy skillet over medium heat, turning occasionally, until soft (they'll blacken in spots), about 15 minutes; cool and peel. While the garlic is roasting, toast the chiles on another side of the griddle or skillet: 1 or 2 at a time, open them flat and press down firmly on the hot surface with a spatula; in a few seconds, when they crackle, even send up a wisp of smoke, flip them and press down to toast the other side. In a small bowl cover the chiles with hot water and let rehydrate 30 minutes, stirring frequently to ensure even soaking. Drain and discard the water.

Combine the oregano, black pepper, cumin and cloves in a food processor or blender, along with the chiles, garlic and ⅔ cup of water (or broth if you have some extra). Process to a smooth puree, scraping and stirring every few seconds. (If the mixture won't go through the blender blades, add a little more liquid.) Press through a medium-mesh strainer into a bowl. Taste and season with salt, usually about 1 teaspoon.

2. *The rice.* In a 2-quart saucepan, heat the oil over medium. Add the rice and onion and cook, stirring regularly, until the rice is chalky looking and the onion is soft, about 5 minutes.

Heat the broth, 5 *tablespoons* of the ancho seasoning (refrigerate the rest to make more rice or to use as a great marinade for grilled chicken, fish or meat) and the salt (½ to 1 teaspoon depending on the saltiness of the broth) in a small saucepan. When the liquid boils, add it to the rice, stir once, scrape down any rice kernels clinging to the side of the pan, cover and cook over medium-low for 15 minutes. Uncover and check a grain of rice: It should be nearly cooked through. If the rice is just about ready, turn off the heat, re-cover and let stand for 5 to 10 minutes to complete the cooking. If the rice seems far from done, continue cooking for 5 minutes or so, retest, then turn off the heat and let stand a few more minutes.

Use a fork to fluff the rice, then scoop it into a warm serving dish, sprinkle with the cilantro, and it's ready to carry to the table.

ADVANCE PREPARATION—The rice can be made several days ahead: Turn out the fluffed rice onto a baking sheet to cool, transfer to a storage container, then cover and refrigerate. Reheat the rice in a steamer; sprinkle on the cilantro just before serving.

VARIATIONS AND IMPROVISATIONS

For a spicier rice, substitute guajillos for anchos, or for something spicier yet (but smoky and alluring), replace the Ancho Seasoning Paste with 2 or 3 tablespoons of Essential Sweet-and-Smoky Chipotle Seasoning Salsa (page 52) or finely chopped canned chipotles (the former will make a brown rice, so you may want to add a little paprika to bring up the reddish color). Stir in shreds of roast lamb or slices of lamb sausage just before serving, for a heartier pot of rice.

Red and Black Rice—When the rice is finished stir in 3 cups of slightly soupy seasoned black beans (see Classic Mexican "Pot" Beans, page 234) and ½ pound warm, sliced smoked sausage. Serve in soup bowls as a Mexican "jambalaya," topped with slivers of green onion.

GREEN POBLANO RICE

Arroz Verde al Poblano

HERE ARE MANY VERSIONS of special-occasion green rice in Mexico. My current favorite is this one, green with the richness and welcoming spiciness of poblano chiles, backed up by herbal cilantro and sweet onion and garlic. This full-flavored rice can accompany a simple grilled fish or chicken, Spicy Tomato-Sauced Enchiladas (page 176) or any dish that weaves a little green chile into its sauce. It also is a great accompaniment to Roasted Mexican Vegetables in Green Sesame *Pipián* (page 221) for an all-vegetable dinner.

The rice is made pilaf style, like most Mexican rices, meaning that the raw rice is fried first so that the grains will be separate when cooked. Dependable as that method is, this rice comes out a touch sticky because of all the poblano pureed into the broth. I make it ahead, spread it onto a baking sheet to cool and allow excess moisture to evaporate, so the rice will fluff up into separate grains. Then I reheat it in a steamer.

MAKES ABOUT 3 CUPS, SERVING 4

1⅔ cups chicken broth or water

2 fresh poblano chiles, stems and seeds removed, and roughly chopped

12 sprigs cilantro, plus extra for garnish

Salt, about ½ teaspoon if using salted broth, 1 teaspoon if using unsalted or water

1 tablespoon vegetable or olive oil

1 cup rice, preferably medium grain

1 small white onion, cut into ¼-inch dice

5 garlic cloves, peeled and finely chopped

1. *The flavoring.* In a 2-quart saucepan, combine the broth and chiles, bring to a boil, then partially cover and simmer gently over medium to medium-low heat for about 10 minutes, until the chiles are very soft. Pour the chile mixture into a food processor, add the cilantro (stems and all), and process to a smooth puree. Press through a medium-mesh strainer into a bowl and stir in the salt.

2. *The rice.* Wipe the pan clean, add the oil and heat over medium. Add the rice and onion, and cook, stirring regularly, until the rice is chalky looking and the onion is soft, about 5 minutes. Stir in the garlic and cook a minute longer.

Add the warm (or reheated) chile liquid to the hot rice pan, stir once, scrape down any rice kernels clinging to the side of the pan, cover, and cook over medium-low heat for 15 minutes. Uncover and check a grain of rice: It should be nearly cooked through. If the rice is just about ready, turn off the heat, re-cover and let stand for 5 to 10 minutes longer to complete the cooking. If the rice seems far from done, continue cooking for 5 minutes or so, retest, then turn off the heat and let stand a few minutes longer. Fluff with a fork, scoop into a warm serving dish, decorate with cilantro sprigs and it's ready to serve.

ADVANCE PREPARATION—The rice can be made several days ahead; turn out the fluffed rice onto a baking sheet to cool, transfer to a storage container, then cover and refrigerate. Reheat the rice in a steamer basket set over boiling water.

VARIATIONS AND IMPROVISATIONS—An obvious variation is to use 3 or 4 long green (Anaheim) chiles, or to mix poblanos and long greens with hotter chiles like jalapeño, manzano or habanero. Grilled corn cut from 1 cob or 1 large grilled zucchini (cubed) are tasty vegetable add-ins. About 1 cup coarsely shredded roast (or barbecued) pork or smoked salmon, mixed in toward the end of cooking, will make green rice a full meal.

green tops

fresh-dug white onions

BLACK BEAN RICE

Arroz Negro

WHEN YOU MAKE those Classic Mexican Fried Beans (page 237) from a long-simmered pot of *frijoles negros*, save the extra broth for a batch of Black Bean Rice. It offers an earthier flavor that goes well with dishes like seared Chipotle Shrimp (page 334).

I've only eaten this dish in the Yucatan as part of the classic *frijol con puerco* dinner. But it's popular throughout the Caribbean. My recipe is based on three from regional cookbooks from Mexico (one from Quintana Roo called *arroz cubano,* a Oaxacan one called *arroz enfrijolado* and an *arroz negro* from Sinaloa). This one requires a really *black* black bean broth (not like the gray broth drained from canned beans) to have the dramatic color and rich flavor.

MAKES ABOUT 3 CUPS, SERVING 4

1 tablespoon vegetable or olive oil

1 cup rice, preferably medium grain

1 small white onion, diced into ¼-inch pieces

5 garlic cloves, peeled and finely chopped

1½ cups broth from cooking black beans (page 234)

Salt, about ½ teaspoon if using salted bean broth, 1 teaspoon if using unsalted

In a 2-quart saucepan, heat the oil over medium. Add the rice and onion, and cook, stirring regularly, until the rice is chalky looking and the onion is soft, about 5 minutes. Stir in the garlic and cook a minute longer.

In a small saucepan, bring the bean broth to a boil, stir in the salt, then pour into the hot rice pan. Stir thoroughly, scrape down any rice kernels clinging to the side of the pan, cover and cook over medium-low for 15 minutes. Uncover and check a grain of rice: It should be nearly cooked through. If the rice is about ready, turn off the heat, re-cover and let stand 5 to 10 minutes. If it seems far from done, cook for 5 minutes or so, retest, then turn off the heat and let stand a few minutes. (Cooking takes longer if the black bean broth is thick.)

Use a fork to fluff the rice, then scoop it into a warm serving dish.

ADVANCE PREPARATION—The rice can be made several days ahead; cool on a baking sheet; cover and refrigerate. Reheat in a steamer.

Add chipotle chile to the rice as it cooks. Crumbled cooked bacon, ham or sausage are tasty, as are diced fried plantain and crumbled fresh cheese.

Black Bean Rice Cakes—Mix the cooked rice with 2 eggs, ¼ cup flour, 1 tablespoon chopped canned chipotle chiles and ⅓ cup crumbled *queso añejo* (the mixture should just hold together). Drop good-size dollops onto a lightly oiled nonstick skillet heated over medium. Flatten to ¼ inch thick, let brown, flip and brown the other side. Serve with Thick Cream (page 165) or *crème fraîche* and Essential Roasted Tomatillo-Chipotle Salsa (page 45).

ACHIOTE RICE SUPPER WITH PORK *CARNITAS*

Arroz Amarillo con Carnitas

A RICE ALMOST LIKE THIS was one of the first dishes I learned to cook in Mexico. María Villalobos, a Juchitecan I met when doing linguistics work in Mexico City some 20 years ago, was the teacher, and her enthusiasm for cooking seared this delicious one-dish dinner into my memory. Achiote paste, the primary flavoring here, contains fewer spices in Juchitan than in Yucatan. Personally, I gravitate to the garlicky, spicy Yucatecan paste. I like this rice so much that, without the meat and chiles, we use it as our "house" rice at Frontera.

SERVES 4 AS A MAIN DISH

FOR ⅓ CUP ESSENTIAL GARLICKY ACHIOTE SEASONING PASTE

2 tablespoons achiote seeds

2 teaspoons whole allspice, preferably freshly ground

1 teaspoon black pepper, preferably freshly ground

1½ teaspoons dried oregano, preferably Mexican

3 tablespoons cider vinegar

6 garlic cloves, peeled

Salt, about 2 teaspoons

1 pound boneless pork shoulder, trimmed and cut into 1½-inch cubes

1 tablespoon fresh lime juice (optional)

1 fresh long green (Anaheim) or poblano chile

1 cup fresh (or defrosted frozen) peas

1 cup rice, preferably medium grain

1 small white onion, finely chopped

1¾ cups broth, preferably pork or beef broth

2 medium carrots, chopped into ¼-inch dice

A little chopped cilantro, for garnish

1. *Making ⅓ cup of Essential Garlicky Achiote Seasoning Paste.* Very finely pulverize the achiote in a spice grinder, then transfer it to a small bowl and mix in the allspice, pepper, oregano and vinegar. Roughly chop the garlic, sprinkle with a generous *1 teaspoon* of the salt, then, working right on your cutting board, use the back of a spoon or the side of a knife to work the two into a smooth paste. Scoop the achiote mixture onto the garlic, work the two together, then dribble on and work in enough water (usually about a tablespoon or 2) to give it all the consistency of a thick but spreadable paste.

2. *The* **carnitas.** Place the pork cubes in a 2-quart, heavy-bottomed saucepan. Cover with water by ½ inch. Add lime juice (if you're using it) and ½ *teaspoon* of the salt. Set over medium heat and simmer, partially covered, until all the liquid is absorbed and the meat begins to fry in its own rendered fat, about 1 hour. Reduce the heat a little and cook uncovered, turning meat frequently, until evenly browned, about 10 minutes. Remove the meat, pour off all but enough fat to lightly coat the bottom of the pan and set the pan aside.

3. *The vegetables.* While the meat is cooking, prepare the vegetables. Place the chile directly over the gas flame or 4 inches below a very hot broiler and roast until blistered and blackened on all sides, 5 to 10 minutes. Cover with a kitchen towel, let stand 5 minutes, then peel, cut out the seed pod, scrape out the seeds and cut into ¼-inch dice.

   Cook fresh peas in a pot of boiling water until tender, 4 to 20 minutes, depending on their size and maturity; drain and set aside. Or, simply measure out frozen peas.

4. *The rice.* Return the pan in which you made the *carnitas* to medium heat and add the rice and onion. Cook, stirring regularly and scraping up any sticky bits from the bottom of the pan, until the rice is chalky looking and the onion is soft, about 5 minutes. Meanwhile, in a small saucepan heat the broth with *2 tablespoons* of the achiote seasoning and the remaining *½ to 1 teaspoon* of salt, depending on the saltiness of the broth. (Refrigerate the rest of the achiote seasoning for more batches of rice or to use as a flavorful marinade for grilled or broiled meat, chicken or fish.) Whisk the broth mixture well, then add to the hot rice pan along with the browned pork, roasted chile and carrots. Stir once, scrape down any rice kernels clinging to the side of the pan, cover and cook over medium-low for 15 minutes. Uncover and bite into a grain of rice: It should be nearly cooked through. If the rice is just about ready, turn off the heat, stir in the peas, re-cover, and let stand for 5 to 10 minutes longer to complete the cooking. If the rice seems far from done, cook for 5 minutes or so, retest and then add the peas, remove from the heat, and let stand a few minutes. Fluff the rice, scoop it into a warm serving dish, sprinkle with cilantro and serve.

ADVANCE PREPARATION—This rice is best finished shortly before it's eaten, so all the vegetables will look fresh. Or make it without the peas, cool, refrigerate covered, then reheat covered in a 350-degree oven. Stir in the peas, garnish with cilantro and serve.

SHORTCUTS—The easiest option is to buy the achiote paste and *carnitas* (¾ pound) at a Mexican grocery. You'll start your preparations with step 3, if you've chosen these shortcuts.

TOMATO-RICE CASSEROLE
WITH POBLANOS AND MELTED CHEESE

Arroz Gratinado

*T*HIS MAIN-DISH recipe offers great everyday flavors: roasted tomatoes and green chiles baked with shreds of beef, tender rice and gooey cheese.

Without the meat, this casserole is a substantial side dish to serve with grilled or roasted meats or poultry. To set on a buffet, double the recipe and bake it in a 13 x 9-inch dish.

SERVES 6 AS A CASUAL ENTREE

FOR 2 CUPS ESSENTIAL ROASTED POBLANO *RAJAS*

1 pound (6 medium-large) fresh poblano chiles

1 tablespoon vegetable or olive oil

1 large white onion, sliced ¼ inch thick

3 garlic cloves, peeled and finely chopped

½ teaspoon dried oregano, preferably Mexican

1 pound (2 medium-large, 6 to 8 plum) ripe tomatoes

Salt, about 2 teaspoons

1 cup rice, preferably medium grain

1 cup (about 4 ounces) grated Mexican Chihuahua, or other melting cheese such as brick or Monterey Jack

1½ cups (about 6 ounces) boneless, shredded, cooked beef (grilled skirt steak works wonderfully here) (optional)

1. *Making 2 cups Essential Roasted Poblano* **Rajas.** Roast the chiles directly over a gas flame or on a baking sheet 4 inches below a very hot broiler until blackened on all sides, about 5 minutes for open flame, about 10 minutes for broiler. (If using a broiler, the tomatoes from step 2 can be roasted at the same time.) Cover with a kitchen towel and let stand 5 minutes. Peel, pull out the stem and seed pod, then rinse *briefly* to remove bits of skin and seeds. Slice into ¼-inch strips.

In a medium-size (8- to 9-inch) skillet, heat the oil over medium to medium-high, then add the onion and cook, stirring regularly, until nicely browned but still a little crunchy, about 5 minutes. Add the garlic and oregano, toss a minute longer, then stir in the chiles and remove from the heat.

2. *The tomatoes.* Roast the tomatoes on a baking sheet 4 inches below a very hot broiler until blackened on one side, about 6 minutes, then flip and roast the other side. Cool, then peel, collecting all the juices. Chop tomatoes coarsely, and combine with the juices.

Return the chiles to medium-high heat, add the tomatoes and their juices, and stir until the juices are nicely reduced, 3 to 4 minutes. Season with salt, usually 1 teaspoon.

3. *The rice*. In a large (6-quart) pot, bring 3 quarts water to a boil and add the remaining *1 teaspoon* of the salt. Add the rice and simmer, uncovered, 15 minutes, until the grains are tender but not mushy or splayed. Pour into a strainer, then spread onto a tray to cool.

4. *The casserole*. Turn on the oven to 350 degrees. Spread *half* of the rice over the bottom of a lightly greased 8 x 8-inch baking dish. Spoon on *half* the chile-tomato mixture, spreading it to the edges, then sprinkle over about *half* of the cheese. If you're using any meat, distribute it over the cheese at this point.

Cover with the remaining rice, chile-tomato mixture and cheese (in that order), and bake until bubbling and brown, 20 to 30 minutes. Let stand 10 minutes and serve.

ADVANCE PREPARATION—Steps 1, 2 and 3 can be completed several days in advance; refrigerate sauce and rice separately, covered. The whole casserole can be assembled (and refrigerated) several hours before baking; the baking time will be slightly longer.

VARIATIONS AND IMPROVISATIONS

Long green (Anaheim) or chilaca chiles can replace the poblanos; 2 cups of *al dente* pasta can replace the rice; and shreds of chicken or pork can replace the meat. An interesting option for fish fanciers would be to layer about 8 ounces of cubed raw monkfish in the middle.

Scalloped Potatoes and Chiles—Slice 1½ pounds of boiling potatoes ⅛ inch thick and layer them in the casserole where rice is called for. Bake the casserole until the potatoes are very tender, about 30 minutes or so.

Creamy Rice Casserole with Poblanos and Corn—Mix the *rajas* in step 1 with 1 cup Thick Cream (page 165), whipping cream or *crème fraîche* or 1¼ cups plain yogurt and *omit* the tomatoes (step 2). Then, assemble the casserole as directed in step 4, adding 1½ cups corn kernels and ¼ cup chopped cilantro to the casserole before adding the optional meat layer.

MEXICAN RICE SUPPER
WITH CHORIZO, ZUCCHINI AND CORN

Arroz con Chorizo

*H*ERE'S A SIMPLE one-pot supper that combines the traditional flavors of chorizo and chopped tomato salsa in the homey confines of a good pot of rice. I concocted this for a class a few years ago, to show the uses of Essential Chopped Tomato-Serrano Salsa (page 25). It is so classic I'm sure something similar has been made in many households across Mexico. Pair it with some dressed greens (or a spinach salad), warm tortillas and, perhaps, a small bowl of beans, and you've got a supper to savor.

MAKES ABOUT 5 CUPS, SERVING 4 AS A CASUAL MAIN DISH

FOR 2 CUPS ESSENTIAL CHOPPED TOMATO-SERRANO SALSA

12 ounces (2 medium-small round or 4 to 6 plum) ripe tomatoes, chopped into ¼-inch dice

Fresh serrano chiles to taste (roughly 3 to 5), stemmed, seeded if you wish, and finely chopped

1 large garlic clove, peeled and very finely chopped

3 tablespoons chopped cilantro, plus a little extra for garnish

1 small white onion, finely chopped

8 ounces (about 1 cup) chorizo sausage, casing removed

1 cup rice, preferably medium grain

¾ cup chicken or beef broth, or even water

Salt, about ½ teaspoon for salted broth, 1 teaspoon for unsalted broth or water

2 small zucchini, cut into ⅜-inch dice

The kernels from 1 large ear corn (about 1 cup)

1. *Making 2 cups Essential Chopped Tomato-Serrano Salsa.* Mix together the tomatoes, chiles, garlic and cilantro. Scoop the onion into a strainer, rinse under cold water, shake off excess and add to the mixture.

2. *The rice.* Break up the chorizo into a medium (2- to 3-quart) heavy-bottomed saucepan and set over medium heat. Stir regularly, breaking up any lumps, until the sausage is thoroughly cooked, about 10 minutes. Remove it with a slotted spoon, then pour off all but a tablespoon or so of the fat. Add the rice to the pan, return to the heat and stir regularly until the rice is lightly browned, about 7 minutes. Add the salsa, raise the heat to medium-high and cook, stirring every once in a while, until very thick and reduced, about 7 minutes.

While the mixture cooks, combine the broth (or water) and salt in a small saucepan and bring to a boil. Add to the rice mixture, stir once, scrape down any rice kernels clinging to the side of the pan, cover and cook over medium-low for 10 minutes. Add the cooked chorizo, zucchini and corn, re-cover and cook 5 minutes longer. Uncover and bite into a grain of rice:It should be nearly cooked through. If the rice is just about ready, turn off the heat, re-cover and let stand for 5 to 10 minutes longer to complete the cooking. If the rice seems far from done, continue cooking for 5 minutes or so, retest, then turn off the heat and let stand a few more minutes.

Scoop into a warm bowl, sprinkle with the extra cilantro, and serve.

ADVANCE PREPARATION—The dish can be made a day or so ahead; the zucchini will suffer a bit in the reheating. Turn out the fluffed rice onto a baking sheet to cool, transfer to a storage container, then cover and refrigerate. Reheat the rice in a steamer.

Rice

During the first years Deann and I traveled through Mexico, I collected rice samples nearly everywhere I went. Though rice is rarely labeled as to its length, I determined at the end of my journey that a medium-grain white rice (there is virtually no brown rice in Mexico) is the standard. When I moved all my rice cooking into the medium camp (at first in order to be "authentic"), I discovered I love its texture: less dry and mealy than long grain, less sticky than short. For me it produces the perfect, toothsome, moist kernel.

Medium grain rice needs a little less liquid than long grain, so don't be surprised by my quantities. (If you can only get long grain, try adding 2 or 3 tablespoons of extra liquid for each cup of dry rice.) And take note of the pan sizes: they are specified to ensure that you'll have the right depth and density for perfect cooking. If you decide to double recipes, don't use a pan that's much larger and don't use double the liquid—*usually* 1½ times will do.

I like my rice fully cooked, with no chalky interior, but not overcooked (splayed at the ends). To avoid overcooking by the residual heat of the pan, I suggest you turn the cooked rice out onto a tray to cool. That's what we do at the restaurant, reheating whatever quantity we need in a steamer.

EGG DISHES

· · · · ·

Being uncertain about where to put egg dishes in today's fat-free climate, I've chosen to include them with meatless (or little-meat) dishes. Twenty years ago I would have featured them prominently by themselves, but then again those were the days when I taught gourmet egg-cooking classes and they sold better than anything else. Today I wouldn't even offer the class for fear of no students, which is sad, since eggs are not only delicious but economical and nutritious—maybe not as the focus of your diet, but certainly as *part* of the diet. So I'm including a good smattering of the very, very delicious egg dishes from Mexico. (To tell the truth, we opened Frontera on Saturdays for *almuerzo* (breakfast/lunch) because I couldn't imagine *not* having these wonderful eggs somewhere on the menu.)

There's a new take here on *Huevos Rancheros* (we're calling it Rustic Red-Sauced Eggs). It is a lighter version of the standard, utilizing toasted (rather than fried) tortillas and a warmed salsa (rather than the classic cooked sauce).

Following are two regional specialties: A Oaxacan Omelette that's bathed in a brothy mix of roasted tomatoes, roasted chiles and Mexican herbs, and the baroque Motul-Style Eggs that include everything from black beans and tomato-habanero sauce to fried plantains, peas, cheese and ham.

The last returns us to the most classic Mexican egg dish, *Huevos Revueltos a la Mexicana*. It starts by searing the classic chopped tomato-serrano salsa in a hot skillet with dots of avocado, then scrambling in the eggs. A deliciously luxurious take on familiar flavors.

RUSTIC RED-SAUCED EGGS ON CORN TORTILLAS

Huevos Rústicos

*H*UEVOS *RÚSTICOS* are a simple version of the ever-popular, oh-so-Mexican *huevos rancheros,* soft corn tortillas replacing the standard quick-fried ones. The sauce here is the classic Essential Roasted Tomato-Jalapeño Salsa, that lusciously textured blend of rich, roasted flavors, spooned over eggs done sunny-side up, with only a sprinkling of racy cheese and cilantro to make life interesting. A spoonful of Classic Mexican Fried Beans (page 237) is the typical accompaniment, though you might want guacamole or a bowl of cut-up fruit drizzled with lime. On Sunday morning or evening, food should be what you want to eat, not what you feel you "ought" to.

SERVES 4 AS A NICE BREAKFAST (IF YOU'RE ALSO SERVING FRUIT, BREADS OR BEANS), PERHAPS 2 IF YOU WANT SOMETHING REALLY SUBSTANTIAL

FOR 2 CUPS ESSENTIAL ROASTED TOMATO-JALAPEÑO SALSA

1 pound (2 medium-large or 6 to 8 plum) ripe tomatoes

2 to 3 fresh jalapeño chiles

3 garlic cloves, unpeeled

Salt, a scant ½ teaspoon

½ small white onion, finely chopped, plus a little extra for garnish

A scant ½ cup loosely packed chopped cilantro, plus a few sprigs for garnish

4 corn tortillas

1 tablespoon vegetable or olive oil

4 eggs

2 tablespoons finely crumbled Mexican queso añejo, dry feta or Parmesan

1. *Making 2 cups Essential Roasted Tomato-Jalapeño Salsa.* Roast the tomatoes on a baking sheet 4 inches below a very hot broiler until blackened on 1 side, about 6 minutes, then flip and roast the other side. Cool and peel, collecting all the juices with the tomatoes. While the tomatoes are roasting, roast the chiles and unpeeled garlic directly on an ungreased griddle or heavy skillet over medium heat, turning occasionally, until soft (they'll blacken in spots: 5 to 10 minutes for the chiles, about 15 minutes for the garlic). Cool, then pull the stems from the chiles and peel the garlic.

In a large mortar (or small food processor/grinder), pound (or whir) the chiles, garlic and salt into a coarse-textured puree. Add the juicy tomatoes (a few at a time, if using a mortar) and work them into a coarse, rich-textured salsa. Rinse the onion in a strainer under cold water, shake off the excess and add to the tomato mixture, along with the cilantro. Taste and season with salt.

2. *The tortillas.* Lightly toast the tortillas directly over a gas flame or in an ungreased nonstick skillet over an electric burner, turning once, until heated through, 30 to 45 seconds. Wrap up in a thick clean towel to keep warm.

3. *Finishing the dish.* In a medium-size (2- to 3-quart) saucepan bring the salsa to a simmer, cover and keep warm over low heat.

Heat the oil in a large (10- to 12-inch), well-seasoned or nonstick skillet (you'll need a lid) over medium to medium-low. Crack the eggs into the skillet, cover and cook 1 minute. Uncover and continue cooking until the whites are set but the yolks are still runny, 1 to 2 minutes more (at least that's how I like them).

Lay a tortilla on each of 4 warm plates. Top each tortilla with an egg and spoon the warm salsa over everything, keeping the yolks uncovered if you like that look. Sprinkle with a little onion and the cheese, decorate with cilantro sprigs and the *huevos rústicos* are ready.

ADVANCE PREPARATION—The salsa and garnishes can be prepared a few hours in advance (a day in advance if you leave the raw onion out of the salsa); refrigerate everything separately, covered. Heat the tortillas, warm the salsa and cook the eggs just before serving.

SHORTCUTS—The salsa may be made with ⅔ of a 28-ounce can of tomatoes, though you'll really notice the lack of sweet roasty flavor.

VARIATIONS AND IMPROVISATIONS—You can use the same approach to eggs and tortillas with a variety of salsas: Essential Simmered Tomato-Habanero Sauce (page 31), Essential Quick-Cooked Tomato-Chipotle Sauce (page 34), Essential Roasted Tomatillo-Serrano Salsa (page 42) and Essential Roasted Tomatillo-Chipotle Salsa (page 45). For a very different presentation, make simple enchiladas from steaming hot tortillas filled with scrambled eggs and crumbled bacon, doused with the salsa and sprinkled with the cheese and cilantro.

OAXACAN OMELETTE
WITH ROASTED TOMATOES AND GREEN CHILES
Huevos a la Oaxaqueña

*A*s SOON AS I ARRIVE in Oaxaca, I'm ready for *huevos a la oaxaqueña*. This fast-cooked, free-form omelette reminds me that folks there aren't afraid of fire; the brothy roasted tomatoes put me in touch with the year-round warmth of Oaxaca's sun; and the special roasted green chiles, *epazote* and crumbled fresh farmhouse cheese let me know that I'm nowhere other than that beautiful colonial town with age-old Indian roots.

Huevos a la oaxaqueña are really just an omelette with a brothy tomato sauce, so it's easy to recreate a dish very similar to the original in an American kitchen. Serve it as is, or with black beans as they do in its homeland, or with small pieces of roasted potato, as I like it. If I'm really homesick for Oaxaca, I'll buy some sweet Mexican breads (*conchas* and the like) and a very ripe pineapple to put out with the omelettes.

SERVES 4 AS A HEARTY BREAKFAST OR SUPPER

FOR 1 CUP ESSENTIAL ROASTED POBLANO *RAJAS*

8 ounces (3 medium-large) fresh poblano chiles

About 3 tablespoons vegetable or olive oil

1 small white onion, sliced ¼ inch thick

2 garlic cloves, peeled and finely chopped

¼ teaspoon dried oregano, preferably Mexican

⅛ teaspoon dried thyme

1½ pounds (3 medium-large, 9 to 11 plum) ripe tomatoes

1¼ cups chicken broth, plus a little more if needed

A dozen epazote leaves (or ⅓ cup chopped cilantro), plus extra for garnish

Salt, a generous teaspoon

8 eggs

¼ cup crumbled Mexican queso fresco or pressed, salted farmer's cheese

1. *Making about 1 cup Essential Roasted Poblano* **Rajas.** Roast the chiles directly over a gas flame or on a baking sheet 4 inches below a very hot broiler until blackened on all sides, about 5 minutes for open flame, about 10 minutes for broiler. (If using a broiler, the tomatoes from step 2 can be roasted at the same time.) Cover with a kitchen towel and let stand 5 minutes. Peel, pull out the stem and seed pod, then rinse *briefly* to remove bits of skin and seeds. Slice into ¼-inch strips.

In a medium-size (8- to 9-inch) skillet, heat ½ *tablespoon* of the oil over medium to medium-high, then add the onion and cook, stirring regularly, until nicely browned but still a little crunchy, about 5 minutes. Add the garlic, herbs and chiles, and mix thoroughly; remove from the heat.

2. The sauce. Roast the tomatoes on a baking sheet about 4 inches below a very hot broiler until blistered and blackened on one side, about 6 minutes, then flip and roast on the other side. Cool, peel (reserving any juices) and coarsely puree in a large mortar, food processor or blender. Add to the chiles.

Set the pan with the chiles over medium-high heat and when hot, add the tomatoes and cook, stirring regularly, until the sauce reduces to a thick mass, about 5 minutes. Stir in the broth and *epazote* (if using cilantro, add it later, along with the salt) and simmer, partially covered, for about 15 minutes. Thin with additional broth, if necessary, to bring the sauce back to a brothy consistency. Taste and season with salt, usually a generous ½ teaspoon (and cilantro, if you are using it), and keep warm over low heat.

3. The eggs. Turn the oven on to the lowest setting. Lightly beat the eggs with ¼ cup water and ½ *teaspoon* of the salt in a medium-size bowl. Set a small (7- to 8-inch) nonstick or well-seasoned skillet (or omelette pan) over medium-high to high heat. When quite hot, add *a scant tablespoon* of the oil, wait a few seconds for it to heat, then add ¼ of the egg mixture. Stir every few seconds to create large curds, and, when *nearly* done (it will still look creamy but will hold together), turn the free-form omelette into a deep dinner plate or wide soup or pasta bowl. Keep warm in the oven until all four omelettes are made in the same manner, adding additional oil to the skillet for each omelette.

Ladle about ⅔ cup of the brothy tomato sauce over each omelette. Sprinkle with crumbled cheese and garnish with *epazote* or cilantro and carry to the table.

ADVANCE PREPARATION—The recipe can be made through step 2 several days ahead; cover and refrigerate. Reheat and adjust the consistency before making the omelettes.

SHORTCUTS—One 28-ounce can of tomatoes can replace the roasted ones.

VARIATIONS AND IMPROVISATIONS—Other sauces, like Essential Simmered Tomatillo-Serrano Sauce (page 38), can replace the tomatoes (I'd still use the *rajas*). And, if you'd like to use fewer eggs, scramble only 4, mix them with the tomato-*rajas* sauce, and toss all that with about 8 ounces of cooked fettucini; garnish with the cheese.

MOTUL-STYLE EGGS
WITH ROASTED TOMATO, BLACK BEANS AND PLAINTAINS
Huevos Motuleños

*L*ATE SUNDAY MORNING is a time I enjoy inviting friends for a meal. It's relaxed, my work week is finished and no one is expecting a big production. That's when these Motul-Style Eggs really shine. They're made from crispy tostadas topped with black beans and eggs sunny-side up, doused with robust roasted tomato sauce flamed with habanero chiles, then strewn with ham, peas, crumbled fresh cheese and slices of sweet fried plantain. Though it sounds like quite a mouthful, be assured that it's a harmonious and very delicious one, full of lively flavors and rich textures that are just made for a group of good eaters.

My recipe is the classic one that I put together after having eaten *huevos motuleños* in numerous places throughout the Yucatan Peninsula (you can taste almost exactly this version at El Anfitrón in Merida).

SERVES 6 AS A HEARTY BREAKFAST OR SUPPER

FOR 3 CUPS ESSENTIAL SIMMERED TOMATO-HABANERO SAUCE

2¼ pounds (4 large round, 14 to 17 plum) ripe tomatoes

¼ to ⅓ cup vegetable oil

1 medium white onion, thinly sliced

1½ fresh habanero chiles, halved

Salt, a generous ¾ teaspoon

2 very ripe plantains

1½ to 2 cups Classic Mexican Fried Beans (page 237)

OR coarsely mashed, seasoned black beans (homemade or canned)

6 ounces good ham (I love dry country-style ham), cut in thin strips

1⅓ cups frozen peas, defrosted (or fresh peas, steamed until tender)

½ cup (2 ounces) crumbled Mexican queso fresco or pressed, salted farmer's cheese

6 eggs

6 crisp fried tostadas (store-bought or homemade, page 87)

1. *Making 3 cups Essential Simmered Tomato-Habanero Sauce.* Roast the tomatoes on a baking sheet 4 inches below a very hot broiler until blistered and blackened on one side, about 6 minutes; flip and roast the other side. Cool, then peel, collecting all juices with the tomatoes. In a food processor or blender, coarsely puree the tomatoes and juices.

In a medium-size (2- to 3-quart) saucepan, heat *1 tablespoon* of the oil over medium. Add the onion and fry, stirring regularly, until deep golden, about 8 minutes. Add the tomatoes and chile halves and simmer over medium-low 15 minutes or so, stirring often, until the sauce is beginning to thicken but is still juicy looking. Season with salt; remove the chile halves.

2. *Completing the basics.* Peel the plantains, then cut them into diagonal slices ¼-inch thick. Heat *2 to 3 tablespoons* of the vegetable oil in a large (10- to 12-inch) well-seasoned or nonstick skillet (you'll need a lid) over medium, and lay in the plantain slices in a single layer (or, fry them in 2 batches). Fry for 3 or 4 minutes per side, until richly browned. Drain on a baking sheet lined with paper towels and keep them in a warm oven.

In a small pan, warm the beans over low heat. Mix together the ham strips and the peas in another small pan or dish, and warm them over low heat or in a microwave oven. Crumble the cheese into a small bowl and set aside. Set the pan of tomato sauce over low heat.

3. *Finishing the dish.* Measure *1 to 2 tablespoons* of the oil into the large skillet and set over medium to medium-low heat. Crack the eggs into the skillet, cover and cook 1 minute. Uncover and cook until the whites are set, 1 to 2 minutes longer, but the yolks are still soft (if you like them that way). If they won't all fit in the pan, cook them in batches, remove from the heat and keep warm in a low oven.

Spread a portion of beans over each tostada, then set in the middle of each of 6 warm dinner plates. Carefully slide an egg onto each, drizzle the sauce over and around the eggs, letting it run off onto the plate around each tostada. Sprinkle each plate with the ham, peas and cheese, decorate with plantain slices.

ADVANCE PREPARATION—The sauce, plantains and beans may be done ahead; refrigerate everything separately, covered. Warm each component (heat plantains on a baking sheet in a 350-degree oven), then complete step 3.

SHORTCUTS—Use commercially made tostadas (found in large supermarkets and Mexican markets) and canned beans rather than taking shortcuts with the sauce.

VARIATIONS AND IMPROVISATIONS

A Casserole of **Huevos Motuleños**—Line a 13 x 9-inch baking dish with 6 quick-fried tortillas, overlapping slightly. Spread on the beans, lay on a single layer of 6 barely set fried eggs, top with half the sauce, 6 more tortillas, the remaining sauce, peas, ham, cheese and plantain. Bake at 350 degrees until bubbling.

DELUXE SCRAMBLED EGGS
WITH SERRANO, TOMATO AND AVOCADO

Huevos Revueltos a la Mexicana, de Lujo

THE FLAVORS HERE are pure Mexico: a seared salsa of ripe tomatoes, spicy serranos, garlic and fresh cilantro all stirred with beaten egg and avocado over a good strong heat. Strong heat? I like fast-scrambled eggs with big curds, rather than small curds cooked slowly *a la francesa*. In Mexico, it's typical to scramble the eggs well-done, but you can stop anywhere along the way. These are lovely Saturday or Sunday breakfast or supper fare with corn tortillas and Classic Mexican Fried Beans (page 237).

MAKES ABOUT 3 CUPS, SERVING 4 (ENOUGH TO FILL 12 SOFT TACOS)

FOR 2 CUPS ESSENTIAL CHOPPED TOMATO-SERRANO SALSA

12 ounces (2 medium round or 4 to 6 plum) ripe tomatoes, cut into ⅛-inch dice

Fresh serrano chiles to taste (roughly 3 to 5), stemmed and finely chopped

1 large garlic clove, peeled and finely chopped

3 tablespoons chopped cilantro, plus a little more for garnish

1 small white onion, finely diced

1½ tablespoons vegetable or olive oil (or even chorizo or bacon drippings)

8 eggs

Salt, about 1 teaspoon

1 small ripe avocado, peeled, pitted and chopped into ⅜-inch pieces

1. *Making 2 cups Essential Chopped Tomato-Serrano Salsa.* Mix together the tomatoes, chiles, garlic and cilantro. Scoop the onion into a strainer, rinse under cold water, shake off excess and add to the mixture.

2. *Finishing the eggs.* Heat the oil (or drippings) in a large (10- to 12-inch) well-seasoned or nonstick skillet over medium-high. Add the salsa and cook, stirring frequently, until nicely browned, about 7 minutes. While the salsa is cooking, crack the eggs into a bowl and add the salt. Beat just enough to break up the yolks and whites. Add the eggs to the skillet, then scoop in the avocado. Stir thoroughly about every 5 seconds, creating large curds, until the eggs are done to your taste. Sprinkle with more chopped cilantro and serve.

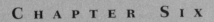

CHAPTER SIX

. . . . .

CLASSIC
FIESTA
FOOD

WE'VE ALL HEARD A THOUSAND TIMES THAT MEXICO IS THE LAND OF FIESTA. It is, though that word *fiesta* may carry different connotations on the two sides of the border. In Mexico, I sense it means a celebration of spirits and joyful sharing of life's simple pleasures. Here in America, many of us think a fiesta is just a party where everyone gets wild, drinks too much tequila and eats lots of cheesy, spicy food.

Though times are changing rapidly, Mexico is a lot less reliant than the U.S. on industrialized food, which means people still see a big difference between what's to be eaten at the everyday table and what's on the fiesta groaning board. The old-fashioned, everyday rural Mexican diet of lots of beans and lots of tortillas, punctuated by bits of meat, vegetables and vegetable-based salsas and sauces, made folks yearn, I'm sure, for richness and variety. The culture responded with an abundant calendar of special occasions (town saint's days, individual saint's days, many religious and political holidays) that have come to be commemorated with feasts that focus mostly on rich meat. (Celebration foods the world around have always been rich, because their denser concentration of calories give you a special sense of satisfaction for a longer period of time—unlike the everyday high-carbohydrate diet most developing countries live on.)

If you're invited to a typical fiesta in Mexico, know that they are as lively as Mexican food is. They're relaxed (unless you're at a more formal, big-city baptism, first communion, girl's fifteenth birthday party or wedding) and flexibly large (with spirited food that's equally flexible). And fiestas are not considered a luxurious frivolity. They are an integral part of Mexican life, the stage on which much of Mexican culture is retold, reconfirmed and played out for all present, mostly with old customs, occasionally with innovations and new relationships.

You can usually expect tamales at a fiesta: They're rich, they're filled with uniquely Mexican sauces and they're so much work (usually communal work) that they're reserved for special occasions. There is very often a huge pot of *pozole* (pork and hominy soup/stew with lots of fresh garnishes (I've included several recipes in *Authentic Mexican*) and often big chunks of golden pork *carnitas* to pull apart for making small tacos. When I've been at fiestas where folks are going all out, they also include a big pot of the local (usually dried-chile) *mole* with chicken (occasionally turkey), though it would be either *mole* or *pozole* and *carnitas* at most parties.

When *barbacoa* is the featured fiesta food, the party is usually in a rural setting. Traditionally *barbacoa* consists of a fresh-slaughtered pig, goat or lamb that's marinated or not, wrapped in aromatic leaves and cooked in a wood-fired pit in the ground—a cross between steaming, roasting and smoking. *Pozole* and *carnitas* wouldn't usually be on the same menu with *barbacoa* (tamales and *mole* may be or not, depending on how special the occasion).

Tortillas and salsas are players at any of these fiestas, as are *botanas* (little snacky appetizers) like pickled vegetables and chiles, pickled pig skin (*cueritos*), cubes of fresh or aged cheese, a Mexican steak tartare cured with lime and chile, salted (and often chilied) pumpkin seeds and peanuts, lime-drizzled crispy fried dried smelt, and little fried quesadillas filled with potatoes or brains or tubular fried tacos of shredded beef. Any or all of these delicious little morsels could be on the table when you arrive, to nibble with the celebratory salutes of mezcal or tequila, or with beer or fresh-made soft drinks like limeade, fruit coolers, rice cooler (*horchata*), tamarind cooler (*tamarindo*) and jamaica cooler (*jamaica*). Frequently, you're issued your own little *mezcalero* or *tequilero* (a tiny cup that, in the versions I'm most familiar with, holds a little more than a tablespoon), so you'll be ready to drink toasts as they are made.

In this chapter, I present a variety of festive *moles* and *tamales*—both those that are served in typical fiestas in Mexico, as well as those that are right for formal entertaining. All the dishes are very special; most are rich, satisfying and complex in the way celebration cooking should be, and all of them embody the essential spirit of the Mexican kitchen. I look forward to these more than any other dishes in this book.

MOLES

· · · · ·

In my cooking classes, students ask "What is *mole*?" more than any other question. So let's start there. If we Americans carry *any* concept of *mole* in the States, it's usually of a red *mole,* the one that gets loosely translated as chicken in chocolate-chile sauce—sweet, bitter and shiny umber, and, for many, close to unfathomable. "*Mole*?" I've heard customers say to servers at Frontera and Topolobampo, "No, I don't eat *mole*."

It's unfortunate that most people's first experience with *mole* is usually in a tourist-oriented restaurant in Mexico. *Mole* is Mexico's national dish, but what most travelers taste is frequently made from a commercially prepared paste, cooked with too much oil and overly sweetened to balance the bitterness that lurks in those commercial preparations.

Luckily that's not all there is to red *mole*. When it's made from scratch, no matter what regional version you're tasting, the sauce will offer the silken fullness of a 20-piece dance band, the intricacy of a Persian rug and the intensity of a Siqueiros mural. The toasted, rehydrated chiles that are the soul of this *mole* create a core of fruity depth, spice and complexity that is spun into a masterpiece of baroque harmony with a dozen herbs and spices (including, in most recipes, a little chocolate), pureed nuts, seeds, bread and tortillas, and sweet-and-tangy tomatoes and tomatillos. And like most main dishes in Mexico, this one is called by the name of the sauce, not the meat or poultry.

What I've just described is more or less the skeletal recipe for red *moles* that are made throughout the Republic (not too much in Yucatan, where cooks march to a different drummer). Each area has its own slant on specific ingredients, proportions and procedures, though it's generally agreed that the most famous, perhaps the original, is *mole poblano* from the town of Puebla. But there are many other *moles,* including the famous gang of seven (from green to yellow to every rusty shade of red to black) of Oaxaca, plus numerous green *moles* all through the country.

So what, then, *is* a *mole?* Looking at the history of the word shines a little light on the subject. *Mole* is the hispanization of a Nahuatl word (*molli*) that means "sauce." So, first, I think of it as a sauce that has strong native roots. Second, related to those native roots, *moles* are usually thickened with ground nuts, seeds or corn (certainly a distinctive technique of the Mexican kitchen). Third, *moles* are sauces that usually feature chiles (again reflecting back on the native Mexican seasoning/vegetable). And fourth, *moles* are almost always thought of as dishes for a special occasion.

I'm starting off our journey through *moles* with the most well-known ones, the ones made from dried chiles. The first is from Teloloapan, Guerrero, a town that's famous (at least in Chicago) for exporting their *mole* pastes. In the recipe I've included, though, everything's made from scratch and the pot gurgles away with the flavors of guajillo and ancho chiles, plus all the regional embellishments (including grated avocado pit); as red *moles* go, this one is truly exceptional.

On the other end of the spectrum from the lighter Teloloapan version is the black *mole* from Oaxaca. It's fabulous (one of the wonders of the culinary world), though to achieve its special balance of burnt-black and rich-sweet requires carefully following the directions.

An elegantly balanced, simple *mole* is my *mole de cacahuate.* It's thickened with a good amount of peanuts, has a light touch of ancho chile and includes a fancy fillip of red wine. Spooned around grilled quail, as I've outlined, the impression is more elegant still.

In other sections of the book, you'll find three more *moles* (the Oaxacan yellow, page 196, the Oaxacan Brick-Red, page 247, and Simple Red, page 178), and they, too, can be utilized as a main dish with meat, poultry, even fish.

And then there are the green *moles.* I'm including two here, because each is so distinctive. The first is related to the nut-and-seed–thickened green *moles* of Central Mexico, though this specialty of Queretaro includes a good amount of fruit (similar to the fruit in red *moles*); if you've tasted the standard green *moles* with their rich nuttiness, this one will be a delicious revelation.

The remaining green *mole* isn't thickened with nuts and seeds. The Oaxacan green *mole* is thickened with corn *masa* (the dough used to make tortillas) and flavored with a puree of very distinctive green herbs (cilantro, *epazote, hoja santa*). It's a special pork-and-vegetable stew, really, but one worthy of the most special occasions.

BRAISED TURKEY IN TELOLOAPAN RED *MOLE*

Guajalote en Mole Teloloapense

MY MIND OFTEN roams the earthy, color-sparked market in Tixtla, Guerrero, high in the mountains above the state capital of Chilpancingo. Deann and I wandered those rambly aisles regularly during the time we lived nearby with friends Sue and Cliff Small. As I look through the ingredients for this most classic of Guerrero fiesta dishes, I'm taken to every section of that market, which seems appropriate for a dish that presents such a clear profile of local tastes. It's a perfect red *mole:* robust and round, but without all the darkness of *mole poblano;* as rich with nuts and seeds as anything in its class; and wonderfully complex with all the seasonings, including that customary dollop of chocolate and grated avocado pit—reported to add a balancing bitterness.

Why Teloloapan? Not only have I had the good fortune to live in Guerrero, but I've had the pleasure of working with Geno Bahena, long-time colleague of Frontera Grill and Topolobampo, and native of Teloloapan.

This is cooking for people who love to cook and who love to share their creations with enthusiastic eaters. It's cooking that takes up the greater part of a day (or parts of several days)—definitely special-occasion fare. So I recommend that you read the recipe carefully before you start, get everything organized, and find great ingredients, which for me means rich-tasting pork lard (though vegetable oil will work, I'd miss the meaty flavor lard adds to the sauce). Frying the chiles, nuts and so forth (rather than dry-toasting) adds a rich roasty character and silky texture that can't be achieved any other way.

Your turkey in *mole* should be the main focus of the celebration. Serve it with Classic White Rice (page 251) and plenty of tortillas, starting, if you wish, with Chilied Tortilla Soup (page 117) and ending with Celebration Cake (page 394).

16 medium (about 8 ounces total)
    dried ancho chiles

22 medium (about 5 1/2 ounces total)
    dried guajillo chiles

1/3 cup (about 1 1/2 ounces) sesame seeds

1 small avocado leaf (or 1 teaspoon
    aniseed)

3 bay leaves

About 1 1/2 inches cinnamon,
    preferably Mexican canela (you'll
    need enough to yield about
    1 1/2 teaspoons ground)

1 teaspoon whole black pepper

1 teaspoon dried thyme

A heaping 1/2 teaspoon dried marjoram

1/3 teaspoon whole cloves

The pit from 1 avocado

2 slices dry firm white bread
    (or 1/2 dry Mexican bolillo roll,
    sliced 1/2 inch thick)

2 stale corn tortillas

2 cups rich-tasting lard or vegetable
    oil (you need this much for
    effective frying; not all goes into
    the sauce)

1/3 cup unskinned almonds

1/3 cup unskinned or Spanish peanuts

1/3 cup hulled pumpkin seeds

1/3 cup raisins

1 medium white onion, sliced

9 garlic cloves, peeled

2 large (about 5 ounces total)
    tomatillos, husked, rinsed and cut
    into quarters

1 medium-large (8-ounce) tomato,
    cut into quarters

7 to 8 cups chicken or turkey broth

1 large whole, boneless (about
    3 3/4-pounds) turkey breast
    (skin still on), split into 2 halves

1 scant cup (about 5 ounces) finely
    chopped Mexican chocolate

Salt, about 3 tablespoons, depending
    on the saltiness of the broth

Sugar, about 1/3 cup

A bunch of flat-leaf parsley, for garnish

1. *Getting started.* Pull the stems from the ancho and guajillo chiles, tear them open, and shake out the seeds, collecting them as you go. Pull out the seed pods (if they didn't come out with the stems), remove any clinging seeds and tear the chiles into flat pieces.

Measure 4 tablespoons of chile seeds into a small skillet, along with 3 1/2 *tablespoons* of the sesame seeds; set over medium heat. Stir for about 2 minutes, as the seeds toast to a golden brown and release a toasty spiciness into the kitchen—a good way to begin *mole* making. Scoop them into a spice grinder or mini-food processor. Return the skillet to the heat and toast the avocado leaf (if you're using one) until aromatic, a few seconds on each side; crumble the leaf (or measure the aniseed) into the spice grinder, then add the bay leaves, cinnamon, pepper, thyme, marjoram and cloves. Pulverize everything and transfer to a large bowl. With a small hand grater, finely grate about 1 teaspoon of the avocado pit (don't be alarmed if the grated pit turns bright orange) and add to the bowl.

If the bread and tortillas are not dried out, dry them on a rack in a 350-degree oven.

2. *The browning.* Set out a large tray lined with several layers of paper towels. Heat a generous ½-inch depth of lard or oil (it should take about 2 cups) in a deep, medium-size (8- to 9-inch) skillet set over medium. When hot, fry the chiles a few at a time, turning nearly constantly with a slotted spoon, until toasted (you'll notice a change in color and a deliciously spicy aroma), about 20 to 30 seconds per batch. Reduce the temperature to medium-low if the chiles start to toast too quickly (there shouldn't be an acrid, burnt smell). As they're fried, drain them well on the towel-lined tray, then transfer to a large bowl. Cover them with hot water to rehydrate and let stand 30 minutes, stirring frequently to ensure even soaking. Strain over a bowl and taste the chile soaking liquid: if it's bitter, discard it.

Meanwhile, one item at a time, fry the almonds, peanuts, then pumpkin seeds in the same skillet over medium heat until thoroughly toasted (about 1 minute for almonds, and ½ to 1 minute for peanuts and pumpkin seeds); use a slotted spoon or skimmer to remove each to the towel-lined tray for draining. In the same fashion, fry and drain the raisins: they'll puff quickly and be browned in 20 to 30 seconds; watch closely—they burn easily.

Fry the bread, turning regularly, until golden, then fry the tortillas. Drain both on the tray, then add bread, tortillas, almonds, peanuts, pumpkin seeds and raisins to the bowl with the pulverized seeds.

Pour the lard remaining in the skillet through a fine-mesh strainer into a very large pot (preferably a 9-quart Dutch oven or large Mexican *cazuela*). Wipe the skillet clean and add back just enough lard to coat the bottom. Return the skillet to medium heat, and add the onion and garlic. Fry, stirring regularly, until soft and richly brown, about 10 minutes. With the slotted spoon or skimmer, remove to the bowl with the pulverized seeds.

Finally, add the tomatillos and tomato to the skillet and cook, stirring, until soft and browned, about 12 minutes. Add to the pulverized seeds. Stir in 2½ cups of the broth.

3. *Browning the turkey.* Set the Dutch oven or *cazuela* over medium-high heat. When hot, sprinkle the turkey breast halves all over with salt, then lay in the pan skin-side down. (If your pan can't comfortably accommodate both halves, brown them one at a time.) When well-browned underneath, about 10 minutes, flip and brown the other side. Remove to a rack set over a plate and set the pan aside to be used at the end of the following step.

4. *From ingredients to* mole. Place ⅓ of the chiles in a blender and add ½ cup of the soaking liquid (or, if it was discarded because of bitterness, use chicken broth). Process to a smooth puree, then press through a medium-mesh strainer into a bowl; discard the strained out chile skins. Repeat two more times to puree and strain the remaining chiles.

Scoop half of the seed mixture (with half the broth) into your blender (no need to wash the blender), process to a smooth puree, then strain (as you did the chiles) into a separate bowl. Puree and strain the remaining seed mixture in the same fashion, and add to the bowl.

Pour off all but a thin coating of the lard from the pan used to brown the turkey and set over medium-high heat. When quite hot, add the chile puree all at once and cook, stirring nearly constantly, until reduced to a thick pastelike mixture that is much darker, 10 to 15 minutes. Add the seed puree, reduce the heat to medium-low and cook, stirring frequently, until everything is very reduced once again, about 30 minutes.

Stir in *4 cups* of the broth and the chocolate, partially cover and simmer over medium-low heat, stirring frequently, for 45 minutes or so, to meld the flavors. Taste and generously season with salt and sugar, remembering that it should be slightly sweet and that the turkey will absorb some of the salt as it braises. (If you prefer a smoother sauce, this is the time to reblend it in batches in a loosely covered blender until smooth and satiny.)

5. *Braising and serving the turkey.* Turn on the oven to 325 degrees. Nestle the turkey into the *mole,* basting it generously if any is exposed. Cover with a lid or foil and bake, basting exposed turkey frequently, until cooked through, about 40 minutes (the USDA tells us it should cook to 170 degrees, though I am personally willing to assume responsibility for eating my turkey cooked to 145 or 150 degrees—the right temperature, I believe, for the moistest breast). Let cool for half an hour in the sauce to finish cooking and reabsorb juices, then, with the help of tongs, meat forks and/or spatulas, transfer the turkey to a cutting board, leaving as much sauce as possible in the pan. Cut into thick slices and lay them partially overlapping onto a large serving platter. Spoon the *mole* over and around the turkey, sprinkle with the remaining sesame seeds and decorate with big tufts of flat-leaf parsley. Serve with a celebratory flourish, and lots of extra *mole* and warm tortillas on the side.

ADVANCE PREPARATION—If I were trying to fit *mole* into a busy schedule, I'd consider each step self-contained and doable within 4 or 5 days of serving; cover and refrigerate each preparation or combination separately. *Mole* is actually better if made a day or two ahead, so you can feel comfortable completing the *mole* and browned turkey through step 4, then braising the meat with the sauce shortly before serving.

VARIATIONS AND IMPROVISATIONS—Though I wouldn't modify the sauce, what goes in it seems easily varied. You can poach chicken breast in the *mole* (allow about ½ cup per breast and follow step 3 on page 284) or make enchiladas with it as described on page 178. Grilled pork chops are wonderful with this *mole,* as are (you may not believe this) grilled tuna steaks. A batch of *mole* will yield plenty of leftover sauce to experiment with. (Package it in 2- or 3-cup batches and freeze; defrost, reblend to smooth out, and warm.)

OAXACAN BLACK *MOLE* WITH BRAISED CHICKEN

Mole Negro Oaxaqueño

I'D VENTURE TO SAY that anyone who has traveled to Oaxaca, the beautifully preserved colonial city in Southern Mexico, has eaten black *mole* at least once. It is *the* regional specialty—on every restaurant menu, at every fiesta. And, quite expectedly, not all black *moles* are crafted equally. At the touristy *zócalo* ("central square") restaurants, it is a lacquered-looking blackness (ever seen drying tar?) that's all sweetness, burn and chocolate. At Abigail Mendoza's now-famous Tlalmanalli restaurant in Teotitlan del Valle, its near-blackness draws you into the layers of complexity, the perfect piquancy, the delicately balanced dulcet char of real *mole negro*. Her version is what dreams are made of.

Black *mole* has to be the star of the meal, so serve it simply with a spoonful of Classic White Rice (page 251—you may want to add a little diced cooked carrot and zucchini to the rice as Abigail does) and plenty of hot tortillas. In summer, I'd work hard to locate squash blossoms for Golden Squash Blossom *Crema* (page 138) or serve Mushroom-Cactus Soup (page 128) to start. Dessert should stay classic and Oaxacan like Mango-Lime Ice (page 393) or Tropical "Trifle" of Mango and Almonds (page 396).

Even in Oaxaca, chilhuacle chiles are expensive and not always available, so folks have learned to make black *mole* with 6 ounces mulato, 2½ ounces pasilla, 1 ounce guajillo and 1 chipotle. For years I collected black *mole* recipes that yielded mediocre results to the point that I just wouldn't offer it at our restaurants. Not until my favorite chile seller, Panchita, in the Oaxaca market really explained the details and her proportions could I get it right. Here's what she taught me.

11 medium (about 5½ ounces) dried
   mulato chiles

6 medium (about 2 ounces) dried
   chilhualces chiles

6 medium (about 2 ounces) dried
   pasilla chiles

1 dried chipotle chile (preferably the
   tan-brown chipotle meco)

1 corn tortilla, torn into small pieces

2 ¼-inch-thick slices of white onion

4 garlic cloves, unpeeled

About 2 cups rich-tasting lard or
   vegetable oil (for frying the chiles)

½ cup sesame seeds, plus a few extra
   for garnish

¼ cup pecan halves

¼ cup unskinned or Spanish peanuts

¼ cup unskinned almonds

About 10 cups chicken broth (canned
   or homemade, page 137)

1 pound (2 medium-large or
   6 to 8 plum) green tomatoes,
   roughly chopped

4 ounces (2 to 3 medium) tomatillos,
   husked, rinsed and roughly chopped

2 slices stale bread, toasted until very
   dark

¼ teaspoon cloves, preferably freshly
   ground

½ teaspoon black pepper, preferably
   freshly ground

½ teaspoon cinnamon, preferably
   freshly ground Mexican canela

A scant teaspoon oregano, preferably
   Mexican

½ teaspoon dried thyme

½ ripe banana

½ cup (about 3 ounces) finely
   chopped Mexican chocolate

2 or 3 avocado leaves (if you have
   them)

Salt, about 1 tablespoon, depending
   on the saltiness of the broth

Sugar, about ¼ cup (or a little more)

2 large (3½- to 4-pound) chickens,
   cut into quarters

1. *Getting started.* Pull out the stems (and attached seed pods) from the chiles, tear them open, and shake or scrape out the seeds, collecting them as you go.

Now, do something that will seem very odd: Scoop the seeds into an ungreased medium-size (8- to 9-inch) skillet along with the torn-up tortilla, set over medium heat, turn on an exhaust fan, open a window and toast your seeds and tortilla, shaking the pan regularly, until burned to charcoal black, about 15 minutes. (This is very important to the flavor and color of the *mole.*) Now, scrape them into a fine-mesh strainer and rinse for 30 seconds or so, then transfer to a blender.

Set an ungreased skillet or griddle over medium heat, lay on a piece of aluminum foil, and lay the onion slices and garlic cloves on that. Roast until soft and very dark (about 5 minutes on each side of the onion slices; about 15 minutes for the garlic—turn it frequently as it roasts). Cool the garlic a bit, peel it and combine with the onion in a large bowl.

While the onion and garlic are roasting, turn on the oven to 350 degrees (for toasting nuts), return the skillet to medium heat, measure in a scant 2 cups of the lard or oil (you'll need about ½-inch depth), and, when hot, begin frying the chiles a couple at a time: they'll unfurl quickly, then release their aroma and piquancy (keep that exhaust on and window open) and, after about 30 seconds, have lightened in color and be well toasted (they should be crisp when cool, but not burnt smelling). Drain them well, gather them into a large bowl, cover with hot tap water, and let rehydrate for 30 minutes, stirring regularly to ensure even soaking. Drain, reserving the soaking liquid.

While the chiles are soaking, toast the seeds and nuts. Spread the sesame seeds onto a baking sheet or ovenproof skillet, spread the pecans, peanuts and almonds onto another baking sheet or skillet, then set both into the oven. In about 12 minutes the sesame seeds will have toasted to a dark brown; the nuts will take slightly longer. Add all of them to the blender (reserving a few sesame seeds for garnish), along with 1½ *cups* of the chicken broth and blend to as smooth a puree as you can. Transfer to a small bowl.

Without rinsing the blender, combine the green tomatoes and tomatillos with another ½ *cup* of the broth and puree. Pour into another bowl. Again, without rinsing the blender, combine the onion and garlic with the bread, cloves, black pepper, cinnamon, oregano, thyme, banana and ¾ *cup* broth. Blend to a smooth puree and pour into a small bowl.

Finally, without rinsing the blender, scoop in *half* of the chiles, measure in ½ *cup* of the soaking liquid, blend to a smooth puree, then pour into another bowl. Repeat with the remaining chiles and another ½ *cup* of the soaking liquid.

2. *From four purees to* mole. In a very large (8- to 9-quart) pot (preferably a Dutch oven or Mexican *cazuela*), heat 3 *tablespoons* of the lard or oil (some of what you used for the chiles is fine) and set over medium-high heat. When very hot, add the tomato puree and stir and scrape for 15 to 20 minutes until reduced, thick as tomato paste, and very dark (it'll be the color of cinnamon stick and may be sticking to the pot in places). Add the nut puree and continue the stirring and scraping until reduced, thick and dark again (this time it'll be the color of black olive paste), about 8 minutes. Then, as you guessed, add the banana-spice puree and stir and scrape for another 7 or 8 minutes as the whole thing simmers back down to a thick mass about the same color it was before you added this one.

Add the chile puree, stir well and let reduce over medium-low heat until very thick and almost black, about 30 minutes, stirring regularly (but, thankfully, not constantly). Stir in the remaining 7 *cups* of broth, the chocolate and avocado leaves (if you have them), partially cover and simmer gently for about an hour. Season with salt and sugar (remembering that sugar helps balance the dark, toasty flavors). Remove the avocado leaves.

In batches in a *loosely* covered blender, puree the sauce until as smooth as possible, then pass through a medium-mesh strainer into a large bowl.

3. *Finishing the dish.* Return the *mole* to the same pot and heat it to a simmer. Nestle the leg-and-thigh quarters of the chicken into the bubbling black liquid, partially cover and time 15 minutes, then nestle in the breast quarters, partially cover and simmer for 20 to 25 minutes, until all the chicken is done.

With a slotted spoon, fish out the chicken pieces and transfer them to a large warm platter. Spoon a generous amount of the *mole* over and around them, sprinkle with the reserved sesame seeds, and set triumphantly before your lucky guests.

ADVANCE PREPARATION—The *mole* can be completed through step 2 several days ahead (it gets better, in fact); cover and refrigerate. Complete step 3 shortly before serving.

My Soapbox: Reflections on Celebration in a Land of Plenty

As a player in our quickly evolving society at the end of the twentieth century, I've noticed that my celebrations are different. They're facing challenges that are brought on by a couple of changes we've seen recently in modern America.

The first is the now year-round availability of practically all fruits and vegetables, beautiful looking and (mostly) brought from great distances. The second is the technology we've developed to manufacture sweets that are not calorie laden, and unctuously tender delights that have no fat—both accomplished in a culture whose appetite for consumption is exceeded only by its ability to produce.

I think most everyone would agree that our familiarity with the always-available fruits and vegetables has bred a certain amount of contempt, or at least lack of interest. Yes, we can have them all the time, but what draw do they have if their prettiness isn't accompanied by flavor? Hasn't our demand for supply relinquished the opportunity to enjoy ripe, local, just-picked taste, and to celebrate the arrival of the season?

The allure of always-available produce is weak compared to the magnetism of fat-free, reduced-calorie prepared foods that offer all the sweetness, all that buttery tenderness without our having to think, balance, fear overdoing or play any role other than that of enjoying consumer. But they're not particularly tasty either; so, as with the fruits and vegetables, we miss out on how good fresh food can be. And having no hand in their preparation, we can forget what ingredients they're made with. Since different ingredients directly affect our health in different ways, I personally don't feel comfortable abdicating so much responsibility for our health to the manufacturers.

Most important for me, food manufacturers blur the distinction between everyday eating and celebration feasts. They offer us those once-in-a-while childhood treats every day of the week by making them fat-free, reduced calorie, cheap and easy. And getting used to a steady diet of the once-special has confused us, I think. We're forgetting both what our bodies feel like when we eat old-fashioned small portions of fresh-by-necessity, everyday cooking, as well as what satisfaction there is in spending the whole day in the kitchen making huge quantities of inimitable, rich, dishes for the most special times.

Special food, seasonal and lovingly crafted, has been the focus of celebrations throughout history. In our age of manufactured food, are celebrations less to look forward to, or will yesterday's "special food" be replaced by something else with the same draw?

. . . .

SMOKY PEANUT *MOLE* WITH GRILLED QUAIL

Codornices Asadas en Mole de Cacahuate

*T*HIS IS A DISH I've come back to frequently over the years. It is the easiest *mole* I know, and its crowd-pleasing flavors work well with everything from chicken, quail and duck to pork, swordfish and grouper. Having made it so long, I had to search my books to rediscover the original recipe I started with. It is from a series of books called . . . *y la comido se hizo.*

The smokiness of the quail (a typical game bird in Mexico) brings out the chipotle in the sauce, and, in addition, the presentation is stunning.

SERVES 6 WITH ABOUT 2 1/2 CUPS MOLE

2 medium (about 1 ounce total) dried ancho chiles, stemmed and seeded

4 tablespoons vegetable or olive oil

1/2 small white onion, sliced

2 garlic cloves, peeled

8 ounces (about 1 medium-large round or 3 to 4 plum) ripe tomatoes

1 cup dry roasted peanuts, plus a few tablespoons chopped for garnish

2 slices firm white bread (or 1/2 dry Mexican bolillo roll), torn into pieces

2 canned chipotle chiles en adobo, seeded

1/8 teaspoon allspice, preferably freshly ground

1/2 teaspoon cinnamon, preferably freshly ground Mexican canela

About 3 1/2 cups chicken broth

1/2 cup fruity red wine

1 tablespoon cider vinegar

2 bay leaves

Salt, about 1 1/2 teaspoons, depending on the saltiness of the broth

Sugar, about 1 tablespoon

12 partially boned, good-size quail (I like ones that are at least 4 ounces each)

A little freshly ground black pepper

Sprigs of flat-leaf parsley, for garnish

1. *The peanut* mole. Tear the ancho chiles into flat pieces, then toast a few at a time on an ungreased griddle or skillet over medium heat: press flat with a metal spatula for a few seconds, until they crackle and change color slightly, then flip, and press again. (If they give off more than the slightest wisp of smoke, they are burning and will add a bitter element to the sauce.) In a small bowl, cover the chiles with hot water and let rehydrate for 30 minutes, stirring occasionally to ensure even soaking. Drain and discard the water.

Meanwhile, heat *1 tablespoon* of the oil in a heavy, medium-size (4-quart) pot (preferably a Dutch oven) over medium. Add the onion and garlic cloves, and fry, stirring regularly, until well browned, about 10 minutes. Scrape into a blender jar. Set the pan aside.

Roast the tomato on a baking sheet 4 inches below a very hot broiler until blackened, about 5 minutes, then flip it and roast the other side; cool, then peel, collecting all the juices with the tomato. Add the tomato to the blender, along with the peanuts, bread, chipotles, drained anchos, allspice and cinnamon. Add *1½ cups* of the broth and blend until smooth, stirring and scraping down the sides of the blender jar, and adding a little more liquid if needed to keep everything moving through the blades. Press the mixture through a medium-mesh strainer into a bowl.

Heat *1 tablespoon* of the remaining oil in the pot over medium-high. When hot enough to make a drop of the puree sizzle sharply, add it all at once. Stir as the nutty-smelling, ruddy-red amalgamation thickens and darkens for about 5 minutes, then stir in the remaining 2 *cups* broth, the wine, vinegar and bay leaves. Partially cover and let gently simmer over medium-low heat for roughly 45 minutes, stirring regularly for the flavors to harmonize. If necessary, thin the sauce with a little more broth to keep it the consistency of a cream soup. Taste and season with salt, about 1½ teaspoons, and the sugar. Cover and keep warm.

2. *Grilling and serving the quail.* Thirty to 45 minutes before serving, light a gas grill or prepare a charcoal fire and let the coals burn until they are covered with gray ash and medium-hot. Position the grill grate about 8 inches above the coals and lightly oil.

While the grill heats, lay the quail on a baking sheet. Tie the legs together with kitchen twine, then brush both sides with some of the remaining oil; sprinkle with salt and pepper.

Lay the quail on the hottest portion of the grill, breast-side down. Cover the grill and cook about 8 minutes, checking once or twice to ensure that they are not browning too quickly. Flip the quail and move to a cooler portion of the grill (quail finished over a cooler fire always seem juicier). Cover and continue grilling until the leg meat will separate from the bone quite easily when you squeeze a leg between two fingers, 4 to 6 minutes more.

Remove to a plate and keep warm in a low oven while you set up your plates. Ladle a generous ⅓ cup of the earthy-colored sauce onto each of 6 warm dinner plates. Set 2 quail over the sauce. Garnish with chopped peanuts and sprigs of parsley.

ADVANCE PREPARATION—The *mole* may be made up to 5 days ahead; cover and refrigerate. If oil separates from sauce when reheated, either skim it off or blend the sauce in a loosely covered blender. The quail are best cooked just before serving.

CHICKEN BREASTS IN NUTTY QUERETARO GREEN *MOLE*

Mole Verde Queretano

*T*HE COMPELLING NATURAL fruitiness of this savory golden-green *mole* makes it a real plea-sure to spoon out for company. The background of plantain and raisins is charged with poblano chiles and tangy tomatillos, balanced with spices like cinnamon, anise, cloves and black pepper, and burnished with the lustre of smooth-ground almond and sesame. It com-bines the freshness of a classic Central-style green *mole* (though no pumpkin seeds) with the complex spicing and fruitiness of a red *mole* (though no dried chiles).

This Queretaro-style green *mole* is based on Martha Chapa's version in *Cocina de Queré-taro*. For drama, you could serve it with Black Bean Rice (page 256); for tradition's sake, go for Classic White Rice (page 251).

SERVES 4 TO 8 WITH 8 CUPS OF *MOLE* (YOU'LL HAVE LEFTOVER *MOLE*)

½ pound (3 medium-large) fresh poblano chiles

12 ounces (8 to 9 medium) tomatillos, husked and rinsed

½ cup sesame seeds, plus a few extra for garnish

½ cup whole blanched almonds

1 small soft-ripe plantain, peeled and sliced ½ inch thick

1 corn tortilla, torn into pieces

2 large garlic cloves, peeled and roughly chopped

½ cup raisins (I suggest golden raisins to preserve the green color of the sauce)

½ cup roasted skinless peanuts

1 large leaf of romaine lettuce

8 good-size sprigs of flat-leaf parsley, plus a few extra for garnish

½ teaspoon cinnamon, preferably freshly ground Mexican canela

½ teaspoon black pepper, preferably freshly ground

A scant ½ teaspoon aniseed, preferably freshly ground

A big pinch cloves, preferably freshly ground

5 cups chicken broth, plus a little more if needed

1 tablespoon vegetable or olive oil

Salt, about 2 teaspoons, depending on the saltiness of the broth

8 small (2 to 2½ pounds total) boneless, skinless chicken breast halves, trimmed

1. *Roasting, toasting and browning.* Roast the chiles directly over a gas flame or on a bak-ing sheet 4 inches below a very hot broiler until blackened on all sides, about 5 minutes for open flame, about 10 minutes for broiler. Cover with a kitchen towel and let stand 5 min-

utes. Peel, pull out the stem and seed pod, then rinse briefly to remove bits of skin and seeds; roughly chop and place in a large bowl.

Roast the tomatillos on a baking sheet 6 inches below the broiler until softened and a little brown and soft on one side, about 3 minutes, then turn them over and roast the other side. (We don't blacken them here as in other recipes, so the sauce will be more green.) Transfer the tomatillos (including all juices) to the bowl with the chiles.

Heat a small skillet over medium and add the sesame seeds. Stir nearly continually until golden and aromatic, 2 to 4 minutes. Scrape in with the chile mixture, then toast the almonds in the same manner (they'll toast a little irregularly and take 2 to 4 minutes); scrape them in with the sesame.

2. *Finishing the* mole. To the bowl with the growing pile of ingredients, add the remaining riot of aromas and flavors—the plantain, tortilla, garlic, raisins, peanuts, romaine, parsley, cinnamon, pepper, aniseed and cloves. Stir in 2 *cups* of the broth, then, in a blender, in batches, process to a smooth puree. Into a large bowl, press the batches of puree through a medium-mesh strainer into a bowl.

Set a medium-size (4-quart) pot (preferably a Dutch oven or Mexican *cazuela*) over medium heat and measure in the oil. When the oil that's still there is hot enough to make a drop of the puree sizzle sharply, add it all at once. Stir for 3 or 4 minutes, as the mixture sears and thickens. Stir in the remaining 3 *cups* of the broth, partially cover the pot, and gently simmer over medium-low, stirring regularly, for about 30 minutes to allow the variety of flavors to come into harmony. At this point, the sauce should have the consistency of a thick cream soup. Taste and season with salt, usually about 2 teaspoons.

3. *The chicken*. Turn on the oven to 350 degrees. Coat the bottom of a 13 x 9-inch baking dish with some of the *mole,* lay in the chicken breasts in a single layer, then ladle the remaining sauce over them. Bake until the chicken is just done, 20 to 30 minutes. With tongs or a slotted spoon, transfer the chicken to a warm serving platter. Stir the sauce to incorporate any accumulated chicken juices, then add a little more broth if necessary to give the sauce the consistency of a *light* cream soup. Ladle the *mole* over the chicken, sprinkle with a few sesame seeds and decorate with parsley.

ADVANCE PREPARATION—The *mole* can be made several days ahead through step 2; cover and refrigerate. Bake the chicken in the sauce shortly before serving.

OAXACAN GREEN *MOLE*
WITH PORK, WHITE BEANS AND MEXICAN VEGETABLES
Mole Verde Oaxaqueño

*T*HE SAUCE OF THIS Oaxacan classic is one of the most beautiful spring-green colors you've seen. Infused with an alchemical combination of traditional herbs (cilantro, *epazote*, and *hoja santa*), this simple pork-and-white-bean stew with chayote and green beans has the freshest flavors of any cooked dish on the Mexican roster. But don't just turn the page if *epazote* and *hoja santa* aren't at the ready. Just increase the cilantro, use the green fennel tops and add in a handful of flat-leaf parsley. It will have a similarly delicious punch.

My recipe for this *masa*-thickened green *mole* (*masa* rather than the standard nut thickening of Central Mexico) is a compilation of several from my favorite Oaxacan cookbooks. It is a meal in itself—usually not served with any accompaniment.

SERVES 6, WITH ABOUT 10 CUPS OF FINISHED STEW

⅔ cup (about 4½ ounces) small white (navy) beans

2 pounds lean, boneless pork shoulder, cut into 1½-inch pieces

1 pound pork bones (such as neck bones, back bones or the like), cut into 2-inch pieces (if they're not already cut when you buy them)

8 garlic cloves, 4 peeled and 4 unpeeled

1 medium white onion, diced

1 pound (10 to 12 medium) tomatillos, husked and rinsed

Fresh green chile to taste (roughly 3 serranos, 2 jalapeños or 1 Oaxacan chile de agua), stemmed

½ teaspoon cumin, preferably freshly ground

½ teaspoon black pepper, preferably freshly ground

A pinch of cloves, preferably freshly ground

1½ tablespoons rich-tasting lard or vegetable oil

2 medium (1 pound total) chayotes, peeled, seeded and cut into ¾-inch chunks (about 2 cups)

1½ cups (about 6 ounces) tender, young green beans, trimmed and cut in half

⅔ cup (about 5 ounces) fresh masa OR a generous ½ cup masa harina mixed with 6 tablespoons hot water

Salt, about 2 teaspoons

4 large sprigs of flat-leaf parsley, plus a few for garnish

2 small sprigs of epazote (or 5 to 6 sprigs of cilantro, if no epazote is to be found)

2 leaves hoja santa (or 1 cup roughly chopped green tops from fresh fennel bulb)

1. *The stew base.* Place the beans in a heavy, large (6-quart) pot (preferably a Dutch oven or Mexican *cazuela*), along with 3 quarts water, the pork and the bones. Bring to a boil. Skim off any gray foam that rises during the first few minutes of boiling. Finely chop the *4 peeled cloves* of garlic and add to the pot along with the onion; partially cover and gently simmer over medium-low heat, stirring occasionally, until the beans are wonderfully soft and meat is fall-apart tender, 1½ to 2 hours. If the liquid drops below the level of the beans and meat, add enough hot water to keep everything floating freely.

2. *The basic flavorings.* Roast the tomatillos on a baking sheet 4 inches below a very hot broiler until blackened and soft on one side, about 5 minutes; turn them over and roast on the other side. Transfer tomatillos and any accumulated juices to a food processor or blender.

On a heavy griddle or skillet set over medium, roast the unpeeled garlic and whole chiles, turning frequently, until soft and blackened in spots, about 5 minutes for the chiles, 15 minutes for the garlic. Peel the garlic, then roughly chop it and the chiles, and add to the food processor or blender, along with the cumin, pepper and cloves, and process to a smooth puree.

3. *Finishing the stew base.* When the beans and meat are tender, pour them into a colander set over a large bowl. Remove the bones, pick off any meat you find on them, add it back to the colander, and set aside. Skim the fat from the top of the broth—there should be at least 5 cups of broth; if you're shy any, add water to bring it to that quantity.

Wash and dry your pot, set over medium-high heat and add the lard or oil. When hot enough to make a drop of the tomatillo puree sizzle sharply, add it all at once. Stir constantly for 4 or 5 minutes as the mixture sears and thickens. Add *4 cups* of the pork broth, partially cover, and simmer over medium-low heat, stirring regularly, for 15 minutes. Uncover, add the chayote and the green beans and simmer 5 minutes longer.

In a small bowl, thoroughly mix ⅔ *cup* of the remaining broth into the fresh or reconstituted *masa*, then strain into the simmering stew base, whisking the stew constantly until thickened. Add the beans and meat, taste and season with salt (usually about 2 teaspoons) and let the pot gently gurgle away while you prepare the herb puree.

4. *The herb puree and finishing the stew.* Puree the parsley, *epazote* (or cilantro), and *hoja santa* (or fennel) with the remaining ⅓ *cup* broth in a food processor or blender. Stir the puree into the stew, then add a little more broth or water, if necessary, to thin the whole mixture to a medium-thick, stewlike consistency. Ladle the aromatic, emerald-sauced stew into warm deep plates or wide soup bowls, lay on sprigs of flat-leaf parsley, and carry to the table.

ADVANCE PREPARATION—The dish may be prepared ahead through step 3; cover and refrigerate for up to 4 days. Just before serving, reheat the stew, thin if necessary, add the herb puree and serve.

VARIATIONS AND IMPROVISATIONS—The simplest, dressiest variation is to replace the 2 pounds of pork shoulder with 6 pork chops: Prepare the recipe as directed (you'll get pork flavor in the sauce from the bones), ignoring any mention of the cubes of pork shoulder. Grill the pork chops (I would marinate them with green chile, garlic, olive oil, and salt), then serve them atop a generous pool of the finished white bean–studded green *mole*. Also, you can make a chicken version, cooking the beans as described in step 1 (omit pork and bones but use chicken broth as part of the liquid, if you have it). When the beans are tender, add the thighs and legs from 2 small chickens and cook 10 minutes; add the breasts and simmer about 15 minutes, until chicken is tender. Continue with steps 3 and 4.

TAMALES

. . . . .

Perhaps your only experience with tamales started at the frozen-food counter or at a Tex-Mex chain restaurants, where they can be heav and often not worth much energy or enthusiasm. I grew up loving these Tex-Mex tamales, and I still get a hankering for them, but they are not nearly as interesting or varied as those from Mexico.

Below the Rio Grande, when some tamales are plucked from the steamer, they're as light as good corn bread and filled with vegetables (like my Spicy Mushroom Tamales), or they're compact, tender and flecked with herbs (like the Juchitcan-Style Black Bean Tamales flavored with *epazote*). Others are thick with texture (the other Yucatecan Tamales are studded with chopped greens, hardboiled eggs and toasted pumpkin seeds) and since tamales have been made longer than we have recorded history, some versions show their ancient roots: My recipe for Pre-Hispanic-Style Tamales, made without the tenderizing fat that the Spaniards brought, proudly sets before us what is essentially a steamed tortilla, tender and quivery.

Tamales are occasionally not individually wrapped. A homey *tamalón* is made by rolling all the dough into a big cloth- or banana leaf–wrapped log, tying it neatly and steaming it. The texture of my Great Big Chard Tamal Roll isn't quite as light as that of the Mushroom Tamales, but sliced up as a snack, first course or accompaniment, it's always a crowd pleaser.

Sometimes tamales are baked rather than steamed. Back in the chapter on casseroles, I offered a recipe for Crusty Baked Tamal (page 210) that shows how tamal dough can turn out crispy-crunchy on the surface, tender and cakey within. Here, there's a very coarse-textured tamal patterned after the enormous *Zacahuiles* of Veracruz that are baked in wood-fired ovens. My pork-filled beauty is very satisfying, even without the smokiness of the fire.

Tamales are a main attraction at most every party in Mexico. For me, they're a perfect example of special-occasion food: They're rich and they involve individual handcrafting.

A few cooking notes: You'll notice that some recipes call for *masa* that's been ground smooth for tortillas, others for *masa* that's been ground coarse for tamales. This is a regional (or cook's) preference, so you can feel free to use what you like or can get.

One thing that makes those Tex-Mex tamales heavy is that most are made from the dehydrated, powdered *masa harina* that is used occasionally for tortillas. It simply won't make as fluffy a tamal as the fresh-ground *masa*. Recently, a special coarse-ground dehydrated *masa harina* for tamales has come into the American market from Mexico (I've only seen Maseca brand). It works well and tastes good, though the texture it gives is more commercial seeming.

Tamales freeze beautifully, or the fresh *masa* can be frozen before making them (frozen *masa* makes good tamales but not very good tortillas). Many Mexican markets in Chicago carry fresh *masa* (both smooth- and coarse-ground) on weekends.

Corn husks are available most everywhere, banana leaves less so. Though I've included many banana leaf–wrapped tamales, you can, if banana leaves aren't available, make most of them in corn husks; you'll just need to make them smaller.

SPICY MUSHROOM TAMALES

Tamales de Hongos

THESE LOOK LIKE what most of us think of as tamales—corn husk–wrapped stogies of yellowish corn *masa* hugging a little spicy something. This recipe produces Central-style tamales, so they may be a little lighter than what you are used to. Right out of the steamer, they're meltingly tender, wonderfully rich. And with flavorful mushrooms, roasted poblanos and tomatoes as the filling, as is typical in the wild mushroom-filled forests high around Mexico City, they have a contemporary freshness.

Tamales like these are the most commonly prepared ones in Mexico, light from vigorous beating and filled with practically anything edible (meat in red chile, chicken with tomatillo, and poblanos with tomato and fresh cheese are typical).

Tamales mean special occasion to all Mexicans. They may be the only food served (you can easily double or triple the recipe), accompanied by a mug of *atole,* the traditional warm *masa*-thickened drink (plain, cinnamon, chocolate, fruit-flavored) or soda pop. There may or may not be salsa to daub on, but there will always be a good time.

MAKES 16 MEDIUM-SIZE TAMALES

½ of an 8-ounce package dried corn husks

4 ounces (½ cup) to 5½ ounces (⅔ cup) chilled rich-tasting lard (or vegetable shortening if you want to)—depending on how tender you want your tamales

1 teaspoon baking powder

1 pound (2 cups) coarse-ground masa for tamales

> *OR 1¾ cups dried masa harina for tamales mixed with 1 cup plus 2 tablespoons hot water, then allowed to cool*

About ⅔ cup cool chicken broth, plus up to ⅓ cup more for optional second beating

Salt, about 2 teaspoons

1 pound (2 medium-large round or 6 to 8 plum) ripe tomatoes

About ½ pound (3 medium-large) fresh poblano chiles

1 tablespoon vegetable or olive oil

1 small white onion, sliced

2 garlic cloves, peeled and finely chopped

¼ teaspoon dried oregano, preferably Mexican

¼ teaspoon dried thyme

8 ounces (about 4 cups) sliced flavorful mushrooms (shiitakes are excellent, as are chanterelles or other wild mushrooms, when available), stems removed

1. *The corn husks.* Bring the corn husks to a boil in water to cover in a large saucepan, then weight with a plate to keep them submerged and let stand an hour or so.

2. *The batter.* With an electric mixer, beat the chilled lard or shortening with the baking powder until light in texture, about 1 minute. Continue beating as you add the *masa* (fresh or reconstituted) in three additions. Slowly pour in a generous ½ cup of the broth, beating all the while. Continue beating for another minute, until a ½-teaspoon dollop of the batter floats in a cup of cold water (if it floats you can be sure the tamales will be tender and light).

Beat in enough additional broth to give the mixture the consistency of soft (not runny) cake batter; it should softly hold its shape in a spoon. Season with salt (yes, it will involve tasting raw batter), usually 1 scant teaspoon, depending on the saltiness of the broth.

For the lightest-textured tamales, refrigerate the batter for an hour or so, then rebeat, adding enough additional liquid to bring the mixture to the consistency it had before. (You may find it necessary to add a little salt, too.)

3. *The filling.* Roast the tomatoes on a baking sheet set 4 inches below a very hot broiler until blackened and blistered on one side, about 6 minutes; flip and roast the other side. Peel and roughly chop, collecting all the juices with the tomatoes.

Roast the chiles directly over a gas flame or 4 inches below the very hot broiler until blackened on all sides, about 5 minutes for open flame, about 10 minutes for broiler. Cover with a kitchen towel and let stand 5 minutes. Peel, pull out the stem and seed pod, then rinse *briefly* to remove bits of skin and seeds. Slice into ¼-inch strips.

In a large (10- to 12-inch) skillet, heat the oil over medium-high, then add the onion and cook, stirring regularly, until nicely browned but still a little crunchy, about 5 minutes. Add the garlic and herbs, toss a minute longer, then stir in the chiles, tomatoes and mushrooms. Cook, stirring regularly, until everything is reduced to a thick mixture that easily holds it shape in a spoon, about 5 minutes. Season with salt, usually about 1 teaspoon, and cool.

4. *Forming and steaming the tamales.* Pick out 16 nice corn husks for forming the tamales, then use ⅔ of the remainder to line a steamer (you'll need one that's at least 4-inches deep—a Mexican tamal steamer or a vegetable steamer in a deep pot); fill the bottom of the steamer with 1 to 2 inches of water. Tear 16 long, ¼-inch-wide strips of corn husks for tying the tamales.

One by one form the tamales: Lay a corn husk in front of you, lightly dry it, then spread about a scant ¼ cup of the batter into a 4-inch square, leaving at least a 1½-inch border on the pointy end of the husk, a ¾-inch border along the other sides. Spoon a good 2 tablespoons of the filling down the center of the batter. Pick up the two long sides of the husk and bring them together (this will cause the batter to roll around the filling, enclosing it). Roll the flaps of the husk in the same direction around the tamal. (If the husk is so small that the tamal doesn't seem very well wrapped, roll it in another husk.) Fold up the empty, pointy, 1½-inch section to close off the bottom, then secure it by loosely tying one of the strips of husk around the tamal and folded flap. Stand the tamal on the folded end in the steamer (the top of the tamal will be open).

Continue spreading, filling, rolling and folding until all the tamales are made (you may have a little filling left). Fill in any gaps in the steamer with loosely wadded foil to keep the tamales from sliding down. Lay any unused husks over the tamales. Cover the pot; bring to a boil and steam over medium heat for 1 to 1¼ hours (ones made from reconstituted *masa* will take a little longer than those made from fresh); make sure that the water stays at a steady boil and never runs out—otherwise your tamales won't be as light.

The tamales are done when the husk peels away easily. Let them firm up a few minutes in the steamer, off the heat, before setting your fragrant creations before your guests.

ADVANCE PREPARATION—Tamales hold beautifully, covered and refrigerated for several days; reheat them in the steamer.

VARIATIONS AND IMPROVISATIONS—If you have about 2 cups of shredded cooked meat or lightly cooked vegetables mixed with a salsa or sauce, you can use it as a filling for tamales. From this book, look specifically at the Essential Roasted Poblano *Rajas* (page 62), Spicy Pasilla Mushrooms (page 156), Tacos of Tomatillo Chicken (page 146), Smoky Shredded Pork (page 150) or Chicken or Pork with Simple Red *Mole* (page 178). It is typical to mix a little of the dried chile sauces, achiote paste or chopped or pureed green herbs into the *masa*.

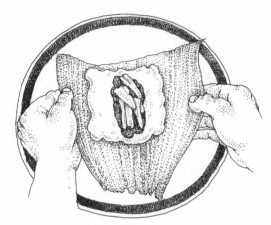

Dough and filling on corn husk.

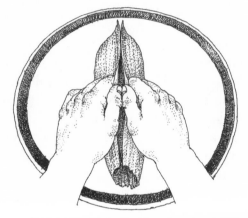

Bringing up sides to enclose dough and filling

Folding and tying husk-wrapped tamal

Steamers and Steaming

With as much steaming of tamales as is done in Mexico, you'd think every house would have a big commercially made steamer in the kitchen. Truth is, many people improvise with something like a 5-gallon metal bucket or stock pot in which they position supports in the bottom, then top with a metal rack and fill with tamales. You can do the same with a big pot: If you have a collapsible vegetable steamer to fit into the bottom, that's great; otherwise, set in some custard cups, top with a roasting rack, and you've got a steamer.

Most of the commercially made Mexican tamal steamers are pretty much the same set up, with a stationary rack to set the tamales on (and often several divisions in the chamber, so you can separate tamales with different fillings) and an opening on the side toward the bottom for adding water. Some are more like the aluminum Chinese steamers (which is what I use at home), with a base for the boiling water that detaches from the steamer top.

When you're steaming, if your steamer allows it, bring the water to a boil before adding the tamales or whatever. Many cooks put a little something in the bottom of the pot (like a coin), so you can hear when the pot's about to go dry. And if that were to happen before the tamales are finished cooking, they'll come out heavier (like a cake that's removed from the oven before it's done). So keep a good amount of water steadily boiling in your steamer and, if it gets low, pour in *boiling* water so you won't lose your heat.

JUCHITAN-STYLE BLACK BEAN TAMALES

Tamales de Frijol, Estilo Juchiteco

A̶LL I HAVE TO DO is think of these toothsome little packages and I can see Ofelia Toledo in her riotously colored Juchitan tunic and long skirt, gold earrings dangling and slender hands spreading the green-flecked dough over squares of banana leaves. She deftly dollops on spoons of black beans and makes the quick folds, then speeds on to the next. I just love black beans with anything made from *masa,* and these small tamales are extra special because the tender dough is flavored with fresh herbs.

MAKES 15 TAMALES

1 pound banana leaves, defrosted if frozen

4 ounces (½ cup) to 5-½ ounces (⅔ cup) rich-tasting lard (or vegetable shortening if you want to), depending on how tender you want the tamales (I recommend the larger amount because these are more compact tamales)

1 pound (2 cups) coarse-ground masa *for tamales*

> OR *1¾ cups* masa harina *for tamales mixed with 1 cup plus 2 tablespoons hot water, then allowed to cool*

10 good-size leaves of epazote *(or half a small bunch of cilantro, if you can't lay your hands on* epazote)

About ⅔ cup cool chicken broth

Salt, about 1 teaspoon

2 cups seasoned, cooked black beans, preferably cooked as Ofelia does them with a couple of red jalapeños and a spoonful of good lard

About 1½ cups salsa (I love these with Essential Roasted Tomatillo-Chipotle Salsa, page 45), for serving

1. *The leaves.* Unfold the banana leaves and cut off the long, hard sides of the leaves (where they were attached to the central vein). Look for holes or rips, then cut leaves into unbroken 8-inch segments (you will need 15). Either steam the segments for 20 minutes to make them soft and pliable, or one at a time run them over an open flame or hot electric burner until soft and glossy.

2. *The batter.* With an electric mixer, beat the lard or other shortening for a few seconds until smooth. Continue beating as you add the *masa* (fresh or reconstituted) in three additions. In a blender, puree the *epazote* (or cilantro) with ½ *cup* of the broth, then slowly pour it into the *masa* mixture, beating all the while.

Beat in enough additional broth to give the mixture the consistency of soft (not runny) cake batter; it should softly hold its shape in a spoon. Season with salt (yes, it will involve tasting a little raw batter), about 1 scant teaspoon, depending on the saltiness of the broth.

3. *The filling.* If the level of the bean broth just covers the beans, pour off about half of the broth, then mash the beans with the remaining broth using a bean masher or the back of a spoon (they should wind up soft-textured, but not soupy). Season with salt, if needed.

4. *Forming and steaming the tamales.* One at a time, form the tamales: Lay a leaf on your work surface so the long side is horizontal, and smear a scant ¼ cup of batter into a 4 x 4-inch rectangle as indicated in the accompanying drawing. Spoon about 2 tablespoons of beans over the batter. Fold the right third of the leaf over the middle third (this will enclose the filling in the batter), then fold over the uncovered third of the leaf. Fold the two ends in at roughly the point where the batter begins and lay folded-side down into a steamer (a Mexican tamal steamer or Chinese steamer gives the greatest surface over which to distrib-

Dough and filling on banana leaf

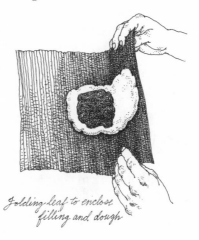

Folding leaf to enclose filling and dough

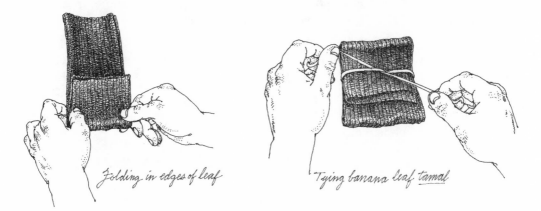

Folding in edges of leaf

Tying banana leaf *tamal*

ute the tamales) lined with half the remaining banana leaves. As tamales are made, place in the steamer, stacking when necessary, though not over two high.

Cover with remaining banana-leaf scraps. Set the steamer over 2 inches of boiling water, cover and steam over a medium heat for 1 to 1¼ hours (tamales made from reconstituted *masa* may take a little longer).

Let the steamer stand off the heat for a few minutes, then remove a tamal: If the leaf peels off easily, the tamales are done, if not, return them to the heat for a few minutes.

For a dressy presentation, untie the tamales and fold back the leaves, tucking them under to form a little boat. Spoon the salsa over them and be prepared for raves from your guests.

ADVANCE PREPARATION—The finished tamales can be refrigerated, covered, for several days; reheat them in the steamer. They can also be successfully frozen.

L-A-R-D

I feel like I'm stepping on a land mine whenever I mention the word *lard*. It elicits the most visceral of reactions from the nicest people. If lard is part of Mexican cooking, I've been told by a few, then they want nothing to do with it. Period. I haven't heard that said of French cooking, even though it relies heavily on another animal fat: butter. And butter has *more* saturated fat and *more* cholesterol than lard. So, it is not just health concerns that causes these exaggerated responses.

You can tell by my recipes that I'm a careful cook, especially when it comes to the amount of fat I use in everyday cooking. And I support the nutritionists and physicians who've proven that reducing our intake of saturated fat can make us healthier. But my recommendation is to achieve that reduction by relying less on processed foods, eating smaller amounts of meat, feasting only on special occasions and enjoying the roasty flavor of pork lard when traditional wisdom tells us it will enhance a dish.

Lard in Mexico usually is rendered at a higher heat than in the States, giving it a roast-pork flavor. That is the flavor in tamales and *moles,* among other traditional dishes, that is inimitable. If finding a rich-tasting lard is your difficulty, try buying it from a Mexican, German or other ethnic butcher (that is what we do at Frontera). Or, you can render cubed pork fat in a 350-degree oven until the remaining bits (cracklings) are brown. (I recommend you stay away from commercial, hydrogenated lard: it tastes like bad vegetable shortening). Or, for use in small amounts, you can substitute a little of the fat rendered from bacon or chorizo sausage.

YUCATECAN TAMALES
WITH GREENS, PUMPKIN SEEDS AND EGG

Dzotobichay

I HAVE NEVER experienced as weighty a heat as the late afternoon I tasted my first *dzoto-bichay* in Merida. There were twenty-something of us (it was our yearly staff trip to Mexico) huddled in Doña Lupita's 98-degree kitchen around a steaming steamer of tamales, watching her coolly pat out the dough and form the packages; she must have been drawing on a personal reserve of internal refreshment that I'd long since exhausted.

We were ushered into Doña Lupita's living room, where she'd set up tables and chairs, plus a fan to help shoulder the heavy air. And then she poured a round of her renowned *hot chocolate*. Honest. To a group whose collective dehydrated daydream was only for bottles of icy water, she served hot chocolate. And, of course, the hot tamales.

Today, away from all but the memory of that momentary discomfort, I know that these Yucatecan tamales are real gems. They're studded with greens (*chaya* there, a leaf that looks like grape leaf and has a chardlike taste), so they have a lovely balance of flavors. With Simmered Tomato-Habanero Sauce, these tamales are as delicious as Merida is hot in July.

MAKES 12 TAMALES

⅔ cup hulled, untoasted pumpkin seeds (pepitas)

2 eggs

1 pound banana leaves, defrosted if frozen

1 pound (about 2 cups) masa for tortillas

> OR *1¾ cups dried masa harina for tortillas mixed with 1 cup plus 2 tablespoons hot water, then allowed to cool*

4 ounces (½ cup) to 5½ (⅔ cup) rich-tasting lard or vegetable shortening—depending on how tender you want your tamales

¾ teaspoon salt

2 cups chopped chaya or green chard leaves (¼-inch pieces)

About 2 cups Essential Simmered Tomato-Habanero Sauce (page 31), for serving

1. *Getting started.* Heat a medium-size (8- to 9-inch) skillet over medium-low for several minutes, then pour in the pumpkin seeds. When the first one pops, stir them constantly for 4 to 5 minutes, until all have toasted and popped from flat to oval (don't let them brown too much or they'll be bitter). Cool completely. In a food processor, coarsely grind the seeds.

Put the eggs into a small saucepan filled with cold, salted water and bring to a boil. Reduce the heat so the water simmers gently for 11 minutes. Drain, set the pan under cold running water for a minute or so, then let the eggs cool in the water. Peel and coarsely chop.

2. *The leaves.* Unfold the banana leaves and cut off the long, hard side of the leaf (where it was attached to the central vein). Look for holes or rips, then cut the leaves into unbroken 10- to 12-inch segments (you will need 12 of these). Either steam the segments for 20 minutes to make them soft and pliable, or one at a time slowly run them over an open flame or hot electric burner until the oils rise to the top (the leaves will look glossy) and they soften; if they spend too long over the heat, they'll be crispy rather than soft—definitely not what you're looking for. Cut 12 long strips from the leftover leaves to use for tying the tamales.

3. *The batter.* If the *masa* is stiff, work in tablespoons of cool water to give it the consistency of rather soft cookie dough. In the large bowl of an electric mixer, combine the *masa*, lard and salt. Beat until combined, then mix in the chopped *chaya* or chard.

4. *Forming and steaming the tamales.* Using a rubber spatula, spread out ¼ cup of the *masa* over the center of 1 banana-leaf segment into a 4- to 5-inch circle. Sprinkle with about 2 teaspoons of the ground pumpkin seeds and a generous teaspoon of the chopped egg. Using the leaf, fold the right ⅓ of the *masa* circle over the center third, gingerly peel back the leaf (leaving that ⅓ of the circle folded over), then fold the left ⅓ over so the *masa* completely encloses the pumpkin-seed-and-egg filling. Fold in all the sides of the banana leaf even with the enclosed *masa* and tie with one of the banana leaf strips. Continue spreading, filling and folding until all 12 tamales are made.

Set up a large steamer (a Mexican tamal steamer or Chinese steamer gives the greatest surface) with 2 inches of water and spread *half* of the remaining banana-leaf scraps over the bottom. Arrange the tamales in the steamer folded-side down, stacking when necessary (but not more than 2 high). Cover with the remaining banana-leaf scraps. Bring the water to a boil, cover tightly, and steam over medium heat for about 1 hour (tamales made from reconstituted *masa* may take a little longer). Remove a tamal, open it and see if the leaf pulls away—the sign it is done. Let the tamales stand in the steamer off the heat for a few minutes, to firm up.

5. *Serving the tamales.* Remove ties from tamales. For a decorative presentation, open out each banana leaf, gather one end together and tie with another banana-leaf strip to make a "shell." Spoon on a little sauce and sprinkle with ground pumpkin seed.

ADVANCE PREPARATION—Though most tender when first made, these can be done several days ahead, covered, refrigerated, then reheated in the steamer.

Banana Leaves

Once, in Guerrero, in the middle of preparing Yucatecan Achiote Roasted Pork (page 170) in banana leaves, I realized banana leaves aren't used in cooking in that part of Mexico. Determined to accomplish my task, I drove up to a house with a banana tree in the back yard and asked to buy some of the leaves. We cut down a couple of big ones and I took them home. The tender part of the leaves had to be cut from the main stalk, then slowly passed over a gas flame until soft and shiny-looking (you can also steam them for 20 minutes or so to soften them). I was ready to wrap my marinated pork. Banana leaves impart a very special herby-green flavor that you can't get from any other leaf.

In Chicago, we generally get one-pound packages of frozen banana leaves (these dryish leaves freeze perfectly well); most come from Indonesia or the Philippines and, luckily, they're available in lots of the Mexican and Asian markets. Be careful to completely defrost them before unfolding, so the leaves won't break up. Cut off the less flexible brownish strip of the central stalk still left on the leaves, before softening them over the flame or in the steamer.

If you can't find banana leaves, most tamales (except the Pre-Hispanic Tamales) can be done in corn husks. They can be left out of practically every other dish I've included here; you won't have that herbaceous flavor, but the dish will be very good.

Stats: Expect to get 10 (or 12) 12-inch squares of banana leaf from each 1-pound package. Leftovers will keep in the refrigerator for a month or so (wipe off any surface mold that develops); they'll have an off smell if they've gone bad.

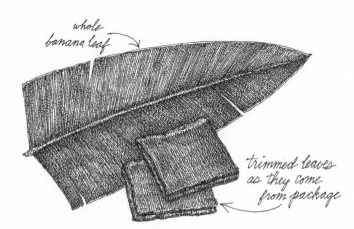

whole banana leaf

trimmed leaves as they come from package

PRE-HISPANIC-STYLE TAMALES
WITH BLACK BEANS OR YELLOW *MOLE*

Tamales de Frijoles Negros o Mole Amarillo

Ｐʀᴇ-ʜɪsᴘᴀɴɪᴄ? Tʜᴇ ʀᴇᴀsᴏɴ I'm calling these tamales *pre-Hispanic* is because of their lack of any fat. They are made the way tamales were before the Spaniards brought pigs and cattle, fat and all. Pre-Hispanic tamales, you see, were really steamed tortillas with a filling. Though in Oaxaca corn leaves (the leaves from the stalks, not the corn husks) are the common wrapper, I've called for the more accessible banana leaves—the leaf sometimes used in Guerrero.

These tamales are very simple, especially if you choose black beans as the filling. They have a toothsome texture—not light and fluffy, but tender, sort of like those wonderfully thick Asian rice noodles.

Every time folks talk about *tamales de amarillo* in Oaxaca, their faces light up. They unwrap the little packages regularly in market stalls, unassuming restaurants and at special occasions. These are based on those made by Zoyla Mendoza in Teotitlan del Valle.

Mᴀᴋᴇs 12 ᴛᴀᴍᴀʟᴇs

1 pound banana leaves, defrosted if
frozen

1 1/2 pounds (3 cups) fresh masa for
tortillas

OR 2 2/3 cups dried masa harina
mixed with 1 3/4 cups hot water

1 teaspoon salt

1 1/2 cups cooked, seasoned black beans

OR 1 1/2 cups Yellow Mole
(page 196) mixed with 1 cup

shredded cooked chicken and
1/2 cup coarsely chopped hoja santa
or cilantro, plus an additional
1 1/2 cups or so mole for serving

About 1 1/2 cups salsa (I like
Essential Roasted Tomatillo-
Serrano Salsa, page 42),
for serving with black
bean tamales

1. *The leaves.* Unfold the banana leaves and cut off the long, hard side of the leaf (where they were attached to the central vein). Look for holes or rips, then cut into unbroken 12-inch segments (you will need 12). Either steam the segments for 20 minutes to make them pliable, or one at a time slowly run them over an open flame or hot electric burner until the leaves will look glossy and soften.

2. *The dough.* Cut 2 pieces of plastic (preferably the weight of a plastic garbage bag) to cover the plates of your tortilla press. Knead the salt into the *masa* (fresh or reconstituted),

plus, if necessary, a few drops of water to give it the consistency of a soft cookie dough; roll into 12 balls. Cover with plastic.

3. *Forming and steaming the tamales.* If you're using beans and they're covered with broth, drain off about *half* of it, then mash together beans and remaining broth with a bean or potato masher or the back of a spoon (they should be soft, but not soupy). Season them with salt if they need it. If you're using the yellow *mole* mixture and it's cold, stir it vigorously to loosen up the texture.

One at a time, form the tamales: Use the tortilla press to press out the dough between the 2 sheets of plastic, peel off the top sheet, then flip the tortilla onto your hand, exposed-side down. Carefully peel off the plastic. Spoon a portion of the filling down the center third of the tortilla, then fold the 2 uncovered sides in, to more or less cover it. Lay in the middle of a banana-leaf segment, fold in the 2 sides, then fold up top and bottom. Lay folded-side down and continue forming the remaining tamales.

Set up a large steamer (a Mexican tamal steamer or Chinese steamer will give you the greatest surface over which to distribute the tamales) with a couple of inches of water and spread *half* the remaining banana leaf scraps over the bottom. Arrange the tamales in the steamer folded side down, stacking when necessary (but not more than 2 high). Cover with the remaining banana-leaf scraps. Bring the water to a boil, cover tightly and steam over medium heat for about 15 minutes (tamales made from reconstituted *masa* may take a little longer).

Remove a tamal from the center of the steamer: If the leaf peels off easily, the tamales are done and ready to serve; if not, return them to the steamy heat for a few more minutes.

To serve, open up the tamales, folding the leaf under on all sides, set on plates, then spoon a little warm *mole* or salsa over them and they're ready to dig into.

ADVANCE PREPARATION—These tamales, more so than any others, are best eaten right after they're steamed.

VARIATIONS AND IMPROVISATIONS—South of Mexico City, in the states of Morelos and Guerrero, cooks make something very similar with no filling, called *tamales nejos* (the name refers to the fact that the corn is boiled with ashes). They are usually about 8 inches long and 3 or 4 inches wide. Folks get very excited about eating them topped with green pumpkin-seed *mole*.

GREAT BIG TAMAL ROLL WITH CHARD

Tamalón de Acelgas

$\mathcal{Y}$OU DON'T SEE these big tamales offered in restaurants in Mexico, but my Mexican friends all know them and think of them as comforting and homey. I like them because they are easy (none of the individual leaf wrapping), and in this version, I've made them even easier by mixing the filling (green chard) right in with the batter. Fanned out slices look stunning on a platter, sitting on a spicy-looking salsa. It can be a main dish, side dish or snack.

To keep this batter thicker (and easier to work with in this larger format), I do not suggest the second beating with additional liquid that I recommend in other tamal recipes. The *tamalón* won't be fluffy-light, but it will be tender and toothsome, especially with all the flecks of chard. If you like the flavor of banana leaves, lay a section over the towel (it'll need to be softened over the flame) before you add the batter.

SERVES 4 TO 6 AS A MAIN DISH, 8 TO 10 AS AN ACCOMPANIMENT OR SUCH

4 ounces (½ cup) to 5½ ounces (⅔ cup) chilled, rich-tasting lard (or vegetable shortening if you want to), depending on how tender you want the tamalón *(I recommend the larger amount since the* tamalón *has a more compact texture)*

1 teaspoon baking powder

1 pound (2 cups) coarse-ground masa for tamales

   OR 1¾ cups dried masa harina for tamales mixed with 1 cup plus 2 tablespoons hot water, then allowed to cool

About ⅔ cup cool chicken broth

Salt, about a scant teaspoon

About 3 loosely packed cups of coarsely chopped chard leaves (you'll need about ½ of a 12-ounce bunch)

About 1½ cups of practically any salsa (the tamalón *is particularly good with the Essential Roasted Tomato-Jalapeño Salsa, page 21), for serving, unless you're using it as an accompaniment to a saucy main dish*

1. *The steamer.* My first choice is a large (at least 12-inch) Mexican tamal steamer or Chinese steamer; second choice would be to use a large (at least 12-inch) oval roasting pan or Dutch oven with a tight-fitting lid and a roasting rack that roughly fits it. If using one of the steamers, pour an inch of water into the base; if using one of the second choices, set the rack on upside-down custard cups and pour in a couple of inches of water.

2. *The batter*. With an electric mixer, beat the lard (or shortening) with the baking powder until light in texture, about 1 minute. Continue beating as you add the *masa* (fresh or reconstituted) in three additions. Slowly pour in a generous ½ *cup* of the broth, beating all the while. Continue beating for another minute or so, until a ½-teaspoon dollop of the batter floats in a cup of cold water (if it floats the *tamalón* will be tender and light).

Beat in enough additional broth to give the mixture the consistency of soft (not runny) cake batter; it should softly hold its shape in a spoon. Season with salt, usually about 1 scant teaspoon, depending on the saltiness of the broth. Stir in the chopped chard.

3. *Forming and steaming the roll*. Lay a damp cotton kitchen towel on your counter; you'll need one about 25 x 18 inches and it shouldn't be terrycloth. Spoon the mixture down the length of the center, making a log shape about 12 inches long and 5 inches wide. Fold one long side of the towel over the mixture, then continue rolling gently, being careful that the mixture doesn't work its way out toward the ends. Now, carefully tie the ends with two pieces of kitchen string, squeezing the mixture in at each end to plump the roll. With 4 more strings, tie the tamal at intervals to give it as round a shape as possible. The roll will be about 12 inches long and 3 inches in diameter when it is tied.

Bring the water in your steamer to a boil, carefully lay in the tamal roll, cover tightly and steam over medium heat for about 1¼ hours, making sure the water never runs out. Let stand a few minutes, then cut the string and unroll the tamal onto your cutting board. If it won't pull away from the towel, roll it up again and steam an additional 15 minutes. Slice the tamal about 1 inch thick and lay on a warm, bright-colored serving plate. Drizzle the salsa all around, if you've chosen to serve salsa with it.

ADVANCE PREPARATION—The *tamalón* can be made ahead, cooled, wrapped in plastic and refrigerated for several days. It reheats beautifully, whole or in slices, in a steamer.

VARIATIONS AND IMPROVISATIONS

Use other greens (spinach, *quelites*, amaranth, collard, arugula), meat, even sundried tomatoes and herbs or olives for the *tamalón*.

Black Bean Tamalón, *Guerrero Style*—At the restaurant we do versions of *tamalón* that involve gently rolling the dough ¼ inch thick between sheets of plastic, removing the top piece of plastic, spreading on a filling, then rolling it up jellyroll style (peeling back the plastic as you go), wrapping it described above and steaming it. Geno Bahena (managing chef of Topolobampo) invited his mother from Guerrero to show us how to do her black bean version. Instead of wrapping it in a cloth, she cut the uncooked roll into 2-inch sections, nested each slice in a corn husk, stood her tamales in the steamer and cooked them—exactly what Sahagún described in the early 1500s as being sold in the Tenochtitlan market.

RUSTIC BAKED TAMAL OF COARSE-GROUND CORN, PORK AND RED CHILE

Zacahuil en Miniatura

*I*F THIS MINIATURE version of the enormous classic *zacahuil* weren't so delicious, I would never have scaled it down to include in this collection. The original, you see, is 4- or 5-feet long and 8 inches thick, swaddled in layer upon layer of banana leaves and baked for hours in a wood-fired oven. Eating slabs of it in the bare little open-air dining rooms around Papantla, Veracruz, in the Huastec region of the state, is a memorable experience to say the least—much more than simple gustatory pleasure. This is food of generations, perhaps centuries, and to "refine" it would never be an improvement.

So why a miniature *zacahuil* here? Because there's no doubting that you'll enjoy the rough texture and red-chile goodness this tamal has to offer. And the preparation teaches how to make your own coarse-ground *masa* from half-cooked hominy (*nixtamal*)—the *maíz martajado* of the original. Though you'll miss the smokiness of the wood-fired oven, you can capture some of the original's herbaceousness by lining your pan with banana leaves.

I buy *nixtamal* at a local tortilla factory (*nixtamal* is the half-cooked corn they grind to make *masa* for tortillas or tamales); occasionally they carry it at a nearby Mexican market on the weekends. If you're interested in making your own *nixtamal*, I describe the whole process in my first book, *Authentic Mexican*.

SERVES 8 AS A FIRST COURSE, 4 TO 6 AS A CASUAL MAIN COURSE

4 medium (*about 2 ounces total*) *dried ancho chiles, stemmed and seeded*

OR 6 dried New Mexico chiles, *stemmed and seeded*

3 large garlic cloves, peeled and *roughly chopped*

1/2 teaspoon black pepper, preferably *freshly ground*

1 1/2-inch-thick slice of white onion

1/2 pound boneless pork shoulder, *trimmed and cut into 1-inch cubes*

Salt, *about 2 teaspoons*

1 pound (*about 2 3/4 cups*) half-cooked *hominy* (nixtamal)

OR 1 pound (2 cups) coarse-ground fresh masa *for tamales*

OR 1 3/4 cups dried masa harina *for tamales mixed with 1 cup plus 2 tablespoons hot water, then allowed to cool*

4 ounces (1/2 cup) chilled rich-tasting *lard (or vegetable shortening if you want to)*

1 teaspoon baking powder

About 1/2 cup cool beef broth, plus up *to 1/3 cup more for the second beating (if you choose to do it)*

A 2-foot length of banana leaf (*defrosted if frozen*), *if you can get it*

1. *The filling.* One at a time, toast the chiles on an ungreased griddle or heavy skillet over medium heat: Tear into flat pieces, use a metal spatula to press them flat against the hot surface, then, in a few seconds (when they crackle and change color, even send up a wisp of smoke), flip them, and press down to toast the other side. In a small bowl, cover them with hot water and let rehydrate 30 minutes, stirring frequently to ensure even soaking. Strain, reserving the soaking liquid.

In a food processor or blender, combine the garlic, black pepper and onion with the chiles and just enough of their soaking liquid to barely cover everything. Process to a smooth puree, then press through a medium-mesh strainer into a medium-size (2- to 3-quart) saucepan. Add the pork, 1½ cups of water and ½ *teaspoon* of the salt. Bring to a boil, partially cover and let gurgle away over medium-low heat until the kitchen is filled with a rich, spicy aroma and the meat is fall-apart tender, about 1 hour.

With a slotted spoon, remove the meat to a plate and shred with two forks (or cool and shred with your fingers). Taste and season the sauce with salt, usually about ½ teaspoon, then let it cool completely. There will be about 1½ cups shredded meat and 2 cups of sauce.

2. *The batter.* If using the *nixtamal,* rinse it very well to ensure that all the yellow skins are off the corn, then grind in a food processor to the texture of a damp, very coarse meal. Scoop ⅔ of the corn into a bowl and continue grinding the remainder until it is as fine as possible—almost powdery. (It will look like processor-ground almonds; this fine grinding will ensure that the tamal will hold together.) Scrape the fine ground corn in with the more coarsely ground. Fresh or reconstituted *masa* doesn't need to be processed. With an electric mixer, beat the lard (or shortening) with the baking powder until light in texture, about 1 minute. Continue beating as you add the ground *nixtamal* or *masa* (fresh or reconstituted) in three additions. Slowly pour in a generous ⅓ *cup* of the broth, beating all the while, then beat in *3 or 4 tablespoons* of the cooled sauce.

Beat in additional broth, if necessary, to give the mixture the consistency of soft (not runny) cake batter; it should softly hold its shape in a spoon. Season with salt (yes, it will involve tasting a little raw batter), usually about 1 scant teaspoon, depending on the saltiness of the broth.

For the lightest-textured *zacahuil,* refrigerate the batter for an hour or so, then rebeat, adding enough additional broth to bring the mixture to the consistency it had before. (You may find it necessary to add a little more salt, too.)

3. *Forming and baking the* zacahuil. Turn on the oven to 375 degrees. If you have the banana leaf, slowly run it across a gas or electric burner set on medium (you're moving at the right speed when the leaf becomes shiny and limp as it crosses the heat), then cut a 9-inch section that you can drape into a 9 x 5-inch loaf pan to line it (the two ends will still be

exposed). Generously grease the pan, then drape the leaf in it, pressing it snugly against the sides and bottom, leaving two flaps hanging over the sides.

Scoop *half* of the batter into the pan, then distribute the shredded meat over it. Splash with several tablespoons of the sauce, spoon in the remaining batter, and smooth it to cover the filling evenly. Fold the banana leaf flaps over the top and cover tightly with foil.

Bake for about ½ hour, then reduce the heat to 325 degrees and bake 1 hour longer. Uncover, peel back the foil and banana leaf: The tamal should feel nearly firm in the center; if it still feels quite soft (like there is uncooked batter in there), cover, and return to the oven for a few minutes longer.

Let the tamal stand for 10 or 15 minutes to firm up completely while you warm the remaining sauce. Gently turn the tamal out onto a cutting board, peel off the leaf if you used one, cut into thick slices (it's rustic—somewhat crumbly—so the slices won't be perfect), and serve on warm plates with a little sauce spooned over the top.

ADVANCE PREPARATION—The tamal can be baked a day or two ahead, cooled, removed from the pan, covered, and refrigerated. It slices better cold. You can lay the slices out on a baking sheet and heat them in a 400-degree oven until hot and crusty.

VARIATIONS AND IMPROVISATIONS—You can use this tamal-baked-in-a-loaf-pan idea with a variety of fillings (shredded chicken, beef, venison, moist fish like sea bass) and sauces. (I love *moles* here, but tomato and tomatillo–based sauces are excellent, too.)

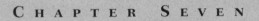

CHAPTER SEVEN

. . . . .

MAIN DISHES

THESE MAIN-DISH RECIPES MAKE ME FEEL WE'RE ON FAMILIAR TURF. They're closer to the kinds of dishes we regularly made for dinner (or for a casual dinner party), almost every one of them utilizes one of the essential recipes (so they're a good place to learn about traditional Mexican flavor and technique), and they're all quite simple (many are very quick).

But are they Mexican? Yes, definitely, because each resonates with flavors and textures you'd spoon up from practically any Mexican plate. Yet they are dishes at home in my American kitchen, exactly the dishes I like to set before my guests, dishes I like to eat.

When you ask what's for dinner in Mexico (or when you ask a Mexican waiter what's good on a restaurant's menu), the response will most likely be a main dish, as it would be in the States. Main dishes on both sides of the border are the heart of the meal. The one difference I note between our two approaches, however, is that in Mexico main dishes are frequently not labeled by the "hunk of beast" (as my partner in the restaurant Zinfandel, Susan Goss, is fond of saying). Rather than "chicken," "shrimp" or "pork," they may be *mole* or *pipián* or *adobo,* leaving unspecified the item we think of as the "center of the plate." In Mexico, you see, the *mole* (or whatever sauce) can welcome most any meat or chicken that is available or cheap or preferred; during religious fasts it welcomes fish or vegetables.

That kind of flexibility would be helpful in our country, I think, as we are striving to rethink the proportions of what we eat. It's certainly the perspective I'm trying to build into these main-dish recipes: from big celebratory steaks and whole roasted fish to main dishes that combine small amounts of meat with lots of vegetables. All, of course, enveloped in that attractive Mexican fullness of flavor that we find so satisfying these days.

I encourage you to look in other sections of the book for main dishes as well. Many of the soups can be served as main attractions, as can most of the *antojitos* (corn *masa*–based dishes), a good smattering of the vegetable, bean and rice dishes, and all of the *moles* in the fiesta food chapter.

When putting together a meal, I've included my suggestions for accompaniments in many recipe introductions. Generally, a traditional Mexican meal will start with a soup, then proceed to the saucy main dish that will have some vegetables cooked with it or a spoon of rice (occasionally beans) on the side, then conclude with a creamy dessert, poached fruit or a plate of typical candies. If the meal is a bit more formal, there may be an appetizer like seviche or little tostadas of something vinegary, and after the soup (the "brothy soup course") there might be a rice dish (the "dry soup course"). At Topolobampo, our set menu includes an appetizer, soup, main dish and dessert; I love that run of courses for a special-occasion meal. Of course, you'll want to put on your table what *you* like to eat, in the order and with the variety that is right for your occasions and your guests.

POULTRY

· · · · ·

If you've ever bitten into Mexican chicken, you know (to borrow a line from *The Wizard of Oz*) you're not in Kansas anymore. It has a muscley texture that let's you know it's toured the chicken yard, and in my opinion that's not a bad thing. Our striving to make chicken fork-tender has never seemed to me an honorable goal, nor has our desire to breed the bird to blandness. Tastelessness is certainly not a problem with market chickens in Mexico, so choose free-range chicken for a more authentically Mexican flavor and texture.

One of the glorious classics of the Mexican kitchen, in my opinion, is chicken or pork in *adobo* or any other simple red chile sauce for that matter. My version of Red Chile–Braised Chicken is pretty classic, except that rarely do you see the garlic and spice–sweetened, rich red-chile sauce harboring wilted greens and tender potatoes; the chicken's browned flavor adds another layer of satisfaction, giving this homey chicken braise an elegant flavor.

Different from the sesame-thickened green *pipián* with salmon (page 351) or from the complex green *mole* I included in *Authentic Mexican,* the chicken in Pueblan Green Pumpkin Seed Sauce is simple and herby. There are no tomatillos, so it's richer, less sharp; the focus stays almost completely on pumpkin seeds, green chiles and cilantro. Made in the classic Mexican fashion (poaching the chicken, using the broth for the sauce, then simmering the chicken in the sauce), this dish is about as traditional as you can get.

Back in the traditional bent are the Grilled Chicken Breasts in Tomato-*Guaje* Sauce. The sauce, which blends a little-known seed with roasted tomatoes and green chiles, is a simple classic from Puebla; I think its toasted nuttiness goes particularly well with anything cooked over embers, so I've paired it with grilled chicken breasts.

Also in Puebla reign the *tingas* of sweet tomatoes, garlic and chipotle chiles. They're served on plates or in tacos or sandwiches, usually with a garnishing dice of avocado and fresh cheese; I've included the coarsely shredded version here; keep this preparation in mind when you're searching for a buffet dish for a crowd or for a taco or sandwich filling.

Two creamy, very simple chicken breast recipes are perfect for entertaining when time is of the essence. The first combines the smokiness of chipotle chiles with creamy spinach, while the second features classic roasted poblanos and mushrooms (to really give your friends a special treat, buy wild mushrooms when they're in season). Neither is really traditional, though both of these quick dishes spotlight very classic flavors.

The final two recipes in this section wander away from chicken. Achiote Grilled Turkey is classic Yucatecan cooking that weaves together the flavor of the grill with an unusual, spicy "white sauce" spiked with tomato, garlicky achiote and mint; sounds exotic, I know, but the effect is comforting and very satisfying. Squab may not be part of your normal repertoire, but they are available from many specialty groceries and butchers nowadays. Squab is a regional specialty in Guerrero, and this simple, typical tomato-chipotle sauce (simmered with dark beer and sweet spices) is a perfect match for the rich dark-red meat.

RED CHILE-BRAISED CHICKEN
WITH POTATOES AND GREENS
Adobo de Pollo, de Lujo

TYPICAL MEXICAN *adobos* are stewlike presentations of meat in savory red chile sauce. Don't confuse the noun *adobo*, referring to the sauce or whole dish, with the adjective *adobado*, which is used for something marinated in a punchier version of this sauce—though the use of these two words for some cooks is not so distinct.

When the *adobo* is made with ancho chiles, as it is here, rather than the tangier guajillos, it needs the zing of something zesty. Here I prefer vinegar; other recipes use orange juice. Simmer that with chicken, potatoes and greens and you have a one-dish meal that is as earthy and elegant as the red-brick color of its sauce.

You will need nothing besides a deep, nice-looking serving platter to complete your main course. A creamy soup (squash blossom for special meals, fava bean or black bean for other times) or a frisee salad with *queso fresco*, plus a cooling dessert like homemade Mango-Lime Ice (page 393) will frame a beautiful dinner.

SERVES 4

1 ½ tablespoons vegetable or olive oil

A 2 ½- to 3-pound chicken, cut into quarters

1 medium white onion, sliced ¼ inch thick, plus 2 slices broken into rings, for garnish

FOR 1 CUP ESSENTIAL SWEET-AND-SPICY ANCHO SEASONING PASTE

8 garlic cloves, unpeeled

8 medium (about 4 ounces total) dried ancho chiles, stemmed and seeded

1 ½ teaspoons dried oregano, preferably Mexican

½ teaspoon black pepper, preferably freshly ground

⅛ teaspoon cumin seeds, preferably freshly ground

A scant ¼ teaspoon cloves, preferably freshly ground

2 ⅔ cups chicken broth, plus a little more if necessary

1 ½ tablespoons cider vinegar

8 small (about 1 pound) boiling potatoes (like the red-skin ones), halved

4 cups sliced (½-inch slices), full-flavored greens (choose chard, beet or turnip tops, lamb's quarters, collards or the like), well rinsed

Salt, about 1 ¼ teaspoons, depending on saltiness of the broth

1. *Browning the chicken and onions.* Heat the oil in a medium-to-large (4- to 6-quart) pot (like a Dutch oven or Mexican *cazuela*) over medium-high. Pat the chicken dry, then brown in a single uncrowded layer (in batches if necessary), about 4 minutes per side. Remove the chicken to a plate, reduce heat to medium, add onion and fry until soft and richly browned, about 10 minutes. Set aside.

2. *Making 1 cup Essential Sweet-and-Spicy Ancho Seasoning Paste.* Roast the unpeeled garlic directly on an ungreased griddle or heavy skillet over medium heat, turning occasionally, until soft (they'll blacken in spots), about 15 minutes; cool and peel. While the garlic is roasting, toast the chiles on another side of the griddle or skillet: 1 or 2 at a time, open them flat and press down firmly on the hot surface with a spatula; in a few seconds, when they crackle, even send up a wisp of smoke, flip them, and press down to toast the other side. In a small bowl, cover the chiles with hot water and let rehydrate 30 minutes, stirring frequently to ensure even soaking. Drain and discard the water.

Combine the oregano, black pepper, cumin and cloves in a food processor or blender, along with the drained chiles, garlic and ⅔ *cup* of the broth. Blend to a smooth puree, scraping and stirring every few seconds. (If the mixture won't go through the blender blades, add a little more liquid.) Press through a medium-mesh strainer into a bowl.

2. *The sauce.* Return the chicken-browning pot to medium-high heat and, when very hot, add the ancho chile seasoning. Cook, stirring until thickened and noticeably darker, about 5 minutes, then stir in the remaining 2 *cups* broth and the vinegar. Simmer for 15 minutes, stirring occasionally.

3. *Finishing the dish.* Add the chicken thigh and leg quarters and the potatoes to the sauce. Partially cover and simmer over medium-low for 15 minutes. Stir in the greens and add the chicken breasts. Partially cover and simmer until the chicken is cooked through, about 20 minutes. Use a slotted spoon to transfer the chicken to a warm, deep serving platter.

Bring the sauce and vegetables to a boil over medium to medium-high heat and reduce until the mixture reaches a medium consistency, about 5 minutes. Season with salt.

Ladle the sauce over the chicken, arranging the greens and potatoes around the edges. Strew the onion rings over the vegetables and you're ready to serve.

ADVANCE PREPARATION—The recipe may be prepared up to several days in advance through step 2, covered and refrigerated. The finished dish reheats quite well, too, though the chicken won't have that just-cooked texture, and the sauce may need a little thinning with water.

CHICKEN IN PUEBLAN GREEN
PUMPKIN SEED SAUCE

Pipián Verde de Pollo

*T*HOUGH AN ALMOST identical dish of chicken in creamy-textured, nutty, herby pumpkin seed sauce will be called *mole verde* in much of Central and other parts of Mexico, in Puebla it is *pipián*. Celebrating the fresh greenness of all things herbal (cilantro, lettuce, even the easy-to-find bitey leaves of radishes), as well as sprightly green chiles, there's an honest simplicity here that is very appealing. A typical *mole verde* made with tomatillos and numerous spices, like the one I detailed in *Authentic Mexican,* is rich, complex, and very satisfying; but on a recent trip to Puebla I was struck again with the perfect balance of this very easy sauce. My version is based on the one in *Comida poblana,* a gastronomic guide published by the magazine *México Desconocido.* I added the spicy, herby radish leaves to the pot, since they are commonly used in *moles verdes* and *pipianes verdes*.

Adding some blanched vegetables like cubed zucchini and chayote or green beans to the sauce just before returning the chicken to the pot will turn the dish into a complete meal. A spoonful of Classic White Rice (page 251) or Green Poblano Rice (page 254) is always welcome, as is the Tropical "Trifle" of Mango and Almonds (page 396) for dessert.

SERVES 4, WITH ABOUT 5 CUPS SAUCE (SO YOU'LL HAVE LEFTOVERS FOR ANOTHER ROUND OF CHICKEN OR FOR ENCHILADAS OR VEGETABLES)

1 large white onion, sliced

4 garlic cloves, peeled and roughly chopped

1 large carrot, peeled and thinly sliced

Salt, about 1½ teaspoons

1 good-size (3-pound) chicken, cut into quarters

2 bay leaves

¼ teaspoon dried thyme

¼ teaspoon dried marjoram

A generous 1 cup (about 4½ ounces) hulled pumpkin seeds (pepitas)

12 large sprigs cilantro, roughly chopped, plus a few extra sprigs for garnish

3 small romaine leaves, roughly chopped

2 large radish leaves, roughly chopped

Hot green chiles to taste (roughly 3 serranos or 2 small jalapeños), stemmed and roughly chopped

1 tablespoon vegetable or olive oil

1. *Poaching the chicken.* In a large (6-quart) pot, bring 8 cups of water to a boil. Add *half* of the onion and garlic, all the carrot, *1 teaspoon* of the salt, and the chicken back (if you're lucky enough to have a separated one), neck, heart and giblets. Skim off any foam that rises

after a minute or two, partially cover and simmer over medium-low heat for 20 minutes. Add the dark meat quarters, skim again after a couple of minutes, then add the bay, thyme and marjoram, partially cover and cook over medium heat for 10 minutes. Add the breast quarters, skim when the liquid returns to the simmer, partially cover, and cook 13 minutes. Remove the pot from the heat and let the chicken cool for a few minutes in the broth.

Remove the breast and leg quarters from the broth and set aside. Strain the broth, discarding the solids, and spoon off any fat that rises to the top.

2. *The pumpkin seeds.* In a large (10- to 12-inch), heavy skillet set over medium heat, spread out the pumpkin seeds and toast, stirring regularly, until all have popped (from flat to rounded) and turned golden (no darker or they will be bitter); once they start popping, the whole process shouldn't take longer than 5 minutes. Spread out on a plate to cool; reserve a couple of tablespoons for garnish.

3. *The sauce.* In a blender, combine the cooled pumpkin seeds with the remaining *half* of the onion and garlic, the cilantro, romaine, radish leaves and green chiles. Add *1½ cups* of the chicken broth and blend to a smooth puree.

Heat the oil in a large (4-quart), heavy saucepan over medium. Add the puree and stir constantly until very thick, about 10 minutes. Stir in *2 cups* of the broth (you'll have about 4 cups broth left over for soup or another sauce), partially cover and simmer 20 minutes; the sauce will look coarse at this point.

Scrape the sauce into a blender, *loosely cover* and blend to a smooth puree; if necessary add a little extra broth (or water) to give the sauce a medium consistency. Rinse your saucepan, return the blended sauce to it, taste and season with salt, usually a ½ teaspoon. Add the chicken and warm (don't bring to a simmer) over medium-low, about 10 minutes.

With a slotted spoon, transfer the chicken to a warm serving platter, then ladle the sauce over it, decorate with the reserved pumpkin seeds and cilantro sprigs, and it's ready to serve.

ADVANCE PREPARATION—The dish can be prepared a couple of days ahead: Store poached chicken and sauce separately, covered and refrigerated.

VARIATIONS AND IMPROVISATIONS—The sauce can be made separately and used for rich and delicious enchiladas (try them filled with crabmeat or shredded grilled chicken) or to sauce vegetables. It is good with grilled poultry or pork, or with practically any grilled seafood (especially salmon, squid and scallops).

Pumpkin Seeds

Pumpkin seeds, as is true of all nuts, add a rich and nutritious texture when blended into sauces. Peanut-thick satay sauce or pesto are among the few nut- or seed-thickened sauces we come across regularly in the States, though many such sauces are commonplace in Mexico and have been since pre-Columbian times. Pumpkin seeds (*pepitas*) are the most frequently used thickeners there. Most thick-shelled varieties are sold shelled in Mexico (the inside seed is vibrant olive green); thin-shelled seeds are used shell and all. The latter, when blended into sauces, gives a less oily pulpiness (you might think the sauce is a bit grittier); in some regions that's what's loved.

Hulled green pumpkin seeds are available widely in the States, especially in health-food stores. Untoasted are preferable to the quicker-to-spoil toasted ones you find as snack nuts. Shell-on, mottled white, thin-shelled seeds are rarely available outside Mexican groceries. Both freeze well.

Pumpkin seeds need to be toasted in order for them to have that mealy texture that will puree well into a sauce. Though pumpkin seeds for snacking usually are roasted in oil, for cooking they are best and most commonly toasted in a dry skillet (they come out less oily). Pour them into a skillet in roughly a single layer, set over medium heat, and, when the first one pops, stir constantly for several minutes until all have popped from flat to rounded and picked up a faint toasted hue. Be careful not to walk away while they are toasting—burnt seeds will make a sauce taste, well, burnt. As soon as the seeds are uniformly toasted, pour them out onto a baking sheet to cool completely.

Stats: One cup of pumpkin seeds weighs about 4½ ounces.

BROILED CHIPOTLE CHICKEN
WITH CREAMY SPINACH

Pollo Enchipotlado con Crema y Espinacas

*Y*OU HAVE COMPANY COMING, you want to do something special and there's no time. Here is a simple concoction that practically everyone takes to right away: smoky and spicy broiled chicken with creamy spinach. There is nothing particularly traditional here except the combination of chipotles and cream (considered a little "gourmet" in Mexico). It is just very good (comfort food with a kick) and very easy. Make the quick Rustic Ranch-Style Soup (page 126) to start, buy tropical fruit for dessert and you have a memorable meal.

SERVES 4

2 tablespoons Essential Sweet-and Smoky Chipotle Seasoning Salsa (*page 52*)
OR 2 to 3 canned chipotles chiles en adobo, *finely chopped (about 2 tablespoons)*
1¼ *cups Thick Cream (page 165), whipping cream or* crème fraîche

4 *medium-large (about 1⅓ pounds total) boneless, skinless chicken-breast halves, trimmed of all extraneous fat*
¼ *cup chicken broth*
6 *cups (about 10 ounces) stemmed spinach, well rinsed*
Salt, about ½ *teaspoon*

1. *Marinating the chicken.* Combine the chipotle salsa (or chopped canned chipotles) with *2 tablespoons* of the cream. Smear over the chicken breasts, cover and refrigerate for several hours, if time permits, for the chiles to season the chicken.

2. *Finishing the dish.* Lay the chicken breasts in a broiler-proof baking dish just large enough to hold them comfortably. Set 6 inches below a very hot broiler and cook until richly brown, 4 to 5 minutes. Turn the breasts over, drizzle the remaining *1 cup plus 2 tablespoons* cream *around* them and set under the broiler. Cook until the chicken is deep golden and no longer squishy feeling when lightly pressed, 4 to 5 minutes.

Transfer the chicken to 4 warm dinner plates and keep warm in a low oven. Scrape the cream mixture into a medium-large (3- to 4-quart) saucepan and add the broth and spinach. Bring to a boil over high heat and cook, stirring nearly constantly, until the spinach is wilted and the cream reduced and thick, about 3 minutes. Taste and season with salt, then spoon around the chicken breasts and serve right away.

GRILLED CHICKEN BREASTS IN
TOMATO-*GUAJE* SAUCE

Pollo Asado en Guasmole

*J*HAVE INCLUDED a dish with this simple tomato sauce thickened with the intricate nuttiness of toasted *guaje* seeds because the seeds are so easily available in Mexican markets in Chicago. They are from a tree that is in the legume family, one that produces pods that look like what I picked off a mimosa tree as a kid. We use the dried seeds to make this sauce regularly at Frontera Grill and Topolobampo, serving it with grilled or roasted chicken, pork, beef or lamb.

Sauces like this one are classic preparations from Central and Southern Mexico. I first learned to make it—and various relishy *guaje* salsas—in Guerrero, though this recipe is based on one from Puebla. It couldn't be simpler or the flavor more impressive; my method for searing the chicken on the grill, then baking it with the sauce, marries smokiness with the toastiness of the seeds, while freeing the cook from last-minute grill duty. Serve with black beans and make Modern Mexican Chocolate Flan (page 390) for dessert. You'll have a special meal, every bit of which can be done well ahead.

SERVES 6, WITH ABOUT 4 CUPS SAUCE

1 pound (2 medium-large round, 6 or 8 plum) ripe tomatoes

Hot green chiles to taste (roughly 2 serranos or 1 jalapeño)

2 large garlic cloves, unpeeled

½ cup (about 3 ounces) dry guaje *seeds*

3 cups chicken broth, plus a little more if needed

1 tablespoon vegetable or olive oil, plus a little for brushing on the chicken

¼ cup chopped cilantro, plus a few sprigs for garnish

Salt, about 2 teaspoons, plus some for sprinkling on the chicken

6 medium-large (about 2 pounds) boneless, skinless, chicken-breast halves, trimmed of all extraneous fat

1. *The sauce.* Roast the tomatoes on a baking sheet 4 inches below a very hot broiler until blackened on one side, about 6 minutes, then flip them over and roast on the other side. Cool and peel, collecting all the juices with the tomatoes. While the tomatoes are roasting, roast the chiles and garlic directly in an ungreased, heavy, large (10-inch) skillet over medium heat, turning occasionally, until soft (they'll blacken in spots): 5 to 10 minutes for the chiles, about 15 minutes for the garlic. Cool, then pull the stems from the chiles, peel the garlic and roughly chop the two.

With the skillet still over medium heat, toast the *guaje* seeds, stirring nearly constantly, until toasty smelling and all have darkened a bit (most of them will pop from flat to oval in shape), about 3 to 4 minutes. Save a couple of tablespoons for garnish, then pour the rest into a blender, along with the tomatoes and their juices, chiles, garlic and ½ *cup* of the broth. Blend to a smooth puree.

Set a medium (4-quart) pot (preferably a Dutch oven or Mexican *cazuela*) over medium-high heat and add the oil. When it's hot enough to make a drop of the puree really sizzle, add the puree all at once and stir for about 5 minutes as it sears, concentrates, and darkens. Stir in the remaining 2½ *cups* broth, reduce the heat to medium-low and simmer, partially covered, for 30 minutes. Stir in the chopped cilantro, plus a little more broth if necessary to bring the sauce to the consistency of a light cream sauce, then taste and season with salt.

2. *Grilling the chicken.* Light a charcoal fire and let it burn until coals are all very hot and covered with gray ash. Brush the chicken with a little oil and sprinkle with salt. Lay the chicken on well-oiled grill grates 8 inches from the heat and sear for a minute or so on one side (until nicely browned), then flip and sear the other side; your goal is to sear in that smoky grilled flavor without completely cooking the chicken.

3. *Finishing the dish.* Turn on the oven to 325 degrees. Lay the chicken in a single layer in a baking dish (all the better if it's one you can serve in) and ladle the hot sauce over it. Bake until the chicken is barely cooked through, about 15 minutes, depending on the size and thickness of the breasts. Use tongs or a slotted spoon to transfer the breasts to a warm serving platter (unless, of course, you're serving in the baking dish) and ladle the sauce over them. Sprinkle with the reserved seeds and decorate with sprigs of cilantro before carrying the beautiful dish to the table.

ADVANCE PREPARATION—The dish may be completed a day or two ahead through step 2; cover and refrigerate sauce and chicken separately. Complete step 3 shortly before serving.

SHORTCUTS—Two-thirds of a drained 28-ounce can of tomatoes can replace the roasted fresh ones.

VARIATIONS AND IMPROVISATIONS—A quartered, bone-in chicken may be used here: bake the leg and thigh quarters for 10 minutes, then nestle in the breasts and bake for about 15 minutes longer. Or make the sauce to serve on grilled swordfish, halibut or snapper, or red meat from pork to lamb.

SMOKY SHREDDED CHICKEN AND POTATOES WITH ROASTED TOMATOES

Tinga de Pollo y Papas

*T*HIS CLASSIC BLEND of Central Mexican (especially Pueblan) flavors is popular with just about everyone. We use a dish like this for lots of parties at the restaurant when we don't know the tastes—or the adventurousness—of the guests. The smoky, slightly spicy tomatoes have a broad appeal; the potatoes, onions and chicken comfort even the most timid, while the fresh cheese and avocado garnish place this relaxed dish squarely in the Mexican kitchen. You can turn *tinga* into a piece-of-meat entree simply by leaving the chicken thighs whole or replacing them with chicken breasts (breast will take less time to cook), and, for more sauciness, doubling the sauce.

This dish is good buffet fare (the recipe triples or quadruples easily, though you probably will have to work in batches); it requires no knives for your guests. For an informal meal, serve it with a big green salad and lots of hot tortillas for making tacos.

SERVES 4 AS A LIGHT MAIN DISH (WITH ABOUT 4 CUPS OF FINISHED *TINGA*)

FOR 1 CUP ESSENTIAL QUICK-COOKED TOMATO-CHIPOTLE SAUCE

2 stemmed, dried chipotle chiles or canned chipotle chiles **en adobo**

2 garlic cloves, unpeeled

12 ounces (2 medium-small round or 4 to 6 plum) ripe tomatoes

2 tablespoons olive or vegetable oil

4 medium (1½ pounds total) chicken thighs, skin removed

4 medium boiling potatoes (like the red-skin ones)

1 medium white onion, thinly sliced

1 teaspoon dried oregano, preferably Mexican

Salt, about ¾ teaspoon

⅓ cup crumbled Mexican queso fresco *or pressed, salted farmer's cheese*

1 ripe avocado, peeled, pitted and cut into ⅜-inch dice

1. *Making 1 cup Essential Quick-Cooked Tomato-Chipotle Sauce.* For dried chiles, toast them on an ungreased griddle or heavy skillet over medium heat, turning regularly and pressing flat with a spatula until very aromatic, 30 seconds. In a small bowl, cover the chiles with hot water and let rehydrate 30 minutes, stirring frequently to ensure even soaking. Drain and discard the water. (Canned chiles need only be removed from their sauce.)

While the chiles are soaking, roast the unpeeled garlic on the griddle or skillet over medium heat, turning occasionally, until soft (they will blacken in spots), about 15 minutes;

cool and peel. Roast the tomatoes on a baking sheet 4 inches below a very hot broiler until blackened on one side, about 6 minutes, then flip and roast the other side. Cool, then peel, collecting all the juices with the tomatoes.

In a food processor or blender, puree the tomatoes and their juices, rehydrated or canned chiles and garlic. Heat *1 tablespoon* of the oil in a heavy, medium (2- to 3-quart) saucepan over medium-high. Add the puree and stir for about 5 minutes as it sears and thickens.

2. *The chicken and potatoes.* Nestle the skinless thighs into the sauce, cover, and set over medium-low heat. Cook for about 25 minutes, until the meat is thoroughly tender. Remove the chicken to a plate, leaving as much sauce as possible in the pan. Cool, then pull the meat from the bones in large shreds; there will be about 2 cups.

With a food processor or hand grater, *coarsely* shred the potatoes. Squeeze between your hands to remove as much water as possible.

3. *Finishing the dish.* Heat the remaining *1 tablespoon* of the oil over medium-high in a large (10- to 12-inch) nonstick or well-seasoned skillet. Add the onion and potatoes and cook, stirring and scraping up any sticking bits, until well browned, about 15 minutes. Scrape in the sauce and oregano, bring to a boil, stir in the chicken, and heat through, about 2 minutes. Taste and season with salt.

Scoop the mixture into a warm, deep, decorative serving dish. Sprinkle with cheese, strew with avocado and serve without hesitation.

ADVANCE PREPARATION—The *tinga* can be finished a day ahead, cover and refrigerate. Warm in a 400-degree oven, covered with foil, garnish with avocado and cheese, and serve.

SHORTCUTS—A drained 15-ounce can of tomatoes can replace the roasted fresh ones.

VARIATIONS AND IMPROVISATIONS—Without the potatoes, this is a very common taco, torta and tostada filling (or topping) in Central Mexico (you can even omit the garnishes). I love the texture the potatoes give. A generous pound of pork shoulder (cubed, simmered in salted water until tender, then shredded) can replace the chicken as can shredded cooked duck legs (a personal favorite). If you want the dish spicier, garnish with slices of canned chipotles.

CHICKEN BREASTS WITH POBLANOS, MUSHROOMS AND CREAM

Pollo a la Poblana con Hongos

*T*HESE CHICKEN BREASTS are one of the simplest, dressy (yet gutsy) crowd-pleasers you can prepare. The poblano-cream combination that has popped up in several of my recipes makes an entree appearance now—to great advantage. The mushrooms lend an earthiness to the sweetness of the cream and rich spice of the chiles. I love to spoon a little Classic White Rice (page 251) onto the plate, or Green Poblano Rice (page 254) for a more special touch. Not-too-oaky Chardonnay or Viognier is the perfect libation.

SERVES 6, WITH ABOUT 2 1/2 TO 3 CUPS OF SAUCE

FOR 2 CUPS ESSENTIAL POBLANO *RAJAS*

1 pound (6 medium-large) fresh poblano chiles

2 1/2 tablespoons vegetable or olive oil

1 large white onion, sliced 1/4 inch thick

3 garlic cloves, peeled and finely chopped

1/2 teaspoon dried oregano, preferably Mexican

3/4 teaspoon dried thyme (or 2 teaspoons minced fresh thyme)

1 cup Thick Cream (page 165), whipping cream or crème fraîche

6 large leaves epazote, if you can get them

Salt, about 1 teaspoon, plus a little for sprinkling on the chicken

1/3 cup chopped cilantro, plus a little extra for garnish

6 medium-large (about 2 pounds total) boneless, skinless, chicken-breast halves

3 cups (about 6 ounces) sliced mushrooms (preferably shiitake, oyster or some delicious wild variety—chanterelles are great)

1. *Making 2 cups Essential Roasted Poblano* Rajas. Roast the chiles directly over a gas flame or 4 inches below a very hot broiler, turning occasionally until blackened on all sides, about 5 minutes for open flame, about 10 minutes for broiler. Cover with a kitchen towel and let stand 5 minutes. Peel, pull out the stem and seed pod, then rinse *briefly* to remove bits of skin and seeds. Slice into 1/4-inch strips.

In a large (10- to 12-inch) skillet, heat *1 tablespoon* of the oil over medium-high, then add the onion and cook, stirring regularly, until nicely browned but still crunchy, about 5 minutes. Add the garlic and herbs, toss 1 minute, then stir in the chiles and heat through.

2. *The sauce.* Scoop about ⅓ of the *rajas* out of the pan and onto your cutting board. Roughly chop them and set aside. Add *half* of the cream and the *epazote* to the skillet, simmer over medium for about 5 minutes, then scrape into a food processor or blender. Add the remaining cream and process (loosely covered, if using the blender) until smooth. Taste and season with salt; stir in the cilantro and the reserved chopped *rajas*. If necessary thin with a little water (or chicken broth) to the consistency of a medium-thick cream soup.

3. *The chicken and mushrooms.* Turn on the oven to 350 degrees. Wash and dry the skillet, set over medium-high heat and measure in the remaining *1½ tablespoons* of the oil. Dry the chicken breasts on paper towels, then lightly sprinkle both sides with the salt. When the oil is sizzling hot, lay in the chicken breasts in an uncrowded layer (you may have to brown them in 2 batches). When lightly browned on one side, about 2 minutes, flip and brown the other side. Lay in a single layer in a gratin dish or a 13 x 9-inch glass baking dish.

Return the skillet to the heat (there should be a light coating of oil left; if not add a little more), add the mushrooms, and stir until nicely soft, about 5 minutes, depending on the variety. Strew them over the chicken breasts, then spoon on the sauce.

4. *Finishing the dish.* Cover the baking dish lightly with foil and bake until the chicken is just cooked through and the sauce is beginning to brown at the edges, about 15 minutes. Sprinkle with chopped cilantro (thinly sliced *epazote* is enticingly aromatic as a garnish here, too), and carry right to the table, baking dish and all.

ADVANCE PREPARATION—The sauce may be completed through step 2 a day or two ahead; cover and refrigerate. Step 3 may be completed early in the day you are serving (store everything covered in the refrigerator), then complete step 4 just before you are ready to eat.

VARIATIONS AND IMPROVISATIONS

Use the sauce to make au gratin potatoes or to spoon onto broccoli, asparagus or baked potatoes.

A Less Rich Sauce—Reduce the Thick Cream to ⅔ cup and use it to simmer with the *rajas.* Then process that *rajas*-cream mixture with ⅔ cup chicken broth and 2 tablespoons fresh *masa* or dried *masa harina*. Return the mixture to the skillet and whisk constantly until it begins to thicken. Simmer 2 minutes, season with salt and stir in the cilantro and reserved *rajas.*

ACHIOTE-GRILLED TURKEY BREAST
WITH TOMATO, CHILE AND MINT

Sak Kol de Pavo

*T*HERE IS SOMETHING at once comforting and invigorating about this dish—grilled turkey scented with complex achiote seasoning, served in a Mexican "white sauce" (it is thickened with *masa*, not flour) that in the Mayan dialect of Yucatan is called *kol*. "White sauce" is not the whole story, however, since this one is flecked with tomato, revved up with tiny hot dried chiles, perfumed with mint and burnished to that beautiful rust-red with achiote.

You may have tasted this dish at Los Almendros, the famous chain of Yucatecan restaurants. Their version is served with a simple *kol* plus tomato sauce splashed over the *roasted* turkey. I've followed the lead of the recipe in *Comida familiar en el estado de Yucatán*, bringing the two elements together to give a more harmonious aura to the dish.

Though *Sak Kol de Pavo* is typically served all by itself, black beans (either Classic Mexican Fried, page 237, or in the form of Black Bean Rice, page 256) are a good addition to the plate.

SERVES 10, WITH ABOUT 5 CUPS SAUCE

3 tablespoons achiote seasoning
  paste (homemade, page 66 or store-
  bought)

3 tablespoons vegetable or olive oil

1 whole (about 3-pound) boneless
  turkey breast, skin still on and split
  into two halves

¼ cup (a scant ¼ ounce) small hot
  dried chiles (roughly 15 dried chiles
  japoneses, chiles secos *from*
  Yucatan or dried árbol chiles)

3 cups chicken broth

About 1½ pounds (3 medium-large
  round, 9 or 12 plum) ripe
  tomatoes

1 medium white onion, cut into
  ¼-inch dice

5 leaves of mint, roughly chopped,
  plus extra sprigs for garnish

3 tablespoons fresh masa

  OR 4 generous tablespoons masa
  harina

Salt, about ½ teaspoon, depending on
  the saltiness of the broth

1. *Grilling the turkey.* Light a gas grill or prepare a charcoal fire, letting coals burn until covered with a gray ash and medium-hot. Bank the coals onto two opposite sides of the grill, then position a drip pan in the center (where there are no coals), for indirect cooking. Set cooking grate about 8 inches above coals.

Combine *half* of the achiote paste with *1 tablespoon* of the oil and rub over the turkey breast halves. Position the halves in the center of the cooking grate over the drip pan. Grill, covered, checking coals occasionally and adding more as needed, until done, 1 to 1½ hours. Use a meat thermometer to check the internal temperature. The USDA tells us it should cook to 170 degrees, though I am personally willing to assume responsibility for my turkey cooked to 145 or 150 degrees—the right temperature, I believe, for the moistest breast.

2. *The sauce*. While the turkey is cooking, make the sauce. In a small bowl, cover the chiles with hot water and let rehydrate 30 minutes, stirring frequently to ensure even soaking. Drain and discard the water.

Place chiles in a blender (a small food processor or chopper will work, too) with the remaining *half* of the achiote paste and ¼ *cup* of the broth. Blend until smooth. Push through a medium-mesh strainer into a bowl; there will be about ¼ cup.

Blanch tomatoes in boiling water for 30 seconds, just until skins loosen; drain and peel. Cut tomatoes crosswise in half and squeeze out seeds. Dice into ¼-inch pieces.

Heat the remaining 2 *tablespoons* oil in a medium-size (4-quart) pot (like a Dutch oven or Mexican *cazuela*) over medium. Add the onion and cook until translucent, about 4 minutes. Add the tomatoes, achiote mixture, chopped mint, and 2½ *cups* of the broth. Simmer, partially covered, for 30 minutes.

Dissolve the *masa* in the remaining ¼ *cup* of the broth. Strain into the simmering sauce, whisking constantly as it returns to a simmer and thickens. Simmer 10 minutes, then taste and season with salt, usually about ½ teaspoon; the sauce should be the consistency of light white sauce.

3. *Serving*. Let the grilled turkey rest at least 10 minutes in a very low oven, then slice it about ¼ inch thick, and arrange the slices on a warm platter. Spoon the sauce over (but not completely covering the slices), garnish with mint sprigs and carry to the table.

ADVANCE PREPARATION—While both turkey and sauce are most delicious when just finished, both can be done ahead, cooled and refrigerated (you'll want to take the turkey off the grill just *before* it is done). Heat the sauce, whisking, then thin it a little if it has gotten thicker than a light white sauce. Heat the turkey, covered with foil, in a 300-degree oven until warm through, about 30 minutes.

SHORTCUTS—A drained 28-ounce can tomatoes can replace the boiled fresh tomatoes.

SMOKY BRAISED SQUAB
WITH ROASTED TOMATOES AND DARK BEER
Pichón al Chipotle

BELIEVE IT OR NOT, I came across this recipe in a series of very homey cookbooks put out by the Mexican government (. . . *y la comida se hizo*). I only changed the cooking of the bird, from stew to medium-rare roast (to preserve the light flavor and juciness of the breast). Squab is all dark meat, like a poultry version of venison, and simple to work with. The smoky touch to the sauce, plus the sweetness of the onion against the hint of bitterness from the beer, perfectly dresses up the rich complexity of the meat.

Though in Guerrero, squab is sold in road-side eateries as a regional specialty, you'll have to look for it at a specially butcher. An alternative is to use boneless, skinless duck breast (simmer 7 minutes longer, before removing and letting stand 10 minutes).

For a special meal, I'd start off with Mushroom-Cactus Soup (page 128), accompany the squab with Black Bean Rice (page 256), and finish with Celebration Cake (page 394).

SERVES 4, WITH 2 CUPS SAUCE

FOR 2 CUPS ESSENTIAL QUICK-COOKED TOMATO-CHIPOTLE SAUCE

3 to 4 (*about ¼ ounce total*) *stemmed, dried chipotle chiles (or canned chipotle chiles en adobo)*

4 *garlic cloves, unpeeled*

1½ *pounds (3 medium-large round or 8 to 12 plum) ripe tomatoes*

3 *tablespoons olive or vegetable oil or rich-tasting pork lard*

4 *whole squabs, about 12 ounces each*

1 *medium white onion, thinly sliced*

½ *cup chicken broth*

½ *cup dark beer, such as Negra Modelo*

A generous ½ teaspoon black pepper, preferably freshly ground

¼ *teaspoon cinnamon, preferably freshly ground Mexican* canela

⅛ *teaspoon cloves, preferably freshly ground*

Salt, about ½ teaspoon, plus some for sprinkling on the squab

Sprigs of cilantro or flat-leaf parsley, for garnish

1. *Making 2 cups Essential Quick-Cooked Tomato-Chipotle Sauce.* For dried chiles, toast them on an ungreased griddle or heavy skillet over medium heat, turning regularly, and pressing flat with a spatula, until very aromatic, 30 seconds. In a small bowl, cover the chiles with hot water and let rehydrate 30 minutes, stirring frequently to ensure even soaking. Drain and discard the water. (Canned chiles need only be removed from their sauce.)

While the chiles are soaking, roast the unpeeled garlic on the griddle or skillet over medium heat, turning occasionally, until soft (they will blacken in spots), about 15 minutes; cool and peel. Roast the tomatoes on a baking sheet 4 inches below a very hot broiler until blackened on one side, about 6 minutes, then turn and roast the other side. Cool, then peel, collecting all the juices with the tomatoes.

In a food processor or blender, puree the tomatoes, rehydrated or canned chiles and garlic. Heat *1 tablespoon* of the oil or lard in a heavy, medium-size saucepan over medium-high. Add the puree and stir for about 5 minutes as it thickens. Remove from the heat.

2. *The squabs.* Half-bone each bird: Using a sharp knife, cut down between the leg joint and body on one side. Twist the bone sharply outward to break the joint, then cut the leg free. Cut off the other leg in similar fashion.

With the bird still on its back, slit the skin right down the middle of the breast, along one side of the breastbone; then cut down through the meat to the breastbone. Now, angle your knife and continue cutting along the breastbone and ribs, freeing the breast meat in one piece. When you reach the wing joint cut through it, leaving the wing attached to the breast meat. Cut away the other breast half in like manner. Cut off the last two joints of each wing.

Sprinkle the squab pieces with salt. Heat the remaining *2 tablespoons* of the oil or lard in a heavy, large (10- to 12-inch) skillet over medium. Lay in the leg pieces and breasts, skin-side down, in a single layer. (Do this in two batches if the pan gets crowded.) Fry until the skin side is well browned, about 4 minutes, then remove to a cooling rack set over a plate.

3. *Simmering the sauce.* Add the onion and fry over medium heat until nicely golden, about 10 minutes. Scrape in the tomato-chipotle sauce, stir in the broth, beer, black pepper, cinnamon and cloves, and simmer over medium-low for half an hour. Season with salt.

4. *Finishing the dish.* Add the squab legs and any accumulated juices on the plate to the skillet and simmer over medium-low for 10 minutes. Lay in the breasts, skin-side up (trying not to let any of the sauce splash on—and soften—the skin), and simmer for 3 minutes (no more). Remove from the heat and let stand for 10 minutes.

Remove the squab pieces to a warm platter. Bring the sauce to a boil, then spoon a portion of it onto each of 4 warm dinner plates. Top each with 2 of the legs. To complete each, slice 2 breast halves into several broad slices and fan out over the sauce. Garnish with cilantro or parsley sprigs and serve without hesitation.

ADVANCE PREPARATION—The sauce may be prepared several days ahead; cover and refrigerate. The squab can be browned several hours in advance; refrigerate, covered. Complete step 4 just before serving.

SHORTCUTS—One 28-ounce can of tomatoes can replace the roasted fresh ones.

FISH AND SHELLFISH

· · · · ·

A long the Mexican coasts (there are thousands of miles of them), deliciously fresh seafood is a focus of the cooking, which is what you would expect, unless your concept of Mexican food is pure Tex-Mex enchiladas and such, no seafood at all. I feature quite a number of fish and shellfish dishes here, because most are quick to prepare and the majority of us can get good-quality seafood these days, no matter where we live.

Shrimp *a la mexicana* combines the classic griddle searing (*a la plancha*) with the bright flavors of *salsa mexicana,* that perfect, simple blend of tomatoes, green chile and cilantro. Chipotle Shrimp are turned in a skillet with just enough roasted tomatoes and lip-tingling chipotles to give them a burnished beauty. Guajillo-Sauced Shrimp is simmered with the liveliness of guajillo and the tanginess of quick-fried cactus—the racy flavors I always want in the winter, when I'm trying to forget the cold outside my window.

Shrimp also work their way into the two robust seafood stews typical of the cooking from the Gulf of Mexico, where the most abundant shrimp supply is found. The Seafood-Rice *Cazuela* is like a soupy paella, dressed up with roasted tomatoes and jalapeños; it's flexible (you can use almost any seafood) and stunning for an informal dinner party.

Seven Seas Soup is a brothier, spicier and simpler cousin that harbors in its ocean of red-chile flavors a variety of vegetables, fish, shrimp and shellfish. With chopped white onion, fresh cilantro and a big squirt of lime, it is dazzlingly aromatic and attractive.

Following are five distinctly regional, rather homey, fish dishes. Tabasco-style Seared Fish Fillets in Escabeche is a light and good-looking dish of bright flavors: vegetables, mushrooms, chiles, herbs, spices, vinegar and olive oil. A simple approach that features tomatoes, citrus and redolent habanero comes from Campeche; the saucy flavorings are quick-baked with the fish. While Pan-Roasted Salmon may not be completely traditional, the Central Mexican Aromatic Green *Pipián,* made thick with roasted tomatillos and toasted sesame seeds, is; the crusty pink of the fish against the earthy pale green is beautiful. From Yucatan, comes another baked fish dish, one that adds the intrigue of garlicky achiote, roasted green chile and banana leaf. And for the adventurous, there's a spectacular, red chile–marinated whole roast fish. A good slathering of ancho chile marinade—a little spicy, a little sweet and tangy—gives the fish a lacquered beauty, while roasting the fish on the bone gives it an incomparable succulence.

Grilled Catfish Steaks have no traditional regional affiliation, though here I've marinated them in a traditional salsa, then, when they're sizzling off the grill, I've given them another dollop of the salsa enriched with avocado.

The final recipe is as traditional as you can get, though I've presented it in a novel way.

Platters of slow-simmered salt cod with roasted tomatoes, olives and green chiles is on practically every Christmas Eve table in Mexico. I've packed the old-fashioned flavors into roasted chiles to give the dish an attractive presentation and to balance the *bacalao* flavor (which will likely be new to most).

SHRIMP *A LA MEXICANA*
WITH TOMATOES, SERRANOS, AND CILANTRO
Camarones a la Plancha

SHRIMP SEARED QUICKLY on a hot metal slab—they come out with that perfect crispy texture—are on menus all across Mexico. And one of the simplest, freshest and most flavorful ways to dress up these *camarones a la plancha* ("shrimp on the griddle") is to toss them on the griddle with a *salsa mexicana* of ripe tomatoes, serranos and cilantro, then gild it all with avocado. The searing heat of all this quick cooking forces the delicious aromas both into the shrimp and away from your kitchen toward the table, setting everyone's mouths to watering. Tasting these flavors again with my mind's tongue, I'm right there in one of those beachside seafood restaurants in Tampico or Veracruz, where it seems they always have perfectly ripe tomatoes for a dish like this.

Though I'd welcome the creaminess of Classic Mexican Fried Beans (page 237), a buffet or informal pass-around dinner that includes a platter of shrimp with the Crusty Chayote Casserole (page 224) also would be very pleasing. If you are a wine drinker, here's a good place for a dry Chenin Blanc, Riesling, Gewürztraminer or Spanish Albariño.

SERVES 4

FOR 2 CUPS ESSENTIAL CHOPPED TOMATO-SERRANO SALSA

12 ounces (2 medium-small round or 4 to 5 plum) ripe tomatoes, cored and finely diced

Fresh serrano chiles to taste (roughly 3 to 5), stemmed and finely chopped

3 large garlic cloves, peeled and very finely chopped

1 small white onion, finely diced

Salt, about 1 1/4 teaspoons

1 pound (about 24) medium-large shrimp

2 tablespoons fresh lime juice

1/4 teaspoon black pepper, preferably freshly ground

2 small avocados (optional)

1 to 2 tablespoons olive oil

6 tablespoons chopped cilantro

1. *Making 2 cups Essential Chopped Tomato-Serrano Salsa.* Mix together the tomatoes, chiles and garlic. Scoop the onion into a strainer, rinse under cold water, shake dry and add to the mixture, along with 3/4 *teaspoon* of the salt.

2. *The shrimp.* Peel the shrimp, leaving the final joint and the tail intact. One at a time, devein the shrimp by laying each one flat on your work surface and making a shallow incision down the back, exposing the (usually) dark intestinal tract and scraping it out.

Put the shrimp into a medium-size bowl. Add *1 tablespoon* of the lime juice, the remaining *½ teaspoon* of the salt, and the pepper. Stir well and let marinate about 30 minutes (but no longer than one hour). Pat shrimp completely dry with paper toweling.

3. *The optional avocados.* Cut the avocados in half, running your knife around the pit from stem to blossom end and back up again; twist the halves in opposite directions to free the pits and pull the halves apart. Either scoop out the pits with a spoon, or gently lodge your knife into them and twist to free. With a soup spoon, scoop out the avocado flesh and cut into 3/8-inch dice.

4. *Finishing the dish.* Arrange all the ingredients near the stove. Lightly coat 2 large (10- to 12-inch) skillets (preferably well-seasoned cast-iron ones) or a large heavy griddle with olive oil and set over medium-high heat. When very hot, lay in the shrimp in a single uncrowded layer. When half done, 2½ to 3 minutes, flip them over and divide the salsa and remaining tablespoon of lime juice over all. When the shrimp are done, about 2 minutes more, use a pair of tongs to remove them to warm plates, leaving behind as much salsa as possible. If using avocados, sprinkle them over the salsa and cook, scooping and stirring with a metal spatula, until heated through, 1½ to 2 minutes. Using your spatula, scoop up portions of the salsa and sprinkle over the shrimp. Strew each serving generously with cilantro and carry to the table.

ADVANCE PREPARATION—The salsa can be prepared several hours ahead. The dish doesn't reheat well, but it is good at room temperature if you want to cook it an hour to two ahead for a picnic or summer buffet; add the avocados just before serving.

VARIATIONS AND IMPROVISATIONS—An equal weight of scallops is as good as shrimp (scallops are not common in Mexico). Or follow the same procedure for fat strips or 2-inch squares of substantial fish (tuna, salmon, snapper, mahimahi); they'll take a minute or two longer to cook. Boiled, cubed potatoes (or other root vegetables) can replace the shrimp for a tasty side dish; you'll need about 3 cups and you'll want to leave them on the oily griddle (or skillet) long enough to crust and brown.

CHIPOTLE SHRIMP

Camarones Enchipotlados

*T*HESE SHRIMP WERE a revelation the first time I bit into one at Carmen Ramírez Dego-llado's table! Spicy, garlicky, smoky and (like the best barbecued shrimp) not too saucy. You can pick them up with your fingers and pop them right into your mouth, one after another after another. They are wonderful party food for the not-too-timid, though truthfully I can't imagine that all won't eventually be won over to these glowing flavors.

Like all of Carmen's specialties, this shrimp dish is a great rendition of classic Veracruz cooking. If you take the time to make Carmen's Sweet-and-Smoky Chipotle Seasoning Salsa (page 52), the dish will take on incredible depth of flavor. Still, I'd never turn them down made the quick way with chopped canned chipotles. With Classic White Rice (page 251) to serve alongside the shrimp, you'll have the perfect summer meal. And since they're good at room temperature, carry them on a picnic or pass around a platter sprinkled with chopped cilantro, as the starter for a great feast. This is beer food, in my opinion—icy Bohemia or Negra Modelo taste great here.

SERVES 6 GENEROUSLY

6 garlic cloves, unpeeled

1 small white onion, sliced ¼ inch thick

6 ounces (1 medium-small or 2 to 3 plum) ripe tomatoes

¾ teaspoon black pepper, preferably freshly ground

⅛ teaspoon cloves, preferably freshly ground

2 tablespoons olive oil

2 to 4 tablespoons Essential Sweet-and-Smoky Chipotle Seasoning Salsa (page 52)

OR 2 to 4 tablespoons very finely chopped canned chipotle chiles, drained before chopping

Salt, about ½ teaspoon

2 pounds (about 50) medium-large shrimp

1. *Roasting the flavorings.* On an ungreased griddle or heavy skillet set over medium, roast the garlic cloves, turning occasionally, until soft (they will blacken in spots), about 15 minutes. Cool and peel.

While the garlic is roasting, lay the onion out on a small square of foil, set on the griddle and let sear, brown and soften, about 5 minutes per side.

Roast the tomatoes on a baking sheet set 4 inches below a very hot broiler until black-ened in spots and soft, about 6 minutes; flip and roast the other side. Cool and peel, col-lecting all the juices with the tomatoes.

2. *The sauce.* Combine all the roasted ingredients in a food processor or blender, along with the pepper, cloves and ¼ cup water. Process to a medium-smooth puree.

In a very large (12-inch) skillet, heat the oil over medium-high. When hot enough to make a drop of the puree sizzle noisily, add it all at once. Stir for several minutes as the mixture sears and darkens, then reduce the heat to medium-low and continue to cook, stirring regularly, until very thick, about 5 minutes. A tablespoon at a time, stir in the Chipotle Seasoning Salsa (or chopped chipotles), tasting until the thick salsa suits your own penchant for spiciness. (I think these are best when they've reached the upper levels of heat.) Taste, season with salt and remove from the heat.

3. *The shrimp.* Peel the shrimp, leaving the final joint and the tail intact. One at a time, devein the shrimp by laying them flat on your work surface and making a shallow incision down the back, exposing the (usually) dark intestinal tract and scraping it out.

Return the skillet with the sauce to medium-high heat. Add the shrimp, then slowly stir and turn for about 3 to 4 minutes, until the shrimp are just cooked through. (The sauce should nicely coat the shrimp, though it won't really pool around them.) Taste a shrimp, sprinkle on a little more salt if necessary, then pile up the crustaceans on a rustic platter and carry them to the table.

ADVANCE PREPARATION—The sauce (steps 1 and 2) may be made several days ahead; cover and refrigerate. Finish step 3 just before serving if you want them hot or several hours ahead for room-temperature shrimp.

VARIATIONS AND IMPROVISATIONS—You can take this same approach with scallops (preferably medium-size for even cooking with this method), or with beef (grill about 2 pounds of anything tender enough to be a grillable steak, cut into ¾-inch cubes, toss with the warm sauce and serve). For a casserole to serve on a buffet, toss the sauce with roasted potatoes or spread it on grilled eggplant, sprinkle with melting cheese, and run under the broiler until bubbly and brown.

GUAJILLO-SAUCED SHRIMP
WITH QUICK-FRIED CACTUS
Camarones al Guajillo con Nopales

*I*F YOU LIKE SPICY FOOD and have never had cactus, I recommend you make this your first foray. The flavor of the guajillo sauce is complex and lively (as well as spicy), the shrimp have that crispness that only a hot skillet will impart, and the cactus punctuate everything with their limy dazzle. I jotted down the basics of this dish years ago, while perusing a cookbook in Mexico; sadly, I can't credit the author, since I foolishly didn't record it.

Pass around a platter of these shrimp garnished with steamed or roasted potatoes. Beer is an easy mate for these flavors; wine should stay in the fruity Riesling or Gewürztraminer (or even sparkling) arena. And choose a cooling Modern Mexican Chocolate Flan (page 390) for dessert.

SERVES 4

8 medium (about 1 pound) fresh cactus paddles (nopales)

1 to 1½ pounds (24 to 36) medium-large shrimp

FOR 1 CUP ESSENTIAL SIMMERED GUAJILLO SAUCE

3 garlic cloves, unpeeled

8 (about 2 ounces total) dried guajillo chiles, stemmed and seeded

½ teaspoon dried oregano, preferably Mexican

⅛ teaspoon black pepper, preferably freshly ground

A pinch cumin, preferably freshly ground

1¾ cups fish or chicken broth, plus a little more if needed

3 tablespoons vegetable or olive oil

Salt, about 1 teaspoon, depending on the saltiness of the broth

Sugar, about ¾ teaspoon

8 ounces (1 medium-large round or 3 to 4 plum) ripe tomatoes

1 tablespoon fresh lime juice

1. *Getting started.* Holding a cactus paddle gingerly between the nodes of the prickly spines, trim off the edge that outlines the paddle, including the blunt end where the paddle was severed from the plant. Slice or scrape off the spiny nodes from both sides. Cut into ½-inch squares; there will be about 4 cups.

Peel the shrimp, leaving the final joint and the tail intact. Devein each shrimp by making a shallow incision down the back, exposing the dark intestinal tract and scraping it out. Refrigerate, covered.

2. *Making about 1 cup Essential Simmered Guajillo Sauce.* Roast the unpeeled garlic directly on an ungreased griddle or heavy skillet over medium heat, turning occasionally, until soft (they will blacken in spots), about 15 minutes; cool and peel. While the garlic is roasting, toast the chiles: first, set one chile aside to use later, then 1 or 2 at a time, open the remainder flat and use a spatula to press them down firmly on the griddle or skillet; in a few seconds, when they crackle, even send up a wisp of smoke, flip them and press down to toast the other side. In a small bowl, cover the chiles with hot water and let rehydrate 30 minutes, stirring frequently to ensure even soaking. Drain and discard the water.

Combine the oregano, black pepper and cumin in a food processor or blender, along with the chiles, garlic and *1/2 cup* of the broth. Blend to a smooth puree, scraping and stirring every few seconds. (If the mixture won't go through the blender blades, add a little more liquid.) Press through a medium-mesh strainer into a bowl.

Heat *1 tablespoon* of the oil in a heavy, medium-size (2- to 3-quart) saucepan over medium-high. Add the puree and stir constantly until it reduces into a thick paste, 5 to 7 minutes. Stir in the remaining *1 1/4 cups* of the broth, partially cover and simmer, stirring occasionally, about 45 minutes. If necessary, add more broth to bring the sauce to a medium consistency. Taste and season with about *1/2 teaspoon* of the salt and the sugar.

3. *The tomatoes.* Roast the tomatoes on a baking sheet about 4 inches below a very hot broiler until blistered and blackened on one side, about 6 minutes; then flip and roast the other side. Cool, then peel, collecting all the juices with the tomatoes. Coarsely puree in a food processor or blender.

4. *The cactus.* Turn on the oven to the lowest setting. Cut the reserved chile into very thin strips (almost threads). Heat *1 tablespoon* of the oil in a large (10- to 12-inch) skillet over medium-high. Add the cactus and stir-fry for 2 minutes, then add the chile strips and continue to stir-fry until the cactus is tender, 1 to 2 minutes more. Stir in the lime juice, sprinkle with about *1/4 teaspoon* of the salt, and cook until all the liquid has evaporated. Scrape everything onto a plate, spreading it out; keep warm in a low oven.

5. *Finishing the dish.* Wipe the skillet clean, add the remaining *1 tablespoon* of the oil, and set over medium-high heat. Lay the shrimp into the pan in a single layer (if you are using the larger amount, divide everything between 2 skillets), sprinkle with the remaining *1/4 teaspoon* salt. Cook about 2 minutes, flip over, then add the chile sauce and the tomatoes. Cook for 2 or 3 more minutes, until the shrimp are barely done (cutting into one, you'll see a trace of translucence in the middle).

With a pair of tongs, remove the shrimp to a warm deep serving platter. Taste the sauce and add more salt if necessary, then spoon it over the shrimp. Strew with the cactus mixture and it's ready to serve.

ADVANCE PREPARATION—The recipe can be prepared several hours in advance through step 4; let the cactus cool. Reheat the cactus in a low oven and complete step 5 just before serving.

SHORTCUTS—The cactus may be left out all together or replaced by 1½ cups blanched (or defrosted frozen) peas.

VARIATIONS AND IMPROVISATIONS

Scallops could easily replace shrimp here, as could chicken breasts (for the breasts, sear them in the skillet, flip them, add the sauce and tomatoes, partially cover and simmer over medium-low for about 12 minutes, until the chicken is done). Boiled, cubed potatoes can replace the shrimp (you'll need 3 to 4 cups) for a side dish or vegetarian main dish (it is great with cubes of fresh cheese). If you want to use this dish as a taco filling, remove the tails from the shrimp and boil the sauce until thick enough to cling nicely.

Cactus and Eggs in Guajillo Sauce—The typical dish (I have seen it from Central Mexico north) is usually made with boiled cactus, but you can use fried. Complete step 4, leaving the cactus in the skillet; over medium-high heat add 8 salted, lightly beaten eggs. Stir every few seconds to create large curds, then, when nearly set (still creamy), add the sauce and tomatoes, bring to a simmer and scoop into a warm serving bowl.

SEAFOOD RICE *CAZUELA*
WITH JALAPEÑOS AND ROASTED TOMATOES
Arroz a la Tumbada

*I*F YOU LIVE ON THE COAST (or near a great fish market), this seafood-rice dish can just be "thrown together," as its name, *a la tumbada,* tells us it should be. Like a brothy paella, *arroz a la tumbada* stirs together spicy roasted tomato-jalapeño salsa with quick-cooked seafood and rice. (One exception to "quick-cooked" is the squid; it cooks for about 25 minutes, until it softens into tenderness.)

This typically Veracruz dish is listed on quite a few restaurant menus. My recipe is based on one from the best Veracruz cookbook, *La cocina veracruzana.* For most of us, any seafood dish means a pretty special occasion; this one is perfect for an informal party. All but the final step can be completed ahead. Begin with *Picadillo*-Stuffed Jalapeños (page 104). Chocolate Pecan Pie (page 404) is a festive indulgence.

SERVES 4 TO 6

2½ tablespoons vegetable or olive oil

1 cup rice, preferably medium grain

1 medium white onion, finely chopped

5¾ cups fish or chicken broth

Salt, 1½ to 2 teaspoons

8 ounces cleaned squid (or extra fish or shrimp)

FOR 2 CUPS ESSENTIAL ROASTED TOMATO-JALAPEÑO SALSA

1 pound (2 medium-large round or 6 to 8 plum) ripe tomatoes

2 to 3 fresh jalapeño chiles

3 garlic cloves, unpeeled

½ cup loosely packed chopped cilantro, plus a little extra for garnish

12 medium-large (about 8 ounces) shrimp

8 ounces (about 12) tightly closed fresh clams, well scrubbed

6 ounces boneless, skinless fish fillets (choose a meaty fish like sea bass, mahimahi, cod or halibut) cut into 1-inch cubes

A big sprig of epazote (or use a handful of cilantro or parsley if lacking epazote)

½ cup crab meat (optional)

A lime or two, cut into wedges, for serving

1. *The rice.* Combine *1½ tablespoons* of the oil, the rice and ⅔ of the onion in a small (1- to 2-quart) saucepan over medium heat. Stir frequently for about 4 minutes, until translucent.

In another small saucepan, bring to a boil 1¾ *cups* of the broth and ½ *teaspoon* of the salt if using salted broth or *1 teaspoon* of the salt if using unsalted broth.

Add the hot broth to the rice mixture, scrape down any stray kernels on the side of the pan, cover tightly and cook at barely a simmer over low to medium-low heat for 15 minutes. Let stand off the heat for 5 to 10 minutes, until the rice is completely tender.

2. *The squid.* If using squid, cut it into 1-inch pieces, scoop into a small (1- to 2-quart) saucepan, cover with salted water, and simmer over medium-low heat until tender, about 25 minutes. Strain, reserving cooking liquid (which you may use as part of the broth you need in step 3) and squid separately.

3. *Making 2 cups Essential Roasted Tomato-Jalapeño Salsa.* Roast the tomatoes on a baking sheet 4 inches below a very hot broiler until blackened on 1 side, about 6 minutes, then flip them and broil the other side. Cool and peel, collecting all the juices with the tomatoes. While the tomatoes are roasting, roast the chiles and unpeeled garlic directly on an ungreased griddle or heavy skillet over medium heat, turning occasionally, until soft (they'll blacken in spots): 5 to 10 minutes for the chiles, about 15 minutes for the garlic. Cool, then pull the stems from the chiles and peel the garlic.

In a large mortar (or food processor), pound (or whir) the chiles, garlic and ½ *teaspoon* of the salt into a coarse-textured puree. Add the tomatoes and their juices (a few at a time, if using a mortar) and work into a coarse, rich-textured salsa. Rinse the remaining ⅓ of the onion in a strainer, and stir it into the tomato mixture, along with the cilantro.

4. *Finishing the dish.* Peel the shrimp, leaving the final joint and the tail intact. One at a time, devein the shrimp by laying each one flat on your work surface and making a shallow incision down the back, exposing the (usually) dark intestinal track and scraping it out.

Heat the remaining 1 *tablespoon* of oil in a medium-large (4- to 6-quart) heavy pot (like a Dutch oven) over medium-high. Add the tomato salsa and stir for 2 minutes, until rapidly boiling. Add the remaining 4 cups broth, bring to a boil, then taste and season with salt, usually about ½ teaspoon. Add the clams, fish cubes and *epazote*. Simmer, covered, over medium-high until the clams open, about 2 minutes. Add shrimp and optional crab meat; simmer, covered, about 1 minute, uncover and stir in the cooked rice and squid. As soon as the mixture returns to the boil, spoon into warm, large bowls. Sprinkle with cilantro and serve with lime wedges.

ADVANCE PREPARATION—The rice and salsa may be prepared several days ahead; refrigerate covered. The squid may be cooked, covered and refrigerated a day or so ahead. Complete step 4 just before serving.

HEARTY SEVEN SEAS SOUP

Caldo de Siete Mares

I HAVE BEEN TOLD by many Mexicans that there is nothing more satisfying than a bowlful of rich, spicy broth. In fact, I've noticed that when push comes to shove, everything but the soup can be nudged out of the dinner picture. Understandable, I say, in a culture whose favorite fiesta food is *pozole,* that slow-simmered pork-and-hominy soup.

In coastal seafood restaurants in Mexico, especially along the Gulf, there is a main dish seafood soup or stew listed on most menus as *Caldo de Siete Mares,* "Seven Seas Soup," because it welcomes practically anything that comes from the ocean. Though occasionally made with tomatoes and green chile, my favorite is the dried-chile version. Though bouillabaisselike, there is a big difference: European food always strives to feature the flavor of meat, poultry or seafood enhanced by vegetables (reflect on the importance of stocks in French cooking), while Mexican food features the flavor of vegetables (enhanced by the meat and so forth) with special emphasis on chiles, tomatoes, tomatillos and herbs. *Epazote* shows its rambunctious personality deliciously here.

I have chosen a beautiful, yet rustic presentation, with shrimp tails left on and corn cut into sections, cob and all. Serve your soup with crusty bread and a bottle of fruity but dry Gewürztraminer, Chenin Blanc, Spanish Albariño or Riesling. Crusty Baked *Masa* Boats (page 186) as a starter would dress up the dinner; a Tomatillo-Green Guacamole (page 81) with vegetables or chips would keep it casual.

FOR 1 CUP ESSENTIAL SIMMERED
GUAJILLO SAUCE base

3 garlic cloves, unpeeled

8 medium-large (about 2 ounces total)
dried guajillo chiles, stemmed and
seeded

1/2 teaspoon dried oregano, preferably
Mexican

1/8 teaspoon black pepper, preferably
freshly ground

A pinch cumin, preferably freshly
ground

1 tablespoon vegetable or olive oil

3 quarts fish or chicken broth

2 large sprigs epazote (or use a
handful of cilantro if no
epazote is available)

Salt, about 2¼ teaspoons, depending
on the saltiness of the broth

A little sugar, if necessary

12 medium-large (about 8 ounces)
shrimp

6 small boiling potatoes (like the red-
skin ones), cut into 3/4-inch dice

2 cups diced (3/4 inch) vegetables, such
as zucchini and peeled and pitted
chayote

2 ears of corn, shucked, silk removed
and cut crosswise 3/4 inch thick
(optional)

1 pound (about 2 dozen) tightly closed
fresh mussels or clams, well
scrubbed (and, for mussels, any
stringy "beards" trailing from
between the shells removed)

12 ounces boneless skinless fish fillets
(such as snapper, cod, halibut,
mahimahi and the like—in
Mexico, robalo [snook] is
popular), cut into 3/4-inch pieces

2/3 cup finely chopped white onion

1/2 cup loosely packed, chopped
cilantro

1 large lime, cut into wedges

1. *Making 1 cup Essential Simmered Guajillo Sauce base.* Roast the unpeeled garlic directly on an ungreased griddle or heavy skillet over medium heat, turning occasionally, until soft (they'll blacken in spots), about 15 minutes; cool and peel. While the garlic is roasting, toast the chiles on another side of the griddle or skillet: 1 or 2 at a time, open them flat and press down firmly on the hot surface with a spatula; in a few seconds, when they crackle, even send up a wisp of smoke, flip them and press down to toast the other side. In a small bowl, cover the chiles with hot water and let rehydrate 30 minutes, stirring frequently to ensure even soaking. Drain and discard the water.

Combine the oregano, black pepper and cumin in a food processor or blender, along with the drained chiles, garlic and 1/2 cup of water (or extra broth if you have it). Blend to a smooth puree, scraping and stirring every few seconds. (If the mixture won't go through the blender blades, add a little more liquid.) Press through a medium-mesh strainer into a bowl.

Heat the oil in a heavy, very large (8-quart) pot over medium-high. When hot enough to make a drop of the puree really sizzle, add the puree all at once and stir constantly until it reduces to a thick paste, about 5 minutes.

2. *The soup broth.* Add the broth and *epazote* to the soup pot and simmer over medium heat, stirring occasionally, for about 45 minutes. Taste and season with salt and a little sugar, if necessary, to balance any bitterness.

3. *Finishing the soup.* Peel the shrimp, leaving the final joint and the tail intact. Devein them by making a shallow incision down the back of each shrimp, exposing the (usually) dark intestinal tract and scraping it out.

Add the potatoes to the hot broth. Simmer, uncovered, until potatoes are nearly tender, about 5 minutes. Add the diced vegetables, cook 3 minutes, then add the corn (if you're using it) and mussels or clams, and simmer until the shellfish open, about 2 minutes. Add the fish cubes, cook 2 minutes, then stir in the shrimp. Remove from the heat, cover and let stand 3 to 4 minutes.

While the soup is "resting," rinse the chopped onion in a strainer under cold water. Shake off the excess water and mix with the chopped cilantro in a small serving bowl; place the lime wedges in another serving bowl and set both on the table. Serve the soup in large, warm bowls, passing the garnishes separately.

ADVANCE PREPARATION—The soup can be made through step 2 several days ahead; cover and refrigerate.

TANGY SEARED FISH FILLETS
WITH WOODLAND MUSHROOMS AND PICKLED JALAPEÑOS

Pescado en Escabeche de Hongos

*E*SCABECHE IS AN ANTIQUE IDEA (it showed up in Mexico with the Spaniards), yet the lightness of this dish, augmented with fresh herbs, unexpected spices and vegetables make it taste as though it were created yesterday. In its conception, escabeche is basically a pickle, originally a way to preserve the fish (or whatever) with spices, vinegar and oil.

Fish and shellfish escabeches are made in most coastal areas of Mexico, though southern Veracruz, Tabasco, Campeche and Yucatan seem to put them on the table more frequently than elsewhere. This dish combines the classic Tabasco shellfish escabeche with a recipe for wild mushroom escabeche from *Los hongos en la cocina mexicana*.

Pack this fish on a picnic (keep the green beans and tomato separate until ready to serve). It is also tasty served warm with roasted potatoes. Yucatecan-Style Fresh Coconut Pie (page 402) is a good picnic dessert. Beer is easier to pair with escabeche than wine.

SERVES 6

The juice of 2 limes

Salt, about 1 teaspoon

Six 4- to 6-ounce fish fillets (choose snapper, sea bass, walleye, or one of the stronger fish like bluefish or kingfish), each 1 inch thick

5 tablespoons olive oil

2 medium white onions, sliced ⅛ inch thick

5 large garlic cloves, peeled and halved

3 carrots, peeled and sliced thinly on the diagonal

2 cups shiitake (or other full-flavored) mushrooms, stemmed, caps sliced ⅛ inch thick

1¼ cups fish (or chicken) broth

¼ cup cider vinegar

2 large sprigs fresh thyme (or ½ teaspoon dried), plus a few sprigs for garnish

2 sprigs fresh marjoram (or ½ teaspoon dried), plus a few sprigs for garnish

A 2-inch piece cinnamon stick, preferably Mexican canela

½ teaspoon black pepper, preferably freshly and coarsely ground

3 bay leaves

3 whole cloves

4 pickled jalapeño chiles, stemmed, seeded and thinly sliced

1 cup (about 4 ounces) tender green beans, steamed until crisp-tender (optional)

1 medium tomato, diced (optional)

1. *Marinating the fish.* In a medium-size bowl, mix the lime juice and *¼ teaspoon* of the salt; lay in the fish and turn to coat evenly. Refrigerate, covered, for 1 hour. Remove the fish from the juice and thoroughly dry with paper toweling.

2. *Making the escabeche.* Heat *4 tablespoons* of the oil in a large (10- to 12-inch), deep skillet over medium-high. Add the onions, garlic and carrots; fry, stirring often, until onions are crisp-tender but not brown, about 5 minutes. Stir in the mushrooms, broth, vinegar, thyme, marjoram, cinnamon stick, pepper, bay and cloves. Simmer, covered, over low heat, stirring occasionally, for 30 minutes. Remove from heat, add the jalapeños, and season with the remaining salt, usually about ¾ teaspoon. Pour into a wide baking dish (a 13 x 9-inch glass baking dish works perfectly here).

3. *Frying the fish.* Wipe out the skillet, add the remaining 1 *tablespoon* of the oil and set over medium-high heat. When hot, lay in the fish in an uncrowded layer. Cook, turning once, until browned, about 2 minutes per side (the center of the fish will be medium-rare).

Carefully remove the fish fillets from the skillet and submerge them in the escabeche, moving everything around a bit so that the brothy mixture covers most of the fish. Let cool completely, about 1 hour; cover and refrigerate if not serving right away.

4. *Serving.* If using the optional green beans and tomato, add them to the escabeche. Taste and add more salt if necessary. If you're planning to serve the dish warm, heat it in a preheated 350-degree oven for a few minutes. Warm or at room temperature (if refrigerated, warm long enough to take the chill off), carefully transfer the fish to a large plate, spoon a portion of the vegetable mixture onto each of 6 dinner plates (you may want to remove the bay leaves, cloves and cinnamon if you're looking for a less rustic presentation); then top each with a piece of fish. Garnish with sprigs of thyme and marjoram, if you have them.

ADVANCE PREPARATION—This dish is best if prepared at least a few hours (or up to 1 day) before serving (you'll notice it will get a bit more *picante* the longer it sits).

VARIATIONS AND IMPROVISATIONS—Shrimp or sea scallops, ounce for ounce, can replace the fish; shrimp take less time to cook than fish or scallops. Chicken (or pheasant or guinea hen) is great done this way: Cut it into serving pieces, omit the lime-juice marinade (just use salt), pan-fry until just barely done (breasts will take 7 to 10 minutes and legs and thighs 15 to 20 minutes) and continue as described above. Grilled duck breasts, done to medium-rare, are very tasty when allowed to cool in the escabeche, then sliced and served as a summery main dish.

Hierbas de Olor, Aromatic Herbs

It's customary in Mexican markets, both in Mexico and in many in the States, to find little bundles of fresh marjoram and thyme sprigs tied up with a branch of the skinny little, simple-flavored bay leaves (they're smaller and pointier than the European variety). These are the *hierbas de olor,* the triad of herbs that are always said in a single breath and rarely even listed individually in Mexican recipes. For soups, stews, some sauces, escabeches and broths, they're essential.

Parsley shows up in some lists of *hierbas de olor,* and it may seem out of place to those who only think cilantro when Mexican food comes to mind. Flat-leaf parsley is very common in Mexico, and, in places like Oaxaca, it is *the* garnish on certain dishes—cilantro would seem a sacrilege. Each region has its preferences.

Fish Broth

There are certain soups and stews that simply taste better made with a good fish broth. If you can get to a fish market, fish heads will be available (since fish counters in grocery stores often don't get whole fish, you may need to order them in advance). This broth is a little different from the one in *Authentic Mexican*—here I cook the vegetables first to bring out their sweetness, and I leave the heads in the broth for a longer time, which, contrary to what most of us were taught, really doesn't make the broth bitter.

ABOUT 2 QUARTS

2 pounds fish heads (gills removed) and bones (choose from white-fleshed fish like skate, flounder, sole, bass and snapper, preferably not oily fish like salmon, mackerel and bluefish)

1 rib celery, roughly chopped

1 small white onion, sliced

1 medium-large carrot, roughly chopped

2 large garlic cloves, peeled and halved

2 tablespoons olive or vegetable oil

2 bay leaves

¾ teaspoon dried thyme

¾ teaspoon dried marjoram

4 sprigs cilantro

½ teaspoon black peppercorns, very coarsely ground

RINSE THE FISH heads and bones, then place in a large (6-quart) pot along with the celery, onion, carrot, garlic and oil. Stir to coat everything with the oil, place over medium, cover and cook, stirring occasionally, for 8 minutes or longer if you want a darker, richer stock.

Stir in 2½ quarts water and heat slowly to a simmer. Skim off all the grayish foam that rises during the first few minutes of simmering, then add the remaining ingredients, partially cover and simmer gently over medium to medium-low heat about 30 minutes.

Strain the broth through a fine wire-mesh strainer into a large bowl; discard the solids. If time allows, refrigerate the broth until cold, then skim off the congealed fat. If you intend to use the broth right away, use a wide, shallow spoon to skim the fat from the top.

ADVANCE PREPARATION—The broth will keep, covered and refrigerated, for several days. It also freezes well.

CAMPECHE BAKED FISH FILLETS
WITH TOMATO, HABANERO AND CITRUS
Filetes de Pescado a la Campechana

*T*HE BRIGHT FLAVORS of this simple and quick-to-prepare baked fish are easy to like—that is, if you are drawn to the smoldering glow of habanero chiles. Beyond spicy, the traditional Yucatecan flavors are tangy and "clean," about as far from *mole poblano* as you can roam, but then all this variety is what makes real Mexican food so attractive.

In the first year we opened Frontera, I stumbled on this sauce in Josefina Velázquez de Leon's *Cocina campechana;* I was looking for a dish to bring sparkle to a menu heavy in *moles.* We've woven it into dozens of dishes over the last decade. Alongside Classic White Rice (page 251) tossed with little cubes of fried plantain, the fish seems just right. A salad to start and a fruit ice or ice cream with cookies for dessert will frame a meal that is deliciously spirited and not difficult to turn out.

SERVES 4, WITH ABOUT 2 CUPS OF SAUCE

FOR 2 CUPS ESSENTIAL SIMMERED TOMATO-HABANERO SAUCE

1½ pounds (3 medium-large round or 9 to 12 plum) ripe tomatoes

1½ tablespoons vegetable or olive oil, plus a little more for oiling the baking dish

1 small white onion, thinly sliced

1 to 2 fresh habanero chiles, stems removed and halved

Salt, about ¾ teaspoon

¼ cup fresh sour orange juice or 2 to 3 tablespoons fresh lime juice

2 tablespoons roughly chopped epazote (or cilantro), plus a few sprigs for garnish

Four 5- or 6-ounce fish steaks or bone-less, skinless fillets (choose a fish that's still moist when cooked through, such as snapper, halibut, mahimahi, grouper or sea bass)

1. *Making 2 cups of Essential Simmered Tomato-Habanero Sauce.* Roast the tomatoes on a baking sheet 4 inches below a very hot broiler until blackened on 1 side, about 6 minutes, then flip and roast the other side. Cool, then peel, collecting all the juices with the tomatoes. Coarsely puree the tomatoes (with juices) in a food processor or blender.

In a deep, heavy skillet or medium-size (2- to 3-quart) saucepan, heat the oil over medium. Add the onion and fry until beginning to brown, about 6 minutes. Increase the heat to medium-high, and when quite hot, add the tomatoes and chile. Stir for about 5 minutes as the mixture sears and boils rapidly, then reduce the heat to medium-low and simmer for about 15 minutes, until medium-thick. Season with salt.

2. *Baking the fish.* Turn on the oven to 350 degrees. Lay out the fish fillets in a lightly oiled baking dish without crowding them. Drizzle with the sour orange or lime juice and sprinkle with the *epazote* (or cilantro). Spoon the warm tomato sauce over the fish, cover with foil and bake until the fish just flakes when pressed firmly, 10 to 15 minutes, depending on how thick the fillets are. With a spatula, carefully transfer the fillets to a warm serving platter, thoroughly mix the sauce and juices that remain in the baking dish, then spoon them over the fish. (If the sauce seems too juicy, scrape it into a saucepan and boil it down; if too thick, thin with a little water or broth; taste it and add more salt if necessary.) Garnish with sprigs of *epazote* (or cilantro) and serve at once.

ADVANCE PREPARATION—The sauce may be made a day or two ahead; cover and refrigerate. Warm the sauce, then finish step 2 just before serving.

SHORTCUTS—A drained 28-ounce can of tomatoes can replace the fresh roasted ones, though there will be a noticeable lack of rich sweetness in the finished sauce.

VARIATIONS AND IMPROVISATIONS—You can bake whole fish *a la campechana* following the timing for the Ancho-Marinated Whole Roast Fish (page 356); or use fish steaks if you want the richness the bone and skin give to the sauce. Steaks or fillets can be grilled (first marinated with Essential Garlicky Achiote Seasoning Paste (page 66), then doused with the sauce and garnished with orange segments. Going the other direction, you can omit the sour orange or lime and bake 4 blade pork chops in the sauce (sear them first in a lightly oiled skillet, then bake covered for about 45 minutes).

Sour Orange

I have never understood why sour oranges (also known as Seville or bitter oranges) aren't in every market. They are not simply oranges that didn't turn out very sweet, but rather a separate variety of orange (they're bumpy and not too pretty) that has wonderful acidity (they're as sour as a lemon, but with a mitigating fruitiness). I've been told that sour orange is the strongest, most disease-resistant, most virile member of the orange family (they're used as root stock on which to graft other varieties), but they're simply not utilized in the States. On the other hand, we can buy them year-round through our wholesalers (primarily Caribbean suppliers) for the restaurant. At certain times they're less juicy, indicating, I think, that they're not in season. As far as I know, they're generally harvested year-round in the parts of Mexico that use them (mostly Yucatan, where they're so integral to the cuisine that the word for orange—*naranja*—refers to the sour orange rather than the sweet).

A dressing made from half fruity olive oil, half sour orange, seasoned only with salt, is one of my favorites for watercress and for jícama. It is common for cooks in Mexico to say that fresh lime juice is an acceptable substitute for sour orange, though lime is more potent, especially if it's the juice of the little yellow Mexican key limes. I recommend using less (or diluted) lime juice or mild vinegar if sour orange isn't on the horizon. All the bottled sour orange juice I've seen in the Caribbean markets hasn't really been "sour orange" juice, so I avoid it. If you're set on experiencing a flavor that is very similar to sour orange, try this concoction that I developed for *Authentic Mexican:* Mix ¾ cup fresh grapefruit juice with 6 tablespoons fresh lime juice and ½ teaspoon finely minced orange zest (colored part only), let stand 2 to 3 hours, then strain to remove the zest. This will make 1 cup, which should be used within 24 hours.

PAN-ROASTED SALMON IN AROMATIC GREEN *PIPIÁN*

Salmón Rostizado en Pipián Verde

WHAT I LIKE BEST about this dish is the color: the crusted pink fish laid up against the pale jade of the sauce. The flavors hint at exotic (toasted sesame, roasted tomatillos, *epazote* and *hoja santa*), yet they're as gentle as the roughed-up pastels you see on the plate.

I've made this sauce for so long, I had to scour my cookbooks from Mexico to remember where I found it: It's based on the one from the wonderful 1969 book *México en la cocina de Marichú* by Maria A. de Carbia. There is nothing tricky or time-consuming about the preparations here; I think you'll like this way of roasting the salmon to a delicious crustiness in a hot, heavy pan in a hot oven—a restaurant cooking technique that works really well at home.

This is a dish for the most elegant of dinners—contemporary and dressy, combined with all the earthy goodness of Mexico. If you've eaten at Topolobampo, it's likely you've tasted this dish served with Garlicky Mexican Greens (page 161). You may want to start your meal with Mexican-Style Sweet Roasted Garlic Soup (page 120) and finish with the Creamy Lime Pie (page 410). A full Sauvignon Blanc or Viognier would be my wine suggestion.

SERVES 6, WITH ABOUT 3 CUPS OF SAUCE

FOR 2 CUPS ESSENTIAL SIMMERED TOMATILLO-SERRANO SAUCE base

14 ounces (about 8 to 10) tomatillos, husked and rinsed

Fresh serrano chiles to taste (roughly 2), stemmed

2 tablespoons vegetable or olive oil

1 small white onion, roughly chopped

2 garlic cloves, peeled and roughly chopped

½ cup hulled sesame seeds, plus a few extra for garnish

2¼ cups chicken broth, plus a little more if necessary

1 sprig epazote, plus a few extra leaves for garnish (if no epazote is to be found, replace it with 6 or 8 sprigs of cilantro)

1 leaf hoja santa

  OR ½ cup roughly chopped green tops of fresh fennel bulb

  OR ½ teaspoon anise seed, preferably freshly ground

Salt, about 1 teaspoon, plus some for sprinkling on the fish

Six 5- to 6-ounce salmon steaks or skinless fillets, about ¾ inch thick

1. *Making about 2 cups Essential Tomatillo-Serrano Sauce base.* Roast the tomatillos and serranos on a baking sheet about 4 inches below a very hot broiler. When they blacken and soften on one side, about 5 minutes, turn them over and broil on the other side. Roughly chop the chiles and transfer to a blender, along with the tomatillos and their juice.

Heat *1 tablespoon* of the oil in a medium-size (2- to 3-quart), heavy saucepan over medium. Add the onion and cook, stirring often, until deep golden, about 10 minutes. Stir in the garlic and cook 1 minute more. Scrape into the blender, leaving as much oil as possible in the pan. Cover the blender *loosely* and blend to a smooth puree.

Return the saucepan to medium-high heat and, when hot enough to make a drop of the puree sizzle sharply, pour it in all at once. Stir for a few minutes as the sauce sears and concentrates, about 7 minutes; set aside.

2. *From tomatillo sauce base to green* pipián. In an ungreased small skillet over medium heat, toast the sesame seeds, stirring regularly for about 5 minutes, until golden. Scoop into the sauce, along with the broth, *epazote* (or cilantro) and *hoja santa* (or one of its stand-ins). Partially cover and simmer for about 30 minutes.

In batches pour the mixture into the blender, cover *loosely* and blend for a good minute or so, until the sauce is smooth. (If you'd like an even smoother sauce, push it through a medium-mesh strainer.) Return the sauce to the pan, taste, and season with salt. If it is too thick, thin with a little broth to bring it to the consistency of a light cream soup; if it is too thin, simmer a little longer to reduce it. Cover and keep warm.

3. *The salmon.* Turn on the oven to 425 degrees. Coat a large (10- to 12-inch) cast-iron or other heavy, ovenproof skillet with the remaining *1 tablespoon* of oil and set into the oven. Lightly salt both sides of each fish steak or fillet, and, if you wish, use tweezers to pull out any of the white pin bones. When the pan is very hot, after about 10 minutes, remove it, lay in the fish and return to the oven. In 4 to 5 minutes, when the pieces of fish are crusty and brown underneath, use a thin-bladed metal spatula to carefully flip them over and return them to the oven for 2 to 4 minutes longer, until the salmon is as done as you like it. (I like mine still translucent in the center, which would be the minimum cooking time.)

Ladle a generous portion of warm sauce onto 6 warm serving plates and top with a crusty pink piece of fish. Sprinkle everything with sesame seeds, lay on a sprig of *epazote* or cilantro and you're ready to eat.

ADVANCE PREPARATION—The sauce may be prepared through step 2 several days ahead; cover and refrigerate. Pan-roast the fish just before serving.

VARIATIONS AND IMPROVISATIONS—Of course, this dish can be made with snapper, sea bass, halibut and the like. In Mexico, it is customary to find tender-simmered pieces of pork shoulder or chicken in this sauce (use the pork-simmering broth for the sauce).

Rustic Baked Tamal of Coarse-Ground Corn, Pork and Red Chile (*page 308*)

CHIPOTLE SHRIMP (*page 334*)

HEARTY SEVEN SEAS SOUP (*page 341*)

Tangy Seared Fish Fillets with woodland mushrooms and pickled jalapeños (*page 344*)

LAMB *BARBACOA* FROM THE BACKYARD GRILL (*page 376*)

6   MANGO-LIME ICE *(page 393)*

Warm *Cajeta* Pudding with fresh berries (*page 399*)

Yucatecan-Style Fresh Coconut Pie *(page 402)*

Hoja Santa

The lush-looking, 6- to 8-inch heart-shaped green leaves of *hoja santa* (also known as *hierba santa, acuyo, tlanepa, momo* and other regional names) are soft like ultrasuede, a little thin rather than succulent, and thrillingly aromatic. The viney plant grows abundantly in south Texas (up and over telephone poles and electric wires) where they call it *root-beer plant* because of its flavor resemblance to sassafras. The plant loves a moderate-to-tropical climate; in Texas it will die back during winter months, then sprout up again come spring.

In my opinion, *hoja santa* has an herbier green flavor than sassafras, more like green fennel tops, but considerably richer and more complex. It's in the black-pepper family, and you can note the resemblant spiciness. In Mexico, the leaves are used most often as an herb in sauces (*moles* and *pipíanes*, as well as many regional specialties throughout Veracruz, Tabasco, Chiapas and Oaxaca; fewer are used in Central Mexico, and practically none in Yucatan, Western and Northern Mexico). In some areas, the leaves are folded into tamales or wrapped around fish (as well as poultry or meat) before they are cooked.

Fresh *hoja santa* is what you're looking for, though I've dried the leaves for adding to sauces with fairly good results. Recently, I've seen dried *hoja santa* leaves for sale in Mexican groceries in New York, right beside dried avocado leaves. Rather than drying, my recommendation is to buy a good quantity of fresh leaves (see Sources, page 425), separate them with plastic or waxed paper and freeze them. The leaves don't have a high water content, so they freeze well; their color will darken slightly and they'll become limp.

. . . .

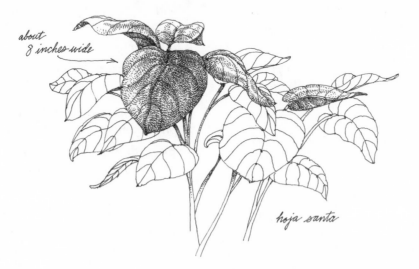

about 8 inches wide

hoja santa

TOMATO-BRAISED GROUPER
WITH ACHIOTE AND ROASTED PEPPERS
Nac Cum de Mero

THERE IS SOMETHING very elegant about the balance of earthy (achiote), tangy (sour orange), sweet (roasted tomatoes and chiles) and herby (banana leaf) in this braised fish. All the flavors are classic Yucatan, so much so that you can almost feel the baking sun when you take a bite. They are echoed in other classic Yucatecan dishes like grilled fish *tikin xik*, chicken and pork *pibil* and many tamales. In fact, the first recipe I collected in Mexico for *nac cum* (the one this version is based on), was told to me as the "fish variation" on chicken and pork *pibil*. I have chosen to brown the fish before baking, because I love the savory richness it adds. Hot banana peppers, by the way, are similar to *xcatic* of the Yucatan and give the most characteristic flavor.

Classic White Rice (page 251) is, yes, the classic accompaniment to most everything in Yucatan. Occasionally I serve *nac cum* in small portions as a special appetizer or fish course topped with matchstick jícama that's been tossed with sour orange and cilantro. The temperature and textural contrast is stunning. Because of the tanginess of this dish, choose wine carefully: a very citrusy Sauvignon Blanc or *very* dry Gewürztraminer, Spanish Albariño or Riesling.

SERVES 4

2 tablespoons achiote seasoning paste (homemade, page 66, or store-bought)

¼ cup fresh sour orange juice
   OR 3 tablespoons fresh lime juice

Four 5- to 6-ounce boneless, skinless fish fillets (choose a fish that is moist when cooked all the way through, like sea bass, grouper, snapper, mahimahi or halibut)

14 ounces (2 medium-small round or 5 to 7 plum) ripe tomatoes

4 hot banana peppers or 2 fresh long green (Anaheim) chiles

A roughly 12-inch square of banana leaf (if you can get one), for lining baking dish

2 tablespoons olive oil

1 medium white onion, sliced

4 bay leaves

2 tablespoons chopped flat-leaf parsley, plus a few sprigs for garnish

½ cup fish broth or water, plus a few extra tablespoons if needed

1. *Marinating the fish.* Combine the achiote paste with the sour orange (or lime) juice in a shallow glass dish. Lay in the fish fillets and turn to coat well with the marinade. Cover and refrigerate about an hour (but no longer than 3 hours).

2. *Roasting the tomatoes and peppers.* Lay the tomatoes and chiles onto a baking sheet and place about 4 inches below a very hot broiler. Roast until blistered and blackened on one side, about 6 minutes, then flip and roast the other side; cool. Peel the tomatoes, then coarsely chop them, reserving all the juices. Peel, seed and slice the chiles ¼ inch thick.

3. *The flavorings.* Lay the banana leaf (if you have one) in a 9 x 9- or 11 x 7-inch baking dish. In a large (10- to 12-inch), well-seasoned or nonstick skillet over medium-high, heat the olive oil. When very hot, use a pair of tongs to remove the fish fillets from the marinade (reserve what is left in the dish) and lay in the hot oil, searing them for about 1 minute per side. Transfer to the baking dish, spreading out the fillets in a single layer.

Reduce the heat under the skillet to medium. Add the onion and fry, stirring occasionally, until softened, about 5 minutes. Add the peppers, tomatoes, bay leaves, parsley, broth and all the marinade remaining in the dish. Heat to a simmer. Taste and season with salt, usually about ½ teaspoon, depending on the saltiness of the broth.

4. *Finishing the dish.* Turn on the oven to 300 degrees. Spoon the warm tomato mixture over the fish and bake until the fish just begins to flake, 5 to 12 minutes, depending on the thickness of the fillets. Use a spatula to transfer each fillet to its own warm dinner plate (if you have more banana leaves, cut squares to line each plate). If the sauce seems too brothy, pour it back into the skillet and boil for a minute or so to reduce it. If it seems thick, simply stir in a little broth or water. Give the sauce a final taste for salt, spoon it over the fish, garnish with parsley sprigs, and serve.

ADVANCE PREPARATION—The tomatoes and chiles can be roasted several days in advance; the fish can be put in the marinade 3 hours before you finish the sauce, assemble the dish and bake it.

VARIATIONS AND IMPROVISATIONS—Personally, I love this dish done with scallops or shrimp; you can simply nestle them back into the skillet of seasoned sauce, cover and gently simmer for a couple of minutes until they are done.

ANCHO-MARINATED WHOLE ROAST FISH, OAXACA-STYLE

Pescado Adobado, Estilo Oaxaqueño

When you roast a fish whole, each bite has an indescribable juiciness and fullness of flavor that you simply won't taste in a fillet. Slathering the fish with the richly flavored ancho chile seasoning paste, then strewing it with sweet-and-crunchy white onions, cilantro and radishes make presenting a whole fish the celebration it should be.

To serve the fish, use a large spoon and fork to cut away the head, then use your fork to carefully lift the meat off the backbone (concentrate on the top half of the fish, working all the way to the tail; on the lower half, where the meat covers the belly cavity, you will encounter small bones jutting into the meat—work with caution there). When the meat has been removed, carefully lift off the backbone with the attached vertical bones and tail, leaving the second fillet on the plate; be aware of the small bones around the belly cavity.

Salted, steamed new potatoes and a Pinot Noir or Grenache (or a bottle of Bohemia beer) are my favorite accompaniments to the fish.

SERVES 4

FOR ¾ CUP ESSENTIAL SWEET-AND-SPICY ANCHO SEASONING PASTE

6 garlic cloves, unpeeled

6 (about 3 ounces total) dried ancho chiles, stemmed and seeded

1 teaspoon dried oregano, preferably Mexican

A scant ½ teaspoon black pepper, preferably freshly ground

A pinch cumin seeds, preferably freshly ground

A pinch cloves, preferably freshly ground

1 cup fish (or chicken) broth, plus a little more if needed

Salt, about ¾ teaspoon, plus a little more if needed

About 3 tablespoons olive oil

2 tablespoons cider vinegar

1 tablespoon sugar

Two 1- to 1¼-pound whole fish (such as snapper, bass or pompano), gutted and scaled

1 small white onion, sliced ⅜ inch thick and separated into rings

2 tablespoons chopped cilantro, plus a few sprigs for garnish

3 radishes, thinly sliced

1. *Making ¾ cup Essential Sweet-and-Spicy Ancho Seasoning Paste.* Roast the unpeeled garlic directly on an ungreased griddle or heavy skillet over medium heat, turning occasion-

ally, until soft (they will blacken in spots), about 15 minutes; cool and peel. While the garlic is roasting, toast the chiles on another side of the griddle or skillet: 1 or 2 at a time, open them flat and press down firmly on the hot surface with a spatula; in a few seconds, when they crackle, even send up a wisp of smoke, flip them and press down to toast the other side. In a small bowl, cover the chiles with hot water and let rehydrate 30 minutes, stirring frequently to ensure even soaking. Drain and discard the water.

Combine the oregano, black pepper, cumin and cloves in a food processor or blender, along with the chiles, garlic and *½ cup* of the broth. Blend to a smooth puree, scraping and stirring every few seconds. (If the mixture won't go through the blender blades, add a little more liquid.) Press through a medium-mesh strainer into a bowl. Taste and season with salt, usually about a generous ¾ teaspoon (it should taste a little salty).

2. *Marinating the fish.* Heat *1 tablespoon* of the oil in a small (1- to 1½-quart) saucepan over medium-high. When hot enough to make a drop of the puree really sizzle, add it all at once, and cook, stirring constantly, until very thick, about 5 minutes. Stir in the vinegar and sugar and cool to tepid. With sharp scissors, trim off all fins and cut out gills from both fish, then make 3 diagonal slashes on each side of the fish, penetrating to the bone. Place the fish in an oiled 13 x 9-inch baking dish, then smear all but 2 tablespoons of the chile paste (reserve the remainder) over both sides of each fish. Cover and refrigerate an hour or two (but not more than 6).

3. *Baking the fish.* Turn on the oven to 400 degrees. With a brush, daub *1 tablespoon* of the remaining oil over the fish. Bake uncovered until the flesh comes away from the bone near the top of the head, 12 to 14 minutes.

4. *Finishing and serving the dish.* While the fish is baking, heat the remaining *1 tablespoon* oil in a medium-size (8- to 9-inch) skillet over medium-high. Add the onion rings and stir-fry until browned but still crunchy, about 5 minutes. Add the reserved *2 tablespoons* chile mixture and the remaining *½ cup* of the broth to the onions. Boil quickly until reduced to a light saucy consistency. Taste and season with salt if necessary; keep warm.

Use 2 metal spatulas to transfer the fish to a large, warm, serving platter. Add any baking-dish juices to the sauce, return to a boil, then spoon over the fish. Sprinkle on the chopped cilantro and radishes. Garnish with sprigs of cilantro, and carry confidently to the table.

Advance Preparation—The ancho seasoning can be prepared several days ahead; cover and refrigerate.

GRILLED CATFISH STEAKS
WITH CHIPOTLE-AVOCADO SALSA

Bagre Asado con Salsa de Aguacate Enchipotlado

A SMOKY BED OF EMBERS (always hardwood charcoal, not briquettes) radiates its searing, redolent heat toward fish in Yucatan (*tikin xik*—marinated in achiote, protected by a banana-leaf wrap) and Nayarit (*pescado zarandeado*—marinated with garlic and spices, slow-cooked far above the glow). Smokiness draws me like a magnet, whether it is emanating from chipotles, charcoal-roasted green chiles, or one of the rustic meat, poultry and fish dishes from Mexico.

There are no tricky techniques or hard-to-find ingredients here. I've simply grilled steaks of marinated fish; the fish then becomes a vehicle for eating lots of the good tomatillo-chipotle salsa that I've enriched with creamy avocado. Spoon some Classic Mexican Fried Beans (page 237) on the plate, toss together a salad, set out warm tortillas, pop open some beer or fizzy water, and you are ready to celebrate grilling season.

SERVES 4 GENEROUSLY, WITH 1 1/2 CUPS SALSA

FOR 1 CUP ESSENTIAL ROASTED TOMATILLO-CHIPOTLE SALSA

3 to 6 (1/4 to 1/2 ounce) stemmed, dried chipotle chiles (or canned chipotle chiles en adobo)

3 large garlic cloves, unpeeled

8 ounces (about 5 medium) tomatillos, husked and rinsed

Salt, about 1 teaspoon

Sugar, about 1/4 teaspoon

Eight 3- to 4-ounce catfish steaks, each about 1 inch thick

1 tablespoon olive oil, plus a little more for the grill grate

2 small avocados, peeled, pitted and chopped into 1/4-inch dice

Sprigs of cilantro for garnish

1. *Making about 1 cup Essential Roasted Tomatillo-Chipotle Salsa.* For dried chiles, toast them on an ungreased griddle or skillet over medium heat, turning regularly and pressing flat with a spatula, until very aromatic, about 30 seconds. In a small bowl, cover the chiles with hot water and let rehydrate 30 minutes, stirring frequently to ensure even soaking. Drain and discard the water. (Canned chiles need only be removed from their sauce.)

While chiles are soaking, roast the unpeeled garlic on the griddle or skillet, turning occasionally, until soft (they will blacken in spots), about 15 minutes; cool and peel. Roast the tomatillos on a baking sheet 4 inches below a very hot broiler until blackened on 1 side, about 5 minutes, then flip and roast the other side.

Scrape the tomatillos (and their juices) and garlic into a food processor or blender, and process to a smooth puree. Transfer to a bowl. With a knife, finely chop the (rehydrated or canned) chiles and stir in, along with enough water (about 3 tablespoons) to give the sauce a medium-thick consistency. Season with about ½ *teaspoon* of the salt, and the sugar.

2. *Marinating the fish.* Lay the catfish steaks in a baking dish. Mix together ¼ cup of the tomatillo-chipotle salsa mixture with the oil, then brush *half* of it over the fish. Flip the fish and brush the other side with the remaining marinade. Cover and refrigerate for several hours, if time permits.

3. *Finishing the dish.* Combine the remaining chipotle salsa with the avocados, taste and add more salt if needed, stirring vigorously to make the sauce slightly creamy. Cover and leave at room temperature.

Light a gas grill or prepare a charcoal fire, letting the coals burn until they are covered with a gray ash and are medium-hot. Position grill grate about 8 inches above the coals and lightly oil.

Remove the catfish from the marinade and lay it on the grill. Sprinkle lightly with salt. Grill, covered, until nicely seared and half-done, 4 to 6 minutes. Flip the steaks, sprinkle with salt, and grill the other side, 4 to 6 minutes more.

Transfer the fish to a warm serving platter, spoon the salsa across the fish, and garnish with sprigs of cilantro. Serve without hesitation.

ADVANCE PREPARATION—The tomatillo-chipotle salsa (without the avocado) can be made and the fish marinated a day ahead. Add the avocado and grill the fish just before serving.

VARIATIONS AND IMPROVISATIONS—If you have to buy a whole catfish, know that a 2-pounder will yield four 1-inch-thick center cut steaks (3½ to 5 ounces each); use a sharp chef's knife to cut straight down through the bone. Other fish steaks or fillets easily can be substituted, though meatier ones (tuna, swordfish, shark) are easier to grill than those with small flakes (like flounder and sole). Skewered grilled scallops are remarkable with this salsa. The chipotle-avocado salsa is good on practically anything off the grill (we use it a lot on grilled quail at Frontera, though it is equally tasty with skirt steak).

BACALAO-STUFFED CHILES
WITH TOMATOES AND OLIVES
Chiles Rellenos de Bacalao

*I*N MEXICO SALT COD is one of *the* Christmas Eve dishes—one that I didn't take to right away, not having been raised with the dried fish myself. After years now of Oaxacan Christmases, the holiday wouldn't be complete for me without my plate of *bacalao*. I've truly come to love the flavors of this Mexican version (notice the jalapeños) of the Mediterranean classic: flakes of long-simmered fish thick with roasted tomatoes, olives, herbs and potatoes.

My twist here is to pack the rough-looking mix into chiles. For *bacalao* first timers, serving the stuffed chiles as a starter course at a holiday meal, with a full Chardonnay, is my favorite way to go. Follow them with the Turkey Breast in Teloloapan Red *Mole* (page 277) and Classic White Rice (page 251). The *bacalao*-stuffed chiles also are delicious as a main course, either warm or at room temperature; they make good picnic fare.

Mostly you will find skinless salt cod in little wooden boxes (oddly enough, often in the freezer) in seafood shops and large supermarkets; at Mexican (and other ethnic) markets look for it in half-fish pieces, skin still on (simply buy a little more than you need and, after the first soaking, pull off the skin).

SERVES 4 AS A MAIN COURSE, 8 AS AN APPETIZER

1 pound good-quality boneless, skin-less salt cod (bacalao)

2 pounds (4 medium-large round or 12 to 16 plum) ripe tomatoes

2 tablespoons olive oil

2 medium white onions, finely diced

3 large garlic cloves, peeled and finely chopped

1/2 cup chopped flat-leaf parsley, plus a few sprigs for garnish

1/2 cup green olives, preferably manzanillo, pitted and sliced

2 to 3 pickled jalapeño chiles, seeded and sliced

1/2 teaspoon dried marjoram

1/2 teaspoon dried thyme

8 small (about 1 1/4 pounds total) fresh poblano or large long green (Anaheim) chiles

4 medium boiling potatoes (like the red-skin ones), cut into 1/2-inch dice

Salt, if necessary

1. *The salt cod.* The day before serving, place the cod in a large bowl, cover with cold water and refrigerate. Every few hours, change the water, to leach out as much salt as possible.

2. *The tomato mixture.* Roast the tomatoes on a baking sheet 4 inches below a very hot broiler until blackened on one side, about 6 minutes, then flip them and roast the other side. Cool, then pull off the blackened skins. Puree tomatoes (and any accumulated juices) in a food processor or blender.

Heat the olive oil in a large (4-quart) saucepan over medium. Add the onions and cook, stirring frequently, until richly browned, about 10 minutes. Add the garlic, cook 2 minutes longer, then add the tomatoes. Cook, stirring occasionally, until the mixture is reduced and thick, about 15 minutes.

3. *Simmering the* bacalao. While the tomato mixture is reducing, drain the cod and place it in a medium-size (2- to 3-quart) saucepan, cover with fresh water and bring to a boil. Simmer 5 minutes over medium heat, then pour off the water.

Add the parsley, olives, jalapeños, marjoram and thyme to the tomato mixture. Stir in enough water (usually about ½ cup) to give it a soupy consistency, then nestle in the cod and simmer, partially covered, over medium-low for about an hour, until the cod has broken up into small chunks.

4. *The chiles.* While the cod is simmering, roast the chiles directly over a gas flame or on a baking sheet 4 inches below a very hot broiler, turning as needed until blackened on all sides (but you don't want them to be too soft), about 5 minutes for the open flame, about 10 minutes for the broiler. Cover with a kitchen towel and let stand 5 minutes. Peel, then make a long slit in the side of each chile and with your fingers carefully remove the seeds. Rinse *briefly* to remove bits of skin and seeds, then pat dry.

5. *Finishing the dish.* Break up any remaining large pieces of cod in the simmering mixture, then stir in the diced potatoes and simmer until they're tender and the mixture is thick enough to hold its shape well in a spoon, about 15 minutes. Season with salt if necessary. (The saltiness of the fish and the olives usually supplies ample seasoning.)

Turn on the oven to 350 degrees. Spoon the cod mixture into the chiles on a lightly oiled baking sheet, packing them loosely. Bake for about 15 minutes, to thoroughly heat everything. Transfer the chiles to warm serving plates, garnish with parsley and they're ready.

ADVANCE PREPARATION—The cod filling and the roasted chiles can be prepared several days ahead; refrigerate them separately, covered.

VARIATIONS AND IMPROVISATIONS—You can serve *bacalao* as a taco filling; or keep the pieces of cod large and serve them on a plate with white rice (as is traditional). About 1½ cups shredded, leftover cooked fish can replace the salt cod.

MEAT

. . . . .

$\mathcal{M}eat$ in $\mathcal{M}exico$ is, for the most part, given a long, slow simmer or braise to soften it up. Yes, the North is known for some good charcoal-grilled slabs of steak, and in other parts there are thin slices of beef that are flash-fried to a chewy tenderness. But broiled or grilled pork chops, beef ribeyes and all the rest of those more expensive, tender, "center of the animal" cuts are not the interest of traditional Mexican cooking.

In this section, I've included dishes from both the traditional (stewed) camp and the more contemporary (broiled, grilled) one. The first recipe, for instance, pairs a spectacularly classic guajillo sauce with grilled steak and onions. You could replace the steak with cubes of beef chuck, simmer everything together in a pot and you'd have something closer to the Mexican original; it wouldn't necessarily be better, only more traditional.

Skirt steak is one of those typical street-vendor cuts (popular especially through Northern Mexico) that is seared on a hot metal slab, then chopped into slivers for *tacos de bistec.* If you don't butterfly the steak into thin sheets as the street vendors do, but you do follow their searing method, skirt steak is a delicious and tender piece of meat. I've outlined the procedure carefully so you'll have instant success—all in the company of a simple chipotle-tomatillo salsa and roasted garlic.

Chipotle is the life of the pot-roast recipe as well, a somewhat interpretive recipe on my part, but one with clearly Mexican roots. If you've made pot roast before, you'll recognize the easy steps; if you haven't (or if you say you've sworn off pot roast because of bad childhood experiences), better take a close look at this one. This is pot roast for our times.

Seared Lamb in Swarthy Pasilla-Honey Sauce couldn't be more traditional. The browned lamb is simmered with the raucous sauce in typical Mexican style, then the rough edges are whittled away with a little honey. And traditional is certainly a description for the Almond-Thickened Veal Stew. It is a classic from Oaxaca and the recipe I give is as close to the original as I could ever get in my stateside kitchen: rich with the flavor of well-browned veal, velvety from the pulverized almonds, exotically perfumed with cloves and cinnamon, and punctuated with olives, raisins, and slivers of pickled chiles.

For this book, I've adapted the classic pit-cooked Central-style Lamb *Barbacoa* to the American backyard kettle-style covered grill. It comes out a little smokier here, but the spirit is the same. If you live where the century plant (*maguey* in Spanish, *agave* in English) grows, you can roast a "leaf" over your coals until soft, tie it around the meat and slow-roast the bundle in the steamy, smoky chamber.

The Chiapas-Style Chile-Seasoned Pot-Roasted Pork is a recipe that in Mexico long ago moved from pit to oven, and it'll demonstrate for you how pot-roasting (roasting with a little liquid in a closed pot) can create an incredibly harmonious blending of flavors.

Though pork country ribs aren't a typical cut to use in Mexico, the juicy variety of textures they pack into every piece reminds me a lot of what I've eaten throughout that country. I've included two recipes that feature them. The first, country ribs *adobadas* (marinated in ancho and guajillo chiles, then slowly baked to allow the marinade to become a very appealing, crusty, sweet-and-spicy glaze) is similar in flavor to the saucy red-chile *adobo* that blankets the chicken on page 314. The second country rib dish celebrates the long-loved Mexican combination of tomatillos, green chile and purslane; it's a one-dish meal that makes you wonder if food can get any better.

To finish up, we come to a dish I almost hesitate to include. It's so simple and tastes so much of its home, Yucatan, that I worry about bringing it to American soil. But every time I make the tangy grilled pork for folks, they seem as thrilled as I was that first time I tasted it in Maní. So here it is, tangy Yucatecan grilled pork—grill-roasted onions, habaneros and all. Just the kind of food that seems right on the Fourth of July.

GRILLED STEAK WITH SPICY GUAJILLO SAUCE

Carne Asada al Guajillo

SMOKY CHARCOALED BEEF lit up by the shimmering spicy richness of slow-simmered guajillo sauce is one of the crowning glories of the Mexican kitchen. Strew around some ribbons of sweet crunchy grilled onions, spoon on some Classic Mexican Fried Beans (page 237) or Garlicky Mexican Greens (page 161), and you have a feast that will live in your memory. Why, seeing the rusty-red of the sauce against a slice of rare steak is worth the price of admission.

SERVES 6, WITH ABOUT 2 1/2 CUPS SAUCE

FOR 2 1/2 CUPS ESSENTIAL SIMMERED GUAJILLO SAUCE

6 garlic cloves, unpeeled

16 (about 4 ounces total) guajillo chiles, stemmed and seeded

1 teaspoon dried oregano, preferably Mexican

1/4 teaspoon black pepper, preferably freshly ground

1/8 teaspoon cumin, preferably freshly ground

3 2/3 cups beef broth, plus a little more if needed

2 1/2 tablespoons vegetable or olive oil

Salt, about 1 1/2 teaspoons, depending on the saltiness of the broth

Sugar, about 1 1/2 teaspoons

1 tablespoon cider vinegar

Six 6-ounce beef steaks, such as tenderloin, New York strip or sirloin, each 1 inch thick

1 large red onion, sliced 1/2 inch thick

Several sprigs of cilantro, for garnish

1. *Making 2 1/2 cups Essential Simmered Guajillo Sauce.* Roast the unpeeled garlic directly on an ungreased griddle or heavy skillet over medium heat, turning occasionally, until soft (they'll blacken in spots), about 15 minutes; cool and peel. While the garlic is roasting, toast the chiles on another side of the griddle or skillet: 1 or 2 at a time, open them flat and press down firmly on the hot surface with a spatula; when they crackle, even send up a wisp of smoke, flip them and press down to toast the other side. In a small bowl, cover the chiles with hot water and let rehydrate 30 minutes, stirring frequently to ensure even soaking. Drain and discard the water.

Combine the oregano, black pepper and cumin in a food processor or blender, along with the drained chiles, garlic and *2/3 cup* of the broth. Blend to a smooth puree, scraping and stirring every few seconds. (If the mixture just won't go through the blender blades, add a little more liquid.) Press through a medium-mesh strainer into a bowl.

Heat *1½ tablespoons* of the oil in a heavy, medium-size (4-quart) pot (such as a Dutch oven or Mexican *cazuela*) over medium-high. When the oil is hot enough to make a drop of the puree sizzle sharply, add the puree and stir constantly until it reduces into a thick paste, 5 to 7 minutes. Stir in the remaining *3 cups* broth, partially cover and simmer over medium-low, stirring occasionally, about 45 minutes for the flavors to come together. If necessary, stir in a little more broth to bring the sauce to a medium, saucy consistency. Taste and season with about *1 teaspoon* of the salt and the sugar.

2. *Marinating the steaks.* Mix ¼ cup of the sauce with the vinegar and ½ teaspoon of salt in a large bowl. Lay in the steaks and turn to coat evenly with the marinade. Let marinate, covered and refrigerated, while you are getting the fire prepared (best not to let them marinate more than about 4 hours, because it will affect the color and texture of the meat).

3. *Grilling the steaks and onions.* Light a gas grill or prepare a charcoal fire, letting the coals burn until they are covered with a gray ash and are medium-hot. Position the grill grate about 8 inches above the coals and lightly oil. Lay the steaks on the hottest portion of the grill and let them sear for 4 or 5 minutes on one side, then turn and finish on the other (4 to 5 minutes more for medium-rare).

While the steaks are cooking, separate the onion into rings and toss them with the remaining 1 tablespoon of oil. Spread them on the grill around the steaks and cook, stirring and turning with tongs or a spatula, until lightly browned and crisp-tender, 6 to 8 minutes.

As the steaks and onions are done, heat the sauce to a simmer. Serve steaks as soon as they come off the grill with a generous ½ cup of the heated sauce and a topping of the onions. Garnish with sprigs of cilantro.

ADVANCE PREPARATION—The sauce may be prepared several days ahead; the steaks can be slipped into the marinade as long as four hours before grilling.

VARIATIONS AND IMPROVISATIONS—Anything tender enough to be grillable can be used in this dish, from all the beef steaks, to pork chops and tenderloin, to chicken, duck and quail, to shrimp, scallops and fish steaks, to vegetables like zucchini, sweet potato and eggplant. A little canned or rehydrated chipotle is welcome blended into the sauce.

SEARED SKIRT STEAK WITH
CHIPOTLE AND GARLIC

Arrachera con Chipotle y Ajo

THE FAJITA PHENOMENON has led us to think Mexican when skirt steak is mentioned. True, skirt steak (called *arrachera* in most of Mexico) is popular in the North and well liked throughout the Republic (mostly it is butterflied into thin sheets to sear on a hot griddle). It can be chewy if you don't cut it across the grain, but it has full beefy flavor.

Like most of you, I find the smoky sting of chipotles irresistible. Against the bright background of roasted tomatillos, beside the sweetness of browned onions, and hugging a morsel of seared steak, the chiles are even better dressed for success. Because I really love roasted garlic's aromatic sweetness, I have studded this mix with whole cloves for a dish that transforms an everyday salsa into a quick dinner for all lovers of full flavors.

SERVES 4

FOR ABOUT 1 CUP ESSENTIAL ROASTED TOMATILLO-CHIPOTLE SALSA

3 to 6 (¼ to ½ ounce) stemmed, dried chipotle chiles (or canned chipotle chiles en adobo)

15 cloves of garlic, unpeeled

8 ounces (about 5 medium) tomatillos, husked and rinsed

Salt, about ½ teaspoon, plus some for sprinkling on the steak

Sugar, about ¼ teaspoon

1 tablespoon olive or vegetable oil or rich-tasting lard

Four 5- to 6-ounce pieces of beef skirt steaks, trimmed of exterior fat

1 medium white onion, thinly sliced

½ teaspoon cumin, preferably freshly ground

½ teaspoon black pepper, preferably freshly ground

⅔ cup beef broth

A little chopped cilantro, for garnish

1. *Making about 1 cup Essential Roasted Tomatillo-Chipotle Salsa.* For dried chiles, toast them on an ungreased griddle or heavy skillet over medium heat, turning regularly and pressing flat with a spatula, about 30 seconds. In a small bowl, cover the chiles with hot water and let rehydrate 30 minutes, stirring frequently to ensure even soaking. Drain and discard the water. (Canned chiles need only be removed from their canning sauce.)

While chiles are soaking, roast the unpeeled garlic on the griddle or skillet, turning occasionally, until soft (they will blacken in spots), about 15 minutes; cool and peel. (If you're lucky enough to have your Tomatillo-Chipotle Salsa made, you'll need to roast 12 cloves of garlic for use in step 2.) Roast the tomatillos on a baking sheet 4 inches below a very hot broiler until blackened on 1 side, about 5 minutes, then flip and roast the other side.

Combine the tomatillos (and their juices), rehydrated or canned chiles and 3 *cloves* of the garlic into a food processor or blender, and process to a rather fine-textured puree. Taste and season with salt and sugar.

2. *Finishing the dish.* Heat the oil or lard in a large (12-inch) heavy skillet (preferably cast-iron) over medium-high. When very hot, pat the steaks dry, sprinkle with salt, and lay in the pan in a single layer. Sear well on both sides until meat is rare to medium-rare, 3 to 4 minutes. Remove to a rack set over a plate.

Add the onion to the skillet and cook, stirring regularly, until it begins to brown (but still stays crunchy), about 5 minutes. Add the salsa to the skillet along with the cumin, pepper, and remaining *12 cloves* of the roasted garlic (yes, left whole). Stir as the salsa reduces for several minutes, then stir in the broth and simmer for 5 minutes. Return the meat to the pan and let it warm through, about 5 minutes or until the meat is done to your liking (skirt steak, like flank, is best done medium or medium-rare in my opinion). Taste the sauce and add a little more salt or sugar if necessary.

With a spatula or slotted spoon, transfer the steaks to a serving platter, then spoon the sauce, onions and garlic over and around them. Sprinkle with the cilantro and you're ready.

ADVANCE PREPARATION—The dish can be prepared through step 1 several days ahead; finish step 2 just before serving.

VARIATIONS AND IMPROVISATIONS

The steak can be replaced by other rather thin-cut steaks (New York/shell, ribeye or sirloin) or thin-cut pork chops. I am wild about the whole garlic, but you could leave it out.

Seared Vegetables with Chipotle and Garlic—This makes a great taco filling, vegetable for a buffet, or accompaniment to anything off the grill. Replace the meat with 3 chayotes (about 1½ pounds total), peeled, pitted and cut into ½-inch dice. Fry with the onions for about 7 minutes, until crunchy-tender. Add the salsa, roasted garlic and seasonings, and stir as the salsa reduces for several minutes, then stir in ½ cup of the broth (or vegetable broth or water) and simmer 5 minutes. Stir in 3 packed cups of roughly chopped spinach or chard, partially cover, and simmer until nicely wilted, 4 to 5 minutes.

CHIPOTLE-SEASONED POT ROAST
WITH MEXICAN VEGETABLES

Carne de Res al Chipotle

I AM SIMPLY TAKEN with the texture and flavorful depth of honest-to-goodness American pot roast, nearly as much as I love the Mexican flavors of roasted tomatillos, garlic and smoky chipotle chiles. In the same pot, with a chorus of Mexican-American vegetables, the meat and sauce become a whole.

Serve your pot roast on a cold afternoon or evening, with Crusty Baked *Masa* Boats (page 186) or *Tlacoyos* (page 190) to start, and Spicy Plantain Pie (page 415) for dessert. A bottle of rustic red wine from France's Rhône Valley or from Italy would be just great.

MAKES 6 GENEROUS PORTIONS

FOR ABOUT 1 CUP ESSENTIAL ROASTED TOMATILLO-CHIPOTLE SALSA

3 to 6 (¼ to ½ ounce) stemmed, dried chipotle chiles (or canned chipotle chiles en adobo)

3 large garlic cloves, unpeeled

8 ounces (about 5 medium) tomatillos, husked and rinsed

Salt, about ½ teaspoon, plus a little coarse salt for the final presentation, if you have it

Sugar, about ¼ teaspoon

3-pound boneless beef chuck roast, 2½ to 3 inches thick (it'll cook best if it's tied into a compact shape)

1 tablespoon vegetable or olive oil

4 medium carrots, peeled and cut into ½-inch rounds

2 chayotes, peeled (if you'd like), pitted and cut into ½-inch pieces

4 medium boiling potatoes (like the red-skin ones), cut into ½-inch cubes

¼ cup finely chopped cilantro

1. *Making about 1 cup Essential Roasted Tomatillo-Chipotle Salsa.* For dried chiles, toast them on an ungreased griddle or heavy skillet over medium heat, turning regularly and pressing flat with a spatula, about 30 seconds. In a small bowl, cover the chiles with hot water and let rehydrate 30 minutes, stirring frequently to ensure even soaking. Drain and discard the water. (Canned chiles need only be removed from their canning sauce.)

While chiles are soaking, roast the unpeeled garlic on the griddle or skillet over medium heat, turning occasionally, until soft (they will blacken in spots), about 15 minutes; cool and peel. Roast the tomatillos on a baking sheet 4 inches below a very hot broiler until blackened on 1 side, about 5 minutes, then flip and roast the other side.

Scrape the tomatillos (and their juices), rehydrated or canned chiles and garlic into a food processor or blender, and process to a rather fine-textured puree. Transfer to a bowl and stir in enough water (3 to 4 tablespoons) to give the sauce a medium consistency. Taste and season with salt and sugar.

2. *The roast.* In a shallow dish, smear the meat with the salsa, cover and refrigerate for several hours (the longer the better—up to 24 hours—to infuse the meat with the smokiness).

When you're ready to cook the meat, turn on the oven to 325 degrees. Scrape as much salsa as possible off the meat and reserve. Dry the meat on paper towels and sprinkle with salt. Heat the oil in a heavy, medium-size (4-quart) pot (preferably a Dutch oven) over medium-high; when hot, add the roast and brown on one side, about 5 minutes, then flip and brown the other side.

Remove the roast to a plate; pour 1 cup of water into the pot and boil over medium, scraping up the browned bits. Stir in the reserved salsa, then return the roast to the pan. Cover tightly and bake for 2 hours, until the meat is just tender.

Distribute the vegetables around the meat, stir to coat them with the pan juices, cover and continue cooking until the meat and vegetables are tender, 30 to 45 minutes.

3. *Serving.* Use two large metal spatulas (or meat forks) to transfer the roast to a large, warm, serving platter. Scoop out the vegetables with a slotted spoon and distribute them around the meat. Skim off the fat from pan juices, and if necessary, boil them to reduce until lightly thickened; there should be about a cup. Taste and season with salt if necessary, then splash the sauce over the meat and vegetables. Sprinkle with cilantro and coarse salt.

ADVANCE PREPARATION—The salsa (step 1) can be made a day or two ahead, as can the whole dish, though the texture of the meat and vegetables is best right out of the oven. If done ahead, refrigerate covered, then rewarm in the oven, adding a little water to the pan juices as they reheat if they have thickened too much.

VARIATIONS AND IMPROVISATIONS—An equal-size pork shoulder roast or equal weight of chicken thighs can be substituted for the beef (chicken and vegetables can cook together—a total of about 40 or 45 minutes). Other cuts of beef to use include sirloin tip, rump, top round or eye of the round, almost all of which are leaner and will need to be very tightly covered to ensure that they don't dry out.

SEARED LAMB (OR PORK) IN SWARTHY PASILLA-HONEY SAUCE

Borrego (o Puerco) al Pasilla Enmielado

*O*NCE I DECIDED to overcome my uneasiness around the broad-shouldered flavor of pasilla chile, this is where I started. Yes, the chile's flavor can resound with the rumble of earthy base notes and persistent spiciness. But simmered with rich, well-browned lamb and sweetened with honey, the garlic-laced pasilla sauce becomes a crowd pleaser.

My starting point was a recipe for pork stewed in *chile macho,* as the recipe christened it. Knowing that lamb is the classic pairing with pasilla in the Central Mexican *barbacoas,* and that a little sweetening is the perfect balance for pure dried chile sauces, I wove together this richly flavored stew. I give a range in the quantity of honey: the smaller amount lets the chile stay in central focus; the larger gives it that sweet-and-hot appeal.

Classic Mexican Fried Beans (page 237) or Classic White Rice (page 251) are the traditional accompaniments, along with a malty Dos Equis or molassesy Negra Modelo. A rough, earthy, fruity Rhône wine would also be welcome.

SERVES 4

FOR ¾ CUP ESSENTIAL BOLD PASILLA SEASONING PASTE

6 garlic cloves, unpeeled

6 (about 2 ounces total) dried pasilla chiles, stemmed and seeded

1 teaspoon dried oregano, preferably Mexican

¼ teaspoon black pepper, preferably freshly ground

⅛ teaspoon cumin, preferably freshly ground

1 to 2 tablespoons vegetable oil

1 to 1½ pounds well-trimmed, boneless lamb (or pork) for stew (preferably cut from the shoulder), cut into 1-inch cubes

1½ cups beef (or other meat) broth

1 medium-size sweet potato, peeled, cut into 1-inch cubes

OR *a peeled 8-ounce wedge of pumpkin, acorn or butternut squash, cubed*

¼ to ⅓ cup honey

Salt, about a scant teaspoon

A few white onion rings, for garnish

Several sprigs of cilantro, for garnish

1. *Making ¾ cup Essential Bold Pasilla Seasoning Paste.* Roast the unpeeled garlic on an ungreased griddle or heavy skillet over medium heat, turning occasionally, until soft (they will blacken in spots), about 15 minutes; cool and peel. While the garlic is roasting, toast the chiles on another side of the griddle or skillet: 1 or 2 at a time, open them flat and press down firmly on the hot surface with a spatula; in a few seconds, when they crackle, even send up a wisp of smoke, flip them, and press down to toast the other side. In a small bowl, cover the chiles with hot water and let rehydrate 30 minutes, stirring frequently to ensure even soaking. Drain, *reserving ¼ cup of the soaking water.*

In a food processor or blender, combine the chiles, *¼ cup* of the soaking liquid, garlic, oregano, pepper and cumin. Blend to a smooth puree, scraping down and stirring frequently. (If necessary, add water a little at a time to get the mixture moving through the blender blades.) Press through a medium-mesh strainer into a small bowl.

2. *The meat.* In a large (10- to 12-inch) heavy skillet, heat *1 tablespoon* of the oil over medium-high. In an uncrowded single layer, brown the meat on all sides. (Do this in batches if your skillet isn't large enough to hold it all at once, adding oil as needed.)

Return all meat to the pan and stir in the chile seasoning. Cook, stirring, scraping and turning regularly, until the chile mixture is very thick, about 3 minutes. Stir in the broth, partially cover, and simmer over low heat for 25 minutes. Add the sweet potato (or pumpkin) and stir to coat with sauce; continue simmering until meat and potato or pumpkin are tender, about 30 minutes.

3. *Serving.* Stir in enough honey to give the sauce a slightly sweet edge, then season with salt. Simmer 5 minutes longer to blend the flavors. Ladle onto a warm, deep platter, decorate with the onion rings and sprigs of cilantro, and you're ready for a hearty meal.

ADVANCE PREPARATION—Covered and refrigerated, the finished dish will keep for several days. Stir gently when reheating to avoid breaking up the sweet potatoes.

VARIATIONS AND IMPROVISATIONS—The sauce (prepared as described, simply leaving the meat out) is delicious with venison (grilled, roasted or stewed), roasted duck legs and grilled eggplant. This dish also works well as a taco filling: Omit the sweet potato and cut the meat into ½-inch cubes; boil, uncovered, until the sauce is thick enough to cling nicely to the meat.

ALMOND-THICKENED VEAL STEW
WITH RAISINS AND OLIVES

Estofado Almendrado

*T*HOUGH IT IS COUNTED among the traditional Oaxacan specialties, this *estofado* has rather shallow roots in Mexican soil. In fact, looking through the list of ingredients, only the tomatoes, oregano and garnishing jalapeño chiles weren't brought by the Spaniards. As elegant as a classic *boeuf bourgignon* (it even follows the same techniques), *estofado almendrado* comes to the table with a medieval aroma about it, with it's ground-almond thickness, sweet spices and flavorful bits of olive and raisins to stud the rich sauce—a dish I wouldn't hesitate to serve to the most timid tongue.

As a typical Mexican "stew" (which is what *estofado* means), it shouldn't be thought of as the hearty, soupy meat-and-vegetable conglomerations that are so good served in large bowls on a cold day. This *estofado* is less saucy and served on a plate; it could be accompanied by a salad or Classic Red Tomato Rice (page 250).

Estofado almendrado is a cousin of all the *almendrado* preparations served in Mexico, though most contain dried chile and many are served with chicken. This recipe utilizing veal (which is usually darker meat than we know here) is based on one from Portillo's *Oaxaca y su cocina*.

MAKES 6 SERVINGS

2½ to 3 pounds lean boneless veal for stew (preferably cut from the shoulder), well trimmed and cut into 2-inch cubes

About 3½ tablespoons vegetable oil or rich-tasting lard, plus more if necessary

1 small and 1 medium white onion, both thickly sliced

¾ teaspoon black pepper, preferably freshly and coarsely ground

Salt, about 2 teaspoons

1½ pounds (3 medium-large or 9 to 12 plum) ripe tomatoes

5 garlic cloves, peeled

1½ cups whole blanched almonds

3 slices white bread, untrimmed, toasted until dark brown

⅛ teaspoon cloves, preferably freshly ground

1 scant teaspoon cinnamon, preferably freshly ground Mexican canela

1 teaspoon dried oregano, preferably Mexican

⅓ cup firmly packed raisins

½ cup meaty green olives, pitted

4 to 6 pickled jalapeño chiles, seeded and cut into strips

1 tablespoon cider vinegar

Sugar, about 1 tablespoon

1. *The veal.* Dry the veal on paper towels. Heat *1½ tablespoons* of the oil or lard in a large, (10- to 12-inch) heavy skillet over medium-high. In batches, brown the veal in the hot oil in a single layer 2 or 3 minutes per side and set aside.

Bring 2 quarts of water to a boil in a large (6-quart) pot (preferably a Dutch oven or Mexican *cazuela*). Add the veal and any juices. Skim off any foam that rises to the top as the liquid simmers for several minutes, then add the small sliced onion, *½ teaspoon* of the pepper, and *1 teaspoon* of the salt. Partially cover and simmer over medium-low until the veal is tender, about 1 hour.

2. *Preparing the flavorings.* Roast the tomatoes on a baking sheet 4 inches below a very hot broiler until blistered and blackened on one side, about 6 minutes; flip and roast the other side. Peel, roughly chop and scoop into a bowl, collecting all the juices.

Return the skillet to medium heat and add *1 tablespoon* of the remaining oil or lard and the sliced medium onion. When the onion looks transparent, about 4 minutes, add the whole garlic cloves, then stir frequently until the onion is nicely browned and the garlic is soft, 4 or 5 minutes. Remove to the bowl with the tomatoes, leaving behind as much fat as possible.

Add a little more oil to the pan if necessary, then scoop in the almonds. Stir nearly constantly for 4 or 5 minutes, until they are a deep golden brown. Remove the almonds; add *half* of them to the bowl with the other flavorings and roughly chop the other half and set aside. Break up the toasted bread into the tomato-flavoring bowl, then stir in the cloves, cinnamon and oregano.

3. *The sauce.* When the meat is tender, remove it; strain the broth and skim off the fat that rises to the top. Scoop the tomato-flavoring mixture into a blender jar and stir in *1⅓ cups* of broth. Blend until a drop of the sauce no longer feels gritty when rubbed between your fingers.

Heat *1 tablespoon* oil or lard in a medium (4-quart) pot (like a Dutch oven or Mexican *cazuela*) over medium-high. When hot enough to make a drop of the puree really sizzle, add it all at once and stir for about 5 minutes, until the mixture thickens and darkens. Stir in 3 cups broth, partially cover, reduce the heat to medium-low and simmer for 20 minutes, stirring frequently.

While the sauce is simmering, soak the raisins in hot water to cover; combine the reserved almonds with the olives and sliced jalapeños. When the sauce is ready, drain the raisins, add them to the almond mixture, then stir *half* this mixture and all of the vinegar into the sauce. Taste and season with the salt (usually 1 teaspoon or so) and the sugar.

4. *Finishing the dish.* Add the meat to the sauce and let it simmer until heated through. If the sauce has thickened beyond a medium consistency (it should be the consistency of a good cream sauce), stir in a little broth or water.

Serve on warm deep plates garnished with the remaining almond mixture.

ADVANCE PREPARATION—All the preparations can be completed in advance—even the final simmering of meat in sauce. Cool, and refrigerate until 15 minutes before serving; then reheat it slowly, thin the sauce if necessary and serve.

VARIATIONS AND IMPROVISATIONS

Tongue in Estofado—Prepare a beef tongue as follows: Soak a medium-large (3-pound) beef tongue in salted water for several hours, drain, then simmer in a new batch of salted water (with a little onion, garlic and herbs), skimming at first, for about 2½ hours, until tender. Strain and *thoroughly* degrease the broth. Strip off the tongue's skin. Pull out the bones from the butt end and slice off ¾ inch where they were; discard. Trim off the fatty section along the bottom. Cut the trimmed tongue into ¼-inch slices. Use the broth to prepare the sauce, steps 2 and 3 above. Lay the tongue slices overlapping in a baking dish, then pour the sauce over the meat. Bake at 350 degrees for 15 or 20 minutes to heat the tongue through. Garnish with the almond mixture and serve.

Swordfish in Estofado—Prepare the sauce as directed in steps 2 and 3, replacing the veal broth with fish (or even light chicken) broth. Broil or charcoal-grill six ½-inch-thick swordfish steaks, basting them with olive oil. Serve each swordfish steak with a ladle of the warm sauce and a sprinkling of the almond mixture. This preparation also works well with halibut steaks; and either fish may be baked directly in the sauce, if you'd prefer.

Mexican Oregano

I'm not a botanist, but I know that Mexican oregano is considerably different from Mediterranean oregano. Simply open jars marked Mediterranean and Mexican (both are easy to find in most grocery stores—just read the fine print) and you'll notice that the Mexican is pungently grassier (think fresh-mown hay) and more floral, the Mediterranean more anisey and sweeter (reminiscent of the aromas from a pizza parlor).

I grow a leggy bush of Mexican oregano at home and I'm confident that when my leaves and flowers are dried they match what's sold commercially. My plant looks very much like verbena, and, in fact, in Maximino Martinez's seminal *Catálogo de nombres vulgares y científicos de plantas mexicanas* from the 1930s, of the nineteen varieties of oregano he lists, six are in the verbena family. There's only one listing for *Origanum vulgare* (the botanical name for Mediterranean oregano) specified as a plant from Europe and listed with no regional distribution in Mexico.

Mexican oregano is always sold dried in my experience (its flavor isn't fully developed when fresh); traditionally it's sold in whole-leaf form with all the delicious blossoms and a few stems mixed in. All Mexican kids learn how to crush the coarse dried herb by rolling it between their palms, releasing all the fragrant oils, before sprinkling it over bowls of soup or *pozole*. From a culinary standpoint, whole leaf is best, since cutting and sifting herbs (the way we're used to buying them) quickly dissipates their flavor.

Two striking regional notes: In Monterrey, years ago, I purchased five different packets of dried herbs, all called *orégano* and none of them from the verbena family or from the Mediterranean oregano family. It seems that the Spaniards called anything *orégano* that had a familiar fragrance or flavor . . . thus we have all these regional Mexican "oreganos." And second, there is a huge-leafed oregano from Yucatan, that gets added by the leaf rather than the teaspoon; if you see Yucatecan recipes that call for several leaves, you'll understand why.

LAMB *BARBACOA* FROM THE BACKYARD GRILL

Barbacoa de Borrego

My FAVORITE PLACE TO EAT this Central-style *barbacoa* is at Mexico City's Restaurante Arroyo, with it's skillful cooks maneuvering golden sheets of *chicharrón* (crispy pork skin) out of the hammered copper caldrons, fresh-baked tortillas and deep bricked pits roaring with fire in preparation for a load of agave-wrapped lamb. Maybe their *barbacoa* isn't as good as what you find at a small country place, but in the country you'd miss the celebrating families, the regional musicians and dancers and the clown making balloon animals for the kids.

This Central-style *barbacoa* doesn't use marinade as further south. The meat is wrapped in agave (rather than avocado or banana leaves used elsewhere) before nestling it onto a rack set over a pot of vegetables and garbanzos bobbing in water, and sealing the whole assemblage into a blazing hot pit. None of which is easily replicated in your backyard.

But agave or not, sealed pit or not, I like the flavor of lamb cooked in a smoky chamber (like one of the kettle-type grills you likely own already) over a pot of aromatic soup. It *is* reminiscent of Central Mexico, so I'm telling you how to do it.

This is really informal food. At Arroyo, I always order *Tlacoyos* (page 190) to start off with. Pouring around little shots of tequila and that tangy tomatoey chaser called *sangrita* customarily starts everyone off with a ¡*salud!* which you can follow with icy beers, sparkling limeade or any of those seemingly omnipresent soft drinks: *horchata, jamaica* or *tamarindo.*

SERVES 6 TO 8, WITH 7 CUPS OF SOUP

3 medium red potatoes, cut into ½-inch dice

2 medium carrots, peeled and cut into ½-inch dice

1 medium white onion, halved and thinly sliced

2 garlic cloves, peeled and halved

1 cup cooked (or canned) garbanzo beans

1 large sprig of epazote (*if you can find it*)

One 3-pound rolled and tied boneless lamb shoulder roast

Salt, preferably coarse, about ¾ teaspoon, plus some for sprinkling on lamb

About 3 tablespoons chopped fresh cilantro

1 canned chipotle chile en adobo, seeded and finely chopped

About 1½ cups salsa (such as Essential Roasted Tomatillo-Chipotle Salsa, page 45)

2 tablespoons finely crumbled Mexican queso añejo or Parmesan

Sprigs of flat-leaf parsley, banana leaves or lemon leaves, for garnish

1 cup good-quality manzanillo olives, pitted

1. *Preparing the grill and soup ingredients.* About 30 minutes before cooking, prepare a charcoal fire, letting the coals burn until they are covered with a gray ash and are medium-hot. Bank the coals on two sides of the lower grate to prepare for the indirect cooking that follows.

In a 12 x 9-inch heavy-duty aluminum-foil pan (or something similar), combine the potatoes, carrots, onion, garlic, garbanzos and *epazote.* Position the pan in the center of the lower grate and surround with the coals. Pour water into the pan to about 1 inch from the top (it'll take about 5 cups). Position the cooking grate 8 inches above the coals and set an oven thermometer on it, if you have one.

2. *Grilling the meat.* Sprinkle the lamb liberally with salt. Lay the roast in the center of the cooking grate directly over the soup, cover the grill and cook, maintaining a moderately low temperature (between 250 and 300 degrees), checking every 30 minutes and adding coals as needed. The lamb will be beautifully smoky-roasted—it'll register about 170 degrees on a meat thermometer and be fall-apart tender in about 2½ hours. Be sure to check periodically the slow-simmering soup that's capturing all those aromatic lamb juices to ensure the liquid level remains more or less the same, adding more water if it's needed.

3. *Finishing the dish.* With a couple of meat forks or spatulas, remove the roast to a platter. Sprinkle with salt and let rest, tented with foil, in a warm place for about 20 minutes.

Meanwhile, with the precision of a steady-handed circus performer, carefully remove the pan of soup from the bottom of the grill. Skim off the fat that is floating on the surface, then taste and season with salt, usually about ¾ teaspoon. Stir in the cilantro and finely chopped chipotle and ladle into small, warm soup cups.

Scrape salsa into a serving dish and sprinkle with cheese. Remove strings from lamb. Slice into good thick slabs and arrange on a warm platter that's lined or decorated with parsley, banana leaves or lemon leaves. Strew the olives around the platter and carry to the table with a flourish. Serve each guest a cup of soup, and pass the meat, salsa and lots of warm tortillas for everyone to make delicious soft tacos.

ADVANCE PREPARATION—Though the whole thing can be done a day or two ahead and refrigerated, it would be somewhat like Thanksgiving turkey you cooked in advance and rewarmed.

VARIATIONS AND IMPROVISATIONS—If you live where agave grows, break off one of the "leaves" (called *pencas* in Spanish) at the base, and roast it briefly over your charcoal fire, just until it becomes limp. Use it to wrap your salted raw lamb, tying everything together securely with heavy twine. There are regional Mexican *barbacoas* and their cousins that utilize everything from goat to chicken, pork, beef, even fish.

CHILE-SEASONED POT-ROASTED PORK
Cochito Chiapaneco

I HAVE SEVERAL TIMES had the opportunity to sit down to a plate of *cochito* at Las Pichanchas restaurant in Tuxtla Gutierrez, Chiapas. The crispy-edged meat was rolled in tortillas, doused with the cooking juices and adorned with lettuce, tomato and radish. It's good eating-out food, like hamburgers or corned beef sandwiches, not easy for everyone to make at home.

I went in search of recipes from the chile and spice sellers in the Tuxtla market and was surprised by what I came up with: You simply make pot-roasted pork, they told me, with a little red chile. "Well, of course," they added, "plus the *recado*—the flavorings." Everything there is flavored with allspice, cloves, herbs and such. Cooking without them is as unthinkable as cooking without salt and pepper in our kitchens.

This pork makes a grand taco filling or it can be sliced and served as an informal main course with Classic Mexican Fried Beans (page 237) and a green salad. A Mexican Chocolate Flan (page 390) or fresh fruit would be the perfect dessert.

I've directed you to soak *untoasted* chiles, as I was taught. For pork that's cooked this long, you won't notice much difference in flavor between toasted and untoasted.

MAKES 6 SERVINGS (THERE IS ENOUGH MEAT FOR 20 GOOD-SIZE TACOS)

2 medium (about 1 ounce total) dried ancho chiles, stemmed and seeded

4 medium (about 1 ounce total) dried guajillo chiles, stemmed and seeded

2 bay leaves

2 tablespoons cider vinegar

½ small white onion, roughly chopped, plus a couple of slices (broken into rings) for garnish

2 garlic cloves, peeled and roughly chopped

1 teaspoon mixed dried herbs (such as marjoram, thyme and Mexican oregano)

A scant ¼ teaspoon allspice, preferably freshly ground

A pinch of cloves, preferably freshly ground

1½ tablespoons vegetable oil or rich-lasting lard

Salt, about ½ teaspoon

3 pounds lean, boneless pork shoulder or (Boston) butt roast

OR 4½ pounds fresh picnic ham with the skin on (for classic crispy skin)

8 leaves romaine lettuce, for garnish

3 radishes, thinly sliced, for garnish

1. *The chile paste.* Place the chiles in a small bowl, cover with hot water, and let stand 30 minutes to rehydrate, stirring occasionally to ensure even soaking. Drain, reserving ⅔ cup of liquid, then transfer chiles and reserved liquid to a food processor or blender.

Pulverize the bay leaves in a spice grinder or a mortar, then add to the blender, along with the vinegar, onion, garlic, mixed herbs, allspice and cloves. Process to a smooth puree (adding a little more water if needed to keep the mixture moving through the blades); press through a medium-mesh strainer into a small bowl.

Set a large (6-quart) pot with a lid (preferably a Dutch oven) over medium-high heat and add the oil or lard. When hot enough to make a drop of the puree really sizzle, add it all at once. Stir constantly as the puree sears, concentrates and darkens into a spicy-smelling paste, about 5 minutes. Remove from the heat and season with salt.

2. *Seasoning and pot-roasting the meat.* Turn on the oven to 325 degrees. If you are using pork shoulder or butt, cut it into slabs roughly 3 inches thick (try to get them all about the same thickness so they'll cook evenly); leave a picnic ham whole, but make 1-inch-deep incisions every few inches all over the meat. Lay the meat into the pot with the chile paste, then flip it over to cover with the chile (slathering with a spoon or spatula to give an even coating). Pour ½ cup water around the meat, cover tightly and place in the oven.

Baste the meat every 30 minutes with the liquid and rendered fat that accumulates around it. After about 2½ hours (the fresh ham may need another ½ to 1 hour), the meat will be fork-tender and will have darkened to an appetizing and crusty, rich, red-brown. If all the liquid evaporates during the cooking, leaving only chile paste and fat, dribble a little more water into the pan so you can go on basting. If time allows, let the pork stand, covered, for 20 to 30 minutes to reabsorb juices before serving.

3. *Serving the meat.* Line a serving platter with the lettuce leaves. With the help of tongs, spatulas or meat forks, transfer the meat to the platter, then taste the pan juices and add a little more salt if necessary. Spoon the juices over the meat, then scatter the onion rings and radish slices over all, to create a riot of color and texture.

ADVANCE PREPARATION—The pot-roasted pork holds well in a low oven for an hour or so before serving. It can be done ahead and rewarmed in a 350-degree oven, though the texture of just-cooked pork is the best.

CHILE-GLAZED COUNTRY RIBS
Costillas Adobadas

I HAVE MADE VERSIONS of pork *adobado* for years, and every time that flavor crosses my tongue, life seems in balance. The pork, the red chile, the sweet and the tang—they are all flavors I grew up with in my family's barbecue restaurant.

Unlike the saucy chicken in *adobo* (page 314), these country ribs *adobadas* are cooked with a little punchy red chile until any sauciness becomes a glaze. I love country ribs for their meatiness and the variety of textures you discover in each piece.

The perfect configuration on my plate is a rib or two, a little heap of salad (watercress, when its spiciness appeals) and a spoon of Classic Mexican Fried Beans (page 237). If it is an informal party, I will make Guacamole (page 78 or 81) and a taco filling or two to serve with warm tortillas while we all stand around and chat, then I bring on the main plates and finish with a rich Celebration Cake (page 394). Everything would go with an earthy white wine from the Rhône Valley in France or a rustic, fruity red wine like a Syrah or Zinfandel.

SERVES 4 TO 6

4 garlic cloves, unpeeled

3 (about 1 1/2 ounces total) dried ancho chiles, stemmed and seeded

6 (about 1 1/2 ounces total) dried guajillo chiles, stemmed and seeded

3/4 teaspoon dried oregano, preferably Mexican

1/2 teaspoon cinnamon, preferably freshly ground Mexican canela

1/8 teaspoon black pepper, preferably freshly ground

A pinch of cloves, preferably freshly ground

A pinch of cumin, preferably freshly ground

2 tablespoons cider vinegar

1/2 cup beef broth or water, plus a little more if needed

1 1/2 teaspoons salt

1 teaspoon sugar

3 pounds (about 6 good-size pieces) pork country ribs

1 1/2 tablespoons honey

Romaine lettuce leaves, for lining your serving platter

Sliced radishes, for garnish

Sprigs of cilantro, for garnish

A few slices of white onion, separated into rings, for garnish

1. *Making the chile marinade.* Set an ungreased griddle or heavy skillet over medium heat, lay in the unpeeled garlic and roast, turning occasionally, until blackened in spots and soft,

about 15 minutes; cool, then peel. Toast the chiles a few at a time: open them flat on the hot surface, press flat for a few seconds with a metal spatula (until they start to crackle, even send up a faint wisp of smoke), then flip and press down to toast the other side. In a small bowl, cover the chiles with hot water and let rehydrate 30 minutes, stirring frequently to ensure even soaking. Drain and discard the water.

Place the chiles and garlic in a food processor or blender along with the oregano, cinnamon, pepper, cloves, cumin and vinegar. Measure in the broth or water, then blend to a smooth puree, scraping and stirring every few seconds. (If the mixture won't move through the blender blades, add a little more broth to get things going.) Press the puree through a medium-mesh strainer into a bowl and stir in the salt and sugar.

2. *Marinating the ribs.* Place the ribs in a large bowl, smear *half* of the chile marinade over them, cover and refrigerate for several hours (preferably overnight). Combine the remaining chile marinade with the honey, cover and refrigerate.

3. *Cooking the ribs.* Turn on the oven to 325 degrees. Transfer the ribs and all their marinade to a baking dish large enough to hold them in a single layer (a 13 x 9-inch dish works perfectly). Drizzle ¼ cup water around them, cover with foil and bake for 45 minutes. Uncover and baste with the liquid in the pan. Return to the oven uncovered and bake until tender, another 15 minutes or so. Carefully pour off the fat and any remaining juices.

4. *Glazing and serving the ribs.* Raise the temperature of the oven to 350 degrees. Brush the ribs heavily with the marinade-honey mixture. Bake until the ribs are burnished cranberry color, about 15 minutes. Line a serving platter with the romaine leaves, then pile on the ribs. Strew with radish slices, cilantro sprigs and onion rings.

ADVANCE PREPARATION—The chile marinade can be made a couple of weeks in advance; marinate the ribs (step 2) overnight or as long as 2 days. The ribs may be cooked a day in advance, but save the final glazing for serving time.

TOMATILLO-BRAISED PORK COUNTRY RIBS
WITH MEXICAN GREENS

Costillas de Puerco con Verdolagas

THIS IS A TYPICAL Mexican one-pot meal that could not be more authentic or widely embraced by just about everyone. If you like lemony flavors, you will be taken with the combination of purslane and roasted tomatillos. The browned pork, of course, brings richness to the pot, and the potatoes add that wonderfully gentle foil to all this boldness.

Purslane, sadly, is not in many grocery stores yet, so you probably will be making this when purslane is in the farmer's market, or you will use chard, which makes a great dish, though one that is not as lemony and soft-textured. The dish needs only a Golden Squash Blossom *Crema* (page 138), Corn-*Masa Crepas* (page 110) or a salad with creamy dressing to start, and a comforting Spicy Plantain Pie (page 415) or rich Chocolate Pecan Pie (page 404) to finish. For wine, I would recommend a full, but dry, Gewürztraminer.

SERVES 4 TO 6

FOR 2¼ CUPS ESSENTIAL SIMMERED TOMATILLO-SERRANO SAUCE BASE

1½ pounds (15 to 18) tomatillos, husked and rinsed

Fresh hot green chile to taste (roughly 5 serranos), stemmed

½ cup chopped fresh cilantro, plus a few sprigs for garnish

Salt, about 1½ teaspoons, plus some for sprinkling on the meat

2 tablespoons vegetable or olive oil

3 pounds (about 6 good-size pieces) pork country ribs (or 1-inch-thick pork blade chops)

2 small white onions, finely chopped, plus a couple of slices separated into rings, for garnish

3 garlic cloves, peeled and finely chopped

8 medium boiling potatoes (like the red-skin ones), quartered

3 cups (about 12 ounces) fresh purslane (verdolagas), rinsed and thick bottom stems removed

OR 6 cups loosely packed, sliced (½-inch pieces) chard leaves (you'll need a 12-ounce bunch)

1. *Making 2¼ cups Essential Simmered Tomatillo-Serrano Sauce base.* Lay the tomatillos and chiles on a baking sheet and place about 4 inches below a very hot broiler. When they darken and soften, about 5 minutes, turn them over and broil the other side.

Roughly chop the chiles, then transfer them and the tomatillos (along with any liquid) to a food processor or blender. Puree, then add the chopped cilantro, ¾ cup water and salt.

2. *The meat and potatoes.* Over medium-high, heat the oil in a Dutch oven or Mexican *cazuela* large enough to hold the meat in a single layer. Sprinkle the meat with salt, then brown on all sides, 10 to 15 minutes. Transfer to a plate.

Turn on the oven to 325 degrees. Pour off all but a thin coating of oil from the pan. Add the onions and cook until translucent, about 4 minutes; add the garlic and cook 2 minutes longer. Stir in the tomatillo sauce base, let come to a rolling boil, then return the meat to the pan. Cover and bake in the oven until the meat is just tender, about 45 minutes. Remove from the oven and skim off any fat that has risen to the top of the sauce.

Add the potatoes to the hot pot, push them down into the sauce, cover and continue baking until potatoes are tender, about 20 minutes.

3. *Finishing the dish.* Stir the greens into the meat and potatoes, set the cover in place again, and bake 10 more minutes. Taste and season with a little more salt if necessary.

Transfer the ribs to a warm, deep, serving platter. Arrange the potatoes around them, then spoon the sauce and greens over and around the meat. Strew the onion rings over the top, garnish with cilantro, and carry the impressive platter to the table.

ADVANCE PREPARATION—The dish may be prepared very successfully through step 2; cover and refrigerate. Bring to a simmer on top of the stove before continuing with step 3.

SHORTCUTS—Two 10-ounce packages frozen leaf spinach, thawed, squeezed dry and roughly chopped, can replace the fresh greens; add them just before serving.

VARIATIONS AND IMPROVISATIONS—This classic combination of purslane, potatoes and tomatillos can be made as a great vegetable dish or taco filling: Omit the meat, simply fry the onion and garlic, add the sauce base, then let reduce until thick; stir in 1 cup broth (I prefer beef broth for flavor). Simmer until medium-thick, then add the potatoes, simmer 15 or 20 minutes, add the greens, simmer 5 to 10 minutes more, season, and serve (this is good with cubes of *queso fresco* as a garnish). An equal weight of chicken thighs or beef short ribs can replace the pork, as can thick tuna or swordfish steaks (thin the sauce base to a spoonable consistency with broth once it has come to a boil; add the potatoes—but not the browned fish—and bake 20 minutes, then nestle in the greens and fish and bake until both are as done as you like).

TANGY YUCATECAN GRILLED PORK
WITH ROASTED ONIONS AND FRESH GARNISHES

Poc Chuc

$\mathcal{W}$HERE I GREW UP, you could get chicken-fried steak in practically any restaurant or diner. A few were good, really good, the stuff dreams are made of; but most were just food, better not remembered. If I were from Yucatan, I would be writing that about the ubiquitous *poc chuc*. There are various versions, from saucy to plain, but until I tasted the one at El Príncipe Tutul Xiu in Maní, I never thought the dish more than an example of the utterly simple side of Mexican cooking, food to fill your stomach.

Still, even the best *poc chuc* is the simplest of dishes, and you need all the parts in place or you won't hear the band: You need the charcoal fire, the grill-roasted onions, the sharp marinade for the pork, the plateful of lightly seasoned vegetables, and the explosive dribble of roasted habanero salsa. Start with a batch of margaritas (page 422) and some Crusty Griddle-Baked Quesadillas (page 194) from a griddle set right on the grill—then, with the pork, serve a cup of Classic Mexican "Pot" Beans (page 234; the beans served with this dish in the Yucatan are customarily blended to a medium-thick puree and strained, *frijoles colados*). These are very rustic, *al fresco* flavors, so margaritas may be too refined; you may think they cry out for a cold beer.

SERVES 4 GENEROUSLY

2 medium white onions, unpeeled

1½ pounds well-trimmed, thin-cut, boneless pork steaks, cut from the shoulder or leg

OR 1½ pounds thin-cut, boneless pork chops

¾ cup fresh sour orange juice, plus a little more if needed

OR a generous ½ cup fresh lime juice, plus a little more if needed

Salt and freshly ground black pepper, for seasoning the meat and vegetables

3 cups thinly sliced cabbage

⅓ cup roughly chopped cilantro, plus a few sprigs for garnish

1 pound (2 medium-large round) ripe tomatoes, cored and sliced ¼ inch thick

1 large avocado, peeled, pitted, and sliced ¼ inch thick

1. *Roasting the onions.* Light a charcoal fire and let it burn until all the coals are medium-hot and covered with gray ash. Nestle the onions directly in the coals and let them roast until charred on the outside and soft within, about 20 minutes.

2. *Preparing the meat and vegetables.* While the onions are roasting, pound the meat with a flat mallet to about ⅛ inch thick. Drizzle with ¼ *cup* of the sour orange (or 3 tablespoons lime) juice, cover and set aside.

Cool the onions until handleable, peel the charred outer layers off, then cut what remains into ½-inch squares. Toss with ¼ *cup* of the sour orange (or about 3 tablespoons lime) juice and season with salt and pepper.

Toss the cabbage with the cilantro and the remaining ¼ *cup* of the sour orange (or 3 tablespoons lime) juice; season with salt and pepper. Spread onto a large serving platter about 14 inches or so in diameter. Decorate the perimeter with alternating slices of tomato and avocado, and sprinkle them with salt and pepper.

3. *Grilling and serving.* Stoke your fire with new charcoal and let it get really hot. Sprinkle both sides of the meat generously with salt and pepper. Working with a couple of pieces at a time, grill the pork: Let it sear about 2 minutes on one side, then flip it over and sear on the other. (The total cooking time for ⅛-inch pork steaks over a very hot fire will be no more than 3 or 4 minutes.)

Lay the meat slightly overlapping down the center of the platter and strew the onions over the meat. Decorate with a few cilantro sprigs and serve without delay, accompanied by salsa and baskets of hot tortillas.

VARIATIONS AND IMPROVISATIONS—This simple dish could easily be made with butterflied, pounded, boneless, skinless chicken breasts or with skirt steak. If you like spicy food and want more flavor in the marinade, smear a little of the habanero salsa over the meat in place of the sour orange.

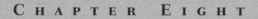

CHAPTER EIGHT

· · · · ·

DESSERTS

MEXICO DOESN'T HAVE A DESSERT CULTURE LIKE THAT OF NORTH AMERICA. It doesn't have the rich history of oven baking, the *homemade* baked goods on the breakfast table, that cakey something hot from the oven to slice up and serve with coffee when friends come over. Rather than out of the oven, a great many of Mexico's classic sweets come off the stovetop.

And those classic Mexican sweets are sweet. Their descendants are Spanish (native Americans had no segregated category of sweets), whose descendants were Arab (just before its conquest of Mexico, Spain had been under more than seven centuries of Arab rule). All who've tasted Arab sweets know what sweets are all about.

At the end of a restaurant meal in, say, Oaxaca, Michoacan, Puebla or Chiapas, the local specialty dessert plate will be a selection of candies and little sweet snacks—not slices of cakes, pies, tortes and such. All this is perfectly understandable in a culture whose cuisine doesn't rely on an oven, whose history involves religious conquest by nuns accustomed to supporting themselves by making and selling candies and whose geography and climate yield little wheat and tremendous amounts of sugar and tropical fruit.

Yet all these cultural considerations may not be helpful when you are planning a nice Mexican dinner and you're searching for a typical dessert and candylike sweets just don't seem appropriate. I suggest you turn your search first toward the traditional custards.

The most classic Mexican custard is the caramel-coated flan, which combines the intensity of caramel syrup with a "baked" custard (baked is in quotation marks here, since flan was originally cooked in a hot water bath on the stovetop). The texture and flavor can be varied infinitely, making it a marvelous candidate for many modern interpretations while staying within a traditional framework. I've provided a recipe for a modern Mexican chocolate flan, as well as many variations.

Or search for your "right" dessert among the traditional ices and ice creams, the kind that are sold from storefronts and pushcarts nearly everywhere in Mexico. Many are locally made from fruits, Mexican chocolate, *cajeta* and such, and they boast a lovely homemade quality that makes them as appealing as any American "super premium frozen confection." Though the ices and ice creams are usually an out-and-about sweet treat, I love to serve them at the end of a substantial meal. The one ice recipe I've given, Mango-Lime Ice, has an incredibly silky texture. It can easily be made by the still-set method (putting the seasoned fruit puree into the freezer, then beating it periodically as it sets), rather than using an ice-cream machine. From its thick texture, you'd swear this sweetened fruit ice contains cream; by its refreshing, light taste, you'll know it doesn't.

Today, at practically every birthday or other special occasion (both in Mexico and among Mexicans in large Mexican communities in the States), the rage is to serve a bakery *tres leches* cake, that wonderful sponge cake soaked with a caramely three-milk "syrup." With the same lusciously moist texture as the original, my version offers the complex dimension of almonds, the scent of orange and a deep caramel.

Continuing in the traditional vein, but based on a much older recipe (I've read similar recipes from as far back as the early seventeenth century), I suggest you consider an *ante*, that versatile, comforting layering of tender, moistened sponge cake and pureed fruit. For a more elegant dessert, I created a lighter spin on Mexico's bread-pudding theme. I replaced the bread with crisped cubes of the same cake used for the *ante* and I baked it all with berries in a rich custard flavored with *cajeta*.

More in the modern vein are pies (they're called *pays* in Spanish, a transliteration of their English ancestral name). A dense, chewy one of fresh coconut from the Yucatan is one of my favorites. The work of hulling and shredding a fresh coconut is well rewarded. Chocolate Pecan Pie, our house dessert at Frontera Grill, combines a sticky-rich molassesy pecan pie with chunks of bittersweet chocolate.

My inspiration for the most exotic dessert in this collection comes from the age-old, sweet *alegrías* (puffed amaranth bars). The first Spaniards to walk on Mexican soil wrote about little cakes made from these tiny puffed seeds; they survive today as street sweets. Once you acquire the knack of working with the seeds and syrup, they can be made into numerous shapes, including little tart shells as I've done here. Fill them with ice cream and you have a deliciously interesting dessert.

Creamy Lime Pie is elegant and rich, a simple custardy pie I developed to show off the ripe, thick cream and key limes we cook with in our classes in Oaxaca; served with spoonfuls of simple sauces made from pureed fruits like guava, papaya and zapote, the dessert tastes of Mexican life. My plaintain pie looks and tastes a little like sweet potato or pumpkin pie, but the tanginess of the cooking bananas adds a nice dimension.

MODERN MEXICAN CHOCOLATE FLAN
WITH KAHLÚA

Flan de Chocolate con Kahlúa

$\mathcal{T}$HERE IS NOTHING more welcomed than the silkiness of a perfectly baked custard at the end of a full-flavored meal. And when each bite is shrouded in unadorned caramely sweetness, as it is for flan or caramel custard or *crème caramel*, the glow of spiciness fades happily to sweet memory.

Mexican flan was traditionally made with boiled-down milk spiked with sugar and *canela* until sweetened condensed milk came along. Now, many cooks rely on that canned milk's stickiness to give body and boiled-milk flavor to flan—but it's a flan that comes out dense. Truth is, I prefer the lighter texture of whole egg yolks, mostly milk rather than cream and no boiling.

Historically, Mexico's native chocolate has never moved from its well-established role as beverage. Mexican chocolate doesn't really melt, making it difficult to use in desserts. But steeping the chocolate in the milk for this modern twist on a classic helps to dissolve it. Be careful in the baking: too high a heat or too long in the oven will turn the custard firm and curdy, with little holes all around.

MAKES 6 INDIVIDUAL FLANS

1/2 cup plus 1/3 cup sugar

1 cup half-and-half

1 cup milk

A generous 3/4 cup (4 1/2 ounces) chopped Mexican chocolate

1 inch cinnamon stick, preferably Mexican canela

4 large eggs

1 tablespoon Kahlúa or other coffee liqueur

1/2 teaspoon pure vanilla extract

1/4 teaspoon pure almond extract

1. *Caramelizing the molds.* Set six 5- to 6-ounce custard cups into a baking pan deep enough to hold about 2 inches of water.

Measure 1/2 *cup* of the sugar into a small (1- to 1 1/2-quart), heavy saucepan. Dribble in 1/4 cup water and stir several times. Bring to a boil, wash down any sugar crystals clinging to the sides of the pan with a brush dipped in water, then simmer over medium heat without stirring, until the syrup begins to color. Swirl the pan continually over the heat until the syrup is an even, deep amber. Working carefully, immediately divide the caramel among the custard cups, then tilt the cups to distribute the caramel over the bottom and a bit up the sides.

2. *The custard.* Pour the half-and-half and the milk into a medium-size (2½- to 3-quart) saucepan. Pulse the chocolate in a food processor until pulverized. Add to the milk, along with the cinnamon stick and remaining ⅓ *cup* of the sugar. Bring to a simmer over medium heat, stirring occasionally, then cover, remove from the heat and let steep for 20 minutes.

Whisk the eggs, Kahlúa, vanilla and almond extracts in a large mixing bowl until combined, then slowly whisk in the hot-milk mixture. Pour through a fine-mesh strainer into a large measuring cup or pitcher with a spout, then divide the mixture among the molds.

3. *Baking the flans.* Turn on the oven to 325 degrees. Pour about 2 inches of very hot water into the pan around the filled molds. Lay a sheet of foil over the molds (don't crimp or seal it—too much heat will build up), and bake in the middle level of the oven just until the custard has barely set (a knife inserted halfway between the edge and the center will come out clean), about 25 minutes. Let cool in the water bath, then refrigerate to chill thoroughly.

To unmold, run a nonserrated knife around the edge of each mold, penetrating to the bottom, then twist the mold back and forth to ensure that the custard will move freely. Invert a serving plate over each mold, then reverse the two and listen for the flan to drop. Scrape out any clinging caramel onto the flans and they're ready to serve.

ADVANCE PREPARATION—Flans keep several days refrigerated and covered.

VARIATIONS AND IMPROVISATIONS

Classic Vanilla Flan—Omit the chocolate and increase the sugar in step 2 to ½ cup. Replace the Kahlúa with brandy, increase the vanilla to 1½ teaspoons and omit the almond extract.

Coffee Flan—Replace the chocolate with ¼ cup dark-roasted ground coffee and increase the sugar in step 2 to ½ cup; steep and strain as directed.

Double Caramel Flan—After caramelizing the molds, caramelize an additional ½ cup sugar, then pour in the half-and-half and milk. Stir over medium heat until the caramel is dissolved. Omit the chocolate, but steep with the cinnamon. Replace the Kahlúa with brandy, increase the vanilla to 1½ teaspoons and omit the almond extract.

Tangerine Flan—Omit the chocolate and increase the sugar in step 2 to ½ cup. Replace ½ cup of the milk with fresh tangerine juice and add the zest from 2 tangerines before steeping. Replace the Kahlúa with orange liqueur and omit the almond extract.

Mexican Chocolate

Though chocolate's birthplace is Mexico, most botanists agree it certainly changed its ways once away from home. Originally the royal court beverage of the Aztec emperors (dressed up with chiles, herbs or, occasionally, honey), chocolate is best known today as a confection that literally melts in your mouth. I encourage everyone to read of this remarkable transformation, as well as chocolate's royal Mexican beginnings, in Sophie and Michael Coe's book *The True History of Chocolate*; chocolate is an integral player in—and mirror of—world history in the fifteenth through the eighteenth centuries.

The flavor of chocolate, like most crops, changes depending on where it's grown. And for whatever reason, chocolate seems to develop more richness and complexity in other lands. In Mexico, the beans are toasted very dark to give added character, then coarsely ground over heat with sugar (and often cinnamon, almonds and vanilla), all with the purpose of making into a disc that more or less dissolves in water or milk, to drink. Mexican chocolate is never "conched," that endless mixing and rocking between cylinders, to smooth it out for that melt-in-your-mouth texture.

Mexico, Oaxaca, Michoacan and Tabasco are the states famous for chocolate production. The best is usually handmade and called *chocolate de metate*, "chocolate from the hand grinding stone." You can easily bring Mexican chocolate back from a trip—customs officials let small quantities pass free—or you can look for the more commercial brands sold here. The most widely distributed brands are Ibarra and Abuelita, though I don't think they're particularly special. El Popular, distributed by Garza from East Chicago, Indiana, is very good (it's made in Tabasco, they tell me).

The vast majority of Mexican chocolate is made into a beverage, though its most talked-about use is probably in *moles*, where it's thought of as a spice. If you can't find Mexican chocolate in your local market, making a substitute to use as a beverage would seem a little beside the point. You can always jazz up your favorite cocoa recipe with cinnamon and vanilla, but it still won't taste much like Mexican chocolate; for the *moles*, however, you can substitute unsweetened cocoa for Mexican chocolate, using about one-third the volume.

MANGO-LIME ICE

Nieve de Mango con Limón

$\mathcal{T}$ROPICAL FRUIT ICES, fruit popsicles called *paletas,* ice milks and ice creams are a way of life in Mexico. Places like Oaxaca are legendary for their slushy ices and ice milks in every flavor imaginable (avocado, corn, roses, burnt milk, even crumbled crispy pig skin), canisters of which are spun in salty ice baths, stirred occasionally with big paddles, then served as a thick slush or soupy granita.

Mango is the perfect fruit to choose when making an ice by the still-set (rather than an ice-cream machine) method, since its dense flesh turns out an almost creamy textured ice that's tangy from the lime and just sweet enough to soothe a tongue that has enjoyed a lot of spiciness. My thanks goes to Harold McGee in *The Curious Cook* for explaining the intricacies of making fruit ice. Using this method, you'll want to start the night before serving, or at least early in the day of your dinner.

MAKES ABOUT 4 CUPS, ENOUGH FOR 6 TO 8 HEALTHY SERVINGS

4 large (2¼ pounds total) mangoes, peeled, fruit cut away from the pit and coarsely chopped (you need about 2 heaping cups)

The finely chopped zest (colored rind only) of 1 orange
1¼ cups sugar
⅓ cup fresh lime juice

In a food processor, combine the mangoes, orange zest, sugar, lime juice and 1 cup of water. Process to a smooth puree, then press through a strainer into a stainless steel bowl or 9 x 9-inch pan. Freeze until the mixture is firm 2 inches in from the sides, about 2 hours. Whip with an immersion blender or scrape into a food processor and process until slushy. Repeat the freezing and beating 2 more times, then freeze at least 1 hour before serving.

It is best to eat the ice within a day, because it will become progressively more icy. If the finished ice has been in the freezer for several hours, soften it in the refrigerator for half an hour before serving.

VARIATIONS AND IMPROVISATIONS—This same process works well with 2 heaping cups of coarsely chopped, not-too-watery tropical fruits like mamey, guanabana, chirimoya, black zapote and chico zapote; they may not need as much lime juice to bring out their flavor. Guava is best cooked with the sugar until tender, then strained; it will need less lime juice. Juicier fruits like papaya, nectarine and peach should be used in larger proportions (2½ heaping cups) with less water (about ⅔ cup). Sugar in all these versions can be varied, depending on the sweetness of the fruit, though if you eliminate too much, the ice will be icy.

CELEBRATION CAKE

Pastel de Tres Leches

*T*HIS CAKE, popular both in Mexico and other parts of Latin America, has a wonderful caramely moistness soaked into a light cake. Today it has risen to stardom as *the* special-occasion cake in Mexico, though mostly a bakery cake, I assume, since recipes for it are scarce in cookbooks.

Recently, I pulled together several recipes, then gave the resulting recipe my own spin. The classic Mexican sponge cake is made by beating egg whites until stiff then folding in egg yolks and flour. Here I've started with a whole-egg sponge cake textured with almonds and flavored with a little browned butter (thanks to Rose Beranbaum in *The Cake Bible* for basic proportions and methods). The classic "three milks" from the title are sweetened condensed milk, evaporated milk and whole milk; I've replaced the first with *cajeta* (the goat-milk caramel so famous in Mexico), the last with heavy cream (to give it a little more custardiness). I've perfumed everything with orange. And the result is beautifully balanced, I think you'll agree: not too moist (though you may be surprised at how much of the milky "syrup" is absorbed by the cake) and not too sweet.

Frosted with whipped cream, everything stays creamy and light. Some cooks choose a buttercream or meringuelike seven-minute frosting, which are too heavy or too sweet for my taste. My favorite way to serve the cake is with chopped fresh fruit on the side; the lively flavors of the fruit complement the rich cake nicely.

MAKES A RICH 10-INCH CAKE, SERVING 12 TO 15

FOR THE CAKE

¾ cup (about 3 ounces) whole blanched almonds

1 cup (3½ ounces) cake flour, sifted before measuring

10 tablespoons (5 ounces) unsalted butter

1½ teaspoons pure vanilla extract

6 large eggs, room temperature

¾ cup plus 2 tablespoons sugar

The finely grated zest (colored rind only) of 1 orange

FOR THE FLAVORING AND FROSTING

2 cups heavy (whipping) cream

¾ cup evaporated milk

⅔ cup cajeta (goat-milk caramel), ~~sweetened~~ either store-bought or homemade ~~condense~~ (page 401)

¼ cup orange liqueur

1. *The cake.* Turn on the oven to 325 degrees. Grease a 2-inch deep, 10-inch round cake pan or springform pan. Line the bottom with a round of parchment paper, then grease the paper and flour it all—pan and paper. Spread the almonds on a baking sheet and toast in the oven, stirring them occasionally, for about 12 minutes, until aromatic and golden. Cool,

then transfer to a food processor along with the flour. Run the machine until the nuts are pulverized. In a small pan, melt the butter over medium heat, stirring and swirling until nut brown, about 5 minutes. Remove from the heat, cool a little, then stir in the vanilla. Raise the temperature of the oven to 350 degrees.

Combine the eggs, ¾ *cup* of the sugar and the orange zest in the large bowl of your electric mixer (you will need a heatproof bowl, preferably stainless steel), then choose a saucepan that the mixer bowl will fit snugly into. Fill the saucepan with 1 inch of water and bring to a simmer. Set the mixer bowl over the simmering water (you'll need to regulate the heat so the water no more than simmers), and whisk for several minutes, until the mixture is very warm to the touch and foamy, and the sugar is completely dissolved. Transfer the bowl to the electric mixer and beat for a full 5 minutes (the mixture will be as thick as whipped cream that almost holds peaks). With the mixer on the lowest speed, add the almond mixture a couple of spoonfuls at a time, letting one addition just disappear before adding the next. Thoroughly mix ¼ cup of the cake batter into the butter mixture. Then, in 2 additions, use a whisk to fold the butter mixture into the remaining cake batter.

Immediately and gently scoop the mixture into the prepared pan and bake until the cake feels slightly springy on top and the sides just begin to pull away from the pan, about 35 minutes. Cool 10 minutes, then turn out onto a rack and cool completely.

2. *The flavoring*. Mix ¾ *cup* of the cream with the evaporated milk and the *cajeta* in a small bowl. Slowly brush or spoon *half* of the mixture over the cake while on the cooling rack. Carefully invert your serving plate over the cake and flip the two. Remove the cooling rack from what is now the top and slowly brush or spoon on the remaining mixture. (Soaking the cake will take 10 to 15 minutes, letting each addition soak in before adding more.)

3. *Frosting the cake*. With an electric mixer on medium-high speed, beat the remaining 1¼ *cups* of the cream with the remaining 2 *tablespoons* of the sugar and the orange liqueur until very stiff. Spread the whipped cream over the sides and top of the cake. Save a little to pipe a border around the top and bottom edges of the cake. Refrigerate until ready to serve.

ADVANCE PREPARATION—The cake layer can be made several days in advance, wrapped in plastic and refrigerated; it may be wrapped and frozen for up to 3 months. The cake can be soaked a day ahead, but do not frost until the day you are serving.

TROPICAL "TRIFLE" OF MANGO AND ALMONDS

Ante de Mango y Alemendras

I LOVE THIS LIQUEUR-LACED sponge cake and pureed fruit or custard for its delicious texture and long history in Mexican cooking. My earliest Mexican cookbooks, from the 1830s, have recipes for it. When working on a benefit seventeenth-century-style dinner for Chicago's Mexican Fine Arts Center Museum, I found a recipe almost identical to this one in the pages of culinary writings left by Sor Juana Inéz de la Cruz, a nun who was also Mexico's greatest poet and mystic of that period.

Unlike most trifles, this version utilizes fruit rather than cream, making it lighter, fresher and more satisfying after a spicy meal. I am indebted to Mexican cooking teacher and author María Dolores Torres Yzábal who showed me how vital a dessert *ante* can be.

SERVES 8 TO 10

FOR THE CAKE

¾ *cup cake flour (measured by scooping and leveling)*

1 teaspoon baking powder

6 large eggs, room temperature

½ *cup plus 2 tablespoons sugar*

1 teaspoon pure vanilla extract

FOR THE FRUIT

4 large (2¼ pounds total) mangoes

⅓ *to* ⅔ *cup sugar, plus a little more if needed*

2 tablespoons fresh lime juice

½ *teaspoon pure almond extract, optional*

FOR THE SYRUP AND FINISHING THE DISH

⅓ *cup sugar*

About ⅓ *cup dry sherry or orange liqueur*

½ *cup lightly toasted sliced almonds*

About 1 cup Sweetened Whipped Cream (page 406), for serving

1. *The cake.* Turn on the oven to 350 degrees. Grease and flour a 17 x 11-inch jelly-roll pan. Lightly grease the pan, then line with parchment paper; grease and flour the paper. Sift together the flour and baking powder. Separate the eggs: In the large bowl of an electric mixer, place the 6 yolks; in another bowl, place 4 of the whites (refrigerate or freeze the remaining 2 whites for another preparation.) To the yolks, add ½ *cup* of the sugar, the vanilla and 3 tablespoons hot water, then beat at medium-high speed for 5 full minutes, until light in color and texture. Using a whisk or rubber spatula, gently fold in the flour mixture in 2 additions. If you have only one bowl, scrape the mixture into a large bowl, wash the mixer bowl and beaters or whisk attachment and transfer the whites to the mixer bowl.

Immediately beat the whites at medium speed until they hold soft peaks. Add *1 table-spoon* of the remaining sugar; beat for 1 minute, then add the remaining *tablespoon* of sugar and beat for a minute or so longer, until the whites hold nearly firm (but not stiff) shiny peaks. Fold into the batter in three additions.

Gently spread the batter in an even layer onto the prepared pan. Bake until nicely browned and springy to the touch, about 15 minutes. Cool 10 minutes on a cooling rack, then turn out onto the rack and carefully peel off the paper. Cool completely.

2. *The fruit.* With a knife, peel the mangoes, then cut the flesh from the pit. Chop it into 1-inch pieces, scoop into a bowl and mash with a fork (there should be 2 generous cups). Add ⅓ *cup* of the sugar, mix well and let stand about 30 minutes to draw some of the juice from the fruit. Strain the mixture and put the liquid into a medium saucepan. Simmer over medium heat until reduced to ½ cup, then stir in the mango and simmer gently 5 minutes longer, stirring often. Remove from the heat and stir in lime juice, almond extract (if you are using it), and enough of the remaining ⅓ *cup* of the sugar to sweeten the fruit nicely.

3. *The syrup.* In a small saucepan combine ⅔ cup water and the ⅓ *cup* sugar. Bring to a boil, stirring to dissolve the sugar. Cool slightly, then stir in the sherry or liqueur.

4. *Assembling the* ante. Cut the cake into two 8-inch circles (you can freeze the cake scraps to use later in making a half recipe or 3 or 4 individual *cajeta* puddings (page 399). Place one circle on a shallow serving dish 10 or 12 inches in diameter. Brush thoroughly with the syrup. Spread on *half* of the fruit mixture, then top with the other cake circle. Brush with remaining syrup and spread on the remaining fruit mixture. Smooth the top and refrigerate for several hours for the texture to become more compact and homogeneous. Sprinkle the top with toasted almonds and cut into wedges. For a dressier presentation, pipe lightly sweetened whipped cream around the edge of the dish.

ADVANCE PREPARATION—This is one dessert that actually gets better with age; make it a day ahead if possible, or up to 3 or 4 days. Store it well-covered in the refrigerator.

SHORTCUTS—About 30 (14 ounces) sponge cake–type ladyfingers can replace the cake.

VARIATIONS AND IMPROVISATIONS—This recipe welcomes a variety of interpretations. Regional Mexican liqueurs (from Toluca, Veracruz, Yucatan and Oaxaca) lend a wonderful flavor of place. And tropical fruits like guanabana, chirimoya and mamey are typical and delicious (none will need the sugaring and boiling in step 2; simply sweeten the coarse puree and continue). Ripe papaya and peaches can be used, but they will need the same treatment as the mango. You may stir cream into the fruit or substitute pastry cream for the puree, with or without pieces of fruit. The almonds easily can be omitted.

Cinnamon and Vanilla

The cinnamon that is used to give distinctiveness to both sweet and savory Mexican dishes isn't what we call cinnamon in the States. We use cassia here, a cousin to real cinnamon. True cinnamon (*canela* in Mexico, sometimes Ceylon cinnamon here) has a lighter, more floral, more complex and less aggressive flavor than cassia. Go to a well-stocked spice store or practically any ethnic market to find true cinnamon. This bark of an Asian evergreen is thin and flaky, while cassia is much thicker and darker (think of what they sell as cinnamon sticks at your grocery store). You'll find *canela* whole, but it's easy to grind and will taste wonderfully fresh.

Vanilla, the other of Mexico's favorite sons, has had the same kind of expatriate success as the native chocolate. Living as we do in an era that values dark flavors like balsamic vinegar, Tahitian vanilla, a cousin to the Mexican, is highly prized. Madagascar vanilla, on the other hand, is the bean many consider the most complex vanilla flavor on earth, while Mexican vanilla now languishes in near anonymity. Truth is, like true cinnamon, Mexican vanilla is very floral and rich, albeit a lighter richness than Madagascar. At the turn of the century, Mexican vanilla was considered the benchmark. Today, Mexican vanilla is in small and somewhat inconsistent supply, and suffers a bad reputation because the bulk commercial varieties have been laced with coumarin, the vanilla-like flavor fixative that the FDA says shouldn't be ingested.

Luckily, we *can* find a number of well-made Mexican vanilla extracts. If you travel to Mexico's beach communities, you often find them for sale there. My favorite is from our country's premier vanilla company, Nielsen Massey (see Sources, page 425), which makes all the main varietal vanillas, including the very best Mexican—on either side of the border. In Mexico, near the famous vanilla orchid-growing town of Papantla, I've enjoyed extract from Fábrica de Vainilla Orlando Goya.

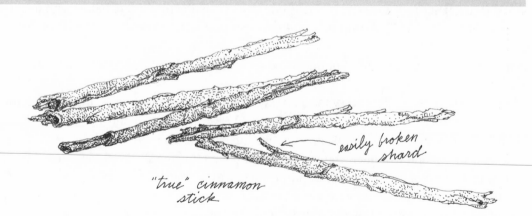

easily broken shard

"true" cinnamon stick

WARM *CAJETA* PUDDING WITH FRESH BERRIES

Budín de Cajeta con Moras

*H*ERE'S MY TAKE on the squares of bread pudding sold in Mexican bakeries. The original is dense, but this one is light (but rich) and tender, working the gutsy caramel of *cajeta* (long-simmered goat-milk caramel) and cream into very light sponge cake, then studding it all with tangy berries. I think you'll like the balance. Though the recipe is one I put together, both the flavors and approach are very Mexican.

SERVES 6 TO 8

FOR THE CAKE

¾ cup cake flour (measured by scooping and leveling)

1 teaspoon baking powder

6 large eggs, room temperature

½ cup plus 2 tablespoons sugar

1 teaspoon pure vanilla extract

FOR THE PUDDING

¾ cup heavy (whipping) cream

4 large eggs, room temperature

1½ cups cajeta (goat-milk caramel), (page 401) or store-bought

2 cups fresh berries (such as blackberries or raspberries), plus a few extra for garnish

About ½ cup Thick Cream (see page 165), crème fraîche, or sour cream, for serving

1. *The cake.* Turn on the oven to 350 degrees. Grease and flour a 17 x 11-inch jelly-roll pan. Lightly grease the pan, then line with parchment paper; grease and flour the paper. Sift together the flour and baking powder. Separate the eggs: In the large bowl of an electric mixer, place the 6 yolks; in another bowl, place 4 of the whites (refrigerate or freeze the remaining 2 whites for another preparation). To the yolks, add ½ *cup* of the sugar, the vanilla and 3 tablespoons hot water, then beat at medium-high speed for 5 full minutes, until light in color and texture. Using a whisk or rubber spatula, gently fold in the flour mixture in 2 additions. If you have only one mixer bowl, scrape the mixture into a large bowl, wash the mixer bowl and beaters or whisk attachment and transfer the whites to the mixer bowl.

Immediately beat the whites at medium speed until they hold soft peaks. Add *1 tablespoon* of the remaining sugar; beat for 1 minute, then add the remaining *tablespoon* of sugar and beat for a minute or so longer, until the whites hold nearly firm (but not stiff) shiny peaks. Fold into the batter in three additions.

Gently spread the batter in an even layer onto the prepared pan. Bake until nicely browned and springy to the touch, about 15 minutes. Cool to room temperature, remove from the pan (it doesn't matter if the cake rips as you are removing it), break or cut into ½-inch bits and spread out on a baking sheet.

Bake, stirring every 5 minutes, until cake is dry and crispy, about 15 minutes. Allow to cool. You will need ⅓ of the cake pieces (about 4 cups loosely packed) for this recipe; you can store the remaining pieces in an airtight container to crumble over ice cream, to mix with crushed fruit and whipped cream as a last-minute topping on poached fruit or for another round of pudding.

2. *Preparing and baking the pudding.* Lightly butter an 8 x 8-inch baking dish. In a large bowl, whisk together the heavy cream and eggs, then add the *cajeta* and whisk well to combine.

Distribute *2 cups* of the cake pieces over the bottom of the prepared dish. Cover with berries, then top with remaining *2 cups* of the cake. Slowly pour the egg mixture over all, evenly moistening everything. Let the pudding stand about 15 minutes, periodically pressing the cake into the custard to ensure that the top is moistened.

Bake at 350 degrees until the pudding is bubbling around the edges, crusty and richly browned, about 40 minutes. Cool slightly, then serve warm in small bowls with a dollop of thick cream and a sprinkling of berries, if you wish.

ADVANCE PREPARATION—The cake may be prepared up to a week in advance, dried out and stored in an airtight container. The finished pudding can be made a day ahead, covered and refrigerated. Warm in a 350-degree oven 15 minutes before serving.

SHORTCUTS—Good-quality store-bought sponge cake can replace the homemade cake.

VARIATIONS AND IMPROVISATIONS—I like this recipe best baked in 5- to 6-ounce souffle dishes, little *cazuelas* or custard cups (use 6 if you want them nicely full); they will take about half the time to bake. Though the berries are easiest to use, diced apricots, peaches, mangoes (or anything equally substantial, not too watery, and tasty when cooked) will be delicious here. If you are looking for pudding for a crowd, double this recipe and bake it in a 13 x 9-inch baking dish.

GOAT-MILK CARAMEL

Cajeta

CAJETA IS ONE OF THE GLORIES of the Mexican sweets kitchen, and you know why if you've tasted one made from goat's milk that has been simmered with *canela* (true cinnamon) until thick and caramely. This isn't the typical caramelized sugar that's diluted with cream; that approach never develops the complexity of flavor or silky texture that *cajeta* has. For *cajeta,* the milk slowly reduces to a third of its original volume as the natural milk sugars brown. Though *cajeta* can be successfully made with cow's milk, the distinctiveness goat's milk brings to the pot will be missing.

I've given many details about *cajeta* in *Authentic Mexican.* Here I simply repeat the wonderful recipe for those interested in making it.

MAKES 1 1/2 CUPS

1 quart goat's milk, cow's milk, or a
   mixture of the two

1 cup sugar

1 tablespoon light corn syrup

1/2-inch cinnamon stick, preferably
   Mexican canela

1/4 teaspoon baking soda

1 tablespoon cream sherry, rum
   or brandy

Stir together the milk, sugar, corn syrup and cinnamon stick in a medium-size (4-quart) heavy pot or Dutch oven. Bring to a boil. Dissolve the baking soda in 1 tablespoon water, remove the milk from the heat, and stir in the soda mixture, having a spoon ready to stir the mixture down if it bubbles up. Cook, stirring frequently, over medium heat, until the mixture thickens into a pale-gold syrup, about 25 minutes. At this point, begin stirring very frequently as the mixture thickens into a caramel-brown syrup that's the consistency of maple syrup, about 10 minutes more.

Strain the *cajeta* through a fine-mesh strainer set over a large measuring cup. Let cool for a few minutes, then stir in the sherry, rum or brandy (plus a little water, if necessary, to bring it to 1 1/2 cups). Refrigerate covered. When cold, the *cajeta* should have the consistency of thin corn syrup.

ADVANCE PREPARATION—*Cajeta* will keep a month or more, covered, in the refrigerator.

YUCATECAN-STYLE FRESH COCONUT PIE

Pay de Coco, Estilo Yucateco

I CAN EASILY GET rapturous about dense fresh coconut stuck together with a little richness, packed into a nutty crust and baked to caramely brown. It's all texture and tender freshness, unlike anything you could make from desiccated packaged coconut. Yes, it is work to hull, peel and grate the coconut, but the payoff is enormous.

Pay de Coco is a Yucatecan specialty I first tasted in Merida, where it was stuck together with sweetened condensed milk. Though there are cultural and historical reasons to use the canned product, I decided to make my own condensed sweetness in order to utilize the water from inside the fresh coconut.

The pie has other virtues: It can be made several days ahead and it travels well (it's not at all fragile). Just rewarm it before serving to restore all the unctuous goodness.

MAKES ONE 9-INCH TART, SERVING 8

FOR THE CRUST

1 cup (4 ounces) slivered almonds

3 tablespoons sugar

4 ounces (about 5 slices) firm white bread, torn into pieces (or 2 cups fine, fresh bread crumbs)

3½ tablespoons (about 1¾ ounces) unsalted butter, melted

FOR THE PIE

1 medium-size coconut with lots of liquid inside

1 cup heavy (whipping) cream

⅔ cup sugar

3 large egg yolks

1 teaspoon pure vanilla extract

About ½ cup Thick Cream (page 165), crème fraîche or sour cream thinned with a little milk, for serving

1. *The crust.* Turn on the oven to 325 degrees. Toast the almonds on a baking sheet in the oven, stirring occasionally, until golden, 7 to 10 minutes. Cool; set *½ cup* of the almonds aside. In a food processor, pulverize the remaining almonds with the sugar. Add the bread and pulse the machine until reduced to fine crumbs. Drizzle in the melted butter and pulse to mix thoroughly. Evenly pat the mixture over the bottom and sides of a ¾-inch deep, 9-inch tart pan with a removable bottom. Refrigerate several minutes to set.

2. *The coconut.* Twist a corkscrew (or drive an ice pick or screwdriver) into 2 of the coconut's "eyes" (the dark indentations on one end), then drain the trapped liquid into a cup (strain if it contains any bits of coconut shell). Place the coconut on a baking sheet and put

into the oven for about 15 minutes to help loosen the flesh from the shell. With a hammer, crack the coconut into several pieces, then use a small knife or screwdriver to pry the flesh from the shell. Use a paring knife or a vegetable peeler to peel away the dark brown skin. In a food processor (or, with determination and stamina, using a four-sided grater) grate the coconut into medium-fine shreds. Measure out 2½ cups for the pie; reserve the remainder for the garnish.

3. *The pie.* Raise the oven temperature to 350 degrees. In a small (1- to 1½-quart) saucepan, combine the coconut water, cream and sugar. Simmer over medium heat, stirring frequently, until reduced to 1 cup, 10 to 15 minutes. Pour into a large bowl, then stir in the 2½ cups of coconut, the reserved ½ cup almonds, the egg yolks and vanilla.

Set the prepared crust onto a baking sheet, scoop in the coconut filling and bake in the middle of the oven until set and lightly browned on top, 30 to 35 minutes. Cool on a wire rack.

While the pie is baking, toast the reserved coconut on a baking sheet in the oven, stirring occasionally, until nicely browned, 7 to 10 minutes.

It's easiest to cut the pie when cool (easier still when refrigerated), so I cool or chill it, cut it, then warm the pieces in a 350-degree oven for about 10 minutes, since I like this pie served warm. Though it's gilding the lily, I'm partial to a dollop of thick cream and a sprinkling of coconut as a garnish.

Advance Preparation—The pie can be made several days ahead, wrapped in plastic and refrigerated.

Variations and Improvisations—If you have tart pans, you can make these small (you will need extra crust mixture—make double) to put out onto a dessert buffet. The almonds can be replaced with other nuts (hazelnuts and macadamias are particularly good), and, if you are so inclined, the finished pie can be drizzled with melted chocolate.

FRONTERA GRILL'S CHOCOLATE PECAN PIE

Pay de Nuéz y Chocolate, estilo Frontera Grill

Over the years, we've made more than 8,000 of these pies at Frontera, each crust rolled out by hand by Gonzalo de Santiago, our pastry chef of nine years, and his crew. I put together the recipe a dozen years ago, because I love pecan pie and thought that stirring in chunks of chocolate could make this favorite from both sides of the border seem less cloying. It does, though the result is still rich—almost like a not-too-sweet candy bar packed into a flaky crust. Barely sweetened whipped cream (laced with a little Kahlúa) plays the welcome role of counterbalance.

Makes one 10-inch pie, serving 12

FOR THE CRUST

1 1/2 (6 3/4 ounces) all-purpose flour
   (measured by scooping and leveling)

6 tablespoons (3 ounces) chilled
   unsalted butter, cut into
   1/2-inch bits

3 tablespoons vegetable shortening or
   rich-tasting lard, chilled, and cut
   into 1/2-inch bits

3/4 teaspoon sugar

1/4 teaspoon salt

1 egg yolk, beaten slightly

FOR THE FILLING

2 cups (about 6 ounces) pecan halves
   (make sure they're fresh and richly
   flavorful)

6 ounces semisweet or bittersweet
   chocolate

3 tablespoons all-purpose flour

3/4 cup (6 ounces) room-temperature
   unsalted butter

1 cup firmly packed dark brown sugar

5 large eggs, room temperature

3/4 cup light corn syrup

1/4 cup molasses

1 1/2 tablespoons Kahlúa or brandy

2 1/4 teaspoons pure vanilla extract

1/2 teaspoon salt

2 cups Sweetened Whipped Cream
   (page 406) flavored with Kahlúa for
   serving

1. *The dough.* Measure the flour, butter and shortening (or lard) into a bowl or a food processor fitted with the metal blade. Quickly work the fats into the flour with a pastry blender or pulse the food processor until the flour looks a little damp (not powdery) but *tiny* bits of fat are still visible. If using the food processor, transfer the mixture to a bowl.

Mix together the sugar, salt and 3 tablespoons of ice water. Using a fork, little by little work the ice-water mixture into the flour mixture. The dough will be in rough, rather stiff clumps; if there is unincorporated flour in the bottom of the bowl, sprinkle in a little more ice water and use the fork to work it together. Press the dough together into a flat disk, wrap in plastic and refrigerate at least 1 hour.

On a lightly floured surface, roll the dough into a 12-inch circle. Transfer to a deep 10-inch glass pie pan (I find it easiest to roll the dough onto the rolling pin, then unroll it onto the pie pan). Decoratively crimp the edge and trim excess dough. Refrigerate 30 minutes.

2. *Prebaking the crust.* Heat the oven to 400 degrees. Lightly oil a 15-inch piece of foil and lay it, oiled-side down, into the crust (heavy duty foil is too stiff to work here); press down to line the crust snugly. Fill with beans or pie weights and bake about 15 minutes, until beginning to brown around the edges. Reduce the oven temperature to 350 degrees. Carefully remove the beans (or weights) and foil, return the crust to the oven and bake 8 to 10 minutes, until it no longer looks moist. (If it bubbles at this point, gently press it down with the back of a spoon.) Brush the beaten egg yolk over the crust, then let cool completely.

3. *The nuts and chocolate.* While the crust is cooling, spread the pecans on a baking sheet and toast in the 350-degree oven until fragrant, about 10 minutes. Cool, then break into small pieces and transfer to a large bowl. Chop the chocolate into rough, 1/2-inch pieces and add to the bowl, along with the flour. Stir until everything is well coated.

4. *The filling.* In a food processor (or in the large bowl of an electric mixer), cream the butter and brown sugar until light and fluffy, about 3 minutes in the food processor, 5 minutes in the mixer. With the machine still running, add the eggs one at a time, letting each be completely incorporated before adding the next. Beat in the corn syrup, molasses, Kahlúa or brandy, vanilla and salt.

5. *Baking.* Pour the filling over the chocolate and pecans and stir well to combine. Pour the mixture into the prebaked pie shell, set onto the lower shelf of the oven and bake until a knife inserted into the center is withdrawn clean, about 1 hour.

Cool completely on a wire rack. Serve slices of the pie at room temperature or slightly warm, topped with a dollop of Kahlúa-spiked, sweetened whipped cream.

ADVANCE PREPARATION—The pie can be made several days ahead, wrapped in plastic and refrigerated. It freezes well. Because the pie is easiest to cut when cold, I suggest making it ahead, refrigerating it, cutting it, then warming just before serving.

VARIATIONS AND IMPROVISATIONS—Other nuts can be substituted for the pecans. Honey can replace the molasses for a lighter flavor. If you like the crystalline crunch of Mexican chocolate, reduce the semisweet chocolate to 5 ounces and sprinkle the pie with 1/3 cup rather finely chopped Mexican chocolate before baking.

Two 9-Inch Pies—Prepare 1½ times the dough, divide it and roll out each half to line 2 shallow 9-inch pie pans; crimp and refrigerate. Divide the filling between the crusts and bake at 325 degrees for 45 to 50 minutes.

Sweetened Whipped Cream

There are two approaches to whipping cream. To dollop on or over a dessert: Beat the cream at a moderate speed, or by hand, until it holds luscious soft peaks, then whip in a little powdered sugar and vanilla or liqueurs.

To use as a filling or frosting: Place everything in your mixer bowl (granulated sugar works fine here since it's going in from the beginning), turn the mixer on medium-high and beat until very stiff—a couple of steps away from butter, stiff enough to pipe easily into a firm shape, but not so stiff that liquid is beginning to weep out. For a cup of cream, sugar can vary from 1 tablespoon to 4, vanilla 1 to 2 teaspoons, and liqueur about double that. A cup of cream will yield nearly 2 cups whipped.

Mexican Chocolate Whipped Cream—Prepare the whipped cream using one of the two approaches described above, replacing the sugar with 2 or more tablespoons of finely pulverized Mexican chocolate (it's best to pulverize it in a food processor); a little vanilla is good here, plus a little rum or Kahlúa.

CRUNCHY AMARANTH TART

Postre Alegría

$\mathcal{W}$HEN I DISCOVERED a source for puffed amaranth (see Sources, page 425) several years ago, I culled recipes from my regional Mexican cookbooks for the classic street sweet called *alegrías:* They are a lot like flattened popcorn balls, if popcorn were the size of the head of a pin. When I watched the snack cakes being made last year near the town of Puebla, complete from the popping of the tiny grain on a steel griddle (*comal*) to the boiling of the syrup and the slapping of the hot mixture into round molds, I was taken by the ancient-looking process and how I imagined it related to the way the indigenous people made the ceremonial puffed amaranth forms the Spaniards saw and wrote about when they first arrived.

It's unfortunate that the Spaniards all but did away with amaranth cakes (the cakes had strong native religious significance). Amaranth is one of the most nutritious grains on earth, yet one that's little utilized in Mexico nowadays—except in these snack cakes, which sport a wonderfully happy name, *alegría* (Spanish for "joy").

The ones I learned to make near Puebla were stuck together either with boiled-down honey (this makes them stay pliable) or with nearly caramelized refined sugar (these set up more rigid). I prefer the deep flavor of the *piloncillo* (unrefined sugar) called for in the early recipes I collected, mixed with a little honey for texture and complexity of flavor.

I've never seen anyone in Mexico form these into any shapes other than round, square or rectangular cakes, to serve as a sweet snack (like a cookie or Rice Krispie treat). The mixture is easy to mold, though, so I took the liberty of making tart shells out of it (by pressing it into custard cups) to fill with ice cream (I'm sure you'll think of other fillings you'd like). It's a simple but unusual and elegant-looking dessert.

MAKES 12 INDIVIDUAL TARTS

FOR THE CRUSTS

4 cups puffed amaranth, plus up to a cup more if necessary

7 ounces (1 large cone, or 7 small cones) piloncillo (Mexican unrefined sugar)

OR *1 cup dark brown sugar plus 1 tablespoon molasses*

⅓ cup honey

2 teaspoons fresh lime juice

FOR FINISHING THE DESSERT

1 quart ice cream (I suggest caramel-pecan, Mexican chocolate, toasted almond or a really good vanilla)

Chopped Mexican chocolate, for sprinkling

6 cups chopped fruit (typical Mexican choices are mango, papaya, strawberries, blackberries, banana and the like), for serving

Fresh mint leaves, for garnish

1. *The crusts.* Turn on the oven to 200 degrees, lightly oil six 6-ounce custard cups and measure the amaranth into a heatproof bowl. In a large (3- to 4-quart) saucepan, combine the *piloncillo* (or brown sugar and molasses), honey and lime juice with 1½ cups water. Cover, set over medium heat and simmer, stirring occasionally, until the sugar is completely dissolved (the *piloncillo* will take longer than the brown sugar to dissolve). Uncover and boil over medium-high heat until the syrup is reduced and thick, 10 to 15 minutes: The bubbles will change from small and quick to burst to larger, glossier, and slow to burst; a drop of the syrup in cold water will yield a firm ball that does not flatten when removed, and the temperature on a candy thermometer, if you have one, will be 245 degrees.

Immediately remove the syrup from the heat and pour onto the amaranth. Use a large wooden spoon to stir and combine well. The amaranth should be lightly coated with the syrup, though the mixture shouldn't look heavy and sticky. If necessary, stir in up to another cup of amaranth to lighten the mixture. Quickly form the crusts one by one by scooping about ⅓ cup of the mixture into a custard cup, and, using lightly oiled hands, pressing it into an even layer to line the mold. (I find it easiest to work next to the oven, keeping the unmolded amaranth mixture in the low oven to keep it warm and pliable). When the first 6 crusts have hardened a minute or two in the cups, gently dislodge them, then make the second batch. Cool them completely, and store in an airtight container until ready to serve.

2. *Finishing the dessert.* Just before serving, let the ice cream soften a few minutes in the refrigerator. Scoop into large balls, placing one into each of the shells. Sprinkle the tops with a little Mexican chocolate. Set the tarts out on dessert plates and spoon about ½ cup chopped fruit around each one. Stand a leaf of mint on top of each tart and carry right to the table.

ADVANCE PREPARATION—The crusts can be made a day or so ahead (store them in an airtight container); or freeze them, well wrapped, up to several months.

VARIATIONS AND IMPROVISATIONS—If you just want to make this as a sweet snack or cookie, flatten the amaranth mixture onto an oiled baking sheet (½-inch thickness is common) and cut into squares while warm (a long knife or pizza wheel seems to work best); if the flattened mixture gets too hard to cut easily, warm it briefly to make it malleable. Chopped nuts or diced dried or candied fruit are commonly added to the mixture before flattening it.

Piloncillo

In the olden days of our country, sugar was sold in huge cones. That's still the case for the Mexican unrefined sugar called *piloncillo* ("little pylon"). In much of southern Mexico the same sugar is formed into a round loaf shape and called *panela* or, in some places, formed into an even rougher round or square for the very coarse (usually darker and more molassesy) *panocha*. Any of these can range in color from light brown to almost black (the latter being the stronger flavored).

In sugar making, cane juice is boiled down and, without further refinement (to remove the molasses), poured into molds to cool and crystalize. What comes out is hard and strong flavored, usually stronger tasting than dark brown sugar, but not as strong as molasses.

Piloncillo is sold in Mexican groceries in the States in small cones that weigh about an ounce or large cones that weigh about seven ounces. I find it easiest to let them dissolve in whatever liquid I have in my recipe, though, with determination, they may be chopped with a large knife or cleaver (whole cones can break a food processor, so watch out).

one ounce cones are about one inch tall

piloncillo (cones of unrefined sugar)

CREAMY LIME PIE

Pay de Limón

*A*T OUR COOKING CLASSES in Oaxaca, I guide our students through the markets, buying tastes of the thick cream (it's like milky butter with a cheesey flavor and unctuous texture), the perfumey, greenish-yellow key limes and exotic tropical fruit like guanabana, chirimoya, guava, black zapote and papaya. In order to offer more than a simple taste of these traditional foods after one trip to the market, I combined that incredible cream and lime into a simple pie for our class meal, serving it with an assortment of pureed fruits. Even with our American homemade cream (or *crème fraîche*) and less-tart hybrid Persian limes, the pie makes a lovely special-dinner finale.

MAKES ONE 9-INCH PIE, SERVING 8

FOR THE CRUST

1 cup (4½ ounces) all-purpose flour (measured by scooping and leveling)

4 tablespoons (2 ounces) chilled unsalted butter, cut into ½-inch bits

2 tablespoons chilled vegetable shortening or rich-tasting lard, chilled, cut into ½-inch bits

½ teaspoon sugar

⅛ teaspoon salt

1 egg yolk, beaten slightly

FOR THE FILLING

3 large eggs, room temperature

1½ tablespoons finely chopped lime zest (colored rind only)

⅔ cup sugar

3 tablespoons masa harina

OR 3 tablespoons all-purpose flour

1 cup plus 2 tablespoons room-temperature Thick Cream (page 165) or crème fraîche

6 tablespoons fresh lime juice

6 tablespoons fresh orange juice

1½ tablespoons orange liqueur

Powdered sugar, for garnish

About 2 cups Crimson Prickly Pear Sauce (page 412) or other fruit sauce (page 414), for serving

1. *The dough.* Measure the flour, butter, and shortening (or lard) into a bowl or a food processor fitted with the metal blade. Quickly work the fats into the flour with a pastry blender or pulse the food processor until the flour looks a little damp (not powdery) but *tiny bits of fat are still visible.* If using the food processor, transfer the mixture to a bowl.

Mix together the sugar, salt and 2 tablespoons of ice water. Using a fork, little by little work the ice-water mixture into the flour mixture. The dough will be in rough, rather stiff clumps; if there is unincorporated flour in the bottom of the bowl, sprinkle in a little more ice water and use the fork to work it together. Press the dough together into a flat disk, wrap in plastic, and refrigerate at least 1 hour.

On a lightly floured surface, roll the dough into a 12-inch circle. Transfer to a 9-inch glass pie pan (I find it easiest to roll the dough onto the rolling pin, then unroll it onto the pie pan). Decoratively crimp the edge and trim the excess dough. Refrigerate 30 minutes.

2. *Prebaking the crust.* Heat the oven to 400 degrees. Lightly oil a 15-inch piece of foil and lay it, oiled-side down, into the crust (heavy duty foil is too stiff to work here); press down to line the crust snugly. Fill with beans or pie weights and bake about 15 minutes, until beginning to brown around the edges. Reduce the oven temperature to 350 degrees. Carefully remove the beans (or weights) and foil, return the crust to the oven and bake 8 to 10 minutes, until it no longer looks moist. (If it bubbles at this point, gently press it down with the back of a spoon.) Brush the beaten egg yolk over the crust, then let cool completely.

3. *The filling.* Crack the eggs into a large bowl; measure in the lime zest, sugar and *masa harina* or flour, and beat by hand until thoroughly combined. Stir in the thick cream, lime juice, orange juice and orange liqueur.

4. *Baking the pie.* Pour the filling into the prebaked pie shell, set in the lower third of the 350-degree oven, and bake until nearly set in the center (a knife inserted halfway between the edge and the center should come out clean), about 45 minutes.

Cool slightly; serve warm, dusted with powdered sugar and with sauce dribbled around.

ADVANCE PREPARATION—This delicate pie is best served shortly after it is baked.

CRIMSON PRICKLY PEAR SAUCE

Salsa de Tuna

*T*HIS IS ONE OF MY favorite sauces: Its deep, purpley, cranberry color is reason enough for that designation, but then again so is the bright strawberry/kiwi/watermelon flavor, with its hint of the unbridled tropics. And the fact that you can tell your guests you're serving them cactus fruit (and that it is delicious) gives you a decidedly exotic edge.

The puree is very watery, like watermelon juice, so in order to give the sauce some body but not take away all the fruit's freshness, I've directed you to rapidly boil down part of the puree with the sugar, then cool it and add the remaining uncooked puree. This method works well with watermelon puree, too, should you not be able to find prickly pears. You will need about 3 cups seeded, pureed watermelon pulp.

MAKES ABOUT 2 CUPS

2½ pounds (about 16) fresh prickly pears (tunas)

⅓ cup sugar, plus a little more if needed

About 1 tablespoon fresh lime juice, if needed

About 1 tablespoon orange liqueur

Cut a ½-inch slice off both ends of the prickly pears, then make a ½-inch deep incision down the side of each one. Carefully (remember there are little stickers) peel off the rind, starting from your incision: The rind is thick and, if the fruit is ripe, will peel easily away from the central core. Roughly chop the peeled prickly pears, puree in a food processor or blender, then press through a fine strainer into a bowl. There should be about 3 cups.

In a medium-size (2- to 3-quart) saucepan, combine 2 *cups* of the puree with ⅓ cup sugar, and simmer rapidly over medium to medium-high heat, stirring frequently, until reduced to 1 cup. Cool.

Combine the cooked mixture with the remaining *1 cup* of uncooked puree in a small bowl. Taste and season with lime juice, orange liqueur and additional sugar if needed.

ADVANCE PREPARATION—Covered and refrigerated, the sauce will keep about a week. The finished sauce (as well as the prickly-pear pulp) also can be frozen.

Prickly Pears

These rather exotic-seeming, slightly spiny, egg-shaped fruits are from the prickly-pear cactus, the same plant that yields the paddles to use as a vegetable. Though the flesh grows in a variety of colors, most common are pale green (often called white) and deep crimson; the latter is the most popular. The pulp of the fruit is very juicy (watery like watermelon) and the sweet ones have a watermelon/ kiwi/strawberry flavor with decidedly cactus overtones. The less common sour ones, called *xoconostles,* are yellow-gray green on the outside, yellowish-pink inside with a reddish seed pod at the center that holds lots of tiny black seeds; their flavor is as tart as an underripe plum, and they're mostly used to add a tangy zing to soups.

Prickly pears (also called cactus pears or cactus fruit) are becoming easily available both in Mexican markets and well-stocked grocery stores, though they are occasionally quite expensive. The height of the season in Mexico is late summer and fall; the ones that come from California seem to be available year 'round, except a few months in spring.

Prickly pears are usually picked when they're ripe (slightly yielding to the touch) and keep well loosely wrapped in the refrigerator. It's common to cut off both ends, make a shallow incision down the length of the greenish rind, then peel back the rind leaving an oval of pure prickly pear free for enjoying.

If you puree the prickly pears in a food processor or blender and don't let the machine run too long, the seeds will stay whole and can easily be strained out.

. . . .

skin

sweet prickly pear (tuna)

Fruit Sauces

I'm fond of serving a spoonful or two of fruit sauce alongside most desserts: It offers a fresh counterpoint to baked or simmered sweetness. Except with very juicy fruit like prickly pear or watermelon, if you simply cut up 2 cups of peeled and pitted fruit and whir it in a blender or food processor, you'll have about 1½ cups of fairly thick puree. Thin it out with a little water or liqueur, then sweeten it with sugar or honey (I recommend keeping the sauce on the less-sweet side to offer a greater contrast to the dessert), and rev it up with a squeeze of fresh lime juice. A hint of ground cinnamon or vanilla may be to your liking with some fruits. You may want to strain purees made from fruits that are fibrous (like pineapple or mango) or that have small seeds (like raspberries).

Tropical fruits like chirimoya, guanabana, papaya, mango, pineapple, mamey, passion fruit, white zapote and black zapote work well with this approach, as do the nontropicals like peach, nectarine, kiwi, blackberry, strawberry, raspberry, persimmon and apricot.

SPICY PLANTAIN PIE

Pay de Plátano

*H*ERE'S ANOTHER OF THE PIES I developed to accompany traditional Mexican flavors, this one utilizing a puree of very ripe plantains. Its allure includes the flavor of dark brown sugar, allspice, cinnamon and cloves, plus the consistency of a rich pumpkin pie. But what's so special is that tropical plantain flavor, mellower than a banana and tangier, too.

MAKES ONE 9-INCH PIE, SERVING 8

FOR THE CRUST

1 cup (4½ ounces) all-purpose flour (measured by scooping and leveling)

4 tablespoons (2 ounces) chilled unsalted butter, cut into ½-inch bits

2 tablespoons vegetable shortening or rich-tasting lard, chilled, cut into ½-inch bits

½ teaspoon sugar

⅛ teaspoon salt

1 egg yolk, beaten slightly

FOR THE FILLING

2 medium (1 pound total) very ripe (black-ripe) plantains

⅔ cup firmly packed dark brown sugar

3 tablespoons (1½ ounces) room-temperature unsalted butter

2 large eggs, room temperature

1 tablespoon molasses

1 teaspoon allspice, preferably freshly ground

½ teaspoon cinnamon, preferably freshly ground Mexican canela

A pinch of cloves, preferably freshly ground

1 cup heavy (whipping) cream

¼ cup milk

About 1½ cup Sweetened Whipped Cream (page 406) flavored with brandy, for serving

1. *The dough.* Measure the flour, butter and shortening (or lard) into a bowl or a food processor fitted with the metal blade. Quickly work the fats into the flour with a pastry blender or pulse the food processor until the flour looks a little damp (not powdery) but *tiny* bits of fat are still visible. If using the food processor, transfer the mixture to a bowl.

Mix together the sugar, salt and 2 tablespoons of ice water. Using a fork, little by little work the ice-water mixture into the flour mixture. The dough will be in rough, rather stiff clumps; if there is unincorporated flour in the bottom of the bowl, sprinkle in a little more ice water and use the fork to work it together. Press the dough together into a flat disk, wrap in plastic, and refrigerate at least 1 hour.

On a lightly floured surface, roll the dough into a 12-inch circle. Carefully transfer to a 9-inch glass pie pan (I find it easiest to roll the dough onto the rolling pin, then unroll it onto the pie pan). Decoratively crimp the edge and trim off the excess dough. Refrigerate for 30 minutes.

2. *Prebaking the crust.* Heat the oven to 400 degrees. Lightly oil a 15-inch piece of foil and lay it, oiled-side down, into the crust (heavy duty foil is too stiff to work here); press down to line the crust snugly. Fill with beans or pie weights and bake about 15 minutes, until beginning to brown around the edges. Reduce the oven temperature to 350 degrees. Carefully remove the beans (or weights) and foil, return the crust to the oven and bake 8 to 10 minutes, until it no longer looks moist. (If it bubbles at this point, gently press it down with the back of a spoon.) Brush the beaten egg yolk over the crust, then let cool completely.

3. *The filling.* Peel the plantains and puree in a food processor. Add the brown sugar, butter, eggs, molasses, allspice, cinnamon and cloves. Process until combined, then add the cream and milk, and pulse to incorporate them.

4. *Baking.* Pour the filling into the prebaked pie shell. Bake in the lower third of the oven until *barely* set in the center (a knife inserted halfway between the edge and the center should come out clean), 35 to 45 minutes. Cool on wire rack, then slice and serve, either slightly warm or at room temperature, and preferably with a good dollop of brandy-laced, sweetened, whipped cream.

ADVANCE PREPARATION—The dough can be made several days ahead, or the prebaked crust can be kept for a day or so, covered at room temperature. The pie is best served the day it is baked.

Plantains

Plaintains (*plátanos*), a thick-skinned variety of banana used almost exclusively in cooking, will surprise anyone who grew up eating sweet, tender bananas out of hand or sliced raw over cereal and fruit salads. Plantains are really only delicious when cooked (well, you *could* eat one raw if it were mushy black-ripe), because cooking dissipates their tannin—the acid that makes your mouth feel as if it were coated with sandpaper.

Plantains are not sweet when underripe (underripe ones are enjoyed as a starchy vegetable throughout the Caribbean). Plantains that are yellow-ripe, like regular bananas, aren't soft and sweet enough for the Spicy Plantain Pie (page 415), though at that state they are perfect for Ripe Plantain Turnovers (page 102). When completely ripe, they will be very soft and nearly black; that's when their sugar is highest and their starch lowest.

Plantains can be cooked by a variety of methods: frying, the most common, and boiling, to make a puree. My favorite way of obtaining a generous amount of cooked pulp that is not water-logged (for use in the empanada dough, for example) is to bake them in a 350-degree oven on a baking sheet for about 45 minutes. To allow some of the moisture to escape while they bake, make a shallow incision down the length of the plantain, then cut it crosswise in half. Once baked, use two forks to peel back the skin. The pulp can then be mashed and refrigerated for several days, or frozen; it will not blacken like other bananas.

Nowadays, many Mexican and Latino markets sell plantains in various stages of ripeness; some fashionable produce markets even tag them with stickers indicating they are ready to use. If only green plantains are available to you, let them sit on the counter—it will take a week or so for them to ripen from totally green to black-ripe.

Stats: A medium plantain is about 10 inches long and weighs about 8 ounces. Two pounds of plantains will yield 2 cups cooked, mashed pulp.

black-ripe plantain

green plantain

CHAPTER NINE

. . . . .

WINE AND MARGARITAS

ALTHOUGH MEXICO'S COOKING is complex and extensive, it's most often paired with beer or tequila-powered margaritas (or in Mexico, with sweet soft drinks or cola mixed with brandy). Mexico has produced a small, steady flow of wine since the mid-sixteenth century, but it's still hard to find great examples there, and wine with everyday meals is not common. So why do I put so much energy into matching wine and Mexican food?

It's my conviction that good wine and good food—especially good Mexican food—are natural allies. Cooking that has integrity, finesse and sophistication, no matter what its ethnic origin, deserves a good glass of wine, which, in my book, is the human race's most refined and complex libation.

When Deann and I opened Frontera Grill in 1987, we wanted to open the wine-with-Mexican-food door for our customers. They walked in with visions of margaritas and Corona glazing their eyes—the necessary stuff, they thought, to wash down those cheese-covered plates they'd grown to expect in Mexican eateries. But our food (and the style of the recipes in this book) reflects the true cuisine of Mexico. The flavors on our plates and in these pages—from the rich-and-redolent, slow-simmered *moles* to the lively dance of tomatillos, cilantro and serranos—upset the American stereotypes in a satisfying, compelling sort of way. Our customers began to expect the unexpected, including the right beverage choice for our cuisine.

Contrary to most American expectations, well-made regional Mexican cooking does not (with a few exceptions) burn unbridled with capsicum. Rather, it's notably full flavored and richly complex and, in more cases than not, offers deep-rooted, long-simmered satisfaction. I find myself drawn mostly to reds (to marry with the food's depth and complexity) rather than whites (which complement the tangy tomatillos and perfumy cilantro).

We find the good acidity and concentration we want in Zinfandels, Syrahs, Petite Sirahs and Amarones. Mourvèdres and Tempranillos provide earth and spice. Youthful freshness complements the liveliness of our food; Grenache is great, but Gamay can be almost too light. And some oaky, old-world Spanish and Italian reds also are perfect mates for our rich, smoky food. Because tannins turn smoldering heat into raging fire, Cabernets are less attractive. Perhaps my favorite matches are young Pinot Noirs; they have great structure coupled with that juicy fruitiness and ephemeral impression of sweetness that makes them a most elegant stand-in for the fruity sweet drinks so beloved in Mexico.

Off-dry whites such as Chenin Blancs, Rieslings and Gewürztraminers are good choices, but I often prefer the impression of sweetness that robust, fruity or floral aromas can give a dry wine. Truth is, whites that have good structure and steely acidity, like Sauvignon Blanc, match the tartness on the plate best. And sparklers? Their effervescence gives them the same tactile advantage as beer (important in the multisensory experience of chile-tinged dishes), and they're versatile, but to me never as satisfying as still wines.

Another equally important consideration in our wine list is variety of flavors. At a restaurant that champions the virtues of purslane, *epazote*, hog trotters and *huitlacoche* (corn mushrooms), why not Albariño, Viura, Pinotage and Mencia? The interesting complexity of these different grape flavors resonates perfectly with this cooking.

All this said, I still like a good margarita now and then before dinner or with snacks. Here follows our three restaurant classics—less sweet than most of the slushy versions that are commonly made with sweet-and-sour mix. All are based on fresh-squeezed lime juice and tequila, but each is distinctive.

Frontera's Gold Margarita, which has the most melded flavor (everything steeps together), can be made ahead and requires the least distinctive tequila. The Topolo Margarita combines just-mixed freshness with the rich flavor of brandy-style tequila and orange liqueur. And the Top-of-the-Line Margarita is bright, tangy and best features the true spirit of tequila—a very classic recipe.

FRONTERA'S GOLD MARGARITA

MAKES ABOUT 4 CUPS, SERVING 8

1²/₃ cups Cuervo Especial gold tequila

¼ cup plus 1 teaspoon Gran Torres
    orange liqueur

    OR ¼ cup Grand Marnier

½ cup plus 1 tablespoon fresh lime
    juice, about 2 large limes

Finely grated zest of 1½ limes, about
    1 teaspoon

5 tablespoons sugar

Lime wedges

Coarse salt

1. *Steeping the margarita mixture.* Mix the tequila, orange liqueur, lime juice, lime zest, sugar and 1 cup water in a glass or plastic pitcher until the sugar dissolves. Cover and refrigerate at least 2 hours (but no more than 24 hours). Strain into another pitcher.

2. *Finishing and serving the margaritas.* Rub the rims of 8 martini or other 6- to 8-ounce glasses with a lime wedge, then dip the rims in a dish of coarse salt. Refrigerate the glasses if desired.

    Serve the margaritas either straight-up or on the rocks in the prepared glasses.

TOPOLO MARGARITA

MAKES ABOUT 2 CUPS, SERVING 4

*Finely grated zest of 1½ limes, about
1 teaspoon*

*½ cup fresh lime juice, about 2 large
limes*

¼ cup plus 1 teaspoon sugar

Lime wedges

Coarse salt

¾ cup Sauza Conmemorativo tequila

*2 tablespoons plus 2 teaspoons Gran
Torres orange liqueur*

OR *2 tablespoons Grand Marnier*

About 1 cup coarsely broken ice cubes

1. *Making 1¼ cups of tangy limeade.* Combine the lime zest, lime juice, sugar and 10 tablespoons of water in a glass or plastic pitcher. Cover and refrigerate for at least 2 hours (but no longer than 24 hours). Strain into another pitcher.

2. *Finishing and serving the margaritas.* Rub the rims of 4 martini glasses with a lime wedge, then dip them in a dish of coarse salt. Refrigerate the glasses if desired.

   In a shaker, combine the limeade, tequila and orange liqueur. Add ice and shake 10 to 15 seconds, then strain into the prepared glasses.

TOP-OF-THE-LINE MARGARITA

SERVES 2 GENEROUSLY

Lime wedges

Coarse salt

*¼ cup fresh lime juice, about
1 large lime*

*¼ cup Tesoro silver or other silver
100 percent agave tequila*

¼ cup Cointreau orange liqueur

½ cup coarsely cracked ice cubes

Rub the rims of 2 martini glasses with a lime wedge, then dip the rims in a dish of coarse salt. Refrigerate the glasses if desired.

In a shaker, combine the lime juice, tequila and orange liqueur. Add ice and shake 10 to 15 seconds, then strain into the prepared glasses.

SOURCES

GREAT MEXICAN MARKETS IN CHICAGO

LA CASA DEL PUEBLO
1810 S. Blue Island, Chicago

JIMENEZ ENTERPRISES, INC.
2140 N. Western and 3850 W. Fullerton,
Chicago

SUPERMERCADO CARDENAS
3922 N. Sheridan and 2153 W. Roscoe,
Chicago

MAIL ORDER

BURNS FARMS
16158 Hillside Circle
Montverde, FL 34756
407-469-4490
Huitlacoche, hoja santa

CALIDO CHILE TRADERS
5360 Merriam Dr.
Merriam, KS 66203
800-568-8468, plus retail stores.
Dried chiles, hot sauces

CHILE TODAY HOT TAMALE
919 Highway 33, Suite 47
Freehold, NJ 07728
800-468-7377
Twenty varieties of dried chiles, hot sauces and pure chile powders

THE CMC COMPANY
P.O. Box 322
Avalon, NJ 08202
800-CMC-2780
Avocado leaves, dried and canned chiles, masa harina, canned tomatillos, piloncillo, Mexican oregano, Mexican chocolate, achiote paste, tortilla presses, molcajetes, comales and hot sauces

COMPANION PLANTS
7247 N. Coolville Ridge Rd.
Athens, OH 45701
614-592-4643
Mexican oregano plants, hoja santa *plants*

A COOK'S WARES
211 37th St.
Beaver Falls, PA 15010-2103
412-846-9490
Dried chiles, Mexican vanilla, cookbooks and kitchen equipment

COYOTE CAFE GENERAL STORE
132 West Water St.
Santa Fe, NM 87501
800-866-4695
Dried beans (including heirloom varieties), dried chiles, canned chipotles, masa harina, Mexican chocolate, spices, herbs and hot sauces

DEAN & DELUCA
Catalog Department
560 Broadway
New York, NY 10012
800-221-7714
Dried chiles, canned chipotles, dried pozole, unusual dried beans (including scarlet runners), pumpkin seeds, Mexican chocolate, masa harina, whole spices, sherry vinegar, hot sauces

DON ALFONSO FOODS
P.O. Box 201988
Austin, TX
800-456-6100
Dried chiles, bottled mole *poblano*

GAZELLA MEXICAN CHOCOLATE
3200 Corte Malpaso, #108
Camarillo, CA 93012
888-MEX-CHOC
Oaxacan-style Mexican chocolate

HERBS OF MEXICO
3903 Whittier Blvd.
Los Angeles, CA 90023
213-261-2521
Dried hoja santa *and* epazote

INTERNATIONAL HOT FOODS, INC.
905 N. California Ave.
Chicago, IL 60622
800-505-9999
Canned chipotles, dried chiles, various hot sauces

JOHNNY'S SELECTED SEEDS
Foss Hill Rd.
Albion, ME 04910-9731
207-437-9294
Seeds for tomatoes, tomatillos, chiles, cilantro and epazote

**THE KING ARTHUR FLOUR
BAKER'S CATALOGUE**
P.O. Box 876
Norwich, VT 05055-0876
800-827-6836
Sour salt, unhulled sesame seeds, Mexican vanilla, coarse salt, masa harina, baking equipment, thermometers

LA CUISINE KITCHENWARE
323 Cameron St.
Alexandria, VA 22314-3219
800-521-1176
Kitchen equipment (including tortilla presses and cast-iron pans), unusual dried beans (including scarlet runners), assorted rices and dried chiles

MO HOTTA MO BETTA
P.O. Box 4136
San Luis Obispo, CA 93403
800-462-3220
Dried chiles, canned chipotles, Mexican chocolate, Mexican cinnamon (canela), achiote seeds, Mexican oregano, pumpkin seeds, masa harina, hot sauces

MONTERREY FOODS
3939 Cesar Chavez
Los Angeles, CA 90063
213-263-2143
Dried chiles

MOZZARELLA COMPANY
2944 Elm St.
Dallas, TX 75226
800-798-2954
Fresh cheeses including queso blanco, fresh cream cheese, ancho and epazote-flavored cheeses

NATIVE SEEDS SEARCH
2509 N. Campbell Ave. #325
Tucson, AZ 85719
520-327-9123
Seeds for tomatillos, chilacoyote, *squash, chiles and* epazote

NICHOLS GARDEN NURSERY
1190 N. Pacific Hwy.
Albany, OR 97321-4580
541-928-9280
Seeds for purslane

NU-WORLD AMARANTH, INC.
P.O. Box 2202
Naperville, IL 60567
800-369-6819
Puffed amaranth and other amaranth products

PENDERY'S, INC.
1221 Manufacturing St.
Dallas, TX 75207
800-533-1870
Dried chiles and spices

PENZEY'S SPICE HOUSE, LTD.
P.O. Box 1633
Milwaukee, WI 53201
414-768-8799
Mexican oregano and wide variety of whole spices including canela

SALSA EXPRESS
P.O. Box 3985
Albuquerque, NM 87190
800-437-2572
Dried chiles, fresh New Mexico chiles in season, hot sauces

SEEDS OF CHANGE
P.O. Box 15700
Santa Fe, NM 87506-5700
505-438-8080

Seeds, many heirloom varieties for beans, lambsquarters, amaranth, tomatoes, tomatillos, chiles and herbs including epazote *and* cilantro

SHEPERD'S GARDEN SEEDS
ORDER DEPARTMENT
30 IRENE ST.
TORRINGTON, CT 06790-6658
860-482-3638
Seeds for tomatoes, tomatillos, chiles (including habanero, jalapeño, poblano, pequín and serrano) and herbs (including cilantro and epazote*)*

VELLA CHEESE CO.
315 SECOND ST. EAST
SONOMA, CA 95476
800-848-0505
Dry jack cheese

WILD GAME/THE HERB PURVEYOR
2315 W. HURON
CHICAGO, IL 60612
312-278-1661
Hoja santa

WILLIAMS-SONOMA
MAIL ORDER DEPARTMENT
P.O. BOX 7456
SAN FRANCISCO, CA 94120-7456
800-541-2233
Kitchen equipment including steamers and tortilla warmers

BIBLIOGRAPHY

Andrews, Jean. *Peppers: The Domesticated Capsicums.* Austin: University of Texas Press, 1984.

Beranbaum, Rose Levy. *The Cake Bible.* New York: William Morrow and Company, 1988.

Camou Healy, Ernesto, coord., and Alicia Hinojosa. *Cocina sonorense.* Hermosillo, Sonora: Gobierno del Estado de Sonora, 1990.

Caraza Campos, Laura B. de, and Georgina Luna Parra. *México desconocido guias gastronomicas: comida poblana.* Mexico, D.F.: Editorial Jilguero, S.A. de C.V., 1993.

Carbia, María A. de. *México en la cocina de Marichu.* 3rd ed. Mexico, D.F.: Editorial Época, 1969.

Casas, Penelope. *The Food and Wines of Spain.* New York: Alfred A. Knopf, 1982.

Chapa, Martha, and Martha Ortiz. *Cocina de Querétaro.* Querétaro: Gobierno del Estado de Querétaro, 1990.

Child, Julia. *From Julia Child's Kitchen.* New York: Alfred A. Knopf, 1975.

Coe, Sophie D., *America's First Cuisines.* Austin: University of Texas Press, 1994.

Coe, Sophie D., and Michael D. *The True History of Chocolate.* New York: Thames and Hudson, 1996.

Dolores, Miriam, and Oscar de Luna Alonson. *La cocina mexicana Océano.* Barcelona: Ediciones Océano-Éxito, S.A., 1986.

Fernández, Beatriz L., María Yani and Margarita Zafiro . . . *y la comida se hizo* . . . Mexico, D.F.: ISSSTE/Trillas, 1984–1987.

Guzmán de Vásquez Colmenares, Ana María. *Tradiciones gastronómicas oaxaqueñas.* Oaxaca: Comite Organizador del CDL Aniversario Oaxaca, 1982.

Levín Kosberg, Larry, coord. *Comida familiar en el estado de Yucatán.* Mexico, D.F.: Banco Nacional de Crédito Rural, 1988.

Linares, Edelmira, and Judith Aguirre. *Los quelites, un tesoro culinario.* Mexico, D.F.: Universidad Nacional Autónoma de México, 1992.

Martínez, Maximino. *Catálogo de nombres vulgares y cientificos de plantas mexicanas.* Mexico, D.F.: Fonda de Cultura Económica, 1979.

McClane, A. J. *The Encyclopedia of Fish Cookery.* New York: Holt, Rinehart and Winston, 1977.

McGee, Harold. *On Food and Cooking: The Science and Lore of the Kitchen.* New York: Charles Scribner's Sons, 1984.

———. *The Curious Cook: More Kitchen Science and Lore.* San Francisco: North Point Press, 1990.

Pérez-Silva, Dra. Evangelina, coord. *Los hongos en la cocina mexicana.* Mexico, D.F.: Sociedad Mexicana de Micología, A.C., 1984.

Portillo de Carbillido, María Concepción. *Oaxaca y su cocina.* Mexico, D.F.: Editorial Orión, 1981.

Sahagún, Fray Bernardino de. *General History of the Things of New Spain,* Vol. 9. Translated and annotated by Arthur J. O. Anderson and Charles E. Dibble. Santa Fe: The School of American Research, 1953.

Stoopen, María, and Ana Laura Delgado. *La cocina veracruzana.* Veracruz: Gobierno del Estado de Veracruz, 1992.

Veláquez de León, Josefina. *Antojitos mexicanos.* Mexico, D.F.: Editorial Velázquez de León.

———. *Cocina campechana.* Mexico, D.F.: Editorial Velázquez de León.

INDEX